Also by Sadakat Kadri

The Trial: A History, from Socrates to O. J. Simpson

Heaven on Earth

Heaven on Earth

A Journey Through
Shari'a Law
from the Deserts
of Ancient Arabia
to the Streets
of the Modern
Muslim World

Sadakat Kadri

Farrar, Straus and Giroux   New York

Farrar, Straus and Giroux
18 West 18th Street, New York 10011

Distributed in Canada by D&M Publishers, Inc.
Printed in the United States of America
Originally published, in slightly different form, in 2012 by the Bodley Head, Great Britain
Published in the United States by Farrar, Straus and Giroux
First American edition, 2012

Library of Congress Cataloging-in-Publication Data
Kadri, Sadakat.
    Heaven on earth : a journey through shari'a law from the deserts of ancient Arabia
to the streets of the modern Muslim world / Sadakat Kadri. — 1st American ed.
        p.   cm.
    ISBN 978-0-374-16872-8 (hardback)
    1. Islamic law—History.   I. Title.

KBP50 .K33 2012
340.5'9—dc23

                                                                    2011040217

Designed by Abby Kagan

www.fsgbooks.com

1   3   5   7   9   10   8   6   4   2

For my mum and dad,
with much love

Contents

Heaven on Earth

Prologue: Infinite Justice

The North Indian city of Badaun is barely known beyond the subcontinent, but among the Muslims of India it has a great reputation. Seven ancient Islamic shrines encircle the town, collectively drawing visitors from miles around, and one spiritual specialty has always brought them immense local renown. They are said to facilitate the exorcism of jinns. That is a weighty claim among the poor, the credulous, and the desperate. Genies of the region are not popularly imagined to be the bountiful servants of lamp-rubbing legend. They are mercurial creatures, capable of wreaking havoc, who routinely seize control of people's lives. Victims are suddenly plunged into depression or discontent, possessed of unusual ideas, and urged to speak, to lash out, even sometimes to kill. Entire families suffer as a consequence, and dozens are therefore to be found at the largest of the shrines, where they camp out in a shanty-filled cemetery pending miraculous interventions on behalf of their afflicted relatives. The scene is permanently alive, serviced by a nearby market, and it swells into something of a carnival as day-trippers arrive by the hundreds on the eve of Friday prayers. The spectacle had horrified and fascinated me in roughly equal measure ever since I first visited Badaun—my father's birthplace—in 1979, at the age of fifteen. Elderly relations had warned me then to steer well clear of the place after dark on a Thursday night. In the spring of 2009, I finally got round to disobeying them.

I reached the shrine long after dusk, and its neem tree glades were pulsating to the drums and accordions of an ululating troupe of musicians. Picking my way through knots of pilgrims, past shadowy figures who babbled in the darkness or lunged from wooden posts to which they had been chained, I eventually reached the marble courtyard at the mausoleum's center. The everyday bedlam of India looked to have merged with a scene from *The Crucible*. In a moonlight that was fluorescent, bright-eyed girls were whipping their hair into propellers while older folk, senile or despondent, chattered to tombstones. As I fidgeted with my camera settings, a teenage girl next to me stepped forward, assisted by anxious relatives, to quiver and collapse into the waiting arms of two shrine employees. Others strode forward to swoon in their turn, and were expertly scooped aside to make way for fresh fainters. Whooping children, barely able to believe their luck, cartwheeled around the hysterics and their helpers throughout. It was hours before the chaos gave way to chirrups and a semblance of peace returned to the sepulchres.

Walking back to my relatives' home across a meadow filled with tottering fourteenth-century funeral vaults, I wondered how to make sense of what had just occurred. I had come to India in search of color after a year immersed in libraries, but it seemed almost as though I had found too much. A survey of Islamic legal history demands flexibility if it is to entertain rather than anesthetize, but fitting tales of jinn exorcism into an account of the shari'a* called for the literary equivalent of a crowbar—until a few hours later. By then, I had found another shrine: a postage stamp of a necropolis, comprising a dusty courtyard, an ancient banyan tree, and a chiffon-draped tombstone. In the afternoon heat, the otherworldly excitements it might ordinarily have inspired had slowed to a crawl. Two women were gazing at the central slab, motionless beneath their burkas, as though it might shuffle away at any moment.

---

*In the interests of readability, only two transliteration symbols are used in this book: the opening apostrophe ' signifies the slightly strangulated vowel *ain*, and its closing counterpart ' indicates the glottal stop *hamza*. They are included only when they fall in the middle of a word.

A man stood before the headstone, his palms cupped in prayer, while his young son raced around and kissed surrounding memorials. The only sign of any transcendental goings-on at all came from a woman who was chanting breathlessly as she strode to and fro beneath the lush branches of the banyan tree, watched by a squatting husband and mournful children. But when I lined up the scene for a photograph, it turned out to contain far more than met the eye. A mustachioed man who was tending a smoldering sheaf of incense sticks at the gnarled roots of the tree raised his hand forbiddingly. "No photographs," he ordered. "She is making her plea to the king of the jinns."

Throughout the previous night, I had wondered how, precisely, a person possessed by a jinn could expect to obtain relief, and I obediently lowered my camera. The man clearly possessed some kind of authority, for he was selling a selection of holy knickknacks that were neatly laid out next to the green coverlet of the shrine's main tomb, and I decided to strike up a conversation. Using a combination of quizzical gestures and atrocious Urdu, I asked if he had any charms worth taking on the three-month trek to Syria and Istanbul that I had lined up. His first suggestion was an amulet to ward off the evil eye. When I pondered it skeptically, he proffered a leather pouch containing a secret verse of the Qur'an. It apparently guaranteed good fortune, God willing, so long as the purchaser did not try to read the contents. That seemed a bargain, and as rupees changed hands, I seized the moment. Why no cameras? He nodded solemnly toward the thick cluster of banyan roots and explained that they enthroned the king of the jinns—whose court was now in session.

That explained the photography ban—in a sense—but what, I wondered, was the likely outcome of the woman's complaint? "The king will listen to both sides and make a ruling," replied the shrine's custodian. "Will the jinn then leave?" I inquired. "Maybe, maybe not," he replied with a wiggle of his head. "Or maybe a hanging." Startled, I asked how that would work. He laughed, slapped a hand around my shoulder, and pointed to a colorfully decorated bough of the banyan. "The jinn, not the woman." "Physically hanged?" I asked meaninglessly. "Yes . . . actual fact," he replied. "If that is required by the shari'a."

The claim was as surprising to me as it ought to have been predictable. I already knew that the invisible world is considered no less subject to God's law than the visible one and that jurists have often had occasion to consider the rights and obligations of genies. A tenth-century writer named al-Shibli once wrote about the lawfulness of their marriages with human beings, for example: though aware of unions that had been fruitful, he warned of inevitable antagonisms and urged all readers to stick to their own kind. At many Sunni madrasas, jinns are thought to be so committed to observance of the shari'a that chairs are left empty for them during jurisprudence classes. And as I found out later in the spring of 2009, their activities are still liable to be considered at the very highest level. The realization came in Damascus, at a question-and-answer session chaired by Ayatollah Mohammad Fadlallah. The Lebanese cleric (who has since died) used to be routinely characterized in the Western media as the "spiritual leader of Hezbollah," but opposition to Israel never made him controversial in Syria and Lebanon. There was one aspect of his teachings that did give rise to dispute, however—his relative liberalism when it came to sexual taboos—and at the meeting, the sniggering students of a rival cleric demanded to know whether he thought it lawful to have sex with a jinn outside marriage. "Why are you wasting my time?" he snapped. "It's fine so long as you use a condom. Next question, please."

Some people might find it odd or even offensive that a book about the shari'a should open with a discussion of jinns, let alone a reference to sexual congress with them. Westerners have been exoticizing Islam for centuries, and a work that sets out to scrutinize Islamic jurisprudence by reference to the supernatural can only invite suspicion. But though intercourse with genies is the kind of subject that would certainly have intrigued many an Orientalist scholar in years gone by, the fact that its lawfulness came up for discussion in a twenty-first-century Shi'a seminary is ample proof that it retains legal significance. Ayatollah Fadlallah's response, for all its contempt, also has contemporary relevance—because he was either right or wrong to imply that thousand-year-old legal traditions might have become redundant. And though any respectable Islamic jurist would ridicule the suggestion that jinns should be hanged from a sturdy branch, it is perfectly sensible to wonder what makes an execution so absurd—and what safeguards exist to prevent other people from making similar mistakes about God's law. The question is important. At least eleven of the world's fifty or so Muslim states possess constitutions that acknowledge Islam to be a source of national law—and several invoke the shari'a to punish defendants who are considerably more tangible than a jinn.

I found myself before the king of the jinns in the first place because the tomb at the shrine's center belonged to one of my direct ancestors. Abdullah was an Arab born in Mecca in the twelfth century, and his journey to India had been an eventful one. He left home in around 1192, the same year that Delhi fell to Muslims for the first time, and reached Lahore at the height of a ferocious regional conflict. After marrying off his son and traveling companion and apparently settling down for almost two decades, he then made himself scarce all over again. Crossing the Punjab, he got to Delhi just before the sultan accidentally and fatally impaled himself on his pommel during a polo game in 1210. A succession crisis ensued, and when a battle-hardened slave-general was elevated to replace the sultan the following year, Abdullah set off for the recently conquered outpost in which the new ruler had earned his reputation. It was there, in Badaun, that his wanderings finally came to an end.

Abdullah's journey through war zones to the jungled fringes of the Islamic world was as arduous as it sounds. Although Badaun gave him a wife and at least one more son, it was a very uncongenial place. Two battles, separated by seven years, had left its fields pockmarked by hundreds of graves. Its Muslim conquerors were confined to a garrison, commanders of a militarized cemetery that was surrounded by a seething Hindu sea. But Abdullah was undaunted, because he had come on a mission. He was a Sufi, in an era when Islamic mystics were as fervent as they were introspective—far more like the warrior monks of Christendom than the flying carpeteers of later legend. And though he almost certainly wielded a sword earlier on his journey, his outlook was not a military one. He had come to Badaun to battle for souls.

As far as Abdullah would have been concerned, the task on which he was engaged was a sacred struggle—a jihad—but the way that he and thousands of other Sufis chose to pursue it was distinctive. In their missionary work, they accentuated similarities rather than differences. Instead of condemning Hindus as irredeemable polytheists, they recognized their pantheon to be different expressions of the one God.

They fused Islamic prayer with Hindu mantras to create the ecstatic devotional music known as *qawwali*. And in a country that was littered with pocket temples and accustomed to worship through the senses, they transformed the graves of fallen warriors into the nuclei of magical shrines: incense-wreathed and saffron-threaded portals into an unseen world where it was said that jinns could be tamed, the dead might speak, and supplicants' wishes become saints' commands. The package sold. Bolstered by practical incentives—the enhanced status that Islamic egalitarianism promised low-caste Hindus, for example—Islam won hearts and minds by the thousands. Within a decade of Abdullah's arrival, Badaun itself was on track to become one of the most important centers of Islamic culture in northern India. Abdullah's own legacy was so enduring that eight centuries later, he was still being venerated by descendants of the men and women he had helped to convert.

I had been very pleased to learn about Abdullah from my father, who recited his adventures from an old genealogy shortly before I set off for India. His existence had furnished me with a useful lineage, and though academic texts often insist that Sufism has no connection with the colorful fantasies of Orientalist legend, his reputation turned out to be gratifyingly magical. Abdullah is known in Badaun simply as Pir Makki, or the Holy Man of Mecca, and devout believers assured me that he was a saint of the highest order. His influence over the unseen world was all but unquestionable—why else would the king of the jinns frequent his shrine?—and hundreds of scribbled prayers around his grave testified to intercessory powers that could tackle problems from matrimonial strife to exam nerves. According to the shrine's amulet vendor, his uncanny abilities had been evident even during his lifetime. Anxious not to abandon followers in Mecca, he had taken the trouble to teleport himself back once a week to lead their Friday prayers.

Over the course of my travels, however, it became apparent that Abdullah's standing with the home crowd was no guarantee of admiration farther afield. The saint- and shrine-dominated rituals of Badaun are associated with one particular set of Indian believers—known as Barelvis—and though there are millions of them, they have long been in conflict with another sect named after a famous madrasa town called Deoband. And many Deobandis take the view that pioneers such as Abdullah were actually responsible for vast amounts of damage. Instead of promoting Islam by cleaving to the path laid down in the seventh century by the Prophet Muhammad,* they had borrowed from the sensuality and menagerie temples of Hinduism. The consequence had been terrible spiritual corruption and the incorporation of innovations ranging from musical prayers to incense sticks. According to the Deobandis, asking saints to intercede with God was not Islamic at all; it was an act of idolatry akin to worshipping a monkey or an elephant. Claims to exorcise people according to the shari'a were equally preposterous: jinns inhabited a parallel universe, and insofar as they might sometimes possess human beings, that was the unchallengeable will of God.

Similar complaints about Sufi heterodoxy date back centuries, and they have some history on their side. Among Abdullah's near contemporaries in late-thirteenth-century Cairo and Damascus were mystical sects of a notoriously inventive sort, known for practices that ranged from cannabis consumption to penis piercing. The willingness of early Indian missionaries to accommodate local customs does not lack for circumstantial evidence either. One of the men who led Badaun's conquest is buried in a mosque alongside his horse—as well as a lion, a snake, and, most mysteriously, a parrot. Another mystic of the era known as Mangho is honored in northern Karachi with a shrine that accommodates two hundred sacred crocodiles, all of them supposedly descended from his head lice, and worshippers often wrap up their prayers at the nearby mosque by sacrificing bags of offal to the reptiles. And though signs of sacred penis piercing are nowadays scant, cannabis retains a degree of popularity: in the anarchic shrine of Sehwan Sharif, narcotic potions are liberally shared as religious ecstasy kicks in, and hopes of spiritual communion in the Sufi mausoleums of Lahore inspire would-be mystics to smoke charas by the fistful.

The eclecticism does not prove that cross-fertilization is inherently irreligious, however. The point is made most vividly with architectural examples. The magnificent turquoise-tiled mosques of cities such as Esfahan and Shiraz owe their existence to the encounter of Muslims with an alien people—the Mongols. Istanbul's skyline, a bubble bath of stone

---

*It is conventional among Muslims to add "May God bless him and grant him peace" (*sallalahu alayhi wa sallam*) when referring to the Prophet. This book does not use the phrase, although—in case anyone thinks otherwise—no disrespect is intended.

that is about as emblematically Islamic as any sight on earth, visibly mirrors the domed basilicas of Christian Byzantium, and the Ottomans who produced it were steeped in Sufism. Indeed, Islam would have been *incapable* of developing such traditions without a capacity to learn and borrow. That struck me forcefully when I visited the ghostly ruins of a city called Anjar, built from scratch less than a century after the Prophet's death, which now nestles among garlic fields in a quiet corner of Lebanon's Bekaa Valley. Its lizard-infested villas, palaces, and frescoed bathhouses are perfectly Greco-Roman—not only in terms of inspiration, but also, in the case of dozens of Corinthian pillars lining its grassy *cardo maximus*, in terms of materials.

Such ruminations would belong to a travel diary rather than a book about the shari'a were it not for one fact. Conservatives have imagined Islamic law to be as eternal as any other aspect of the faith, and arguments about authenticity have therefore had tremendous legal consequences. That is, to a certain extent, consequent on the very notion of Islam—with its commitment to a revealed text and an inspired Prophet—but it has affected approaches to historical scholarship as well. The idea has become widespread that God's revelations were built into practical rules by people untainted by impurities—companions of Muhammad, heroic early generations, and omniscient jurists—whose probity transcends the vagaries of place and the passage of time.

That claim raises issues similar to those I once encountered in a very different part of the world—the United States. As a law student at Harvard in the late 1980s, I had learned that many American conservatives consider the Founding Fathers of the United States to be possessed of incontestable wisdom. Some went further, arguing that God had manifested His will through their deeds. According to certain lawyers, that could oblige judges to interpret the federal Constitution according to its eighteenth-century meaning, or even require that they consider the Founders' views when resolving contemporary legal controversies: limits to the death penalty, for example, or governmental restrictions on free speech. Back then, I had felt that the deference to ancient vocabularies and dead people's thoughts had the whiff of a séance about it. Pinning down a person's meaning and motives is hard enough when he or she is alive. The collective intention of a large and diverse group of the deceased is difficult to conceptualize, let alone know. The traditionalist approach toward interpreting the shari'a does not, on its face, look very different. It seems more akin to ancestor worship than any grave-venerating ritual could be—simply because, notwithstanding my personal debt to Abdullah of Mecca, holy wisdom does not automatically pass down through the generations.

My curiosity about the shari'a was not born during my 2009 visit to Badaun. By then, it was almost a decade old, having been sparked off by an odd detail of the U.S. government's response to 9/11. At the time of the al-Qa'eda attacks I had been living in Manhattan, working on a book about the criminal trial in Western history,* and I had watched as anxiously as everyone else while the administration of President George W. Bush geared up to retaliate against Osama bin Laden in Afghanistan. And then, on September 25, 2001, Secretary of Defense Donald Rumsfeld had announced that the military action was being renamed. It was now to be known as Operation Enduring Freedom, because the title originally chosen might offend friendly nations in the Islamic world. It had previously been called Infinite Justice, and that, observed Rumsfeld, was a prerogative that Muslims attributed to God alone.

It had occurred to me even then that the name of the imminent bombing campaign might not be all that would cause offense, but my primary reaction was simply a vague feeling that the rebranding was appropriate. Whatever other qualities posterity was going to attribute to the Bush administration, it seemed a fairly safe bet that omniscience and omnipotence would not be among them. The next few years did not change my opinion in that regard, but following my return to London, another very inauspicious event served both to rekindle my interest in Islamic law and to illuminate another aspect of the Infinite Justice fiasco: the fact that the United States, without knowing it, almost waged its war on terror in the name of the shari'a.

That realization was occasioned by the bombing of London's subway and bus network by four suicidal killers on July 7, 2005. Those attacks were notoriously committed by Muslims who claimed to be inspired by faith, and in their aftermath claims and counterclaims about

*The Trial: A History, from Socrates to O. J. Simpson.

Islamic law reverberated around the media. Having just published the history of Western criminal justice on which I had been working, I was feeling rather redundant—until I realized that no one was actually throwing much light on the subject they were supposed to be talking about. Fiery preachers and more or less random young Muslims were making bellicose assertions about "the shariʿa." People who wanted to be angry with them were assuming the word meant what they said. Noise, rather than information, was filling a void, while critical questions were going not just unanswered but unasked. Where was the shariʿa written down? To what extent was it accepted that its rules had been crafted by human beings? And what gave the men who were so loudly invoking it the right to speak in God's name?

It took a surprisingly long time to establish even basic answers, but they are so central to the rest of this book that it is worth recalling them here. When the Qurʾan was first enunciated by the Prophet Muhammad during the 620s, the term "shariʿa" conveyed the idea of a direct path to water—a route of considerable importance to a desert people— and at a time when no one systematically differentiated between the world that was and the world that ought to be, Islam's straight and narrow described as much as it prescribed. Scholars would not write about it for at least another century, and half a millennium would elapse before legal theories settled into definitive form, but Muslims always thought of the shariʿa in grand terms—infinite ones, even. The fourteenth-century Syrian jurist Ibn Qayyim (1292–1350) set out the vision well:

> [It] is the absolute cure for all ills . . . It is life and nutrition, the medicine, the light, the cure and the safeguard. Every good in this life is derived from it and achieved through it, and every deficiency in existence results from its dissipation. If it had not been for the fact that some of its rules remain [in this world] this world would [have] become corrupted and the universe would [have been] dissipated . . . If God wish[ed] to destroy the world and dissolve existence, He would void whatever remains of its injunctions. For the shariʿa which was sent to His Prophet . . . is the pillar of existence and the key to success in this world and the Hereafter.

As befits so awesome a phenomenon, the science of studying law—jurisprudence, or *fiqh*—came to be considered a duty akin to prayer. No aspect of creation fell outside its scope, and jurists pronounced on questions from the lawfulness of logic to the legal meaning of the moon. They hypothesized fantastically unfortunate dilemmas: what Muslims should do on a desert island, for example, if they ever found themselves pining away alongside a dead shipmate, a pig, and a flask of wine (clue: avoid the pork and alcohol until desperate). While some would always focus on big issues such as criminal justice and jihad, others explored far more specialized aspects of the cosmic order—the calculation of inheritance shares, say, or the jurisprudence of ablutions—and no problem was ever too personal to escape their collective gaze. Al-Ghazali (1058–1111), arguably the greatest of all Sunni theologians, once subjected the intimacies of marriage to rigorous legal scrutiny and attributed to the Prophet himself a commandment on the importance of foreplay. Sex was unholy unless preceded by "kiss[es] and [sweet] words," Muhammad had reportedly warned. "Let none of you come upon his wife like an animal."

By the time I took the plunge and signed up in late 2007 to write an account of Islamic ideas of justice, it was clear therefore that challenges lay ahead. Researching so sprawling a subject posed inherent problems, and the distinction between shari'a and *fiqh*, all too often overlooked in the West, called for careful negotiation. Attempts to critique the shari'a are liable to be perceived by devout Muslims as a denunciation of God rather than an argument. The rules of *fiqh*, on the other hand, can never be more than a human approximation of the divine will. Individual jurists have often tried to blur the difference, but lawyerly ideas in general have never been immune from scrutiny. It was through that gap—the crack between heaven and earth—that Islamic law would have to be explored.

The difficulties moved from the theoretical to the real when, between late 2008 and the spring of 2011, I traveled around South Asia, Iran, and the Middle East and met jurists in person. Suspicion of the Western world in the region has rarely been higher, and my background as a human rights barrister was more often a hindrance than a help: an indictment of the West's hypocrisy rather than an expression of its values. And although I traded shamelessly on my un-English name and paternal roots, suspicions were often intense. The chief law lecturer of a Lucknow madrasa began by warning me that any attempt to understand the shari'a required a fluency in classical Arabic and proficiency in Qur'anic exegesis, and any questions I had in mind were therefore at least a decade premature. The president of Pakistan's Jamaat e-Islami Party complained that my inquiries about Taliban interpretations of Islamic law sounded like those of a NATO stooge, and that I would be better off abandoning my "agenda" and asking instead about "American napalm, daisy cutters, and helicopter gunships." A particularly memorable put-down came from Muhammad Afshani, the director of fatwas at a militant Karachi madrasa called the Jamia Farooqia. As we sat cross-legged on a threadbare mosque carpet, I outlined the nature of my project and told him that, *insh'allah*, I would fill the gaps in my own knowledge by learning from scholars with different opinions— even conflicting ones. He smiled sagely and murmured that I had taken on a difficult project. I nodded, with what I hoped was humility. "And no one," he continued evenly, "should ever embark on such a journey until they know their destination."

The view that questions were inappropriate until the answers were known was one I felt bound to ignore, and as a consequence I did indeed end up with several unforeseen ideas. Mufti Afshani was wrong to the extent that synthesizing them was productive on my own terms, however, and that is reflected in the relatively straightforward structure of this book. The first part sets out the historical events that informed the creation of Islamic jurisprudence, while the second considers its status today, with a particular focus on four themes: attitudes toward war, modernity, criminal justice, and religious tolerance. It seeks unashamedly to entertain as well as inform, but lest it be necessary to say so—and it probably is—it does not intend at any point to challenge the sacred stature of the Prophet Muhammad, the self-evident appeal of Islam, or the almightiness of God. It seeks instead to recall the history that attended the elucidation of Islamic law and to demonstrate that over the years legal rules have often been rewritten or ignored in the name of the shari'a. It also aims to show that many of the people who nowadays claim the clearest perspectives on seventh-century wisdom form part of a revivalist trend that is in important respects just a few decades old. Even people who disagree will, I hope, recognize at least that issues so important are worthy of debate.

It is tempting in conclusion to plagiarize al-Jahiz, the wittiest writer of ninth-century Baghdad, who once demanded full credit for a work's strengths while insisting that any inadequacies were the fault of his audience's unrealistic expectations. I grudgingly accept, however, that my own shortcomings cannot be so easily palmed off. All I ask is that readers bear in mind the words of another great Arab, the tenth-century historian and traveler al-Mas'udi: "If no one could write books but he who possessed perfect knowledge, no books would be written."

Part One

·

The Past

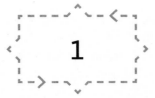

1

Laying Down the Law

"Recite!" The disembodied voice echoed around the cavern. "In the name of thy God who created man from a clot of blood!" With those words, according to the Qur'an, all of humanity was instructed to submit to Islam, but the only person present was a forty-year-old Arab merchant named Muhammad, who reacted by looking around with astonishment. Although it was the holy month of Ramadan and he had come to the cave to meditate, he had never before experienced so uncanny an event. The order was then repeated—"Recite!"—as incomprehensible symbols floated on a piece of cloth before his eyes. Muhammad protested that he could not even read, only to find himself lifted off the ground and crushed until words that he barely understood filled his mouth.

Muhammad was terrified. He came from Mecca, a trading center on the western edge of the Arabian Peninsula that doubled as a place of pilgrimage, and the pagan cults with which he was familiar had no shortage of malevolent deities. Their nymphs, satyrs, and storm gods were constantly up to no good, fighting dusty battles on the desert horizon or shifting villages across its shimmering sands, and Muhammad feared that he was falling victim to one of the most destructive creatures of them all—the jinn, a spirit capable of controlling a person's mind. He scrambled out of the cave, besieged by visions, but as he swayed suicidally on a rocky precipice, he was at last made to realize that he was dealing with no mere demon. A colossal figure now filled the starry sky, and its voice addressed him wherever he turned. "O Muhammad!" it boomed. "You are the Messenger of God and I am Gabriel."

Events on the hillside detained Muhammad for so long that his wife, Khadija, sent out a search party. She was an independently wealthy businesswoman, older than her husband, and when he was found, traumatized and shivering, she swiftly took charge. The region in which Mecca was situated, the Hijaz, was home to a number of faiths, and one of her cousins was an expert in matters spiritual, having studied the Torah and converted to Christianity. A visit was arranged, and Waraqa bin Nawfal's response was both encouraging and ominous. The good news was that Muhammad had encountered the one true God and that the angel Gabriel had been associated with some very auspicious events. The bad news was that Meccans would vilify Muhammad, ridicule his story, and do their utmost to kill him.

Islam so despises the culture it replaced that its hostile claims about Arab paganism always merit a pinch of salt, but there would have been good reasons for Waraqa to be concerned. Although the Meccans considered one of their gods to be paramount, and even called him *the* god—*al-lah*, in Arabic—monotheism ran directly contrary to their traditions. As far as they were concerned, *al-lah* governed the universe in alliance with three daughters and several hundred subordinates, and that belief was fortified by some sound economic calculations. Across the city stood dozens of domed red leather tents, each of them housing holy statuettes and images, and an idol-strewn palace known as the Ka'ba drew thousands of pilgrims annually. The shrine was jointly managed by two branches of the dominant Quraish clan—the Umayyads and the Hashemites—and their partnership was as delicate as it was lucrative. Muhammad was a respected Hashemite, but any attempt to revise the rules would not go down well.

The year was 610, and the channel of communication that had opened between Muhammad and God would transform the world. Thousands of lines of divine wisdom would reach him from the heavens over the next two decades, transmitted by a disembodied voice or heralded by a bell, and as he fell entranced and moved his lips to memorize God's words, he would see far beyond the visible world, far into heaven and deep into hell. Even the jinns that he had initially feared were said to have converted en masse, after several overheard a nocturnal recitation and were struck by its beauty. Among Muslims, Muhammad has become a correspondingly heroic figure, and every child is brought up on stories about his valor, wisdom, and kindness. But though evidence of the admiration is ancient, the process that saw it recorded was far from straightforward. The revelations he received were collected together as a written Qur'an (recitation) soon after his death, but it took another century for the first written accounts of his life to appear, and only in the late ninth century did scholars compile collections of reports (hadiths) that the majority accepted as authentic. Older books were subsequently relegated to irrelevance insofar as they differed. As a consequence, the orthodox version of Islam's origins became definitive only about three centuries after the events it described. Yet for many Muslims, history has turned into an aspect of faith rather than a subject for debate—assumed insofar as it supports the conventional view, and sacrilegious if it seems somehow to undermine it.

Any account of this period therefore faces some serious problems. Not only is there little way to test the received version of events, but the hadiths themselves are contradictory. There is plenty on which the biographers agree, to be sure. No one has ever denied that Muhammad was tall, dark eyed, handsome, fragrant, lustrous, well mannered, soft-spoken, modest, firm of handshake, and purposeful of stride. But the uncertainties quickly multiply. Some hadiths state that he was prone to tears, while others insist that he had an easy smile. There are claims that he once envisioned hell to be full of females, and many others that depict him not just comfortable with but delighted by the company of intelligent and opinionated women. He was a man of unyielding rigor, say some, but he is also supposed to have laughed when told that an arrested drunk had staggered free from a flogging, and to have counseled followers against further action. The truth must lie somewhere, but all that can be said for sure is that the descriptions frequently say more about the describers than they could possibly reveal about Muhammad himself.

A coherent picture does emerge out of the early biographies, however, and it portrays someone who was both resourceful and remarkable. Born after the death of his father, Muhammad lost both his mother and his grandfather during childhood and grew up in the household of an uncle named Abu Talib. Though orphaned and illiterate, he married well and built up a successful trading partnership with Khadija, and his acumen was impressive enough for his fellow Quraish to ask him at one point to arbitrate a dispute over management of the Ka'ba. And even during the first quiet years of his mission, he won supporters. Khadija quickly accepted that her husband was a messenger of God, and though Abu Talib would never acknowledge Muhammad's prophethood, his ten-year-old son, Ali, pledged his allegiance. Slaves and social outcasts also trickled to the cause, along with a prosperous merchant named Abu Bakr. Precisely what Muhammad was divulging at this early stage is not known, but he was clearly already inspirational.

Three years after first making contact, God told Muhammad that the time had come to spread the word more generally. With some trepidation, he duly informed his fellow Meccans that he was a prophet—the last in a line that ran via Jesus and Moses all the way back to Adam. Then, more boldly, he revealed that *al-lah* had neither companions nor daughters. The Quraish were blindly following their ancestors, he declared, "even though their fathers were void of wisdom and guidance," and their activities at the Ka'ba were fundamentally misdirected. They should pray twice daily toward Jerusalem instead and seek peace through submission to the divine—a state encapsulated by the Arabic word *islam*. Only then would they begin to appreciate God's true nature: a spiritual presence "nearer to [man] than his jugular vein."

Although no one would ever doubt Muhammad's eloquence, early reactions were unpromising. Rumors rapidly spread that he had fallen under the spell of a jinn or poetic inspiration (maladies then considered much the same thing), and the first response of Mecca's pagans was to offer Muhammad the best medical treatment that money could buy. But he had found his voice, and it was assuming ever greater urgency. Whereas Meccans seem to have believed that life after death differed little from life before it, Muhammad began to warn that a great reckoning awaited everyone and that earthly deeds carried eternal consequences. In his telling, God was about to snuff out His stars and set seas boiling, and as creation shuddered to a close, trumpet blasts were going to wake all the dead there had ever been. There would then be a time at which commendable deeds would be weighed against sins—the final Hour (*al sa'a*)—and all the signs suggested that Meccans were in line for scorching winds, molten brass, and unquenchable hellfire.

The apocalyptic vision was informed by solid moral arguments. The world into which Muhammad had been born was so stratified that clans did not even intermarry, while women were chattels and slaves bore a shameful status that lasted through generations. Vengeance was as valued as mercy was considered weak, and though the Meccans venerated three goddesses, the birth of an actual girl was so inauspicious that custom allowed for female infanticide. Against that backdrop, Muhammad had begun to claim that his followers were morally equal, regardless of sex or social standing, and to teach that clemency was no flaw but a virtue—so much so that compassion (*al-rahman*) and mercy (*al-rahim*) were the first of God's many names. The killing of a single person was meanwhile tantamount to the murder of all humanity, and at the Hour of Judgment every baby girl ever slaughtered in Mecca would indict her parents from her grave. But there was hope. Penitents might yet spend an eternal afterlife in cool gardens of endless delight.

The attitudes of many Meccans hardened to match. Muhammad's supposed revelations were a mishmash of Jewish and Christian fables, jeered the Quraish. If he was a real prophet, why did he not produce some concrete evidence—a miracle, perhaps, or a public appearance alongside the angel that he talked so much about? Muhammad responded by challenging the naysayers to come up with some verses of their own, if divine inspiration was that easy to fake. He brushed aside charges of inconsistency with the disclosure that God sometimes supplemented His revelations with better ones, and he scorned the demand for miracles. Specific circumstances had required Moses to part the seas and Jesus to raise the dead, but Muhammad's task was to transmit God's final message to humanity—and was that not the greatest wonder of them all?

Many prominent Meccans thought not, and envoys were soon pressing Abu Talib to silence his irksome nephew as a matter of urgency. But though the older man advised Muhammad in private to tone down the revelations, he publicly let it be known that no one could harm his relative without risking retaliation from his household. It was an honorable stand, but its limits were also becoming clear. As conversions grew more frequent, Meccans took to torturing suspect slaves and beating up anyone who was caught trying to pray. Abu Bakr had his beard tugged, and Muhammad himself had the bloody uterus of a sheep hurled at him as he once prostrated. When a group of Muslims fled for Abyssinia, where the Christian king had offered them asylum, the pressure only intensified on those who remained. And crisis then turned to catastrophe—when, in 619, Abu Talib and Khadija both died.

The loss left Muhammad vulnerable as never before. In a hierarchical community where identities were defined by social connections, Muhammad had lost the two people closest to him. It was hard to see how he could recover his position in Mecca, and then, as if by a miracle, the possibility of powerful new allies elsewhere presented itself. As the annual pilgrimage to the Ka'ba proceeded during the summer of 620, six visitors from Yathrib, an oasis situated some two hundred miles to the north, sought a meeting with Muhammad. Having been told by Jewish neighbors that an Arab prophet was long overdue, they were curious to see whether he might be one—and they carried back so favorable a report that many more Yathribis attended the following year's pilgrimage. At a clandestine gathering alongside his own followers in the desert, Muhammad then divulged a momentous revelation. It had long been known that God expected believers to exert themselves—to do jihad—but Muhammad disclosed that spiritual exertions could include the use of force against anyone who opposed the revelations he was transmitting. In the words of an eighth-century biographer:

> The apostle had not been given permission to fight or to shed blood before [then]. He had simply been ordered to call men to God and to endure insult and forgive the ignorant . . . [But now God] gave permission to His apostle to fight and to protect himself against those who wronged [his followers] and treated them badly.

It was the first sign of a phenomenon that would one day inspire fateful ideas about the legal interpretation of divine rules—God's capacity to adjust His revelations—and its practical impact was immediate. On Muhammad's instructions, Muslims began filtering north toward Yathrib. His enemies in Mecca, faced with a local difficulty that was turning regional, simultaneously resolved to terminate the problem at its source. A gathering of clans decided that the prophet in their midst should be murdered, and every family present agreed to assume a share of the blood guilt by contributing a killer to the death squad. But it was too late. After reportedly receiving a tip-off from the angel Gabriel, Muhammad made good his escape through a window, reconnoitered with Abu Bakr, and set off for Yathrib. Both men sheltered together in a cave for three days and then made their way to their destination, which consequently became known as *al-madinat al-nabi* (City of the Prophet)—or, more simply, Medina.

The Prophet's emigration (*hijra*) in September 622 is the seminal moment of Islamic history. It marks the first year of the Muslim calendar, and like Paul Revere's ride or the retreat from Dunkirk it has come to be seen as a portent of triumph rather than a sign of desperation. The righteous exile (*muhajir*) is a figure of Islamic folklore, and countless Muslim revolutionaries with pretensions to holiness have made sure to abandon their homelands during the course of their struggles. Many have gone all the way and spent time loitering around caves— among them Osama bin Laden and Ayman al-Zawahiri, whose post-9/11 publicity material often seemed deliberately to invite comparisons to the travails of the Prophet. But though emulation of the *hijra* was long ago ritualized, it gained its significance in 622 for a very practical reason. An earlier era of wicked ignorance, known to Muslims as the *jahiliyya*, was dispelled forever as they became able for the first time to follow the path toward salvation that God was laying down—the shari'a.

The notion of an absolute break with the past is as easily overstated as that summary suggests. Cultural continuities were legion. To take just one illustration, Arabs would transform their ancestors' practice of circumcision into a religious duty, notwithstanding the absence of any revelation in its support.* An even more specifically pagan Meccan

---

*Although there was a verse mandating circumcision in the Torah, a Muslim consensus on the subject took time to coalesce. Almost a century after the *hijra*, Caliph Umar II would reject an adviser's suggestion that converts be required to prove lack of a foreskin to claim certain privileges under Islamic taxation laws. "God sent Muhammad in order to summon people to Islam," he observed, "not to circumcise them": al-Tabari, *History*, 24:83.

custom—clitoridectomy—has been so tenacious that some Muslims imagine to this day that it was commanded by God. And yet the move to Medina was undeniably momentous, for Islam now metamorphosed from a private faith to a public religion. The process reportedly began at the very moment of the Prophet's arrival. Allowing his camel to choose an auspicious place to kneel, he, along with several followers, is said then and there to have constructed a mosque, and when the last palm frond had been set in place, he turned his attention to the practicalities of prayer. After contemplating whether to summon the faithful with a ram's horn, like the Jews, or a *nakus*—the xylophone-like instrument used by Arab Christians—he settled on the unadorned human voice. Stentorian affirmations of God's greatness, chanted by a freed black slave named Bilal, were soon drifting over the rooftops of Medina. As the duty of submission was broadcast, it also grew more onerous. The custom of fasting during Ramadan was turned into a solemn obligation. By way of another amendment to earlier revelations, Muhammad also revealed that God was requiring followers to increase their daily prostrations from two to three. The number would soon be upped again, to five.

Each step marked out the shari'a a little more clearly, forging the core of a cultural identity that has remained sturdy for almost fourteen hundred years, and the elaborations of worship were complemented by reforms on a wider front. The changes have to be identified and inferred from later sources, but the record points to a genuinely radical program. Provisions in the Qur'an show that Muhammad frequently warned against economic injustice and established the basis for a welfare state: an alms tax (*zakat*) and inheritance rules that automatically granted a deceased Muslim's next of kin a share in his or her estate. Women did not gain equality, but courts came to recognize that they could annul unhappy marriages and go before a judge to vindicate their property rights. As faith in God replaced clan allegiances, a relatively egalitarian outlook also made headway. Muslims remained eligible to hold slaves— as did Christians, Jews, and every other people known to seventh-century history—but believers were forbidden to own each other, and Muhammad repeatedly made clear that emancipation was among the most meritorious acts that anyone could undertake.

The criminal justice provisions instituted at this time, as reflected in the text of the Qur'an, were straightforward enough. God required humanity to punish four sins, known as *haddood* (sing. *hadd*). Theft was said to merit amputation of the right hand, fornication earned a hundred lashes, and falsely accusing someone of the same offense was punishable by eighty strokes. The gravest crime, the "waging of war against Islam or spreading of disorder in the land," was attended by an entire battery of punitive possibilities: exile, double amputation, suspension from a cross, and decapitation. In the case of other acts of violence, a victim or the next of kin was formally authorized to retaliate, pursuant to a passage of the Torah that was reiterated by the Qur'an— "a life for a life, an eye for an eye, a nose for a nose, an ear for an ear, a tooth for a tooth, and, for wounds, punishment." Two additional measures that were not mentioned in the holy book also seem to have been credited to God. The first was a fixed number of lashes, either forty or eighty, for intoxication. The second prescribed that people who had sex outside wedlock, having at some time in their lives been married, should be stoned to death.

The punishments look distinctly premodern from a twenty-first-century perspective, but it would take either naivete or ill will to characterize them in terms worse than that. Corporal punishments were a feature of the age, while crucifixion owed its popularity in the Middle East to centuries of Persian and Roman practice—and among Muslims, at least in later years, it was intended to be a nonfatal means of humiliation rather than a method of execution. Torture, which was routine under the Christianized Roman law of Byzantium, found no place in the Qur'an. And the holy book was suffused with more general concepts of mercy. Repentance was often reason enough to exclude punishment for a *hadd*. Where the offense gave someone else a right to seek vengeance, retaliation was limited by the scale of the original crime, and victims were urged to accept compensation or exercise mercy instead. The rules, for all their rigor, also reflected the ancient notion that responsibility was a matter of honor, and less was expected of those lower down the social pecking order: someone who had unlawful sex having never before been married was subject to lashing rather than stoning, and the number of strokes inflicted for adultery and intoxication was halved if the convict was a slave. The most striking fact of them all was the one that today is most likely to be overlooked: physical punishment was authorized just five times in the entire Qur'an.

The system's relative leniency is paradoxically illustrated by its harshest prescription: the stoning to death of a married or divorced person who had sex outside wedlock. The penalty itself had been known since at least 2350 B.C.E., when a king of Mesopotamia stipulated in the world's oldest known laws that promiscuous women should be executed with rocks bearing their names, and the Israelites notoriously adopted the punishment to kill adulterers—as well as blasphemers, witches, wizards, and disobedient sons. Islamic procedures were novel only insofar as they made it far harder to impose. In order for fornication (*zina*) to be proved against a defendant who denied guilt, four witnesses had to attest to the actual act of penetration—in explicit terms—and the evidential hurdle was as challenging as it sounds. The first written attempt to clarify what it entailed (published about one and a half centuries after the Qur'an's revelation) records that a Muslim once asked Muhammad incredulously whether someone who caught his wife having intercourse was supposed to round up four men to watch. "Yes" was the Prophet's categorical answer.

The actual operation of the system emerges in greatest detail from a story that is still taught to all students of Islamic criminal law. It concerns a young married man named Ma'iz ibn Malik, who is said to have presented himself to the Prophet and declared that he had a confession to make. He was a fornicator. Muhammad reportedly refused to acknowledge the admission and turned away, whereupon Ma'iz repeated himself—three times. The Prophet wondered aloud if Ma'iz might be insane and had his breath smelled for signs of intoxication before tentatively inviting the youth to consider if he might simply have kissed or touched the girl. Ma'iz was adamant that matters had gone further. According to a hadith that has always been held in high scholarly estimation, the Prophet's inquiries then grew even more searching. In the words of a twentieth-century Islamic criminal law textbook (expurgated here, but not there):

Calling a spade a spade, [the Prophet asked,] "Did you ——* her?" [Ma'iz] said "Yes." He asked, "Like the kohl stick disappears into the

*The verb used is *aniktaha*.

kohl container and the bucket into the well?" He answered, "Yes." Then he asked, "Do you know what *zina* means?" He said, "Yes, I did with her unlawfully what a man does with his wife lawfully." Then the Prophet said, "What do you intend with these words?" He answered, "That you purify me." Then he ordered him to be stoned.

The tale of Ma'iz is hard to forget once heard, and whatever anxieties might have prompted his longing for purification, the story of his trial operates as something of a religious Rorschach test. Pious Muslims see only extraordinary restraint on the Prophet's part, and they often point out additional signs of his mercy: the fact that he made no attempt to track down the woman concerned, for example. At the opposite end of the spectrum are people who focus on nothing but the outcome. But a single perspective on a controversial event never makes for balance, and as soon as other hadiths are taken into account, a subtler picture begins to emerge. One of them states that the execution divided Muslims into two camps, and another has Muhammad asking the killers of Ma'iz: "Why did you not leave him alone? He might have repented and been forgiven by God." At least two more suggest that Ma'iz's real offense was not illicit sex but indiscretion. One contemporary was heard to ruminate many years later that the young man had been punished only because he insisted so publicly on his guilt. A second recalled that Muhammad once rounded on several followers who were ridiculing Ma'iz for having been stupid enough to confess, telling them that they would be better off eating carrion than speaking so dishonorably of the dead.

Such stories are a reminder that criminal justice in the seventh century was underpinned by forces considerably more complex than compulsion. Although the Qur'an acknowledges a need to shame criminals in verses that speak of crucifixion as a "disgrace" and amputation as "exemplary," its emphasis on repentance sought throughout to touch a wrongdoer's conscience. It was only when an individual showed an unequivocal refusal to conform that punishment became inevitable, and that was why Ma'iz was killed. In the confines of a desert community, someone who insisted that he had had penetrative sex with someone else's wife, daughter, or slave was trouble personified. There would have been just as great a crisis had four men sworn before God that they had seen penetration taking place. It was not the gravity of the crime so much as the willingness to vocalize an accusation that made remedial action essential. If catharsis was to clear the air in such circumstances, the community needed a victim as much as it needed a verdict. Witnesses and neighbors constituted themselves into a kind of premodern firing squad—reconsecrating the community with blood, at a time when tensions might otherwise have pulled it apart.

There is one more story that, in a very different way, shows how context is essential to make sense of the Qur'an's criminal justice provisions. It involves the offense of sexual slander—and the Prophet himself. As revelations proliferated in Medina, Muhammad received several that addressed his personal circumstances, and after being told that Muslim men could have up to four wives at a time, he learned that God was waiving the limits in his own case. Almost all of the dozen or so women he subsequently married were widows, but there was one exception—a young daughter of Abu Bakr's named A'isha*—and the Prophet's relationship with her was intense and, at one point, almost cataclysmic. That point came following a raid, when she accidentally fell behind. It was common at the time for women to accompany their menfolk on raiding parties, but what followed was far from normal. The teenager rode home on a camel belonging to one of the Prophet's young companions, and though she was demurely mounted and he was on foot when they reentered Medina, rumors of cuckoldry were soon rife. As if that were not enough, allegiances divided down a line that ran straight through the Prophet's household. On one side stood Abu Bakr, publicly defending the honor of his furious, tearful daughter. In the opposing camp was Ali, by now married to the Prophet's daughter Fatima, who tacitly advised his older cousin to contemplate divorce. Worst of

---

*A'isha's age was first recorded a couple of centuries after the Prophet's death, when the biographer Ibn Sa'd and the hadith scholar al-Bukhari wrote that she was nine when the marriage was consummated. Since she was the only wife of Muhammad who was not previously married, they might have been exaggerating her youth to exclude any doubt about her virginity: see Spellberg, *Politics, Gender, and the Islamic Past*, pp. 39–41. They might alternatively have been accurate—not least because child brides were not unusual among rulers of the time.

all, the revelations simply ceased. The Prophet, facing a seismic split in his home, a scandal outside it, and a total silence from God, was left simply to persevere—until, at last, his faith was justified. One cold day, followers noticed with surprise that sweat was forming on his forehead. The long-anticipated communication then came through. A'isha, it turned out, was innocent. The fault lay with the gossipmongers, and slanderers who falsely alleged unchastity against women would henceforth merit a punishment of eighty lashes.

As the Affair of the Lie illustrates, Muhammad was inherently well positioned to tackle any crisis that might come his way, and his status as God's messenger was complemented in Medina by the emergence of great leadership skills. Armed hostilities against the Quraish began in earnest in March 624, when the Prophet led some three hundred men to victory against a Meccan force three times that size at a valley called Badr. As his followers began to feel their strength, the Muslim community also began to distance itself from Judaism and Christianity. Muhammad had originally expressed considerable admiration for both, acknowledging their followers to be fellow "Peoples of the Book," but he now disclosed that they had been seriously misinterpreting the books concerned. At a series of debates, he informed Christians that the prophet Jesus was neither God's son nor part of a holy trinity nor even the victim of a true crucifixion: God had in fact swept him off the cross and substituted a doppelgänger in his place. There was an even more dramatic deterioration of relations with Medina's substantial Jewish population, and one of the spats, as reported by the eighth-century writer Ibn Ishaq, has an acrimony that still all but rises off the page. A group of Jews are said to have approached the Prophet with a question. "Now, Muhammad," they asked. "God created creation, but who created God?" They followed up with an inquiry about the divine physiognomy. "Describe His shape to us, Muhammad; His forearm and His upper arm, what are they like?" Soothing words from the angel Gabriel enabled the Prophet to contain his anger, and a revelation soon confirmed that God was entire of Himself, with a right hand mighty enough to grasp both heaven and earth. But it was a turning point—literally. After one and a half years of uneasy coexistence, Muhammad instructed his followers to cease praying in the direction of Jerusalem and to realign their prostrations toward the Ka'ba. In physical terms, that involved a 180-degree rotation. In theological ones, it was closer to a revolution.

As the rivalry sharpened, the potential for violence mounted, and another incident from this time demonstrates just how tense the situation had become. Muslim women were beginning to wear veils in increasing numbers, because God had recently required them of the Prophet's wives, and a group of Jews supposedly tried to uncover someone's face when she arrived at their market with goods to sell. A prankster then hitched her dress to her back as she squatted on the ground, and after she stood up to reveal considerably more than her face, a retaliatory murder escalated into a melee, which was followed by a full-scale assault by Muslim forces. Although relations remained fluid enough for another Jewish clan then to fight alongside Muslims at a battle on the slopes of Mount Uhud in March 625, communal relations worsened when the joint army went down to a shocking defeat, and several other Jewish settlements were soon being targeted by Muslim forces. Never was that more true than in 627, when one such force killed some seven hundred men from the hostile Qurayza clan—notwithstanding that they had capitulated and given up their weapons.

At the cost of stating the very obvious, troubles between Muslims and Jews did not end there, but the Quraish were still very much the main enemy. Muhammad's followers were steadily gaining in both strength and confidence, however, and that conflict finally came to an end in 630, with the unconditional surrender of the Meccans. As Muhammad returned in triumph to his birthplace, the keys of the Ka'ba were placed in his hand, and followers took pickaxes and sledgehammers to its 360 leaden effigies. And though the Prophet had previously revealed that there should be "no compulsion in religion," God now spoke again. Most Meccans were given one last opportunity to submit, but scores were settled against several supposedly incorrigible enemies, and a new revelation informed Muslims that polytheists now had just four months to see the error of their ways. Once that period was passed, Muslims would be divinely obliged to "fight and slay the pagans wherever you find them. Seize them, beleaguer them, and lie in wait for them [unless they repent]." As emissaries set out to warn pagans across the Hijaz, Muhammad delivered a valedictory sermon and led his followers on the first exclusively Muslim pilgrimage (hajj) to the Ka'ba. The fifth pillar of Islam was thereby set in place—complementing the avowal of faith, prayers, almsgiving, and Ramadan fasts—and after years of conflict the faith looked at last to be secure. And then, with suitably fateful timing, Muhammad died.

The death of a man in his early sixties might ordinarily be considered merely unfortunate, but the demise of the Prophet threatened catastrophe. The Muslim community, in the flush of its extraordinary victory, was suddenly confronted with the prospect of oblivion. Before his body was even in the grave, Medina's two most powerful clans began squaring up against each other, while Muhammad's Meccan followers frantically maneuvered to stake succession claims of their own. A people united by Muhammad's charisma was spinning apart, and at least some of them took the turn of events very hard indeed. One of the Prophet's earliest and most passionate followers, Umar ibn al-Khattab, simply refused to accept that he had gone, and threatened to dismember anyone who denied his imminent resurrection. Only when Abu Bakr gently reminded him that Islam involved submission to God, not a man, did he acknowledge the truth. "My legs would not bear me," he later recalled. "I fell to the ground knowing that the apostle was indeed dead."

There are two versions of what came next. The account accepted by most Muslims records that the Prophet had said nothing about who should succeed him and acknowledges that his followers briefly floundered. It claims that Umar recovered his composure, however, and defused the crisis by boldly acclaiming Abu Bakr as God's vice-regent (*khalifa*, or caliph). The second account did not just differ. It dissented and undermined both men's authority from the very outset. It claimed that Muhammad *had* appointed a successor—his cousin and son-in-law Ali—and that Abu Bakr and Umar had flagrantly disregarded his wishes by capturing the caliphate while Ali was preparing his relative's body for burial.

The conflict would have profound consequences. It reflected the same familial tensions that were apparent during the Affair of the Lie—the crisis surrounding infidelity allegations against Muhammad's young wife A'isha—and it institutionalized them. A'isha's resentment against

Ali hardened as the man who had failed to defend her honor implicitly challenged her father's right to rule. Abu Bakr, meanwhile, alienated Ali's wife and the Prophet's daughter, Fatima, by ruling against her right to inherit property from her father, a decision which so angered her that she never spoke to him again. And though such controversies might seem from a distance to have little connection with religion, they resonated with spiritual meaning among early Muslims. Ali's supporters came to argue not just that he should be caliph but that the Prophet had wanted leadership of the community to remain forever within his family. Their drift from the mainstream would continue for centuries, and Ali's loyalists—the Alids—would eventually coalesce into the faction (*shi'a*) that accounts today for around one in ten of all Muslims. And the conflict's impact on understandings of the shari'a was destined to be equally significant. Legal theorizing remained more than a century away, but rival claims about the Prophet's views had begun to take root from the moment of his death.

It is ordinarily natural to think that fourteen-hundred-year-old arguments belong in the past, but few assumptions are less valid when it comes to Islamic history. I was reminded of that in May 2009 when, in the Iranian town of Esfahan with a couple of hours to kill, I gatecrashed one of its venerable seminaries. After mumbling my way past the doorman, I entered a lush courtyard, its ancient cypresses towering over a riot of rosebushes, and settled into an alcove to read a book. An alert pupil soon guessed that I did not belong, but he seemed delighted to have found a chance to practice his English. I was equally happy to natter, but the small talk ended suddenly when he learned I was researching a book about the shari'a. The disputation skills of a Shi'a seminarian kicked in, and we quickly hurtled back to the seventh century as theological booby traps sprang up all around. If I was writing a history of Islamic law, he observed with a crocodile smile, I obviously knew the identity of the first legitimate caliph—so was it Ali or Abu Bakr? What was my view about the legality of Abu Bakr's willingness to disinherit the Prophet's own daughter? As a teenager, A'isha would clearly have been unbalanced by her husband's death, and how, in my opinion, did that affect any claims about the shari'a she may have made?

It was a good hour before my new friend sensed how much more he was enjoying the conversation than I was. But though the end of my cross-examination came as a great relief, I was also left marveling at the energy with which he had fought his corner—or at least shadowboxed in it. I knew from books that the Shi'a considered themselves historical victims, but I had never before experienced the underdoggery at such close range. Convinced that the world had always been out to tell lies about those loyal to Ali, the seminarian was determined to set the record straight. History to him was the opposite of the cynical cliché: it was not just one damned thing after another but an unfolding cosmic drama, redolent with meaning and pregnant with the possibility of salvation.

A belief that God's wonders are worked out over time can easily produce rigid views and ossified approaches to the present, of course. But over the centuries, countless pious Muslims have subjected received wisdom to scrutiny with a view to clarifying their faith. Although my seminarian friend would not have appreciated the thought, A'isha herself personifies that critical spirit, with a reputation that has survived the fug of centuries and the filter of many men's pens. A well-known story records her contempt when, after Muhammad's death, some of his companions attempted to dignify as divine their belief that women were intrinsically unclean. "You equate us with dogs and donkeys!" she snapped. "But the Prophet would pray while I lay in front of him on the bed." Early Muslims displayed no less honesty when they memorialized her words. Ibn Sa'd and al-Bukhari, whose ninth-century writings helped form the bedrock for more than a thousand years of religious scholarship, had no apparent compunctions about recording her reaction, for example, to a disclosure by Muhammad that God had just extended his unique marital privileges. "I feel," she told him, "that your Lord hastens in fulfilling your wishes and desires."

With the Prophet's death in 632, the community of his followers was faced with a set of crucial choices about its attitude toward the past. The Muslim community had lost its direct access to divine revelations, and unequivocally earthly problems called for immediate responses.

Muhammad's rule over Medina had been an example of the shariʿa in action—of that there could be no doubt—but there were no permanent written records from the time. And what it entailed for the future was anyone's guess. God would doubtless guide believers, but that assumption was destined forever to remain in the realm of faith. The rest is history.

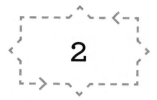

2

From Revelations to Revolution

Abu Bakr's assumption of power in June 632 was followed by a brief but bloody pagan resurgence. As Arab tribes learned that the Muslims had lost their prophet, many decided that they had been overhasty to submit to Islam, and a tax revolt quickly escalated into a series of rebellions. A particularly formidable challenge began to coalesce around Musaylima, a conjurer of some renown, who had previously sent a letter to Muhammad identifying himself as a fellow prophet and offering to go halves on the Hijaz. His initial suggestion having been treated with contempt, Musaylima resolved to make it double or nothing. Unhappily for Musaylima, it was nothing. A Muslim army was dispatched in December to confront his rebel army at its base in the eastern region of Yamama. In the battle that followed, hundreds died on both sides, but it ended with Musaylima dead and Muslim control over the Arabian Peninsula secured.

With the eradication of Arab paganism at Yamama, Islam lost the adversary that had done so much to define its emergence and early growth. And not for the last time in history, the elimination of one enemy led to the magnification of others. A late revelation to Muhammad had suggested that Peoples of the Book had to be subdued by force until they paid "compensation" (*jizya*) for their refusal to accept Islam, and as the threat of idolatry shrank, the importance of that command grew. Subjugation certainly posed a few practical difficulties. To the north and west of the Hijaz stood Christian Byzantium, heir to the glories of Greece and the might of Rome, while Zoroastrian-ruled Persia had been dominating all points east for more than a millennium. But both empires had spent the last three decades pummeling each other to a standstill. The war had notionally ended in 630 with a Christian victory, but both sides were exhausted. If Islam insisted on taking on two superpowers, there could be no better time.

The circumstances surrounding the commencement of hostilities are poorly documented, but Islamic chroniclers have stepped into the breach with a memorable starting point. They record that the emperor Heraclius was stricken one night in his Constantinople palace by a dream that his realm was under attack. When he awoke, one fact had somehow impressed itself on his mind above all others—the assailants had all been circumcised—and he fearfully gathered his priests together for advice. They concurred in a grim conclusion. It would be necessary to kill every male Jew in Byzantium. As preparations for a massacre were laid, the fateful punch line then occurred. An envoy from the southern deserts arrived with news of a great revelation and a demand that Heraclius submit to Islam. The quivering emperor ordered that the Arab be stripped, and the doom of his empire stood revealed.

It would in fact be another eight centuries before Constantinople fell, but Muslims were indeed on the march. By the spring of 634, Byzantium had lost southern Syria, and another Arab force had won a string of victories against the Persian defenders of southern Iraq. When Abu Bakr then died, barely two years after taking over as caliph, the reins of power passed to Umar, who maintained the momentum by annihilating a Byzantine army at the river Yarmuk and driving farther into Iraq. Jerusalem fell in 638, and in 641 Arab forces crossed the Sinai and captured the ancient Egyptian city of Alexandria.

Christian polemicists would in due course transform the warriors sweeping out of the Hijaz into stereotypical fanatics, fiery of eye and bedraggled of beard, who ruthlessly destroyed whatever they could not understand. A Syrian bishop would popularize a particularly tenacious anecdote to that effect at the tail end of the Crusades, almost six and a half centuries later. By his account, the general in charge of the Egyptian campaign asked Caliph Umar for orders with respect to the fabled library of Alexandria and was told to put its works of philosophy to the torch. "If they agree with the Qur'an, they are unnecessary and ought to be destroyed," Umar supposedly murmured. "And if they contradict it, they must be destroyed." As if to add veracity, the chronicler says that the burning scrolls kept the city's extensive network of public baths in fuel for the next six months. In fact, the library was already long gone, razed by either Julius Caesar or the emperor Theodosius I (opinions differ), and letters credited to Umar's general suggest that he became as sensitive to native concerns after Egypt's conquest as he was ruthless toward them before. But though the myth of wanton destruction is unwarranted, it hints at a deeper truth. The caliph was in the habit of questioning the same general about the world beyond the Hijaz and once asked him what the sea was like. The pensive reply— "[it] is a great creature upon which weak creatures ride, like worms upon a piece of wood"—was enough to make Umar abandon naval campaigns for the rest of his reign. Islam was entering unknown territory, and its journey was attended as much by insecurity as by confidence.

One of the earliest manifestations of that polarity, evincing the boldness of seventh-century Muslims but also their unease, was the decision to put the Prophet's message into writing. Repetition of Muhammad's teachings was already widespread at the time of his death, but the revelations were recited from memory, in accordance with an ancient Arab belief that any wisdom worth possessing was worth learning by heart. Orthodoxy dates the turning point to the battle of Yamama and a realization that the carnage had claimed many of the community's most diligent memorizers. An anxious Umar supposedly insisted that Muhammad's revelations be recorded before everyone forgot what they were, and although Abu Bakr was initially perplexed by the thought of reducing God's voice to writing, he invited a former secretary of the Prophet named Zaid ibn Thabit to take on the task. The young scribe was equally amazed, protesting that they might as well ask him to move a mountain, but he overcame his compunctions. In words recorded two centuries later by the great hadith scholar al-Bukhari, the Qur'an was then gathered together "from parchments, scapula, leafstalks of date palms and from the memories of men."

The book that emerged can easily confuse an unprepared reader. Its verses assume an intimate knowledge of the Prophet's mission, and the chapters containing them are structured by theme, and ordered by diminishing length rather than chronology. Several injunctions address Muhammad's household alone: a warning to his wives not to use coarse language, for example, and a stern instruction to visitors not to overstay their welcome. Alongside sublime reflections on the whys and wherefores of creation are eerie tales of worlds disappeared and havoc to come. But to the devout, its mystery has always been part of its magnificence, and its scope has mirrored the immensity of God. Even religiously skeptical Arabic speakers are bound to consider the Qur'an a literary masterpiece, simply because it is the touchstone of Arabic literature: a work without which centuries of Muslim writings would make very little sense. And everyone agrees that its beauty has always rested in the ear as much as on the eye. Not for nothing is its recital said to have stopped jinns in their tracks and melted the hardest of pagan hearts.

The Qur'an's lyricism, like its complexity, speaks of transcendence, however, whereas its physical manifestation was attended by controversy. A belief that became a dogma after the ninth century holds that Ibn Thabit produced an incorruptible copy of a celestial prototype, but even if true, its perfection was not universally appreciated when it first appeared. Alternative versions of the text circulated until at least 651, when Caliph Umar's successor, Uthman, ordered that all variants be gathered together and destroyed, in the world's first Qur'an burning. And though orthodoxy insists that he was simply trying to end certain quarrels over vowel pronunciation, hints abound of more substantial disputes. There is mention in early Muslim sources of revelations that are unknown to any extant Qur'an: A'isha's recollection of a verse on the subject of incest, for example, and a speech by Umar claiming that "God's book" required adulterers to be stoned to death. Some supporters of Ali would later deny that Ibn Thabit had played any role in the Qur'an's compilation at all, insisting instead that the first copy had been handed over directly to their champion by the Prophet himself. A minority of Alids claimed even more daringly that Ibn Thabit had been party to a full-blown conspiracy, or that A'isha had hidden certain revelations favorable to Ali under her bed, where they were eaten by a goat. Such assertions were never taken seriously by the majority, but they are bandied about by sectarians to this day: yet another reminder that eternal perfection is no guarantee of earthly harmony.

Islam's military advance meanwhile continued, and the appearance of the Qur'an served to remedy at least one potentially embarrassing discrepancy. For all that Muslims might complain about the errors of Peoples of the Book, they themselves had previously lacked a book. But the publication of one did not herald any significant change in attitudes toward their rivals, simply because—centuries of anti-Muslim propaganda notwithstanding—forcible conversions were exceptional. Economic calculations did far more to define the trajectory of Islam's early conquests, and the *jizya*, which was always more onerous than the 2.5 percent alms tax applicable to Muslims, was soon producing immense revenues. The spoils of war were simultaneously swelling the caliphal coffers, and Umar then resolved in 638 that every believer was entitled to a share. Islam thereby became as lucrative as it was uplifting, and admission became a privilege, open only to those infidels who could find an Arab to sponsor them.

The financial incentive to limit conversions was complemented by a theological concern. In an age when Muslims collectively assumed that the trumpets of apocalypse might sound at any moment, the urge to avoid spiritual contamination was strong. Consorting with infidels always carried risks, and it would be all too easy for reluctant or false converts to lead a good Muslim astray. Mindful of such concerns, Umar chose to expel Jews and Christians from the Hijaz: a decision that is still cited in Saudi Arabia today to justify a citizenship policy that excludes non-Muslims.* It was harder to keep aliens at bay in those countries that the Arabs had chosen to invade, but isolationist tendencies were strong all the same. Occupying armies constructed isolated reed and clay barracks at strategic locations—sites on the Shatt al-Arab and Euphrates called Basra and Kufa, for example—and kept their social

---

*Interestingly enough, Umar's edict was either entirely ineffective or impermanent. An urbane Palestinian globe-trotter observed in around 985 that "most of the people" in Qurh, a Hijazi town second in size only to Mecca, were Jews: Muqaddasi, *Best Divisions*, p. 82. For the expulsion itself, see Ibn Ishaq, *Life of Muhammad*, pp. 525, 689.

contacts with the natives to a minimum. And yet, as the garrisons turned to towns, the risks of interaction multiplied. Two of Umar's first governors to Iraq obtained recalls after telling the caliph that they had begun to find Iraq "as tempting as a prostitute." Another appointee took to his post rather more easily, only to be dismissed when Umar came to hear a rhapsodic poem he had composed in honor of the drinking dens and dancing girls of Maysan province. There were different ways to confront the new temptations, but whether Muslims met them with caution or robustness, they were not about to go away.

The insularity is yet another reminder that Islam's pioneers were a desert people, suddenly finding themselves in almost fantastic situations and lands. But the very fact that they had entered infidel-dominated territories was to create societies of genuinely remarkable cultural diversity, and though Islamic tolerance began as a necessity, Muslims came to regard their willingness to accept outsiders as a virtue. That is illustrated by countless stories that they told about themselves over the years. A famous speech credited to Abu Bakr, for example, said to have been delivered on the eve of the Muslim invasion of Syria, enumerated a long list of crimes against infidels that Muslim troops were obliged to avoid, from the murder of civilians to the disturbance of Christian hermits whom they might find meditating on pillars. Another well-known report records Umar's personal effort to promote intercommunal harmony during a visit to Jerusalem's Church of the Holy Sepulchre, where he declined its custodians' prudent invitation to join them for worship. "If I had prayed in the church it would have been lost to you," he amicably observed, "for Muslims would have taken it saying: 'Umar prayed here.'"

Although the veracity of such tales is uncertain, there is little doubt about the relatively benign nature of Islamic rule. When Damascus was occupied in 636, Muslims initially commandeered just part of its cathedral, and it was only remodeled into a mosque after purchase from its Christian owners in the early eighth century. The infidel tax was no worse than the impositions of Byzantium and Sassanian Persia, and the civic freedoms permitted minorities were far greater than those offered Jews in Christendom, where they were being expelled, forcibly converted, and killed across a swath of principalities from Gaul to

Byzantium by the early seventh century. And whereas Europe's Jews faced an ever-darkening future of ghettos and pogroms, Islamic clampdowns would always be short-lived, and non-Muslims would often serve as state officials—as viziers, chamberlains, and even as war ministers (twice during the ninth century). Some measure of the big picture emerges from the travelogue of Benjamin of Tudela, a rabbi who roamed North Africa and the Middle East at the height of the Crusades in 1165. By the time his journey was over, he estimated that about three hundred thousand Jews lived under Muslim rule. In Jerusalem, which had been occupied by Christians since 1099, he had found four.

All that is to run ahead with a different story, however, because for all the forbearance that Muslims were exhibiting toward the populations they were subjugating, tensions within the Islamic community itself were about to erupt. The crisis began in 644 when, a decade after taking over as caliph, Umar was mortally stabbed at prayer by a Persian slave. The assassination, by a man reduced to servitude during the conquest of his country, reflected an ethnic conflict that has been in play ever since, but it also reopened the rivalries that had manifested themselves at the time of the Prophet's death. Umar summoned six eminent colleagues to his deathbed and told them to form a consultative council (*shura*) to agree on a successor—on pain of death for dissenters. Ali was among the appointees, but as the collective mood leaned toward a candidate named Uthman, he withdrew his name from consideration. It was another moment of passivity in the face of adversity. That might have signified great patience, as Ali's modern-day admirers claim, but it gave rise to much disappointment at the time—and ominous observations that the failure to assert rightful leadership was itself a betrayal of God.

The new caliph did little to repair the cracks. Uthman belonged to a clan called the Umayyads that had resisted Islam almost to the end, and though his personal record as a close companion of the Prophet was unassailable, he turned out to be a family man through and through. Ali's supporters, already nursing deep grievances about the treatment of the Prophet's household, watched with incredulity as the septuagenarian ruler showered his relatives with largesse, and opposition steadily mounted. Escalating anger in the garrisons of Iraq and Egypt culminated in a major protest in 656, when hundreds of the caliph's opponents converged on his Medina residence. The ugly situation soon became violent as Uthman was besieged in his own home. It then turned lethal, when a mob battered him to death.

The lynching finally tipped the Muslim community from factionalism to fratricide. Ali stepped into the saddle of power, but the atmosphere in Medina was so poisonous that he relocated to Kufa, where he was relatively popular among settlers. His enemies followed. A'isha, still smarting from Ali's advice that Muhammad divorce her, backed a rebellion to the extent that she entered the battlefield on an armored camel, and though that challenge petered out, a simmering threat in Syria then exploded. Uthman had placed an Umayyad cousin in charge of its vast occupying army, and when Ali declined to confirm the nepotistic appointment, the officer concerned—Mu'awiya—took a stand. Legend claims that he did so by brandishing the dead caliph's bloodstiffened shirt and Qur'an, and legend may be right. He certainly condemned Ali for failing to bring his cousin's killers to justice and declared himself duty-bound as an Umayyad to seek vengeance. Twenty-four years after the death of the Prophet, Islam had a civil war (*fitna*) on its hands.

The hostilities began tentatively, but a series of skirmishes in the early summer of 657 developed into a full engagement at a village on the Euphrates called Siffin. As Muslim armies turned on each other for the first time in history, the advantage tilted toward the caliph—until one of Mu'awiya's officers had a brain wave. He instructed his troops to attach passages from the Qur'an to the ends of their lances, and Ali's archers and cavalry, suddenly reminded that God was watching them all, were paralyzed by piety. They withdrew to argue among themselves, some concerned that they were being duped and others contending that the theological issues at stake made that irrelevant, while Ali himself equivocated toward one last compromise. He accepted a proposal from Mu'awiya that each side should empower an arbitrator to negotiate a binding peace, and the deal that ensued left him in a worse position than before. Mu'awiya retained control of Syria, as threatening as ever, while Ali was abandoned by a group of his own supporters. Convinced that he had snatched defeat at the threshold of victory, a group of "seceders" (*khawarij*, or Kharijites) judged him an infidel, and in 661 one of their number set upon him with a poisoned sword as he knelt at prayer. It was another first. Never before had a Muslim presumed to kill a co-religionist for betraying a duty owed to God, and now that that taboo had been transgressed, tragedy loomed.

It manifested itself, as such things often do, after a generational shift. Although Mu'awiya's father had spearheaded opposition to Muhammad for twenty years, he moved effortlessly into the caliphate, and then, as if to parody the Alid veneration for the Prophet's bloodline, he nominated his son as his successor. Yazid took over in 680, and Ali's own younger son Hussein withheld his allegiance. The denouement came during the Muslim month of Muharram, in October, at an Iraqi village named Karbala. Hussein's ragtag force had by then dwindled into an entourage, and when he gave his supporters license to go home, it shrank further. About a hundred men, women, and children remained to be corralled by Yazid's forces, and most were then exterminated. Hussein's head was carried back to Damascus as a prize for the caliph, while his body was robbed and left unburied in the sand.

The slaughter at Karbala was a watershed. The enthroned grandson of a pagan had killed the grandson of the Prophet. To this day, Shi'a clerics and storytellers cannot speak of the injustice without weeping, and its anniversary on the tenth day of Muharram (*ashura Muharram*) is the occasion for mourners around the world to flail and bludgeon themselves into bloody messes. The immediate consequences were even more dramatic. As one of Abu Bakr's grandsons denounced Yazid from Medina, declaring the caliph to be an impostor, a second civil war began. It would last until October 692, by which time thousands more Muslims would lie dead on both sides and Yazid would have cemented his family's hold on power by passing the caliphate on to his own son. The Umayyad clan had transformed the spiritual succession to the Prophet into a hereditary privilege—and taken so tight a grip over expressions of the faith that mosque leaders became obliged to curse Ali during prayers.

Catastrophe and dissension at home did not slow expansion abroad. Quite the opposite. In 663, Mu'awiya began the conquest of Khorasan—a central Asian region that included much of modern Afghanistan, Turkmenistan, and northern Iran—and by the early eighth century Buddhist strongholds and fire temples were toppling as far away as Sind and Punjab. Yazid meanwhile mounted Islam's first assault on the walls of Constantinople in 669, and outposts extended themselves steadily along the African coast. By 711 a general named Tariq ibn Ziyad found himself on the continent's northwest tip, eyeing a rocky outcrop (*jebel*) across the straits, and he then set sail for *jebel Tariq* (Gibraltar), burned his boats, and established Islam's first bridgehead in the land it would call al-Andalus. Christendom gained a respite only after another siege of Constantinople in August 718 and a defeat at Poitiers in 732, each of which Europeans later came to see as pivotal. Edward Gibbon famously speculated that had the fighting at Poitiers gone the other way, "interpretation of the Koran would now be taught in the schools of Oxford, and her pulpits might demonstrate to a circumcised people the sanctity and truth of the revelation of Mahomet." Neither battle ever merited much comment from Muslim chroniclers, however. In just a century, people were being called to prayer from India to Andalusia. The rest of the world could wait its turn.

And yet, for all its military success, the Umayyad dynasty has a deeply dishonorable place in Islamic historiography for one reason: it is said to have abandoned the shari'a. Alid polemicists would transform all its members into figures of unparalleled depravity, and even chroniclers who notionally accepted the family's right to rule came to lay a litany of sins at individuals' doors. Mu'awiya became Islam's proto-outlaw, recalled for having flouted the Qur'an's kinship rules by acknowledging a bastard as his brother. Yazid's crimes were even more enormous: a fondness for incest, and a disregard for proprieties so profound that he gave his favorite monkey (and drinking partner) an ostensibly Islamic funeral. As befitted their pagan roots, the Umayyads were also associated with a dramatic moral decline in the very home of Islam: the Hijaz. Salons opened in Mecca and Medina where it was said that perfumed courtesans would strum lutes while patrons played backgammon and beardless boys recited poems of a licentious sort. A granddaughter of Abu Bakr's named A'isha bint-Talha became notorious for telling a husband—the second of three—that she was not the type to wear a veil. "Since God, may He remain blessed and exalted, ha[s] put upon me the stamp of beauty, it is my wish that the public should view that beauty and thereby recognize His grace unto them." Some libertines even ignored the Qur'an's prohibition on ankle bells—indeed, jangled them openly on horseback.

Hindsight and bias played a fundamentally important part in creating the record of these years, but the reports collectively attest to at least one uncontestable conclusion: Islamic civilization was being pulled in opposing directions. As armies staked down an empire in the name of faith, the Hijaz and Syria were being bloated by unearned wealth. Even officials of the regime were often aware of the contradiction, and some indication of the tensions in play can be seen from the emergence during the early eighth century of that classic symptom of social unease: the scapegoat. In around 712, orders were issued in the holy cities for the closure of all date-wine shebeens, a ban was imposed on transvestites, tambourine shakers, poets, and prostitutes, and several cross-dressers who chose to remain were castrated by force. One of the few Umayyad caliphs who would one day be acknowledged for his righteousness, Umar II (717–20), then turned his attention to infidels. In the course of formally recognizing Christians, Jews, and Zoroastrians as "protected persons" (*dhimmi*), he gave substance for the first time to a Qur'anic verse requiring that anyone paying the infidel tax be made to feel "subdued," by stipulating that they had to remove their turbans, ride bareback, and lower their chants to a whisper during times of prayer. Later legal manuals would prescribe even more inventive humiliations— advising *jizya* collectors to keep infidels standing at all times, for example, and to rise from their divans only when it became necessary to insult the taxpayer concerned, or to tug his beard.*

Another corrective mechanism was in play. As Muslims became increasingly conscious of sins in high places, time-honored hopes of moral renewal began to stir. End-time scenarios multiplied as the eighth century proceeded, invariably credited to the Prophet, which predicted that Jesus and a superhuman savior known as the *mahdi* were soon to wage war against a hideous, one-eyed false prophet called *al-Dajjal*. As

---

*Some perspective is again in order. The social restrictions established by Umar soon fell into disuse, but shortly afterward (in 721 or 722), the emperor Leo III of Byzantium attempted forcibly to convert every Jew in his empire. The Christian Visigoths that Muslim forces were meanwhile ousting from Spain had proscribed Judaism outright for almost a century, and their oldest laws, dating from the fifth and sixth centuries, had made special provision for Jews to be stoned to death or burned alive if convicted of a crime. See Sharf, *Byzantine Jewry*, pp. 55, 61; Scott, *Visigothic Code*, pp. 369, 376.

the anticipation mounted, one belief began to gain particular traction: the old Alid idea that the shari'a would be restored on earth if only the caliphate returned to Muhammad's family. Thousands died in support of a rebellion in 740 led by a grandson of Hussein's named Zaid, and he had barely been crucified when another revolt flared and failed in Kufa. And while Caliph al-Walid II (r. 743–44) supposedly reclined in a wine-filled swimming pool, gulping down its level as he bathed, the most portentous challenge of all was brewing a thousand miles distant, in the still turbulent province of Khorasan. Seers had always expected signs of the Hour of Judgment to come from the east, and soon after June 747 awestruck travelers reported that the provincial capital of Merv had fallen to a band of righteous men. Reports soon confirmed that a vast troop was on the march: long-haired soldiers with immense mustaches and long wool coats, as numerous as ants. Banging drums, they wore clothes as black as their banners. It was, confirmed old-timers, just as the Prophet had foretold.

The uprising in Khorasan was stoked by some very practical griev-ances. Early barriers to conversion had by now fallen away, but as *jizya* revenues declined, attempts to restructure taxation systems were in-creasing resentments in the province among Arab settlers, non-Arab Muslims, and non-Muslims alike. Troops were meanwhile chafing un-der a deployment system that transferred them like pawns from crisis to crisis. But though the hope of change had economic and social roots, it found religious expression. The insurrectionists determined to replace the Umayyads with the Abbasids, a branch of the Prophet's family de-scended from one of his paternal uncles. There was no agreement over precisely who the new ruler should be, but no one doubted what he would do. Umayyad caliphs having deviated so grievously from the straight and narrow, the Abbasid who took over would put the world back to rights by returning to the shari'a.

The revolutionaries were soon well on their way westward, appar-ently unstoppable, and in the summer of 749 they achieved what should have been unthinkable: the capture of Kufa. The erstwhile garrison had grown into the largest city in Iraq, and its loss severed Damascus from its eastern possessions. But as doom loomed for the Umayyads, the re-bellion's leaders were confronted with some urgent questions of their own. Their collective strategy had so far been determined from Khorasan by an ascetic known as Abu Muslim, who had cared little which particular Abbasid swept aside the Umayyads, but that now changed. As a senior Alid in Kufa by the name of Abu Salama took it on himself to open negotiations with various branches of the Prophet's family, Abu Muslim instructed his own men to locate a pliant Abbasid, quickly. In late 749, a previously obscure figure named Abu al-Abbas was duly hustled into Kufa's congregational mosque to receive the requisite oaths of allegiance and stand ready for whatever else his backers might require of him.

As Kufans kissed the ground and tugged his hem, Abu al-Abbas took to his new position rather more eagerly than might have been predicted. After promising to guard the caliphate for the Prophet's family until the final Hour, he supposedly let it be known that he wished henceforth to be called al-Saffah—"the Slaughterer"—and though the name sounds implausibly candid, it was apt. The first indication of that came when, a few months after his accession, he summoned Abu Salama to receive a robe of honor. The failed power broker was keen to build bridges, and he enjoyed the caliph's hospitality late into the night—at which point he was ejected without an escort onto Kufa's deserted streets and done to death. Forces loyal to Abu al-Abbas then destroyed the dregs of the Umayyad army at a tributary of the Tigris in February 750, and the ousted caliph was tracked down six months later to a church in the Nile delta, where his head was chopped off and his tongue fed to a cat. By then, Abu al-Abbas had invited about seventy other members of the Umayyad family to a conciliatory feast, which had ended with the doors being closed and the diners being slaughtered. The new caliph even visited vengeance on enemies who were already dead. Several Umayyads were exhumed, and at least one set of remains was given a whipping. All that could be found of Mu'awiya himself was a bone, and its fate is not recorded, but it is unlikely to have been good.*

*Abu al-Abbas's fury has a couple of postscripts. Years after his own demise, a long-locked chamber of one of his palaces was opened and found to contain a collection of corpses that he had squirreled away at some point, each one neatly identified by a name tag on its ear: al-Tabari, *History*, 29:152–53. One Umayyad meanwhile managed not only to survive but to thrive. After an epic flight across North Africa, Abd al-Rahman

Although Abu al-Abbas then died of smallpox in June 754, he made the new order's presence felt. That in itself was no guarantee of its staying power—for a dynasty is only as good as its next member—but it quickly turned out that fortitude ran in the family. His successor, a brother named al-Mansur, swiftly saw off a rival to the throne by persuading Abu Muslim, the Khorasani architect of the 750 revolution, to perform one more military service for his regime. Once his position was secure, the caliph expressed a desire to thank his savior in person. Abu Muslim, faced with an excruciating choice, eventually concluded that the consequences of insubordination outweighed the risks of obedience. He was wrong. Al-Mansur kept him waiting until the morning after his arrival when, in the freshness of the dawn, he paced his rug-strewn tent and spat out a litany of accusations. "Spare me to battle your enemies!" pleaded Abu Muslim. "What enemy do I have more treacherous than you?" came the reply. A clap of the caliphal hands then produced a retinue of swordsmen, conjured like bad magic from behind a curtain. Abu Muslim was hacked to the ground and rolled into a carpet. The Abbasid dynasty was up and running.

Caliph al-Mansur had met the first challenge that eventually confronts every revolutionary leader: the eagerness of other people to keep the ball rolling. But stabilizing the Abbasid hold on power would require not only ruthlessness. It called for some radical legal reform. Al-Mansur's legitimacy rested on expectations that his regime would enforce God's law, but it was still highly unclear what that required. The Qur'an, in the course of more than six thousand verses, authorized the communal punishment of just four crimes, and though it contained about two hundred commands that differentiated the permissible (*halal*) from the forbidden (*haram*), the practical consequences of confusing the two were rarely spelled out. It was unequivocally impious to eat pork or meat that was not sacrificed to God, but obedience seemed to be its own reward. Respectable dress was urged upon women, lechery was

---

reached Córdoba in 756 and was able to establish a new Umayyad dynasty that would soon become a byword for civilization across Latin Europe: Kennedy, *Muslim Spain and Portugal*, pp. 31–38; Hitti, *History*, p. 505.

condemned in men, and snooping and snideness were compared to cannibalizing a brother's corpse, but indiscretion was simply repugnant. Although usurers were warned of eternal hellfire, the injunctions against exploitation were not backed by so much as a lash. It was reflection rather than compulsion to which Muslims had been invited to apply their minds.

That advice had been well suited to the needs of an oasis community, and there were plenty of contexts in which it still made eminently good sense. No caliph with ambition could simply leave his subjects to ponder their misdemeanors, however, and efficient government certainly needed more than four crimes. The question was how to ascertain and apply the shari'a in detail. The rudimentary administrative system operated by the Umayyads offered no model: it was the Umayyad incapacity to secure justice that had been the main reason for the dynasty's overthrow. And the period that had immediately preceded their ascent was, on its face, not much more promising. After the Prophet's death, the split over Abu Bakr's election had widened into a chasm, two civil wars had raged, and three of the first four caliphs had been murdered.

To restate those facts without qualification is to ignore the rose-tinting power of tradition, however. By the middle of the eighth century, the majority of Muslims were already recalling the pre-Umayyad era as a time of almost impeccable harmony. The first four successors of the Prophet had come to be known as the Rightly Guided Caliphs (*al-Khulafa al-Rashidun*), and they were credited with a dynamic approach toward interpretation of the shari'a that had carried forward the Prophet's legacy unerringly. Their power to improve on preexisting practice was esteemed in fields ranging from inheritance to methods of prayer, and they had made some particularly noteworthy adjustments to application of the *hadd* penalties—those offenses that the Qur'an identified as crimes against God. Abu Bakr was said to have called off an amputation when his aunt had told him that it was not right to lop off someone's hand for stealing a few iron rings. Umar had refused to punish defendants driven to theft by famine, and he had forgiven a slave for opportunistically stealing valuables from his master. Ali's supporters admiringly recalled his decision that thieves convicted of a first offense should be permitted retention of their thumbs, so that they could please God by touching their earlobes during prayer. The Rightly Guided

Caliphs had even acknowledged one *hadd* for the first time—intoxication. The Qur'an itself had made only three observations about wine: that it had its good and bad points; that Muslims should sober up before prayer; and that believers should avoid it "so that you may prosper"—just as they should also steer clear of gambling, idolatry, and fortune-telling. Abu Bakr had ruled, however, that intoxication merited a fixed penalty of forty lashes. That number was then doubled by Umar, who, coincidentally or otherwise, was notoriously fond of date wine before his submission to Islam.

The inventiveness ascribed to the extraordinary wisdom of Abu Bakr and his successors was of limited help, however. The first four caliphs, for all their right-guidedness, were dead. Change, on the other hand, was still coming thick and fast. The territory under Islam's sway now stretched from Seville to Samarkand, and the hesitant insularity of the first expansionists was yielding to cultural mixing on a grand scale. Christian, Persian, and Nubian slave girls were giving birth to freeborn Muslims, foreign customs were being naturalized, and Arab scholars had begun to examine ancient Greek and Zoroastrian texts for the first time. The risks of confusion were multiplying in tandem. No believer could doubt in general terms that the past offered unerring pointers to the shari'a. But if the route of God's law was to be delineated with clarity, some very definite judicial principles would also be required.

3

The Formation of the Law Schools

The wave of expectations that brought the Abbasid regime to power was quick to crash. The hopes of Ali's supporters had soared over the tumultuous summer of 750, and many Alids had even briefly dared to hope that the revolution would end with a descendant of Hussein's on the caliphal throne. Disillusionment hit them correspondingly hard. As Abu al-Abbas settled in, they began to spread slanderous rumors that the man from whom he claimed his pedigree—an uncle of the Prophet's—had in fact died a pagan. Abandoning their tactical position that any member of Muhammad's family would make a better caliph than an Umayyad, they called once again for the caliphate to return to the bloodline of Ali. The dissent then coalesced into a full-scale revolt around two descendants of the Prophet in 762, and when that rebellion was suppressed by Caliph al-Mansur, the schism became definitive. Almost all his successors would from now on pursue a resolutely anti-Alid policy to defend their dynastic claim. Ali's supporters meanwhile turned their backs on the Abbasids once and for all, looking to their own communities for spiritual leadership and pinning their hopes for deliverance on an apocalyptic intervention by God.

One immediate consequence was a major strategic decision by the new regime. No city was more closely associated with the Alid cause than Kufa, and al-Mansur badly needed a capital to call his own. Scouts were dispatched to a number of potential sites, and after receiving feedback on such matters as muddiness and the prevalence of reptiles, al-Mansur settled on a location about a hundred miles north, close to a cluster of Christian villages on the west bank of the Tigris. He decided on a circular town plan, following Buddhist and Zoroastrian precedents, and once a horoscope had been cast, naphtha-soaked cottonseeds were used to burn outlines into the earth on a suitably lucky day in July 762. Within four years, the map had become a municipality. Al-Mansur called his new capital the City of Peace (*al-madinat al-salam*). It was a name that would be used for centuries, but another one, belonging to the original Christian community, has turned out to be even more tenacious—Baghdad.

Not every prediction made for the City of Peace would be vindicated by history. An assurance, for instance, that no Muslim ruler need fear death behind its walls would turn out to be very wrong indeed. But though its fortunes were destined to yo-yo with inauspicious volatility, its marvels were immediately apparent. Awestruck visitors described majestic arcades and tree-lined avenues, a bustling bazaar, houses made of brick rather than mud, and four gates so immense that they could only have been forged by jinns. More than fifty years later, a resident of the city would write that it still looked as though it had just been "poured into a mould and cast." Damascus fell into decline as ambitious Arabs moved eastward, and the shift in Islam's center of gravity was confirmed as Khorasani artisans, traders, and troops flooded west. And the demographic changes heralded others more profound. Arabs who conventionally considered their caliphs God's shadow on earth had to reckon with Persians who expected kings to radiate luminescence. A people tempered by its historic battle against paganism faced a culture steeped in Zoroastrian and Manichaean mysteries. The cultured class of Persia, meanwhile, found itself having to grapple with revelations that were very different from the foreign ideas with which they had previously been familiar: Greek philosophy and Hindu mysticism, for example. It marked the beginning of a story that would run and run: the cultural rivalry that divides Iran from its western Arab neighbors to this day.

None of that mattered much to al-Mansur, of course. He had a far more pressing obligation—to make good on the promise to govern according to the shari'a—and he needed a system that could not only ascertain God's law but show far-flung lands that it was doing so. The solution that might have seemed obvious to any other burgeoning bureaucracy—written rules—was all but unthinkable. It had been controversial enough transcribing the Qur'an, and the men responsible for that momentous step had been the Prophet's closest companions. An attempt to codify laws that God had chosen not to vocalize could have toppled his fragile caliphate. Only one of al-Mansur's advisers even dared suggest such a course of action—a Persian polymath named Ibn al-Muqaffa—and his fate was hard even by eighth-century standards: he fell so badly out of favor that he ended up having to watch his disarticulated limbs being roasted in an oven.

There was another very basic obstacle confronting al-Mansur. Islam simply lacked any settled traditions about how to choose between competing legal claims. Muslim historians would retrospectively record that Caliph Umar had written a letter of advice on the point to one of his Basra governors, but even if such correspondence existed, no one has ever argued that Islamic law was systematically upheld and developed during the century-long Umayyad ascendancy. Religious scholars (who are known collectively as the ulema,* or "possessors of knowledge") had been sidelined throughout, and their conclusions about the shari'a had only rarely affected official policies. And whether that is better seen as a mark of Umayyad corruption or a sign of scholarly scruples, it illustrates an attitude which went to the heart of the problem that now faced al-Mansur: a deep uncertainty among Muslims over whether it was right to judge violations of God's will in the first place. Many members of the ulema were not only reluctant to pronounce on a coreligionist's sinfulness; they were manifestly terrified of doing so. Chronicles of this period are littered with tales of men who underwent floggings or feigned madness to escape the burdens of service as a judge (qadi). The prevalent attitude is illustrated, vividly but not atypically,

---

*The ulema are not a true clergy, because most Muslims consider themselves accountable to God alone. As a matter of practice, they have routinely asserted themselves as privileged interpreters of the divine will, however, and the Shi'a explicitly regard their scholars as spiritual intermediaries.

by the story of a North African scholar who was instructed to decide a case according to the shari'a by the governor of the Maghrib. He had to be escorted under armed guard to the mosque and agreed to hear the litigants only after the governor's guards tied him up, took him to the roof, and threatened to throw him off. Even then, he cried so much that the parties decided it would be better for all concerned if they took their quarrel elsewhere.

The reluctance to judge was rooted in the civil wars of the previous century. The emergence then of Muslim factions who were prepared to battle and kill each other had left many people thoroughly perplexed, because both sides invariably claimed to be fighting for Islam. A movement known as the Postponers (Murji'a) had subsequently sought to resolve the confusion by way of a full-blown theological doctrine. No matter how bad someone's deeds might seem, they argued, God alone knew the secrets of the heart. Any assessment of a person's innocence or guilt under the shari'a was therefore best put off until the day of Resurrection—judged in heaven but not on earth. As was the case with any contentious issue during this period, the concerns also found expression in the form of hadiths. It was said that Muhammad had warned that misinterpretation of the shari'a was a shortcut to hell, for example, and that being asked to judge between believers was tantamount to being "slaughtered without a knife." And whether or not the reports were genuine, the very fact they were circulating was proof that they touched a nerve. An overassertive legal approach was thought to carry some serious risks.

The practical steps taken by al-Mansur to allay the fears are lost to history, but his efforts to circumvent the practical significance of those fears bore fruit in 771, when a respected member of the ulema agreed to serve as the head of the Egyptian judiciary, sworn to uphold the shari'a alone. It was, in its low-key way, a change as revolutionary as the events of 750. Al-Mansur, by forgoing the temptation to ask members of the ulema to pledge allegiance to his regime, had established a precedent that would allow his successors to co-opt them. Religious scholars, for their part, were assured on at least one score, in that they had no obligation to seek guidance from the government when problems arose, as had been the case under the Umayyads. They could instead turn to someone skilled in the nascent science of jurisprudence, and it would soon become routine for legal experts known as muftis to sit alongside judges and offer up detailed opinions about God's law—fatwas. And the new system drew legitimacy from another quarter that was no less independent of political control. Judges relied on witness testimony, honoring the Qur'an's respect for oral evidence. That gave rise to a broader practice of requiring every judicial decision to be witnessed and validated by upstanding men of the Muslim community, bound by oath: a jury, some four hundred years older than its English equivalent.*

The changes did not eradicate the underlying uncertainties about judgment. Scholars would continue dodging judicial appointment for decades, and it remained a convention until the tenth century that anyone recruited as a *qadi* would greet the news by weeping profusely and lamenting his lot. But a partnership between the Abbasids and the ulema had been established, and it was then symbolically sealed by al-Mansur's decision to leave his turquoise-domed palace to suffer the theoretical ignominy of a minor civil suit—an act of ostentatious humility that would gratify chroniclers for generations to come. And as with most compromises, the system had pragmatism at its core. Most day-to-day disputes continued to fall under the jurisdiction of provincial governors, just as they had under the Umayyads, who applied a mishmash of Islamic assumptions and local custom. Complaints against public officials were meanwhile handled by another tribunal, the Court for the Review of Injustice (*nazr al-mazalim*), which was presided over not by a religious judge but by the caliph himself. And the talk of divine justice could become academic when it mattered most. A sweeping

---

*See Tyan, *Histoire de l'organisation judiciaire*, pp. 236–52; Mez, *Renaissance*, pp. 295–96. A twelve-man fact-finding body known as the *lafif*, which first emerged in Fez during the tenth or eleventh century, bore an even greater resemblance to the English jury. It was used where there were not enough men who satisfied the strict criteria required of standing witnesses: Milliot, *Introduction*, p. 569. On the development of juries in early-thirteenth-century England, see Kadri, *Trial*, pp. 70–73. The testimonial incompetence of women arose out of custom incidentally. Although jurists would dignify such discrimination with legal theories over the centuries, the only disadvantage stipulated by the Qur'an arose in financial disputes, where their evidence was said to count for half that of men: Qur'an 2:282; Hussain, *Status of Women*, pp. 242–89. It is perhaps worth noting that female jurors were unknown in England until 1921.

executive power known as the *siyasa* survived alongside all the new judicial arrangements, and it allowed executive officials to override individual rights whenever that was thought to be in the public interest. Its origins were conventionally traced to Caliph Umar, who was said to have deployed the power for the first time to exile a young man whose good looks were inciting unholy passions among the women of Medina. "You have not committed a sin," he archly told the youth. "But I would have committed one if I had not cleansed this town from you."

The balance between religiosity and expediency was reflected on the ground. By the 770s, Baghdad was already spilling beyond its circular walls, with a new market to the south and pontoons across the Tigris connecting the west bank to a new palace district in the east. And everywhere in the rapidly sprawling metropolis, the sacred jostled against the profane. Black-turbaned preachers with shoulder-borne scimitars declaimed from Friday pulpits, and judges held court, resplendent in dark robes and long caps. But the Christian monasteries that ringed Baghdad remained famously convivial places, where the date wine flowed and lutenists and courtesans continued to ply their trades. On the streets, Muslims huddled around chess and backgammon boards, unconcerned by theological arguments over whether they were permissible tests of skill or forbidden games of chance. Virtue had triumphed over iniquity—except where it had not.

Nothing better symbolized the continuing uncertainties surrounding the Abbasid caliphate than al-Mansur's manner of taking leave of it. A fever claimed him in the deserts of the Hijaz in 775 as he headed for Mecca on a pilgrimage, and though he had designated an heir, his chamberlain was so concerned about the possibility of a succession crisis that he initially kept the death secret. That changed only after he had made all the courtiers in the caravan reaffirm their vows to the dead ruler—or, more precisely, to the silhouette of his chain-mailed corpse, propped up behind a curtain in his tent. Even then, it is said that a hundred graves were dug and al-Mansur was deposited in a random pit, concealed like the pea of a gruesome shell game, in case he attracted in death the violence he had staved off during life. The Abbasids had managed to turn God's law to the service of their regime—but enduring legitimacy remained as elusive as ever.

Caliph al-Mansur's somewhat furtive exit notwithstanding, his mark on Islamic legal history was assured by the time of his death. By persuading influential elements of the ulema to engage with the business of government, he had associated his fledgling dynasty with the shari'a and squared Islamic sensibilities and popular expectations with the day-to-day realities of political rule. But that was the beginning of a process rather than its end. Scholarly theories about how best to understand the Qur'an were still in their infancy, and theologians were only just beginning to read between the holy book's lines. A vast expanse of moral high ground therefore remained uncharted, and though a system of empowering judges had been put into place, the rules they were to apply barely existed.

The problems to which that could give rise became acute again and again during the reign of al-Mansur's son and successor, Caliph al-Mahdi (r. 775–85). He was a conscientious ruler who diligently continued the administrative consolidation that his father had begun. A tax on Baghdad's booming bazaars helped finance fortification of the pilgrimage route to Mecca. Armies were raised to suppress ongoing Manichaean revolts to the east, and years of Byzantine raiding on the northern borders of the caliphate were brought to an end by a highly successful military campaign in 782. But every exercise of power was a reminder of its limits. A discretionary tax had no sanction in the Qur'an, and God had laid down detailed provisions about when a Muslim could wage war or end it. Even al-Mahdi's personal pleasures raised legal issues. Hunts had to be accompanied by religious scholars—because only a shari'a scholar could say when a lawful kill turned into the carrion "mangled by beasts of prey" that the Qur'an forbade. His construction of a hippodrome called for equally subtle rulings to distinguish between lawful prizes and unlawful wagers, and a pastime that was particularly dear to al-Mahdi's heart, pigeon racing, once caused an especially notable kerfuffle. Torah-influenced interpretations of the shari'a cryptically insisted that the sport had been invented by the people of Sodom and that no true Muslim would ever race a beast that lacked for hoofs. To al-Mahdi's relief, a scholar was found to affirm that the Prophet had actually authorized the racing of creatures with claws or wings. But it then turned out that the theologian had made up the hadith for the sake of a quiet life, and a panic-stricken al-Mahdi had felt obliged to kill his entire stock. The need for legal certainty—or at least endorsement—was acute.

In response to the challenge, the attempt to render the shari'a into workable rules and regulations—the science of jurisprudence, or *fiqh*—began in earnest during this period. It would be four more centuries before it properly stabilized, by which time five different schools of law, known as *madhhabs*, would be dominant, but the oldest school would always be one of the greatest. Its founder, a Kufa silk merchant named Abu Hanifa (699–767), is still venerated as a saint, and though he left behind no writings of his own, his tomb in Baghdad has been welcoming pilgrims for more than twelve hundred years. His teachings, as developed and expounded by his students, enshrined ideas that went back even further. Influenced by Greek philosophers whose work had been studied for centuries in Persia, Hanafites assumed God's rationality. They proposed that Muslims should therefore seek to discern the purpose underpinning His laws, reasoning by analogy (*qiyas*) where necessary and departing from earlier understandings of the shari'a whenever that seemed just.

The Hanafites were logical, in other words, and though the flaws of logic are familiar enough today, that gave them immense confidence in an age unfamiliar with its shortcomings. One of the earliest fruits of their research was development of the *hila* (pl. *hiyal*)—a word that literally translates as "escape" or "loophole"—which was as inventive as it sounds. It allowed philanthropists to create charitable trusts in violation of the literal terms of the Qur'an's inheritance rules, for example, and it gave would-be tax evaders ways of dodging the *zakat*. But it also meant that the Hanafites were soon redefining the Qur'an's prohibitions on financial speculation in order to lubricate a money economy, complete with paper cash, checks, and letters of credit, half a millennium before canonical lawyers found ways of doing the same in Europe. And their mastery of syllogistic reasoning was capable of accommodating human frailties with equal ease, as early Hanafite arguments about alcohol show. Noting that the Qur'an disapproved specifically of "wine" (*khamr*), jurists proposed that God clearly had no objection to fermented date juice (*nabidh*). Because the holy book warned Muslims against being too drunk to understand their prayers, they reasoned further that the evil of alcohol arose out of the senselessness produced by overindulgence. Intoxication could therefore be defined, they said, as an inability to differentiate between a man and a woman. The route was baffling, but the destination was easily defined. If Hanafites were to be believed, Muslims could down alcohol by the jug until they became incapable of telling a slave girl from a beardless boy.

The malleability impressed many people. As Abbasid officials fumbled to balance piety and convenience, they repeatedly turned to Hanafites for help, and though Abu Hanifa himself was supposedly too God-fearing to serve as a judge,* students were soon wiping away their dutiful tears and settling down to work on divans across the caliphate. Others were considerably more critical, however. Conservatives complained that Hanafites were more interested in expressing their opinions than clarifying God's law, and in the Hijaz, where antagonism toward things Persian had intensified considerably since the Abbasid revolution, that view found a spokesman in Malik ibn Anas (718–96), the founder of Islam's second major school of jurisprudence. Malik was a truculent but highly respected figure in Medina, where he had backed the 762 rebellion against Caliph al-Mansur, and in a work called *al-Muwatta* (The Smooth Path) he set out an approach that differed markedly from that of the Hanafites. Compiled over four decades, it described how the scholars of his city dealt with questions of ritual, etiquette, and civic duty. Their customs, argued Malik, preserved the behavior of the very first Muslims and were therefore incontestable evidence of the way that God expected his followers to live. As Malik wrote to a friend: "When there is a clear practice in Medina and people follow it, I do not see room for anyone to go against it. This is because the people of Medina have in their hands the inherited tradition that no one else can claim or falsely attribute to themselves."

The appeal to the scholarly consensus (*ijma*) of Medina lay some distance from the reasoned arguments being popularized in Kufa and

---

*Chroniclers report that Abu Hanifa declined judicial service by claiming that he was not up to the job and that Caliph al-Mansur's insistence to the contrary led him to point out that if lying, he was even less worthy: Ibn Khallikan, *Biographical Dictionary*, 3:557. It was the kind of argument that annoyed his opponents.

Baghdad, and Malikites and Hanafites of this period traded insults with gusto. Malikites condemned their rivals as toadies and tricksters and jeered that Abu Hanifa would have analogized a stone column into a wooden post while a listener leaned against it. Hanafites responded by characterizing Hijazi jurists as slack-witted donkey drivers and put it about that Malik turned to law only because he was too ugly to succeed as a singer. One of the better Hanafite jibes concerned a custom prevalent in Mecca and Medina that treated possession of a wineskin as a whippable offense. That was justified on the basis that wineskins facilitated intoxication, and the analogy-minded Hanafites wondered why the Hijazis stopped there. "Why do they not scourge themselves, seeing that every man carries with him the instrument of fornication?"

The invective, though heartfelt, can easily mislead. Although the concept of rival schools of jurisprudence might suggest fundamental opposition, the abuse arose as much out of affinity as enmity. The Hanafites could certainly be slippery, but Malikites were also fond of presenting contentious comparisons as common sense and opinionated choices as divine certainties. Some Malikites had even begun to develop their own versions of the trickiest Hanafite innovation of them all: the legal loophole. The truth was that they were both committed to the lawyerly belief in general rules. The real conflict was between the jurists collectively and another group known as traditionists (*muhaddithun*), who took the view that it was not rules but good examples that people should follow. The examples they had in mind were those incidents from the Prophet's life that had been passed down orally over the years in hadiths. They believed such reports to be so clear that they spoke for themselves. Attempts to structure them into general principles or to draw analogies with unrelated matters could only obscure their meaning.

The traditionists were predictably contemptuous of the Hanafites, whom they characterized as "opinion people" (*ahl al-ray*) for overestimating the value of their subjective preferences about the shari‘a. Malikites were also suspect, however, because as far as the traditionists were concerned, their respect for the past, though more reverential, was also tempered by logic. The difference between the two types of conservatism is illustrated by a story told about Malik's teacher, who is said to have asked a Medina traditionist what compensation was due to a woman who had suffered a serious hand injury. He was told that custom entitled her to ten camels for the loss of one finger, twenty for two, and thirty for three—and that if she was left with just a thumb, she should get twenty. When Malik's teacher questioned the math, he was indignantly told that the last figure was the most certain of all, because it was the subject of a specific hadith—and that the concern for consistency made him sound like an Iraqi.

The traditionists' support for emulation of the Prophet certainly had arguments to draw on. The Qur'an observed that his behavior was exemplary, and no self-respecting Muslim would have deliberately disregarded lessons from his life. Muhammad had died almost a century and a half earlier, however, and there was little agreement about how to distinguish truths about his life from falsehoods. One scholar was heard to lament that his colleagues were "never so ready to lie as in matters of the hadith," and a Kufan was executed in 772 after confessing to having told some four thousand fictions about the Prophet. To confuse matters further, storytellers were in the habit of weaving anecdotes about Muhammad into their material, and one Baghdad street entertainer became famous for a routine which warned crowds that the Prophet had foreseen hellfire for all Muslims whose tongues did not reach the tips of their noses. Mystics were meanwhile talking up their stock by passing on wisdom that Muhammad had transmitted to them in a dream—an almost unimpeachable source, given the scholarly consensus that no demon could impersonate the Prophet.

Perhaps unsurprisingly, early Hanafites were uneasy about such stories. Although happy to deploy them against Malikites, they typically took the view that formal invocation of random tales about the Prophet would only confuse their efforts to rationalize the Qur'an. One of Abu Hanifa's most devoted disciples therefore warned students: "Stay away from unusual hadiths . . . A hadith that goes against the Qur'an is not from the Messenger of God even if [reliable] narrators narrate it!"

Malik, for all his conservatism, was equally dismissive. Although he quoted the Prophet more than seventeen hundred times in his *al-Muwatta*, it was the actual customs of Medina rather than reports about the past that were important in his eyes. Thus he considered it obligatory to decapitate Muslims who renounced their faith, but stories crediting the Prophet with a similar attitude toward apostasy were no more than persuasive evidence of God's law; the crucial point was that the jurists of

Medina favored such a punishment. A reported opinion of the Prophet that differed from the city's customs, meanwhile, would be disregarded as legally irrelevant. The question of canine hygiene was a case in point. There were those who said that Muhammad used to insist that dishes licked by dogs had to be washed seven times. Because hunting with hounds was popular in Medina, Malik asserted that a dog's saliva was not unclean and that hadiths to the contrary could simply be ignored.

The jurists' early skepticism toward hadiths could not limit their circulation, however, and as the caliphate stabilized toward the end of the eighth century, they became more common than ever. Fortified highways and the truce with Byzantium made travel easy, and among the many mystics and pilgrims who took to the road were large numbers of pious men in search of information about the Prophet Muhammad. Wandering from hamlet to shrine in search of accounts of his life, asking old men and (rather less often) old women to recount tales they had heard when young, the tradition collectors diligently tried to memorize everything they were told. The more conscientious among them even attempted to remember the names of everyone who had ever passed on the story. And as Muslims racked their brains, hitherto hidden details about the Prophet's life began to proliferate.

Juristically minded Muslims consequently found themselves in a bind. No viable system of moral rules can long afford to ignore popular ideas of right and wrong, and the more hadiths there were, the greater the pressure became to acknowledge their moral significance. At the same time, however, the risks of contamination and contradiction were growing exponentially. The solution came by way of a third monumental tradition of jurisprudence, founded on the ideas of a Cairo-based student of Malik's named Muhammad al-Shafi'i (767–820). Some aspects of al-Shafi'i's thought aimed simply to steer a middle course between existing legal theories. He accepted the distinctively Malikite concept that the shari'a could be illuminated by a scholarly consensus, adding only that it was not just the pious Muslims of Medina but all leading jurists whose opinions were relevant. He simultaneously agreed with Hanafites that it was possible to reason from known rules toward general principles, and he set down systematic ideas about how to exercise a discretion where no clear rule governed the case at hand—Islam's first theory of judgment. But he did far more than restate or gloss existing jurisprudence. He argued that hadiths could also have independent legal value. As long as a report could be sourced back to Muhammad or one of his companions via a near-perfect *isnad*—a supporting chain of named transmitters—it was proof of the shari'a and as authoritative as the Qur'an itself. In certain cases, he implied, it might be even *more* authoritative. The Qur'an specified a penalty of one hundred lashes for extramarital sex, for example, but well-known and venerable hadiths attested to the fact the Prophet had occasionally ordered stonings. Such reports made clear, argued al-Shafi'i, that God had altered the punishment over the course of the Prophet's mission, and the heavier punishment reflected the more developed state of the law.

Al-Shafi'i's jurisprudential contribution went further. By the end of the eighth century, several scholars were attempting to decipher one of the Qur'an's deeper mysteries—what exactly God had meant by revealing that some verses of the Qur'an had been replaced by "better" ones— and a theory of abrogation (*naskh*) had begun to emerge. It had already explained that most of the Qur'an's 114 chapters had been partially overruled—71 of them, according to one authoritative estimate—and al-Shafi'i now gave that analysis a legal spin. God's responses to changing circumstances meant that many older verses of the Qur'an could be legally ineffective, he argued. And because the Prophet had also adjusted his behavior over time, the same was true of many hadiths. In order to discover the law's meaning, scholars therefore had to collect every authentic hadith and assess where it fitted chronologically in relation to the others and the Qur'anic scheme. It was a formidable task, to be sure, but once achieved, the route toward salvation would be forever clear.

Shafi'i's vision, as amplified by later generations of students, was destined to prevail. Although he was insufficiently rational-minded for some Hanafites and too disrespectful of Medina custom for many Malikites, both those schools of jurisprudence would end up with very similar views about the legal significance of hadiths. The most profound conflict was, once again, not with rival lawyerly traditions. It was with the traditionists. The notion of prioritizing reports about the Prophet was inherently objectionable in their eyes, and a scheme to incorporate hadiths into a legal structure raised an even more fundamental objection. They thought it was wrong to write down hadiths at all. Books in their view could only befuddle belief. The assumptions that underlay that opinion are hard to know for sure—not least because no one holding them put them in writing—but countless chroniclers attest to its existence. Abu Bakr had reportedly doubted the wisdom of writing down even the Qur'an. Human literature of a lesser sort seemed pure folly.

Such ideas feel atavistic today, and it is easy to characterize them as superstitions or to reduce them to a fear of change. Invention of the printing press once produced similarly dire predictions; television sets were more recently expected to destroy the moral fiber of baby boomers; and some commentators tut-tut today about the brain-rotting potential of the Internet. But though complaints are always tiresome when they turn into moral panics, the move away from an oral culture carries genuinely far-reaching consequences. That truth was well reflected a thousand years before the advent of Islam in a fable that Plato put into the mouth of Socrates. It told how Thoth, the ibis-headed god of ancient Egypt, had invented writing and offered it up to the king of Thebes (Alexandria) as an elixir of memory and wisdom—only for the monarch to complain that it was actually a recipe for forgetfulness and stupidity. Thoth's innovation would encourage people to remember words rather than what they signified, warned the king, and promote the delusion that knowledge could be acquired without a teacher. Socrates, who famously wrote nothing himself, knew the limits of literature. Once a story has to be structured to convey a lesson, it loses buoyancy. A text read alone is no substitute for social interaction. And attempts to describe a truth can sap energies that would otherwise be used searching for it.

And yet, although such matters are worth bearing in mind when contemplating any premodern culture, their significance is limited by one important consideration. Shifts in information technology are often as inevitable as forces of nature. And on the cusp of the ninth century, such a transformation was rumbling through the caliphate. It had originated near a central Asian town called Talas in 751, when a Muslim force had defeated an army of the Tang dynasty and captured a number of Samarkandi prisoners. They had been privy to a marvelous secret—paper—and in 794 the first linen-pulping mill outside China opened in Baghdad on the banks of the Tigris. Malodorous parchment and brittle papyrus were about to enter the dustbin of history. Jurists such as Abu Hanifa and Malik ibn Anas had established ways of understanding the shari'a, and al-Shafi'i had shown how hadiths could be incorporated into those traditions. The spread of paper would now erode the oral traditionists' monopoly on stories about the Prophet and make it easier than ever for pen-wielding scholars to define fluid traditions and fix them into commandments.

Caliph Mahdi's son Harun al-Rashid (r. 786–809) would be immortalized in *One Thousand and One Nights* as the caliph's caliph: a ruler of mythical proportions who was as eager to walk incognito among his subjects and carouse with louche poets as he was to exalt God and get to the bottom of the paranormal mysteries that endlessly beset his realm. Chroniclers describe a reality that almost makes the fantasies look pale. It was Harun who conducted his father's famously victorious campaign against Byzantium in 782—when, at the age of nineteen, he led a hundred thousand men to the shores of the Bosphorus and subjected the empress Irene to a peace more demeaning than Constantinople had ever known. It was a palace intrigue of the most treacherous kind that then propelled him unexpectedly to the throne: his scheming mother terminated the reign of a less favored elder son by persuading a concubine to sit on his face for just a little too long. And Harun ruled as a true all-rounder. He prostrated himself in prayer a hundred times daily but drank with legendary enthusiasm many a night, and the vigor lasted all the way to the end—when he quelled a Khorasani rebellion, foresaw his death, selected a burial shroud, and supervised the digging of his own grave.

The caliphate went from strength to strength under Harun's energetic guidance. A postal service, modeled on a system inherited from Sassanian Persia, was rolled out across the Islamic world, and though Alid and infidel malcontents perennially mounted minor challenges to his authority, Baghdad's writ ran otherwise unquestioned from central Asia to Sudan. Even the Umayyad emirate of Córdoba was locked into its cultural orbit. A former slave at al-Mahdi's court named Zaryab would take it by storm after he settled there in 821—introducing Andalusians to new table manners, seasonal fashions, and underarm deodorant,

among many other things, and pioneering improvements to the Andalusian lute that would one day lead to flamenco.

But no golden age is complete without storm clouds on the horizon,
and there were major inundations ahead. Some of the challenges to the
caliphate, like the fiefdoms that Alid rebels were beginning to establish
in northern Africa, were both nascent and distant. But one problem
was closer to home and considerably more pressing—the succession.
Harun had designated a son named Muhammad al-Amin as his
heir, but issues quickly gathered over his suitability. According to the
historian al-Mas'udi, they had been present at the very moment of his
conception, when his mother spotted three demons murmuring in
the corner of her bedchamber, and by the time of his adolescence she
was apparently so concerned about his departures from the straight
and narrow that she took to furnishing him with page boys who were
actually slave girls in disguise. That might offer a clue into the nature
of the concerns, but it was hardly beyond the wit of Hanafite jurists by
the end of the eighth century to finesse such deviations. The deeper
problem was that Harun had thirteen other sons, one of whom came to
seem to the caliph a paragon of all the virtues that al-Amin lacked. And
the disparity drove him to a fateful decision. He made al-Amin acknowledge a half brother as his successor and guaranteed young Abu Ja'far
al-Ma'mun his rights by appointing him governor of Khorasan. The
deal was sealed by way of solemn oaths to God at the Ka'ba in December
802. And when the caliph entered his well-prepared grave in 809, the
inevitable civil war kicked off.

The fratricide that followed is a reminder of how much lay beyond
the gift of even God's shadow on earth. In order to show al-Ma'mun
who was boss, al-Amin sent a forty-thousand-strong army eastward, only
for it to be annihilated by a troop a tenth of its size. Al-Ma'mun then
turned the tables by moving on Baghdad. Al-Amin was reduced to
mustering mercenaries and releasing prisoners in his defense, and as
pitched street battles raged across the City of Peace, he was betrayed
and beheaded in September 813 by a treacherous groom. The hostilities
then assumed a momentum of their own. Al-Ma'mun's own army
disintegrated, and violence spiraled for six years as gangs of destitute
freebooters battled to control the city. Al-Ma'mun was little more than

a distant witness, and only in 819 did events stabilize enough for him very belatedly to enter his capital in triumph.

Al-Ma'mun's return to Baghdad drew a line under a decade of war and launched an era that would be at least as glorious as that of his father, but the civil conflict was a defining event. For the next four centuries, writers would blame problems in the capital on the fighters' presumed descendants—who came to be known by Arabic terms that translate roughly as "vagabonds," "vagrants," or "riffraff"—and though the complaints were often as complacent as the language suggests, the social change during these years had genuine significance. Half a century on from the Abbasid revolution, Iraq's capital had once again filled with thousands of Khorasani peasants with an apocalyptic view of the world. And whereas the earlier generation had imagined renewal of the caliphate to preface the emergence of an earthly paradise, fratricide and chaos had left the newcomers with attitudes toward authority that were at least skeptical, and often contemptuous.

That would have one particularly important effect. Toward the tail end of the war in Baghdad, many desperate citizens had organized themselves into vigilante groups to secure the justice that the civil authorities were so comprehensively failing to offer, and they had become associated with a motto drawn from the Qur'an: a formula of words that appears eight times in various forms, which commends or records the Islamic practice of doing good and eschewing evil. And though that sounds uncontentious enough, the imperative to "command good and forbid evil" (*amr bil-ma'ruf wa-nahy an al-munkar*) was destined to give rise to new and radical understandings of the shari'a. Hanafites and Malikites had set out two directions in which legal ideas could evolve— the first of them relatively rationalistic, and the second emphasizing the importance of a communal consensus. Al-Shafi'i had then shown how each of them could be squared with popular ideas about the Prophet that were circulating in the form of hadiths. But the claim that every Muslim was obliged to promote good and forbid evil would give rise to another option. By stressing the duty of individuals to put God's rules into practice, it subverted the very concept of structured jurisprudence and threatened to replace legal order with pious anarchy.

The hostility to constituted authority was confirmation, if such were necessary, that the Abbasid state had not restored the perfections of the Prophet's time. But its significance went further. Caliph al-Mansur had tried to hammer together a governing structure that balanced God's law with political expediency. But the simpler idea that power was a dirty business best avoided, so widespread under the Umayyads, had been reinvigorated. It was no longer just the Alids who were questioning what role government should play in a Muslim community. Many ordinary believers were beginning to think that the shari'a would be far better secured if individuals personally stood up to injustice (*zulm*). Ideas about authority had been unstable since the Prophet's death. They were about to become a lot more so.

4

Commanding the Faithful

The city that Caliph al-Ma'mun (r. 813–33) reentered when civil hostilities ceased in 819 was quickly picking up the pieces. Barricades came down and markets returned, and the dogfighters, the peddlers, and the hucksters brought routine cacophony back to the streets. The Tigris was spanned by new pontoons, and its waters swirled with dhows as Chinese junks began once again to float into town from Basra, buoyed up by inflated sheepskins and weighed down with all the porcelain, ivory, silks, and spices that a decent civilization might need. Scarred by war and seething with underemployed fighters, Baghdad would never again be tranquil, but it was most definitely back in business.

The liveliness was matched by an intellectual resurgence. As paper was popularized, an Arabic literary culture bubbled into life, and a new generation of writers emerged with a taste for paradox and pre-Islamic poetry that brought the language of God down to earth with a bump. The greatest of them all was al-Jahiz (ca. 781–868)—"the Goggle-Eyed." Over the course of a career that lasted half a century, the Basra-born descendant of African slaves carved out conventions of grammar and style that still govern popular Arabic prose, and, as might be expected of a man who was creating a literary tradition from scratch, his monographs make for a roller-coaster read. They plunge from proposition to opposition, lurching and reversing between gossip, polemic, and comedy. Disquisitions on the usefulness of sticks and the best way to hang a door are advanced with as much brio as arguments for the superiority of black skin and accounts of the (apparently insatiable) sexual appetites of the inhabitants of Mecca and Medina. And though al-Jahiz was fascinated by gossip and rumor, the credulity was always balanced by skepticism. Having heard a seafarer's yarn that would one day be immortalized as an adventure of Sinbad, he counsels against believing anyone who claims to have been shipwrecked on the back of a slumbering sea monster. Though open-minded about reports that rhinoceroses gestate for seven years, popping out of the womb only to graze, he warns that so peculiar a phenomenon must be seen to be believed. And instead of merely repeating an unaccountably popular belief about camels—that their scrotums vanish after slaughter—he goes to a butcher and finds a set of testicles.

Al-Jahiz's enthusiasms were very much his own, but his questing attitude was widespread, and no one personified the temper of the times better than Caliph al-Ma'mun himself. Just as al-Jahiz explored questions that no Arab had previously thought to ask, the Commander of the Faithful was constitutionally incapable of scrutinizing a mystery without deepening it. When he visited Egypt's Great Pyramid in 820, he became so intrigued that he broke in—through the urgent gash that has served to admit tourists ever since—and burrowed all the way through to its higher burial chamber. A few years later, he established an observatory to improve on Ptolemy's seven-hundred-year-old star charts and commissioned three astrolabe- and quadrant-laden expeditions to test Greek theories about the earth's circumference, acquiring an estimate that would not be bettered for seven more centuries. And then, at some point during the 820s, al-Ma'mun went even further. The spirit of inquiry was transformed from a habit of mind into an institution.

The caliph's great innovation was to establish an academy known as the House of Wisdom (*beit al-hikma*), committed to translating foreign literature into Arabic. Its polyglot faculty, inspired by weekly meetings with the caliph and remuneration that potentially matched a text's weight in gold, quickly turned the sporadic scholarship of earlier years into a production line. The scholars' collective backlist soon included hundreds of works, and as the knowledge percolated down, Muslims began to learn that foreigners had been thinking the strangest things. From the mathematicians of India or Alexandria, they read about the mysterious *sifr*—a number that was not a quantity—which would one day migrate into English as the cipher, or zero. Books from Byzantium acquainted them with Greek arguments about fate and free will and the notion that human beings, like creation itself, were finely balanced mixtures of fire, water, air, and earth. As they read, they also wrote, on subjects from alchemy to zoology. And each book inspired others: dominoes that would topple down the centuries, crossing continents on the way, and one day set Christendom en route to the Renaissance.

An institution that momentous deserves a decent founding myth, and the House of Wisdom got one. Muslims later claimed that its creation had been inspired by a caliphal dream in which al-Ma'mun had come across a philosopher, "with ruddy complexion . . . joined eyebrows, bald head and bloodshot eyes," reclining on a divan. Aristotle (for it was he) had been in a chatty mood, and the caliph had taken the opportunity to ask him three times to define what was good. One good thing, he had replied, was intellectual achievement. Justice was also good. So too was public welfare. "Then what else?" al-Ma'mun had delightedly wondered. "What else?" the sage had mused. "There is nothing else."

The encounter, legendary fantasy though it was, reflected important truths. Al-Ma'mun was motivated by a desire to seek useful wisdom whatever its source, and the House of Wisdom exposed Muslims to a world that was more sophisticated than many would have thought possible. Ever since the Prophet's followers had triumphed in the Hijaz, conservative Muslims had imagined every other nation, with the qualified exception of Peoples of the Book, to comprise moral primitives. But it was hard to read Aristotle, say, without acknowledging that some pagans had contemplated the meaning of life and the difference between right and wrong. And the new ideas were consequently as dangerous as their study was tempting. The logical techniques developed in Greece might disclose the mechanics of the universe. They could conceivably resolve long-standing moral conundrums. But the answers on offer rested on rational argument rather than revelation. And that threatened to make God look superfluous, if not downright redundant.

Contemporaries were alive to the risks. One of the House of Wisdom's most prolific translators prefaced an early work on classical medicine by warning readers to ignore any "beliefs and opinions" they might encounter in its pages; Greeks expressed them, he explained, "only in order to win people over." But in an era suffused with spirituality, value judgments were not that easy to sideline. Caliph al-Ma'mun's observatory had not been built for love of stargazing alone; it was intended to establish Mecca's longitude and enable Muslims to aim their prayers more precisely toward the Ka'ba. One of the earliest arguments advanced in favor of the Indian science that Arabs called algebra (or *al-jabr*) was that mathematics would allow for the calculation of unprecedentedly accurate Qur'anic inheritance shares. And philosophy was particularly quick to work its magic. A movement known as the Mu'tazilites—very roughly, "dissenters"—began almost immediately to apply Aristotelian concepts to the Qur'an. They spoke of God as the One and His creations as emanations. They differentiated between His essential and His accidental attributes and wondered how Aristotle's ideas about eternity fitted in with the day of Resurrection. And as they studied logic more carefully than Muslims ever had before, they grew notably skeptical of the notion that two-hundred-year-old tales about the Prophet might constitute evidence of God's will. The only hadiths that illuminated the shari'a, they argued, were those which were so widely accepted that arguments over authenticity were irrelevant.

Such claims made for fighting talk. Traditionists were already distressed that Hanafite and Malikite jurists sometimes spoke as if their subjective opinions were a meaningful substitute for the shari'a. To many war veterans, displaced from distant rural communities and unused to sophistication of any sort, the new intellectuals were incomprehensibly more interested in discussing God than in obeying him. Nothing was as enigmatic as it seemed, insisted the conservatives. God was no metaphysical abstraction but a real entity. Any ambiguities that might exist in His revelations and hadiths were His alone to interpret, and insofar as uncertainties remained, Muslims were obliged simply to believe in their words "without [knowing] how" (*bi-la kayfa*).

In an atmosphere so volatile, any number of theological issues could have set off an explosion, and the catalyst turned out to be an esoteric argument about the Qur'an. It was universally agreed that the book precisely transcribed God's revelations, but a dispute had opened up over whether those revelations had always existed. Mu'tazilites claimed that God must logically have preceded His own speech and that no monotheist could believe otherwise. Traditionists countered that the Qur'an had always existed, because it said so. The ramifications of the argument are nowadays difficult to comprehend, let alone resolve, but the stakes could hardly have been higher. If God had created the Qur'an, He had tailored His message to a specific time and place. That would imply that its meaning was liable to change—a conclusion that alarmed conservatives and excited reformists as much in the ninth century as it does in the twenty-first.

The dispute crystallized in 827, when al-Ma'mun came out for the Mu'tazilites by formally announcing that the Qur'an had been created. Over the next few years he busied himself with military and scholarly matters, but in 833 he suddenly gave the proclamation teeth. With a martial zeal of which his father and grandfather would have been proud, he had by then taken to mounting an annual springtime war against Byzantium, and from his field headquarters in northern Syria he mailed letters to all his provincial governors. It had come to his notice, he wrote, that the overwhelming majority of ordinary people were so "feeble in judgment, deficient in intellect, and lacking in the facility to reflect upon things" that they were unable to distinguish between the Creator and His creations. In order to establish whether judges and scholars were similarly incompetent, it would therefore be necessary to interrogate them.

No one knows why al-Ma'mun suddenly made his theological views a matter of public policy. Although caliphs were conventionally honored as Commanders of the Faithful, Abbasid authority rested on an assumption that they would not, in fact, command fidelity at all. The delicate institutional arrangements set up by al-Mansur had left doctrinal controversies for the scholarly ulema to resolve instead. Al-Ma'mun was doubtless concerned to reestablish his authority after the spread of vigilantism during the recent civil war, and his decision to appoint a robustly Hanafite chief judge in 832 had fortified the forces of anti-traditionism in his court. Ill health and an eye on the afterlife might also have played a part, for palace physicians had recently noted with some despondency that he was down to just eighteen mouthfuls of meat a day. But the surest explanation is probably the simplest one. Al-Ma'mun had seized power after facing down his brother's attempt to destroy him. He was temperamentally so inclined to challenge orthodoxies that he had sided with an Alid group at one point during the civil war and contemplated granting full autonomy to his infidel subjects at another. At least one spur must have been self-confidence—and a calculation that he would win.

Initial indications were that he was right. Recital of his letter from pulpits across Iraq aroused fury. A leading traditionist publicly branded al-Ma'mun an atheist in Kufa's congregational mosque and shrugged off the risks of punishment. "All it means is a whipping," he said—"and my head matters less to me than the button of my coat." But he happened to die peacefully before either proposition was tested, and his fellow conservatives turned out to be less than steadfast. Seven of them abandoned their insistence on the Qur'an's eternality as soon as they were brought before the caliph. A second contingent of traditionist scholars, summoned to appear before Baghdad's governor, held firm only until al-Ma'mun dispatched a new letter ordering that they be sent to him in chains. "If they do not then recant and repent," he wrote, "the Commander of the Faithful will consign them collectively to the sword, God willing." All but four chose instantly to recant and repent. A couple of others lasted no longer than forty-eight hours. There were just two holdouts, and as they set off, manacled into camel howdahs, to see al-Ma'mun, it seemed as though traditionist resistance was about to be extinguished with a couple of beheadings in the distant deserts of northern Syria.

If al-Ma'mun was hoping to prove that he was in command of the situation, however, the situation was about to prove him very wrong. Like any good Muslim warrior, he was perpetually ready to meet his Maker— hopeful of it, indeed—and during a fortress-smashing expedition through southern Anatolia in August 833, the opportunity finally arrived. There were contradictory accounts of the cause of his martyrdom—it was either a poisonous date or a fatal chill that he caught when splashed by a fish—but whatever brought it about, the effect was a reprieve for his prisoners. Their camels ambled to a halt twenty-five miles short of their destination, and as a sibling named al-Mu'tasim was sworn in as al-Ma'mun's successor, they reversed course. By the time the prison caravan trudged back through Baghdad's gates, one of the captives had also passed away, and just one man remained to testify to the eternality of the Qur'an. He was Ahmad ibn Hanbal (780–855), whose commitment to traditionism was reportedly so profound that he ignored conversations entirely until they turned to the subject of the Prophet Muhammad. But once they did, there was potentially no stopping him, for he had spent twenty-five years in Anatolia and Arabia memorizing hadiths. And that would be wordiness aplenty for the interrogation that lay ahead.

Although Caliph al-Mu'tasim shared the rationalist sympathies of his predecessor, there are some signs that he was hoping for a quiet end to the fight that he had inherited. Ibn Hanbal was initially left to molder in prison, and the two years that passed before he was produced for trial in September 835 would have killed many a feebler man. But the traditionist was made of stern stuff—as now became clear. For two days, the Hanafites and Mu'tazilites of al-Mu'tasim's court deployed their slyest analogies and syllogisms to prove how illogical it was to disbelieve in the Qur'an's createdness. Ibn Hanbal hurled back hadith after hadith to prove that God's word had neither beginning nor end. The caliph, faced with an opponent who was scoring points according to his own rules, decided on the third day to lash his way to victory instead. But Ibn Hanbal, fortified by two hairs of the Prophet that he had prudently sewn into his shirt, remained resilient. By the time he was cut down from the whipping post, he was unconscious and very bloodied—but also unbowed. Two and a half years after al-Ma'mun had ridiculed his subjects for their feeblemindedness, one of them had battled his successor to a standstill.

Rumors would one day transform Ibn Hanbal's survival into a marvelous triumph. Hagiographers affirmed that 150 evil courtiers had queued up for a turn with the whip and that the scholar had met each of their blows with a prayer. It was said that as the twenty-ninth lash had descended, God had stopped his pants from falling down; some even claimed to have seen a golden hand emerging from the ether to adjust his waistband. The more mundane reality was that the interrogation of traditionists during these years, an inquisition known as the "test," or *mihna*, enjoyed considerable early success. The best evidence of its impact appears in a letter written in around 835 by one of Baghdad's most articulate Mu'tazilites—the writer al-Jahiz. "The [traditionists] have been crushed, reduced and subjected to the inquisition," he wrote to the son of al-Mu'tasim's chief judge. "They have become more amenable and open to argument; their hearts are full and their souls troubled." And yet he felt bound to acknowledge that all the repression was not producing the desired results. "Their numbers have not decreased, the majority have not changed their views, and only a tiny minority are dead," worried al-Jahiz. "This is a situation in which cunning and persuasion are called for, since force and violence are ineffectual."

And, as al-Jahiz feared, the broader battle for hearts and minds was in fact being lost. Caliph al-Mu'tasim's repressive measures bred ever greater opposition, and when he imported four thousand Turkish bodyguards to stabilize the situation, matters simply worsened. The newcomers did what private security forces do, galloping through the city's marketplaces and cutting down innocent women and children, and an outbreak of sustained rioting soon led the caliph to distance himself from his subjects physically as well. Within a year of Hanbal's interrogation, al-Mu'tasim had relocated some sixty miles up the Tigris, where a sumptuous new capital called Samarra was soon rising from the well-irrigated ground. Its palaces, racecourse, and polo field would keep Abbasid rulers entertained for more than half a century, and though the watercourses ran dry long ago, a hint of its splendor survives in a spiraling minaret that still corkscrews out of its sandblasted ruins. But the glory was as insubstantial as a mirage. The caliph's power had come to rest on the protection of foreign mercenaries, and Baghdad had almost slipped out of his control.

The conflict only sharpened after al-Mu'tasim's death in 842. His son and successor, al-Wathiq, made it compulsory to teach the createdness of the Qur'an in elementary schools and refused to redeem prisoners of war from Byzantine hands unless they toed the official religious line. Several recusants were executed, and the caliph personally decapitated a Baghdad insurrectionist in April 846, before displaying his head alongside a placard that praised God for dispatching him to hell. When al-Wathiq then died in his turn in August 847, there was little reason to expect any change. The brother who succeeded him, al-Mutawakkil, was liberal enough to be an inveterate drunk and sufficiently open-minded to appoint al-Jahiz, very briefly, as tutor to one of his sons.* But in a climate of intensifying hostility toward the inquisition, he also turned out to be a thorough pragmatist. An early sign of that came when he had the outgoing and much-despised vizier tortured to death in his own iron maiden. He then pandered to prejudice by reviving legal restrictions on Christians and Jews for the third time in Muslim history, and he exploited anti-Alid sentiment by ordering that the reputed resting place of Ali's son Hussein at Karbala be reduced to farmland. And in August 851, he took the most opportunistic step of all. He jailed the Hanafite judge most closely associated with al-Ma'mun's launch of the inquisition and renounced the orthodoxy of almost two decades.

The official somersault put the caliphate in line with the popular mood after years of escalating repression, and the rapprochement was confirmed when al-Mutawakkil asked Ibn Hanbal to come to Samarra and teach hadiths to the caliphal household. The old introvert lasted just two weeks before returning to Baghdad, where he rent his clothes in anguish at the emptiness of fame, but a timely death in 855 sealed his celebrity status. Eight hundred thousand men and sixty thousand women were said by admirers to have turned out for his funeral, while miracles were so thick on the ground that twenty thousand Jews, Christians, and Zoroastrians adopted Islam on the spot. But the realignment of forces that had been set into motion was less kind to al-Mutawakkil. In the new climate, he contemplated a move to Damascus and made preliminary efforts to disband the mercenary bodyguard that his father had imported during the mid-830s. The mercenaries had other ideas. Late one night in December 861, several hours into one of the caliph's regular drinking sessions, a squad of masked Turkish officers burst into his private apartments. As they stood in the doorway, their swords glinting in the candlelight, they found the Commander of the Faithful so drunk as to be almost comatose. Two eunuchs, charged with keeping the caliph propped up on his cushions, dropped him with a scream and fled the room. A more conscientious aide who attempted

*Al-Jahiz was dismissed as soon as he reported for duty. The writer, whose nickname means "goggle-eyed," genially attributed that to aesthetic factors rather than ideological ones. "[The caliph] found my physical appearance so repellent that he [gave me] 10,000 dirhams and sent me away": al-Mas'udi, Meadows, p. 249.

to shield al-Mutawakkil was skewered alongside him, and both were rolled up within the carpet on which they lay.

It was a pivotal moment. The Prophet's spiritual successor, bound by oath to safeguard the shari'a until the Day of Judgment, had been killed by troops sworn to guard him. Three more caliphs and several high officials were killed by Turkish officers over the next decade—frozen, stifled, or squeezed to death in accordance with central Asian taboos against the spilling of blood. A war against Byzantium that was launched in 862 simultaneously altered the financial structure of the caliphate. Ruinous military expenditures became a nonnegotiable part of the economy, and viziers were soon trying to square the circle by ratcheting taxes to unaffordable heights. Baghdad would be restored as Iraq's capital in just thirty years, but by then the caliphate would have been permanently transformed. The Abbasids were succumbing to vicissitudes that their predecessors had briefly seemed to control, and the tide of their dynasty, surging for a century, had begun at last to recede.

The rise and fall of the ninth-century *mihna* offers a salutary lesson for anyone who might imagine that rationality is inherently benign. Although religious doctrines formed its backdrop, Islam's seminal ideological persecution had been initiated in the name of reason, by a ruler who drew his inspiration from philosophers. That has a flip side, however—simply because the end of the inquisition put the boot on the other foot. Once it ceased to be an offense to assert the eternality of the Qur'an, it became ever more hazardous to claim that it had been created. And that owed relatively little to governmental policies. Traditionists, galvanized by the *mihna*'s collapse and reports of Ibn Hanbal's tribulations, grew increasingly willing to challenge the Mu'tazilites and anyone who contradicted their ideas about God. They did so pursuant to the motto that had first been heard among vigilantes during Baghdad's civil war—the demand that individual believers pursue good and eschew evil—and though their calls for direct action would take time to bear fruit, the consequences would be dramatic.

A more immediate change was a new surge in the popularity of hadiths, which heralded a paradoxical problem. Hadiths were multiplying in suspiciously direct correlation to their utility. Traditionists who feared that Muslims were paying too much attention to opinionated scholars were putting it about that the Prophet used to warn against substituting human opinion for the shari'a. Hanafites, for all their early skepticism toward hadiths, had begun using them to bolster their own jurisprudence, and they also found several that were considerably too good to be true. One even had the Prophet predicting the existence of their founder. "In my community," he had supposedly said, "there will rise a man called Abu Hanifa who will be its guiding light." And though the change is difficult to quantify, because hadiths rested on an oral tradition that was rich to the point of immeasurability, a few numbers speak for themselves. When Malik ibn Anas had written his *al-Muwatta* during the second half of the eighth century, he had attributed just 1,720 statements or deeds to the Prophet. Now it was no longer unusual to hear of people who had collected about a hundred times as many hadiths. Ibn Hanbal was said by admirers to have memorized a round million. It all meant that there was at least one warning on which almost everyone agreed. "There will be forgers," the Prophet had reportedly foreseen, "liars who will bring you hadiths which neither you nor your forefathers have heard. Beware of them."

Some traditionists were relatively unconcerned, still far more interested in memorizing what the Prophet had said and done than they were in analyzing the reports. But with hadith inflation raging, those of a more scholarly disposition were beginning to feel that the reports risked undermining their own cause. Increasingly committed to the view that hadiths were pieces of a great moral jigsaw puzzle, they escalated their long-standing efforts to differentiate accurate hearsay from false rumors. It was already good practice to remember a hadith's sources as well as its substance, and a number of biographers—most notably Muhammad Ibn Sa'd (784–845)—now gathered material on the lives of thousands of early Muslims. Then, at the end of the 840s, a scholar named Muhammad al-Bukhari (810–70) took traditionism into entirely uncharted territory. Having recently returned from a sixteen-year expedition across Khorasan and Persia, he cross-referred his hadiths against the newly published biographical material. Unreliable narrators fell by the wayside, until he had reduced his hadiths—said by admirers to number 600,000—to a core group of 2,762 that had come down to the present through the mouths of men and women with spotless reputations. And then al-Bukhari took the most dramatic step of all: he wrote them down.

That decision was momentous. The Prophet had had more access to eternal wisdom than any other human being who had lived, and tales about his life had always been freighted with otherworldly significance. Even one of Muhammad's contemporaries was said to have been incapable in old age of recalling his words and deeds without breaking into a sweat, trembling, and shaking his cane. And though the spread of paper had made it more likely that traditionists would scribble down temporary memoranda, attempts to compile records more permanent were still considered both presumptuous and dangerous. Ibn Hanbal had expressed the concern with some frankness when reprimanding a student who wanted to take some notes ("I may say something now concerning a juridical problem, then tomorrow go back on it"), and a statement later quoted by his son suggested that he had had no time at all for literary lawyers:

> Whenever a [jurist] comes along, he writes a book . . . Malik wrote a book, al-Shafi'i came and wrote a book, and . . . Abu Thawr has come and written a book. These books . . . are an innovation. Whenever a man comes along, he writes a book and abandons the hadith of the Messenger of God.

The very fact that Hanbal's complaint was recorded is evidence of how swiftly attitudes toward literature were evolving, however, and his approach to traditionism was soon to be eclipsed. Al-Bukhari certainly worried about the supernatural issues at stake, and he made sure to wash and sink to his knees in prayer before every hadith he inscribed, but five similar collections appeared over the next few decades. And the authors' collective willingness to publish and be damned—potentially—transformed Islamic scholarship. By the end of the ninth century, the heroic age of hadith research would be over. Curious students were no longer setting off for the wilds of Khorasan to hear tales about the Prophet, as their grandfathers might have done. They were memorizing and analyzing them at home—by the bookload.

The novelty of the written compilations was no obstacle to their acceptance. Al-Bukhari's work, which is often simply called *Sahih* after the Arabic word for "authentic," soon achieved a status second only to the Qur'an, and all six collections would gain so much authority over the next couple of centuries that they would effectively be canonized. That is made all the more remarkable by the fact that al-Bukhari, like all his fellow hadith compilers, was frequently willing to depart from the literal terms of the holy book. The divergence is most noteworthy on the subject of miracles. Whereas several verses of the Qur'an stated that the Prophet had resisted demands that he work wonders, al-Bukhari recorded that he had acceded to the calls by showing Mecca's pagans a moon split into two; that he had been known to cause water to gush from his fingers; and that he had once invoked rain so successfully that he then had to pray for the clouds to go away. Perhaps most impressively, a visit to God's throne, briefly referred to in the Qur'an as a "vision," was acknowledged by al-Bukhari to have been an actual and event-filled journey. Muhammad was said to have flown on a winged steed to the highest of seven heavens, where he and God had discussed how often Muslims should pray. Although God initially insisted on fifty daily acts of worship, the Prophet had talked Him down to five. Moses, who was also in the vicinity, had urged him to go even lower, but Muhammad was too polite to push his luck.

Such matters possessed a significance that rested deep in the realm of faith, of course, but they also illustrated some fundamental issues of methodology. A story's plausibility was measured only by the names vouching for it, and although al-Bukhari and his fellow authors had taken great care to weed out notorious liars and exaggerators, it was divine providence rather than systematic sampling that structured their research. They had gathered most of their accounts from Persia and Khorasan, thousands of miles away from the Hijaz, two centuries after the events they described. The compilations sourced many claims to people who had been children when Muhammad died, and they collectively credited eleven transmitters who had been unreliable enough to disavow their true beliefs during the recent inquisition. And since the hadith collectors were all men, whose information had been transmitted through male-dominated public spaces, unconscious bias was almost guaranteed. Although Ibn Sa'd had found more than six hundred women to be worthy of inclusion in his biographical collection, they would be forever underrepresented in the hadith compilations. Even

A'isha, who is credited with a total of 2,200 hadiths, made it into al-Bukhari's collection just 128 times. Premodern justifications of sexual segregation and subordination were thereby enshrined, while the views of innumerable early Muslim women were discounted or lost.

The practical importance of such matters was by no means certain when the compilations first appeared. They constituted food for thought rather than instruction manuals. Duties and responsibilities were certainly mentioned, but chapters concerning crimes and commercial transactions, say, were accorded the same prominence as others that addressed eclipses and menstruation. The Prophet's injunctions on subjects such as divorce and inheritance were recorded, but so too were his meditations on the value of toothpicks, the importance of trimming mustaches, and the geographical location of the Antichrist. An entire chapter was devoted to Muhammad's supposed ideas about how to cure illnesses: incense for pleurisy, cumin for all maladies "except death," and honey for diarrhea—a prescription he allegedly maintained even after it made a sufferer feel worse, because "God has uttered the truth, and his abdomen . . . has told a lie." And a few reports seemed barely relevant to human tribulations at all. Al-Bukhari had seen fit to enshrine the recollection of a Hijazi tribesman, for example, that in the dark days before Islam he had been present while a monkey was stoned for adultery by a group of fellow primates. "I too, stoned it," the Arab had enigmatically recalled.*

By the beginning of the tenth century, however, all the conditions were in place for incorporation of the compilations into the wider canons of Islamic jurisprudence. The Hanafites were entrenched across the caliphate, the Malikites were influential in the Hijaz, Africa, and Andalusia, and the Shafi'ites were gaining ground in Egypt and Iraq. They had developed sophisticated theories of legal argument, using

---

*The report, contained in al-Bukhari, 5.58.188, would intrigue jurists for centuries. Although none ever argued that the monkeys were fully competent in the eyes of the law, several toyed with the possibility that they were the descendants of metamorphosed Jews, trying in their rudimentary way to obey the Torah: Michael Cook, "Ibn Qutayba and the Monkeys"; cf. Ibn Qutayba, *Traité des divergences*, pp. 283–85. Interestingly, Catholic jurists would one day be considerably more daring, formulating theories to justify a four-century-long judicial persecution of beasts and insects: Kadri, *Trial*, pp. 146–77.

analogical reasoning and appeals to consensus, and al-Shafi'i had influentially contended that it was for jurists to retrieve and chronologize accounts of the Prophet's mission. They had also developed five categories of moral obligation, distinguishing between activities on the basis of whether they were forbidden, objectionable, permissible, commendable, or compulsory. And that was sufficient flexibility to accommodate even the most recondite hadith.

The upshot was that, among the majority of Muslims, this era saw one version of Islamic history sanctified. Statements and behavior attributed to the Prophet had long been described as *sunna*—a word originally meaning custom in general—and the word gained a force that would increasingly be able to trump any practice opposed to it. Evolving ideas about the lawfulness of imagery offer an example. The Qur'an itself had said nothing about paintings or sculpture, and though all three monotheisms were very familiar with the argument that it was for God rather than humanity to picture creation, an alternative viewpoint certainly existed among Muslims. The Prophet's first biographer recorded in the mid-eighth century that portraits of Jesus and Mary had been allowed to remain hanging at the Ka'ba after its conquest, for example, and the historian al-Mas'udi (896–956) later told how an Arab merchant had seen a Chinese painting of the Prophet Muhammad that had moved him to tears. But such accounts would wither into curiosities. Those recorded in the hadith compilations would come to represent authenticity instead. On the specific question of images, it would consequently become part of the *sunna* that "angels do not enter a house in which there is a dog or there are pictures."

The coalescing narrative could thereby become more traditional than actual traditions themselves, and that was not without its opponents. Vivid proof of that proposition can be found in the writings of al-Jahiz. In a zestful essay on the respective merits of heterosexuality and homosexuality, after quoting some very rude remarks that legends attributed to various eminent early Muslims, he had ridiculed the traditionist approach to the past. "Among those who profess self-denial and poverty there are some who exhibit repugnance and disgust at the sound of the words 'cunt,' 'cock' and 'fuck,'" he complained. "The majority of these people are less learned, high-minded, noble and dignified than they pretend to be . . . These words were created to be used by all Arabic-speaking people, and to hold that they ought never to be uttered would be to make nonsense of their creation. In that case, it would be more logical and better for the purity of the Arabic tongue if these words were to be withdrawn from the language."

The words were blunt, but that was the point, and al-Jahiz's carefully calibrated complaint addressed developments that extended far beyond his concerns for linguistic integrity. As traditionists monopolized the past and jurists adopted their exclusive approach toward the *sunna*, viewpoints that rested on alternative ideas about Muslim history became correspondingly vulnerable. In the first half of the ninth century, the jurist Abu Thawr (d. 854) had taught his students that it was lawful for women to lead prayers because they had been doing so since the Prophet's lifetime. Al-Tabari (d. 923) held that tradition allowed women also to serve as judges, and he was the most celebrated historian of the age as well as a major authority on jurisprudence. But though both doctrines remain an ineradicable part of Islamic legal history, their followers began to dwindle, and by the twelfth century their interpretations would be recalled merely as mistakes.

There was one group, however, that would prove more enduring. Muslims loyal to the memory of Ali had always been instinctively hostile to anyone who had been on the wrong side of their hero, and the notion that A'isha and Umar, for example, had transmitted necessarily reliable information down the years was simply unacceptable. Although that put the Alids at odds with hundreds of hadiths, they had responded with countless reports of their own. Now that the majority was purporting to transform history into holy writ, the conflict was about to move up several notches. The stage was set for the emergence of a distinct faction (*shi'a*) that would stand in direct opposition to the self-proclaimed followers of the *sunna*—the Sunnis.

5

The Sunni Challenge and the Shi'a Response

The violent intrigues that convulsed Samarra in the years following Caliph al-Mutawakkil's murder in 862 eventually settled back into a semblance of stability, and in 892 a successor wrested back the initiative for long enough to engineer a return to Baghdad. That marked a distinct uptick in the fortunes of the City of Peace, and the apparent resurgence of the caliphate was soon being given ceremonial recognition. Tokens of submission rolled in from the provinces—caged falcons, cheetahs on leashes, and so on—and in an era when presents meant power, caliphs gave at least as good as they got. Never was that clearer than in 917, when Caliph al-Muqtadir (r. 908–32) staged a lavish reception in the capital for two Byzantine ambassadors. They had come to pick up a ransom for fifteen hundred Muslim prisoners of war, but Arab chroniclers indicate that the authorities treated them to a display of an empire at the peak of its powers. It was days before they were given an audience—months, according to one account. They were then led through labyrinthine passageways and pavilions, past a hundred chained lions and serried ranks of inscrutable slaves. An artificial garden was shown to them, complete with counterfeit palm trees and a stream made of tin, and mechanical birds warbled for their benefit from a fake tree. Only then did Caliph al-Muqtadir receive them from atop his glittering throne—and authorize release of the cash they had come to collect.

The illusions did not end there. Whatever the Greeks might have made of the extravaganza in 917, the government organizing it had lost its economic and political bearings. Two years later, Baghdad erupted into riots because its citizens could not afford the price the government had fixed for bread, and unknown numbers died under volleys of police arrows as they burned the city's bridges and broke open its prisons. It was a curtain-raiser for eighteen similar uprisings over the next thirteen years, and fiscal mismanagement across the caliphate was as profound as that implies. Powers to tax and spend were being deployed as though part of a vast pyramid scheme: viziers promised Caliph al-Muqtadir phantom revenues, they peddled offices to make the down payments, and when the bills went unpaid and the riots began, arrest or execution would set the whole process in motion all over again. Thirteen viziers rose and fell over the course of al-Muqtadir's twenty-four-year reign, while he himself was temporarily deposed twice by scheming army officers. And all the while, Baghdad's hold over the world beyond crumbled, to the extent that during the 920s the Abbasid regime lost its diplomatic ties to Khorasan, the province that had been so instrumental in its rise to power.

In the face of a corruption so palpable, nostalgia for better times was widespread, and the protests in Baghdad began to ring with the traditionist cry for pious Muslims to promote good and prohibit evil. But though that slogan had a history that by now dated back a century, the hadith-centered conservatism with which it was associated was undergoing an important change. The personification of traditionism, Ibn Hanbal, had been an unassuming figure who had sought neither publicity nor confrontation. But now, a lifetime after his death, his followers were collectively abandoning any traces of contemplativeness they might once have possessed. Hanbalites became known not for their humility but for their obstreperousness. That manifested itself most remarkably with respect to a doctrinal controversy that had been simmering for decades over the meaning of Qur'anic references to God's face and His presence on a throne "as vast as the heaven and earth." Most early traditionists had argued that such mysteries should simply be accepted "without [knowing] how" (*bi-la kayfa*), but the Hanbalites were publicly pronouncing on God's appearance and identifying the bodily features that enabled Him to sit down. And though that might sound like a theological irrelevance, such things did not exist in tenth-century Baghdad. Comprehending the attributes of God was a matter of salvation and damnation, and in a fraught political climate the nature of His throne could, and occasionally did, become a matter of life and death.

The emergence of the Hanbalites as a distinct force would have lasting consequences for understandings of the shari'a. But though they would one day become a fourth major jurisprudential school, alongside the Hanafites, Malikites, and Shafi'ites, that development took almost two centuries to unfold. It was not theories about legal interpretation that characterized their activities during the early tenth century. They were still utterly convinced that the plain words of the Qur'an and the hadiths were all that anyone needed to understand the shari'a— and that it was incumbent on all good Muslims to enforce them, as part of their duty to do good and enjoin evil. Their importance lay in the role they played in consolidating a canonical tradition—the *sunna*. Al-Bukhari's hadith collection had identified specific interpretations of history as sacred. They were doing their utmost to make them binding.

The transformation of hadiths from lessons into rules was reflected by the fact that their reduction into books was now normalized. Whereas Ibn Hanbal had taken the previously common view that human literature was an unholy innovation, his relatives and followers were now recording his hadiths by the thousands. The work of another traditionist named Ibn Abi'l-Dunya (d. 894) shows vividly where that process could lead. Among his 102 books were seven tracts specifically on the subject of censure (*dhamm*), which enumerated sins that the Prophet had supposedly sought to suppress. They made for long lists. In relation to the evils of frivolity alone, Ibn Abi'l-Dunya claimed that Muhammad had reviled chess players, cross-dressers, drummers, dice rollers, the janglers of tambourines, singing girls, pigeon fanciers, and the frequenters of seesaws. Backgammon enthusiasts had apparently sunk so low that "God does not accept their prayers. [They are akin] to people who perform their ablution with pus and swine's blood." And though such assertions spoke far more of tenth-century priorities than of seventh-century ones, publication itself served to give the claims weight. In the

name of commanding good and forbidding evil, Hanbalite vigilantes
began during the 920s to upend board games and trample lutes. They
quizzed lone women and unrelated couples on the street and assaulted
those who could not satisfactorily account for their presence. They were
so contemptuous of the lawyerly consensus that individuals should
not take religious justice into their own hands that there were physical attacks on Shafi'ite jurists. Ibn Hanbal had once insisted that hadiths
merited belief "even if the ears are repelled and the hearer is dis-
gusted" by their contents. For his tenth-century admirers, credulity,
repulsion, and disgust were no longer sufficient. Obedience was also
required.

To add to the dissension, one group of Muslims was not only immune
to the claims being made for the *sunna* but hostile to it. The Alids, as
loyal as ever to Ali's male bloodline, obtained their insights into the
shari'a from sacred reports that were being promulgated by whichever
descendants of the Prophet they happened to support. But tensions
were mounting on their side of the sectarian divide as well. A preacher
who claimed Ali as one of his ancestors had in September 869 roused
the black slaves and East Africans (*zanj*) of Basra to an armed rising
against the caliphate. Tens of thousands had died before the authorities
were finally able in 883 to parade the rebel leader's head on a pole
through Baghdad, and though the excesses of the Zanj alienated ordinary Iraqis across the board, their fight exemplified how potent the
passion for Ali and Hussein remained. A grandson of Hussein's called
Zaid, killed by the Umayyads in 740, still had his followers—known as
Zaidis or Fivers, because he had been a fifth-generation descendant of
the Prophet. Another group believed that Ali's lineage had expired two
generations later with someone called Ismail—hence Seveners, or Ismailis. And a few years into the Zanj rebellion, in 874, the claim favored
by the majority of Alids had culminated in Samarra with the death
of an eleventh-generation descendant. When prophecies of a rounder
number were fulfilled by rumors of a vanished infant son, the Twelvers
concluded that they too had lost their last imam (leader). Such setbacks
might, among lesser sects, have caused despair. But though they all inspired grief and uncertainty at first, Alids never gave up hope. Far from
it. By the end of the ninth century, Ali's supporters everywhere were

convincing themselves that the apparent extinctions were in fact signs of imminent and eternal salvation.

The apocalyptic excitement was epitomized by a Sevener sect known as the Qarmatians. Swelled by veterans of the Zanj revolt, it seized control of the archipelago of Bahrain in 899, and its battalions were soon assaulting pilgrims to Mecca and raiding cities across Syria and Iraq. Violating traditions that forbade Muslim belligerents to mistreat co-religionists, leaders of the sect branded their enemies as infidels and enslaved them, often by the caravan-load. And on January 12, 930, the Qarmatians made the boldest move of all, with an assault on Mecca itself. After slaughtering their way into the Ka'ba and filling the sacred Zamzam well with corpses, they took crowbars to the shrine's Black Stone—reputed to be a remnant of the altar once used by Adam and Eve—and spirited it back to Bahrain, where it would stay for twenty-one years.

No event better symbolized the parlous state to which the Abbasid caliphate had sunk. A regime that claimed to command the faithful had been incapable of protecting Islam's holy of holies. Lesser acts of defiance were meanwhile becoming almost routine. A year before the outrage in Mecca, the Umayyad ruler of Córdoba had formally proclaimed himself to be the legitimate caliph, and a North African upstart would soon be minting coins to prove that he was in fact God's shadow on earth. And they threw their hats into the ring only because dramatic events were unfolding in another part of the Maghreb. The region today occupied by Tunisia gave birth in 908 to a Sevener movement calling itself the Fatimids, and its leader was soon asserting a theoretical right to rule the Muslim world and a practical claim on the fabulously rich Abbasid province of Egypt. His military assaults had failed to dislodge its governor by the time of his death in 934, but his successors would maintain the pressure so effectively that in little more than three decades the country was to fall.

It would have taken a caliph of genius to master the turmoil, and Baghdad's rulers had by now become considerably more likely to fall victim to it. Al-Muqtadir himself was murdered in 932. After a particularly troublesome few years, during which one successor lost his head and a second his eyes, civil administration then collapsed in its entirety in 936. The crisis began when the regime's vizier was thrown into jail and deprived of his right hand and tongue for failing once too often to balance the books. He is said to have eloquently requested reinstatement by tying a pen to his stump, but equilibrium was not to return. Power devolved to an ambitious general who disbanded the standing army, replaced it with a Turkish mercenary force, and announced that he was now the Commander of Commanders (*amir al-umara*). With warrior dynasties circling Baghdad, the title was more optimistic than descriptive. Through a series of intrigues, he was murdered in Mosul, the incumbent caliph was blinded,* and a riot-torn Baghdad went into lockdown. Mutinous officers hustled a new ruler into position, and the capital's citizens, faced with a looming famine, could only pray. Then, even as they were hungrily eyeing the city's cats and dogs, the prayers were answered. But God was moving in a very mysterious way. Baghdad was liberated by a sprawling Persian clan known as the Buyids, who looked for spiritual leadership to the vanished Twelfth Imam.

Pivotal moments had become a disconcertingly regular feature of Islamic history by the middle of the tenth century, but the Twelver take-over of Baghdad in early 946 marked a true turning point. Some three hundred years after Ali had first been denied the reins of power, Muslims loyal to his memory had seized them. Lacking a tangible imam of their own to install as a caliph, Buyid political rulers chose instead to assume the notionally inferior title of sultan. But though they would prop up the Abbasid dynasty, they had no intention of submitting to its authority. That became clear within days of their arrival, when Caliph al-Mustakfi proffered a hand for the traditional kiss, only to be dragged off his throne for the increasingly traditional blinding instead. A pliant successor was soon pursuing policies that ran very contrary to the *sunna* indeed, typified by an order in 962 that the mosques of Baghdad display banner-sized insults against the first three caliphs. That provoked

---

*The amputations and mutilations of this era eventually become numbing even to read about, but it should be noted that blinding was sometimes a calibrated brutality. By the tenth century, most jurists agreed that God required His caliphs to be free from major bodily defects. Poking out a candidate's eyes was therefore a relative mercy, producing an injury no greater than was strictly necessary to disqualify him from his post.

sectarian riots and counter-curses against Ali, but the emergence of a new Shi'a order was then confirmed in 969 by the fall of Egypt to Fatimid forces. The conquerors founded a city they called al-Qahira, or Cairo (the Victorious), close to an existing settlement near the pyramids, and in 973 the sect's leader arrived there in triumphant procession alongside the elephant-borne coffins of his three predecessors. The Fatimid capital quickly became a cultural center on a par with Baghdad—with the consequence that Seveners and Twelvers controlled two of the greatest metropolises in the Muslim world.

The Alid ascendancy did not eliminate rivalries. Cairo's self-proclaimed caliphs would always express contempt for the pretensions of their Sunni counterparts at Córdoba, and although they notionally shared with the Buyids a deep love for Ali and Hussein, they were soon jockeying hard for position against Baghdad. They harbored schemes to conquer the city, and Buyid sultans urgently took steps in response to shore up their Shi'a credentials. By the 980s, they were publicizing the presence of Ali's bodily remains in the Iraqi city of Najaf—squashing the three-hundred-year-old claim of a rival tomb in Medina—and in 981 Karbala also gained a mausoleum, more than a century after Hussein's supposed grave at the site had been tilled into nothingness on the orders of Caliph al-Mutawakkil.

Tranquillity, then, remained elusive, but the upheavals of the mid-tenth century simultaneously generated a remarkable cultural dynamism. All too often, humbled minorities turn out to be viciously intolerant once they get their hands on power, but in those lands where Shi'ism became dominant, philosophers, freethinkers, and deviants of all descriptions thrived. In Persia, for example, three centuries of resentment found voice in the *Book of Kings* (*Shahnama*) by Abolqasem Ferdowsi (ca. 935–1020): a nationalistic epic suffused with contempt for the lizard-eating, camel-milking Arab arrivistes who had dared intrude upon the ancient kingdom of Zoroaster. Among the many writers of Buyid Baghdad was the blind wordsmith Abu'l-'Ala al-Ma'arri (973–1057), famed for versifying a paradise filled with debauched pagan poets and for taking up a challenge in the Qur'an to match the eloquence of God—though even he accepted that his revelations paled against the originals. Mu'tazilite fortunes revived after decades of decline, and the philosophical wisdom of Basrans and the open-mindedness of

Baghdadis began to gain an international reputation. With some dismay, an Andalusian visitor reported that Iraq's Jews, Christians, Zoroastrians, and atheists openly disputed the meaning of truth in public bookstores and that they were even expected to prove their arguments without reference to their holy texts.

At the very center of the ferment were Twelver scholars themselves, and their intellectual efforts would have lasting consequences for Shiʿa theology and law. The death of their twenty-eight-year-old eleventh imam in 874 had set off considerable confusion, and though his closest associates had attested to the existence of a young son who had fled in fear of an Abbasid assassination attempt, years had turned to decades with no sign of his whereabouts. As explanations for his uncommunicativeness ran out, his followers entered a period that they themselves later described as an "era of perplexity." But just when matters were becoming almost unbearably mystifying, Shiʿa theologians had formulated an explanation. Their Twelfth Imam was in occultation—invisibly alive and omnipresent—and would soon be rematerializing as the *mahdi* (guide) in order to eliminate evil, usher in perfection, and prepare humanity for the final Hour. That was not a theory that would escape examination in tenth-century Baghdad, and at a series of debates that began in Baghdad's grandest library after 991, the Muʿtazilites took it on—unsparingly. In the incredulous words of one participant, the Twelvers were following "a man whose birth and existence is not certain, to say nothing of his occultation? And now you say he is a hundred and forty-five years old!" The Twelvers rose to the challenge with a response that has stood them in good stead ever since. They contended that a twelfth imam *must* have existed and gone mystically into hiding, because God would never have left humanity without a living savior. That still assumed at least as much as it proved, to be sure, but it was about as rational as leaps of faith get. If true, God was being not only benign but reasonable. He was acting on grounds that human beings could comprehend, and He was guaranteeing that they would never be left without a guide to the shariʿa.

The theory left one obvious practicality unresolved—how to ascertain what the Twelfth Imam wanted to say—but scholars got to work in that regard as well. Even before the Buyids' arrival, a theologian named

Muhammad al-Kulayni (864–941) had published some sixteen thousand sayings of the Prophet and the imams—the first of four major Shi'a collections—and a volume of sermons and writings credited to Ali then appeared in book form at the beginning of the eleventh century. Under Mu'tazilite influence, Twelvers also moved toward the conclusion that absent their last imam, they themselves would have to establish the material's legal significance. The body of rules that emerged, known as Ja'fari jurisprudence, diverged from Sunni law in several details—granting women slightly larger inheritance shares and recognizing temporary marriages, for example—but another difference was much more far-reaching. As a consequence of their acceptance that God acted for discernible reasons, Shi'a jurists concluded that rational intellect (aql) was itself a source of the shari'a.

The heightened respect for reason that was thereby incorporated into Shi'a jurisprudence had a distinctly premodern quality. It did not stop Twelvers from attributing superhuman powers to their imams, for example, or dim their hopes for the Judgment Hour. The passion with which they recalled the murder of Ali and the slaughter at Karbala would not fade. But jurists gained a yardstick with which to measure revelations and the truth of hadiths, and they were inspired to adopt the Mu'tazilite view that the meaning of the shari'a could change over time—a concession that Sunnis of the tenth and eleventh centuries were becoming increasingly reluctant to make. And as later chapters will show, that intellectual impact has lasted. Shi'a seminaries in Iraq and Iran still turn out more emotional ayatollahs than anyone could safely shake a stick at, but they retain an interest in Islam's encounter with Greek philosophy that Sunni jurisprudence has lost. Ayatollah Khomeini was particularly keen on the writings of a polymath named Abu Nasr al-Farabi (870–950/1), whose many works included a Muslim version of Plato's *Republic—The Principles of the People of the Virtuous City*—and he so liked the notion of an ideal state led by rational and virtuous men that he borrowed it to create the Islamic Republic of Iran.

The meteoric ascendancy of the Shi'a was as quick to plummet as it had been to peak. The Buyids were a busy clan, with many fiefdoms to manage beyond Baghdad, and by the middle of the eleventh century siblings had begun to battle each other ferociously for control of the central Persian province of Fars. As their attention wandered, the sitting caliph quietly solicited support from a Sunni Turkish confederacy known as the Seljuks. Its sultan began elbowing his way toward Baghdad, and by 1060 forces under his control had wrested the city from Buyid hands. The gratified caliph accepted their notional obeisance, and the Seljuks were soon carrying his standard westward and winning a string of momentous victories. They annihilated a Byzantine army at Manzikert in eastern Anatolia in 1071, establishing a Muslim presence in Asia Minor for the first time, and then headed south to oust Sevener forces from the Levant and push them back behind the borders of Egypt. A century of Fatimid expansion came to an end as Baghdad's nemesis was neutralized and sent on a slow decline that would end a century later with its collapse.

The Seljuks' efforts to consolidate their authority in the Iraqi capital, though equally resolute, were considerably less straightforward. The regime's first vizier, Nizam al-Mulk, was an efficient administrator who moved swiftly to reassert Sunni orthodoxies by endowing a new Shafi'ite madrasa and constructing a mausoleum over the grave of Abu Hanifa. Over the course of the previous century, however, Hanbalites had intensified their challenge to jurisprudence in general. Although some were belatedly accepting that legal study had value, many maintained that the shari'a required simply that everyone command good and forbid evil. That idea was inherently anarchic, and the growth of Shi'a power under the Buyids had repeatedly unleashed its violent potential. Nine years before the Seljuk arrival, a sectarian crowd had sought to rebury two Shi'a imams next to Ibn Hanbal, setting a number of teak-domed tombs ablaze in the process, and in 1055 another traditionist mob had egged one another on to do good and forbid evil by decanting a Christian vintner's six hundred jars of wine into the Tigris. Nizam al-Mulk's hopes of calming the mood by encouraging some settled Sunni legalism quickly proved groundless. His new madrasa became a lightning rod for more protests as traditionists demonstrated against visiting lecturers who disagreed with them about the physical attributes of God. When Caliph al-Muqtadi then gave way to agitators during the late 1070s by closing down several brothels and pigeon coops, they simply complained that his efforts to promote virtue and suppress vice were inadequate. Self-righteousness was a tough stance to appease.

The conflicts had innumerable social and economic wellsprings, but they also reflected fundamental arguments about legitimacy that had been shadowing Islam since the Prophet's death. Nizam al-Mulk whole-heartedly believed in the value of Islamic law, but his primary political loyalty was owed to the Seljuk sultan rather than to the Abbasid Commander of the Faithful. The three main Sunni law schools were making strenuous efforts to squeeze out rival traditions and to estab-lish that disputes about the shari'a were best resolved by ascertaining the scholarly consensus (*ijma*)—their own view, in other words. Long-established juristic principles continued to insist, meanwhile, that any attempt to understand the shari'a should be driven by strenuous indi-vidual effort (*ijtihad*) and that blind obedience (*taqlid*) was positively wrong. And across the sectarian divide, Twelver jurists had started to speak for their hidden imam, claiming that his guidance on legal mat-ters would be ascertained through their individual rationality rather than the vagaries of communal consensus. It made for some very com-plicated arguments—but also, a mystery that was simply stated. No one was sure who, apart from God, had ultimate authority over anything.

Similar conflicts afflict societies everywhere, but in the caliphate in October 1092 the stakes were very suddenly raised. Nizam al-Mulk had by then grown old in the service of his Seljuk masters, but he made sure still to take regular soundings from their subjects, and during a tour of northwestern Persia, as he was borne from an audience to his tent, a bedraggled figure approached his litter. The supplicant had the look of a contemplative mystic, but he lacked the manner of one. Pulling a knife from his rags, he hacked the septuagenarian to death. Shock turned to fear a few weeks later when the thirty-seven-year-old sultan died of suspected poisoning, and the mood turned to panic as the cir-cumstances surrounding Nizam al-Mulk's death became known. The killer had not been a deranged hermit on a frolic of his own. He be-longed to an Ismaili sect, and he had been following the instructions of a charismatic leader who claimed an authority to interpret God's will absent the seventh and last imam. The group was almost impregnably secure in a citadel known as Alamut, perched high on a mountain peak in northwestern Persia. And its followers were taught that risking death in order to kill God's enemies was an opportunity to fulfill the shari'a and attain eternal salvation. They called themselves *rafiqan*—Comrades or Missionaries. The world would know them as Assassins.

The sect's precise doctrines are unknown, because they were concealed by adherents and distorted by everyone else, but mythology springs to the rescue with a famous tale that Marco Polo recounted two centuries later. In the travelogue that did more to perpetuate the notoriety of the Assassins than any other single work, the Venetian claimed that the "Ashishin" were named after a potent drug that facilitated and inspired their crimes: a narcotic that Muslims called *hashish*. He described a character called the Old Man of the Mountains who plied his followers with soporific potions before transporting them to a hidden valley of sublime beauty. They awoke to find themselves surrounded by wine, women, and song and were told they were in paradise. When the Old Man determined on homicide—as he often did—a suitable candidate was stupefied once again and returned to the grim surroundings of Alamut. As the youth groggily absorbed the unwelcome turn of events, it was explained that a temporary recall had become necessary. Once he had seen to the murder in question, he could go back to paradise for good.

The story is fantastic in every sense. The sect had emerged out of the embers of the Fatimid ascendancy in Egypt, and though its leaders would include several monomaniacs whose theories about the shari'a were both authoritarian and apocalyptic, its resort to violence began as a practical response to an assault ordered by Nizam al-Mulk against its Persian strongholds. Although Syrians did then come to associate members of the group with hashish and call them *hashishiyyin*, contemporary suggestions of drug use were almost certainly contemptuous rather than descriptive. But though the Assassins' origins were prosaic, their activities were not routine. Ensconced in an expanding network of mountain fortresses, they were soon bringing havoc to the Middle East. Over the course of one and a half centuries, leaders of the sect exercised an influence to rival that of any emir, and as they proselytized among ordinary people, they perfected at a political level the tactic for which they would become legendary: they killed. Preachers and spies would drift like smoke into royal retinues and palace households, suborning courtiers with an ease that seemed incomprehensible to some and diabolical to others. Their luckier victims awoke to find daggers by their bedsides and simply acceded quietly to Assassin demands. Others were stabbed by trusted guards in their privy chambers or murdered by a neighbor as they prayed.

The Assassin challenge to the status quo was therefore profound. Although there are no reliable records of how the sect justified its murder of Nizam al-Mulk in 1092, its willingness to kill Muslims in violation of express Qur'anic prohibitions posed a public order problem against which the Hanbalite protests of previous years paled. Its leader was not just asserting an implicit right to reinterpret the shari'a. He was claiming that his interpretations bound Muslims wherever they might be and trumped any governmental laws to the contrary. The stabbing of a vizier showed where that could lead, and the aftermath of that murder offered an even clearer reminder of the risks. In the wake of the sultan's almost simultaneous death, anxious attempts by the dead ruler's widow to secure the succession for her four-year-old son sparked off another fratricidal civil war. It would last for years, fracturing the Seljuk confederacy forever, and as vigilantism, riots, and barricades returned to Baghdad, the question of legitimacy became as pressing as it had ever been. Someone with authority had to speak up to explain why allegiance was owed to the state.

Cometh the crisis, cometh the man. The recently appointed head of the capital's showcase Shafi'ite madrasa was Abu Hamid al-Ghazali (1058–1111), who owed his post to the dead Nizam al-Mulk, and he now pushed for a social and legal consensus with all the heft at his disposal. Invoking arguments against religiously inspired violence that dated back to the killing of Caliph Ali, he wrote a closely argued condemnation of unthinking obedience (*taqlid*) that was clearly directed at the Assassins: anyone who obeyed a leader on the basis that he had secret knowledge of the shari'a had turned his back on Islam, he warned, and such people merited the death due to apostates. In an attempt to close theological arguments that had been raging for two centuries, he then produced a pivotal Sunni text titled *Moderation in Religious Belief*. It synthesized rationality and traditionism, deploying reams of reasoning to prove not just the attributes of God but also the question that generations of jurists had fudged—whether Muslims had to submit to a regime that they thought sinful. And the answer was bleakly affirmative.

Anticipating an argument that Thomas Hobbes would make half a millennium later during the English Civil War, al-Ghazali argued that the common good demanded obedience, because tyranny was better than anarchy. "It is known that to feed on [carrion] is forbidden, but death is worse than that. Which is better: to dismiss judges, abolish other responsibilities and stop contracting marriages and other social services or to tolerate and acknowledge the authority, defective as it is? It is the duty of wise people to choose the lesser evil."

Al-Ghazali's thoughts on the emergency were in tune with the times. "To kill [the Assassins]," agreed one contemporary, "is more lawful than rainwater." Their significance continues to resonate. According to a 1946 work by an influential Chicago professor named Gustave Grunebaum, they gave early voice to "that disillusionment bordering on cynicism with which the Oriental is still inclined to view the political life," and though intellectuals nowadays tend to avoid committing ethnic general-izations to print, some still theorize about a Muslim affinity for despotic government. Al-Ghazali deserves better than that, however. His fear of strife certainly caused him to argue in favor of stability after 1092, but he was no apostle of authoritarianism. His arguments for the rights of a Muslim ruler were dwarfed by his interest in the other side of the legal coin—the responsibilities of the individual believer.

That was never more vividly illustrated than in July 1095. After almost three years in the stressful service of a crisis-ridden state, he suffered a seismic mental breakdown. Standing before hundreds of students in his Baghdad classroom, he was struck dumb. According to a later autobiography, he remained almost paralyzed by terror for the next two months—teetering "on the brink of a crumbling bank of sand, in imminent danger of hell-fire"—until a luminous vision appeared before him. It told him to leave town and take up Sufism: a spiritual training named after the cloaks of wool (*suf*) worn by its early practi-tioners. The discipline sought to carry a Muslim closer to God, through contemplation and self-denial, lifting the barrier that separates human-ity from the divine. Al-Ghazali needed no further persuasion. He made surreptitious financial arrangements for his family and slipped away on the pretense that he was undertaking a routine pilgrimage to Mecca. After performing hajj and visiting the Prophet's tomb in Medina, he spent some time in meditation at Jerusalem's al-Aqsa Mosque before embarking on a personal quest for salvation that was to last until his death in 1111.

Once on the road, al-Ghazali was beholden only to God and his conscience, and although there is no record of his precise itinerary, his focus switched markedly from the concerns that had occupied him as a quasi-governmental functionary. He wrote extensively, and his magnum opus was a fifteen-hundred-page book called *The Revival of the Religious Sciences*. It was about as close to a deconstruction of Islamic scholarship as an Islamic scholarly text can be. Its opening section was a blistering assault on the small-mindedness, hypocrisy, and avarice that had come to characterize the study of religion, and lawyers came in for the heaviest criticisms of all. The very meaning of their discipline had been corrupted over the years, he asserted. The rules they formulated, though capable of guiding a Muslim's actions, were simply incapable of revealing the sincerity of a person's heartfelt beliefs. A jurist, asked about the lawfulness of betting in archery competitions, would be able to recite voluminous rules "which would never be used or needed," but he would hesitate before venturing so much as an opinion about the meaning of the word "sincerity." According to al-Ghazali, that was why theologians were liable to disparage jurisprudence as "nothing but hair splitting and disputations on menstruation." And though he conceded in another work written during this period that there was "no harm" in studying Islamic law, he made clear that students should first attain all "really useful knowledge" and thoroughly reform their personalities, both outwardly and inwardly.

Anyone raised in a secular culture is likely instinctively to sympathize with an approach toward faith that emphasizes its personal dimensions. To reduce al-Ghazali's critique to the proportions of a self-help manual would be to obscure the extent of its strangeness, however. The onslaught against scholarly pretension was coming from the most eminent scholar of the age, and the *Revival* included plenty of material that could do the hairsplitting cause no harm at all. It contains a long section on religiously correct approaches to sex, for example, with discussions of the sacredness of foreplay, the sinfulness of premature ejaculation, and the jurisprudential arguments that a man was obliged to weigh up when considering coitus interruptus. The companion work that al-Ghazali wrote soon afterward, *The Beginning of Guidance*, was even more ritualistic, laying down how God should be honored throughout a Muslim's day—from the remembrances appropriate in the bathroom before dawn to the prayers against sudden death that were advisable last thing at night.

One explanation for the contradictions is, at the risk of psychoanalysis, personal. The conflict between individual inclinations and communal expectations is a classic source of mental distress, and al-Ghazali's pivotal role during the crisis of the early 1090s—when he effectively became the caliphate's official spokesman for the common good—had a demonstrably catastrophic effect on his health. But such an explanation does not go very far. The anti-scholarly passages in his post-1095 work certainly contain more than a hint of self-loathing, but they were also defined by a consistent theme. Al-Ghazali argued throughout that outwardly correct behavior was a necessary but not sufficient aspect of faith.* It was the *beginning* of guidance—the first stage of the quest for God. Inward piety was the end, however, and Muslims were obliged to look deep into themselves to understand how they stood in relation to God. That cut across every obligation they owed Him, no matter how much it may have been institutionalized by others.

The distinctiveness of al-Ghazali's approach is best illustrated by his attitude toward a legal question that became a matter of great significance during his absence from Baghdad: war. Even as he was musing on God's love at Jerusalem's al-Aqsa Mosque, thousands of Europeans were heading toward Palestine, responding to an appeal for a holy struggle against Islam that Pope Urban II had made in late 1095, and in June 1099 the soldiers of the First Crusade reached Jerusalem's walls. After a five-week siege, they breached them. Christian accounts of what happened next were exultant even by the standards of medieval Latin chroniclers. "Piles of heads, hands, and feet were to be seen in the streets,"

---

*Al-Ghazali's interest in outward ritual, so peculiar from a secular perspective, had many parallels in Jewish thought, and some rabbinical scholars went considerably further than he ever did. When an Egyptian-born rabbi named Sa'adiah Gaon (882–942) once tried to establish what would disqualify someone from being a Jew, every flaw he identified was a ritualistic slipup—the failure to observe the Sabbath or keep a fast, for example—while none concerned beliefs: see Melchert, *Ahmad ibn Hanbal*, p. 84.

wrote one. "Men rode in blood up to their knees and bridle reins. Indeed, it was a just and splendid judgment of God that this place should be filled with the blood of the unbelievers, since it had suffered so long from their blasphemies." According to another: "Nearly ten thousand were beheaded in [the Temple of Solomon]. If you had been there your feet would have been stained to the ankles in the blood of the slain. What shall I say? None of them were left alive. Neither women nor children were spared."

The Christian seizure of Jerusalem marked the beginning of an occupation that would last three-quarters of a century and a regional conflict that would continue for more than a hundred years after that. But when al-Ghazali wrote his autobiography a decade or so after his visit, he chose to dwell on the tranquillity of the holy city and said not a word about the catastrophe that followed his departure. And that was not the end of it. He never once mentioned the Crusades in any of his works. Though he had previously written a textbook reiterating a long-established Shafi'ite principle that Muslim rulers should battle infidels once a year, the only systematic discussion of warfare he published after his breakdown was about as rarefied as talk of combat can be. It came in a section of the *Revival* on "the mysteries of the heart," which lengthily compared the individual to a battlefield and a beleaguered city. The heart had armies of its own, explained al-Ghazali, while angels and demons were constantly battling for the soul of a believer, just as guards and raiders might skirmish over a frontier outpost. And the Prophet himself had apparently thought along similar lines. According to al-Ghazali, he had told Muslims after their first major military victory at Badr that their struggle (jihad) was not won: they had only won a "lesser struggle," while the greater struggle to fortify their spiritual defenses still lay ahead.

Al-Ghazali's stance was far from typical. Islamic jurists had been analyzing the Qur'anic obligation of jihad for three centuries, and although they had identified several spiritual struggles that were covered by the term, none of any note had ever doubted that one of them was holy warfare. And although Baghdad's caliphs were surprisingly reluctant to characterize military resistance to the Christian invaders as a jihad—simply because by the time of the Crusades they lacked the wherewithal to muster an army—their passivity was entirely out of step with prevailing opinion. Caliph al-Mustadhir's inactivity inspired riots in Baghdad on two successive Fridays in February 1111, the year of al-Ghazali's death, and the potentates of Egypt, Syria, and Palestine were soon rallying Muslims against the intruders. Many scholars were equally unconvinced by the notion of equating jihad and psychic struggle. Hanbalites took particular issue with al-Ghazali's methodology, pointing out that he often discussed stories about the Prophet without listing their supposed sources. To this day, there are jurists of a bellicose bent who deny that Muhammad advised his followers to battle their base passions.

Al-Ghazali's concern to show that the shari'a governed the ego would have ramifications that extended far beyond the truth or otherwise of a single hadith, however. It reflected the Sufi mysticism to which he had been drawn after his breakdown, and, despite the controversies that surrounded some of his views, his affirmation of that approach to faith was going to gather force for centuries. In the hurly-burly of the Abbasid caliphate, attempts to collect, collate, analyze, and apply Islam's revelations and hadiths had developed into a highly sophisticated set of legal doctrines. Sufism preserved a far more basic understanding of the behavior required of Muslims. It invited believers to fall back on their own inner resources to strengthen their faith. It insisted, above all, that the shari'a was bigger than a set of orders; it was a path to salvation, which God had given humanity out of love.

The spread of Sufism would enrich Islamic culture immensely, and, for reasons that are set out in the next two chapters, it arguably saved it from evisceration. But its rise was paralleled by a simultaneously regressive development in the field of jurisprudence. Al-Ghazali would be widely recognized among Sunnis in years to come as a *mujaddid*, or "renovator," of the law—a sort of judicial superhero that God sends once a century to clean up the mess that has accumulated since the last one came by. But the darker side of that admiration was an implicit suggestion that he was the last great interpreter of the shari'a. Within a decade of his death, a claim that would become famous in Islamic legal history was recorded for the first time: an assertion that the "gate" through which a scholar had to travel to understand the law had closed and that jurists would never again be able to gain fresh insights into God's will. It was the kind of apocalyptic observation of which gloomier

Muslims had long been fond, and the scholar who jotted down the remark thought it untrue, but it developed a life of its own. Over the next few centuries, Sunni scholars began to treat the *insidad bab al-ijtihad* (closure of interpretation's gate) as a historical fact rather than a poetically pleasing way of saying that jurists were no longer as good as they used to be. Some argued that attempts to interpret the shari'a were not just doomed but presumptuous. Conservatives still invoke the phrase in madrasas today, as and when they think it necessary to explain why settled legal questions should not be revisited.

Attempts to understand the shari'a did not in fact cease in the twelfth century or anytime thereafter, of course. Although conservative Sunni jurists have always pushed for conformity, others would develop imaginative solutions to new problems. Twelver Shi'a scholars meanwhile continued explicitly to struggle with the shari'a's meaning—to do *ijtihad*—pending the return of their invisible imam. But the emergence of the legal pessimism speaks volumes about perceptions. By the early twelfth century, the Muslim world was shrinking for the first time in half a millennium. Crusaders in the Holy Land were not the only ones encroaching on the Islamic world; Norman forces retook Sicily in 1091, and Toledo fell to Alfonso VI in 1085, beginning a process that would see all of Andalusia reconquered by the middle of the thirteenth century. The Seljuk confederacy meanwhile failed to recover from its crisis of the 1090s, and as it fragmented into rival sultanates, the Assassin sect was gathering strength and enfeebled caliphs were having to ignore the infidel armies rampaging through the Levant. It was not a decline in the capacity of scholars to engage with complexity that later inspired the nostalgia for a golden age of legal interpretation. It was hindsight.

Baghdad did not make up the lost ground over the next few decades, if the diary of an Andalusian named Ibn Jubayr (1145–1217) is anything to go by. Ibn Jubayr was a God-fearing man who remorsefully embarked for Mecca in February 1183 after a goblet of wine had been pressed on him by the emir of Granada. He was also curious, however, and once the atonement was done, he decided to squeeze in some sightseeing. Two rollicking years followed. He traversed a war-torn Syria, survived a shipwreck off the Sicilian coast after being rescued by the island's Christian king, and made it all the way across the Arabian Desert, whiling away the longueurs playing chess in his howdah (a pastime he highly recommended, as long as his reader "deems it lawful"). But Baghdad turned out to be not worth the trip. At the time of al-Ghazali's death, it possessed considerable elegance: one resident lyrically described it as a place of groaning waterwheels and gurgling fountains, filled with flower markets, perfumeries, teak balconies, and riverside palaces. Ibn Jubayr found a husk. "Most of its traces have gone, leaving only a famous name. In comparison with its former state, before misfortune struck it and the eyes of adversity turned towards it, it is like an effaced ruin, a remain washed out, or the statue of a ghost." The situation was grim. A caliphate that once held sway from India to Andalusia was reduced to a rump state, while infidels were murdering its notional subjects by the thousands. And the grimness was about to increase exponentially.

6

The Caliphate Destroyed: A Shadowless God

In the spring of 1218, a delegation of foreign traders arrived at a town called Utrar in what is now Pakistan's Swat Valley. It was an outpost on the frontier of Khwarizm province, on the northernmost fringes of the Islamic world, and the foreigners hailed from a little-known heathen land beyond. The ambitious ruler of the province had recently asserted his independence from Baghdad, and Utrar's governor suspiciously accused the newcomers of espionage. With a temerity that was either jumpy or cocky, he then had them executed. When three emissaries from the merchants' homeland arrived to lodge a protest, the governor had one of them beheaded in his turn and ordered that the other two be shaved of their beards and deported back across the border. That, he believed, would show their master that the prince of Khwarizm was not a sovereign to be trifled with. It was a serious miscalculation. Their master had recently breached the Great Wall of China and sacked Beijing. Genghis Khan was unlikely to let the matter lie.

The warlord's response came in the autumn. Countless thousands of horse-borne archers, encased in buffalo hide and iron plate, swept through Khwarizm and surged into the central Asian provinces of the caliphate. Over the next two years, the Mongols overwhelmed cities such as Bukhara and Samarkand, wreaking havoc on an almost unimaginable scale. When Utrar fell, after a six-month siege, Genghis Khan is said to have personally watched as its hapless governor had molten silver poured into his eyes and ears. In Nishapur, the invaders piled their victims' heads into three triumphal pyramids: one for men, another for women, and the last for children. No one will ever know precisely how many died, but even after the exaggerations of chroniclers are discounted, the number undoubtedly runs into the hundreds of thousands. Those spared the saber often survived only until the next battle, when they would be driven ahead of the Mongol siege engines to fill moats and trenches with their bodies.

It was the most devastating assault that the Islamic world had ever experienced, a campaign against which even the Crusades paled, and worse lay ahead. Eastern Europe bore the brunt for a few years after Genghis Khan's death in 1227 while a series of succession disputes divided his descendants, but the clans were soon regathering. And at a convocation of shamans and chiefs during the summer of 1251, they united behind a grandson of Genghis Khan's named Möngke. After the new great khan had taken the precaution of drowning his predecessor's widow in a sack, he charged two siblings with the most ambitious mission yet. Kublai was told to renew the onslaught on China, and young Hülegü was instructed to go west as far as Egypt.

The thirty-four-year-old prepared for his task with a meticulousness that had already come to characterize Mongol campaigns. Chinese engineers were put to work building catapults, rocket batteries, and archery wheels, and scouts went ahead to set aside pasture and make sure that highways were in good repair. Coalitions were assembled no less assiduously. The Mongols had developed surprisingly adroit political skills, far more sophisticated than their slaughtering proclivities might imply, and there was much to divide and rule. Although the Crusades were well past their heyday, Christians remained in control of several city-states across Syria and Palestine. The Assassins had meanwhile multiplied, with strongholds now studding mountains across northern Persia and Syria. The caliphate itself had become a patchwork of autonomous principalities, and Caliph al-Musta'sim (1213–58) was proving dismally incapable of reasserting any authority from Baghdad. Even those rulers who professed loyalty to him were dangerously susceptible to threats and promises, and sectarian tension was so high that a Twelver Shiʻa contingent would eventually sign up to fight alongside the Mongols.

Hülegü's preparations finally began rumbling into action in 1256, with a campaign to disrupt and destroy the Assassin network in Persia. He audaciously announced that he was fighting a war on heresy, demanding assistance from regional emirs and the caliph himself, and his army carried the day. The sect's leader, faced with a force more lethal than any he could ever deploy, yielded up his fortresses on the understanding that his own status and privileges would be preserved. They were not. Having neutralized the Assassin threat, Hülegü issued an order that the imam's personal entourage be executed. When the imam sought desperately to plead their case in person, he was denied an audience and ambushed as he began the long journey home. According to Hülegü's court historian, "He and his followers were kicked to a pulp and then put to the sword; and of him and his stock no trace was left, and he and his kindred became but a tale on men's lips and a tradition in the world." The account was more florid than accurate, in that the Assassin imamate is still claimed today—by the Aga Khan, incongruously enough—but its triumphalist tone was understandable. Hülegü had broken a sect that had seemed invulnerable for almost two centuries. It was a tremendous victory for the Mongol leader—and a very ominous one for everyone else.

By March 1257, Hülegü was contemplating his next move. It was not as obvious as hindsight might suggest. There was a risk that an all-out assault on Baghdad might unite forces against him in a way that Caliph al-Mustaʻsim had been singularly incapable of doing, and one of his astrologers was foreseeing some very dire portents, ranging from the death of all his horses to a failure of the sun to rise. But an accomplished Assassin stargazer that Hülegü had recently spared and taken into his service expressed greater optimism, and the balance was then tipped by a very down-to-earth development. The Mongol ruler received a confidential communication from the caliph's Shiʻa vizier, Muʻayyad ibn al-Alqami, whose loyalties to his supposed master had just been tested to the breaking point. The caliph had used military force to put down unrest in Baghdad's main Shiʻa suburb, and Ibn al-Alqami had been so outraged that he now invited the Mongol ruler to move on the capital. The duplicity has made the vizier's name a byword for treachery among Iraqi Sunnis ever since—in April 2003, Saddam Hussein invoked it in order to explain what underpinned the recent U.S.-led invasion—and its significance was immediately apparent. Hülegü now knew that the caliphate lay within his grasp.

Caliph al-Musta'sim was in an even weaker position than he realized, but it was to his compromised counselor that he anxiously turned for advice. Ibn al-Alqami, with his master's worst interests at heart, warned that attempts to defend Baghdad would be futile and that moneys earmarked for the task should instead be used to buy Hülegü a thousand stallions, a thousand camels, and a thousand donkeys, sumptuously caparisoned and laden with treasure. The bamboozled caliph was not persuaded by that specific suggestion, but he began to contemplate surrender while mouthing defiance, and as he prevaricated, Hülegü's forces moved into position. Clashes across the Tigris and Euphrates in January 1258 led to a major engagement near the town of Dujail, which ended after a day of fierce combat with each side withdrawing for the night. Nocturnal adjournments of battle were customary, but what followed was not. While the Muslims slept, Mongol engineers worked to divert a nearby canal into their camp. Twelve thousand troops awoke in the dark to find themselves awash and surrounded as they sank into a muddy grave. Hülegü had won before Baghdad could even know that it was lost.

The first glimpse that the capital's inhabitants caught of their own fate came in the form of a patch of dust, spotted on the horizon by lookouts on the city rooftops. The dust was soon billowing into a cloud, and as Baghdad locked its gates, it turned into a horde. Engines of war soon surrounded the city, with pontoons linking Mongol infantry divisions on both sides of the Tigris, and the attackers' grip tightened to a stranglehold. For a week, battering rams thundered, arrows hailed, and Greek fire dropped from the sky in luminous streaks. Caliph al-Musta'sim, paralyzed by a final flurry of contradictory suggestions from his vizier, surrendered to the inevitable on February 10, 1258, and half a millennium after its foundation the City of Peace fell into infidel hands.

As the walls of Baghdad were torn down, Hülegü received its vanquished ruler in his former palace. An eyewitness account conveys some flavor of the meeting. It records that the Mongol leader paced the room, as if distracted, before suddenly demanding a gift. Every posses-sion offered up by al-Musta'sim was then waved away, until Hülegü's eyes fell on a golden tray. Snatching it up, he placed the glittering plate in front of the caliph and told him to eat it. Al-Musta'sim replied in confusion that no one ate gold, whereupon Hülegü exploded with rage. "Then why did you keep it, and not give it to your soldiers? And why did you not turn your iron doors into arrowheads and come to the river-bank to stop me from crossing it?" "Such was God's will," replied the terrified caliph. "And what is going to befall you," said Hülegü, "is also God's will."

Destiny was not long in manifesting itself. Hülegü's troops were given the traditional license to pillage, and while their saddlebags filled with booty, Baghdad drowned in blood. Writers would later memorial-ize the end of empire with suitably exaggerated accounts. One reports that wooden palaces went up in plumes of sandal- and aloe-scented flames that could be smelled thirty miles distant; another that the Tigris ran black with ink, as the wisdom of centuries was used to build a bridge across the river for the Mongol cavalry. The caliph's end, when it came on February 20, 1258, was more prosaic. By then, corpses and carcasses were rotting so terribly in the capital's streets that Hülegü had relocated to an outlying village; and al-Musta'sim was made to trudge through the stench on foot. God's supposed shadow on earth was then rolled into a carpet, so as not to invite the earthquake that the Mongols feared from the spilling of royal blood, and extinguished: trampled by galloping horses said some; kicked to death by soldiers, according to others.

The Muslim world was thereby plunged into uncertainties as pro-found as any in its history. An eyewitness later called Baghdad's fall "the most awful catastrophe that has befallen time . . . Histories con-tain nothing that even approaches it." According to the recollections of a writer who was born three years after 1258: "Things happened which I shall not record; imagine them and do not ask for a description." Even Muslims on Hülegü's payroll seem to have been shocked. One of his senior Persian administrators would soon produce a three-volume cel-ebration of Mongol triumphs, but though willing to characterize count-less other massacres as God's wrath manifest, he avoided any mention of Baghdad's conquest at all.

Hülegü, on the other hand, simply gained one more reason to feel optimistic, and by the autumn of 1259 he was on the move again. His forces marched through Kurdistan, accepting capitulations and demolishing resistance as they went, and then headed into Syria to smash the walls and massacre the inhabitants of Aleppo. Damascus, Hebron, and Gaza collapsed in short order, until all that remained of the mission he had undertaken was the conquest of Egypt itself. And that looked unlikely to pose much challenge. Cairo's sultans had recently succumbed to an extreme version of the problem that had been plaguing Muslim rulers since the ninth century—palace guards with political ambitions—and a cabal of notionally enslaved Turkish army officers known as Mamluks had seized power in a violent coup nine years earlier. They had already split into factions, however, and Hülegü, who hailed from a culture with firmly aristocratic views about political order, assumed their moral fiber to be as mean as their social origins. He sent their sultan appropriate notice of his intentions:

> You have heard that we have conquered a vast expanse of land and that we have purified the earth of the disorders which tainted it, and that we have slaughtered the greater part of its inhabitants. It is for you to flee and for us to pursue, and which land will offer you refuge, what road will be able to save you, and what country shall keep you alive? . . . Our horses are very swift, our arrows are sharp, and our swords are like thunderbolts; our hearts are hard as mountains, and our soldiers are numerous as grains of sand. Fortresses cannot stand before us, and arms have no way of stopping us . . . In sending you this message, we have acted nobly toward you. We [wish only] to arouse you from your slumber.

The ultimatum was not well received. The four envoys carrying it were executed, their heads mounted under the turrets of Cairo's Zuweila gate, and a force of twenty thousand men was assembled to meet Hülegü's approaching army. As the sun rose on September 3, 1260, battle was joined at an oasis near Nablus called Ain Jalut. With Mecca and Medina defenseless and the Mongols poised to slot the last remnant of the caliphate into an empire that now stretched from the Mediterranean to the Sea of Japan, the encounter has fair claim to be one of the most consequential clashes of world history. By midday, it was over, and the Mongols had lost. Their commander's head was en route to Cairo, and the body of his army was in suitably breakneck retreat. The Islamic world could breathe again.

The victory at Ain Jalut marked the beginning of a major fightback. Damascus was liberated a few days later, and within weeks the Mamluks had driven the Mongols out of Syria entirely and overrun some of the last crusader strongholds for good measure. But though Ain Jalut postponed a Day of Judgment that had started to seem very nigh indeed, it could not reverse the enormity of Baghdad's collapse or the challenge that now confronted Islamic law. The *khalifa*—the vice-regent of God—had personified righteous rulership ever since Abu Bakr had assumed power in the days after the Prophet's death in 632. Real-life caliphs had never lacked for flaws, but no jurist or theologian of note had ever seriously contemplated that the caliphate might somehow come to an end before the world itself. The unimaginable had now become actual, and the practical question posed by the new situation had already crystallized. As Hülegü had rested his armies in Baghdad, he had gathered a group of jurists together in the city's largest madrasa and invited them to consider the legal status of his conquest. "Who is to be preferred?" he had demanded. "A just, unbelieving ruler, or a Muslim ruler who is unjust?"

Hülegü's inquiry was as tricky as it sounds. The only half-relevant advice in the Qur'an charged Muslims to resolve their political problems through consultation and obey "those charged with authority among you," and the weight of Islamic jurisprudence supported a confrontational conclusion. Sunni jurists had entrusted Islam's most fundamental powers, such as declarations of holy war and the imposition of sacred *hadd* criminal penalties, to the Commander of the Faithful. Al-Ghazali had famously urged Baghdadis to tolerate injustice for the greater good of the caliphate during the civil crisis of the 1090s. In more recent years, the reconquest of Andalusia by Catholic armies had led several scholars in Córdoba and North Africa explicitly to state that Muslim tyranny was always preferable to life under a Christian ruler. Only a handful had ever openly accepted the converse proposition: that fair-minded infidels might merit obedience. But the spokesman of the delegation in Baghdad, Razi al-Din Ali ibn Tawus, had lifted his pen to scratch out its collective and very conciliatory fatwa: "The just infidel is preferable to an unjust Muslim."

It would have taken great courage or profound stupidity to have done any different, and the imperatives of realpolitik were augmented in Ibn Tawus's case by the fact that he was a Shi'a. He started from the assumption that the Abbasid caliphate had ignored historical crimes against Ali and Hussein and compounded them by oppressive measures against many of their descendants. The only authority he acknowledged as truly legitimate was the invisible Twelfth Imam. From his perspective, Hülegü might even have been an improvement on the Abbasids; the Mongol ruler was self-evidently prepared to pay heed to Shi'a interpretations of the shari'a, and he at least had no pretensions to the Prophet's spiritual authority.

Ibn Tawus's ruling possessed a meaning that transcended its sectarian outlook, however. It reflected a legal inventiveness that had suddenly become all but obligatory. The Muslim world had lost its power to define itself according to its own terms, and with the apex of the existing order removed, scholars across the board were going to have to reappraise some of their basic assumptions almost from scratch. New answers would emerge, but an appreciation of their significance requires a digression and a geographical diversion. The reason is that the fall of the caliphate coincided with the tail end of a philosophical debate in faraway Andalusia—an argument about how humanity could know what it knew. It was an old epistemological riddle, but Islamic scholars were formulating answers that would change political fortunes and legal ideas, not only among Muslims, but among European Christians as well.

The Muslim world, for the first five centuries of its existence, had paid almost no attention to the great landmass that lay north of Andalusia and west of Constantinople. While Europeans languished in what they would later call the Dark Ages, Arabic scholars had been synthesizing Hindu mathematics and Athenian philosophy. When the emperor Charlemagne (a man barely able to scratch out his own signature) had sent ambassadors with furs and fabric to Caliph Harun al-Rashid,

Muslim chroniclers had even managed to overlook their arrival. The tenth-century writer al-Mas'udi made only passing mention of the Continent's people in one of his geographical works, and though his observations were probably based on hearsay, no charitable reader would have faulted his failure to gather information firsthand:

> The warm humour is lacking among them; their bodies are large, their natures gross, their manners harsh, their understanding dull, and their tongues heavy. Their colour is so excessively white that they look blue; their skin is fine and their flesh coarse. Their eyes, too, are blue, matching their colouring; their hair is lank and reddish because of the damp mists. Their religious beliefs lack solidity, and this is because of the nature of cold and the lack of warmth. The farther they are to the north, the more stupid, gross, and brutish they are.

Even when Muslims were able to adjust the caricatures, following the first incursions of Christian forces into Andalusia, Sicily, and Palestine at the end of the eleventh century, they found little reason to do so. The foreigners (*faranji*, or Franks) sometimes won grudging respect for their martial prowess, but that assessment did not translate into admiration. The impression they made is well illustrated by the diaries of a Syrian poet and warrior by the name of Usama ibn Munqidh (1095–1188). He portrayed them as a herd of blundering numskulls—"animals possessing the virtues of courage and fighting, but nothing else"—whose physicians killed every patient they touched. Their standards of propriety were typified by the oaf who blithely took his wife to the local bathhouse, where he became so excited to learn about depilation that he ordered the attendant to shave off his pubic hair—and then, "By the truth of my religion, do the same to madame!" The anecdotes are considerably more vivid than reliable, but they speak volumes about the reputation that Europeans were establishing among their reluctant hosts.

Many aspects of *faranji* jurisprudence seemed equally strange to Muslims. The earliest written laws enacted by the Crusaders, a series of statutes approved at Nablus in 1120, imposed several punishments that would have been familiar—amputation for thieves, for example—but there were many that had no Islamic parallel. They prescribed castration for rapists, for example, burnings at the stake for so-called sodomites,* and removal of the nose for those Christian wives who dared fornicate across religious lines. The statutes also provided for a type of trial, then at the cutting edge of Norman and German jurisprudence, that a Muslim was bound to consider bizarre: a procedure obliging any man accused of seducing someone else's wife to prove his innocence by asking God to help him carry a red-hot iron without injury. Few Islamic jurists doubted God's ability to do as He saw fit, but none had ever thought miracles a sound basis for a judicial system. Islamic trials had come to depend instead on elaborate witness qualifications and evidential rules, and if a man swore that his wife had been unfaithful and she denied it on oath, their marriage was simply dissolved. When Ibn Munqidh stumbled across another type of ordeal in Nablus during the 1130s, he was correspondingly contemptuous:

> They installed a huge cask and filled it with water. Across it they set a board of wood. They then bound the arms of the man charged with [crimes against Christian pilgrims], tied a rope around his shoulders and dropped him into the cask, their idea being that [if] he was innocent, he would sink in the water; and . . . [if] he was guilty he would [float]. This man did his best to sink when they dropped him into the water, but he could not do it. So he had to submit to their sentence upon him—curse be upon them! They pierced his eyeballs with red-hot awls.

Such incredulity found its mirror image in the collective European response to Islamic culture. The Christian gate-crashers were as impressed as Muslims were underwhelmed. As a monk observed from early-twelfth-century Palestine, the pillaging opportunities alone were remarkable: "Those who had little money [at home] have countless besants here, and those who did not have a villa possess here by the gift of

---

*On the basis of certain hadiths, Malikite and Shafi'ite jurists, along with some smaller schools of law, believed that male homosexuals should be stoned to death: Farah, *Marriage and Sexuality*, pp. 37–39. There is no account in the hadith collections or later texts of such a penalty ever actually being applied, however.

God a city." Sophistication was not so instantly acquired, but Christians were quick to learn. Although they lacked words to describe many of the luxuries they encountered—from the sofas (*suffa*), lutes (*al-ud*), and guitars (*qitara*) of Andalusia to the damasks of Damascus, the muslin of Mosul, and the gauze of Gaza—they were as swift to adopt them as the vocabulary implies. By the end of the twelfth century, the Norman ladies of Palermo were wearing jewelry, scent, and veils with such elegance that an Arab traveler even dared compare them to Muslim women—though not without begging the forgiveness of God.

There was another type of treasure that, though less tangible, seemed in many European eyes most desirable of all. The wisdom of the scholars of Córdoba and Baghdad had long been the stuff of Christian legend, and rumors about its potency were swirling by the early twelfth century. Monks at Monte Cassino and Salerno had recently laid hands on a number of Arabic medical texts, and Toledo's fall to Catholic forces in 1085 had opened up a way for Christian scholars to gain direct access to Islamic literature for the first time. In the intellectual equivalent of a gold rush, adventurers were heading south, and, despite efforts by panicky Muslim officials to stop people from selling them books, the new arrivals teamed up with bilingual locals to sift through centuries of Arabic writing. As had been the case among the translators at Baghdad's ninth-century House of Wisdom, they focused on information that might be useful, and usefulness in the twelfth century covered a lot of ground. Numbers made their way northward in the form of algebra and algorithms, but so too did the sciences of alchemy, astrology, fortune-telling, and long-distance poisoning. And one discipline was soon commanding particular interest. In another echo of ninth-century Baghdad, Latin Europe gained exposure to a body of knowledge that would transform it forever: Greek philosophy.

It can be hard today to appreciate just how estranged Latin scholars were from the heritage of ancient Athens. Although it has been common in the West for more than three centuries to assert cultural continuities with Greece and Rome, the connections were few and far between in medieval Europe. Monks spoke Latin, and Christendom was littered with institutional relics of the Roman Empire, but Western Europe's real debts were owed to the pagan cultures of Germany and Scandinavia. Constantinople had a more substantial claim, but its influence in the West was minimal, and there had been a decisive theological break with the Latin Church during the eleventh century. And that had very important consequences for the intellectual trajectory of medieval Europe. Although Latin scholars eventually got access to Aristotle's works in the original Greek, that was not how they first became aware of pre-Christian philosophy. Their introduction came courtesy of Muslims.

The roundabout route by which they grew acquainted with Aristotle began with the translation in the third quarter of the twelfth century of a book by al-Ghazali called *Aims of the Philosophers*, which the Baghdadi scholar had written a few years before his nervous breakdown in 1095. Catholics took its author to be a great logician, to whom they gave the name Algazel, but though that reflected well on the mystic's evenhandedness, it obscured the Sufi perspective that had inspired it. Al-Ghazali had written the work as a kind of primer for a polemic called *The Incoherence of the Philosophers*, which sought to expose why Greek logic had no business trespassing onto questions of religion. He had not opposed reason—accepting, for example, that "a rational foe is better than an ignorant friend"—but he had argued that it lacked spiritual relevance. God did as He wished, and it was wrong to assess or predict His behavior according to human ideas of what made sense.

Al-Ghazali thereby raised a fundamental question—whether human beings could rely on reason as well as revelation to understand the cosmos—and answered it in the negative. But his was not the last word on the matter. At around the same time that his work was being translated into Latin, one of Córdoba's most renowned scholars—the jurist and physician Ibn Rushd (1126–98)—was writing a counterblast titled *The Incoherence of the Incoherence*. Although addressed to al-Ghazali's old arguments, it was directed primarily at Andalusian religious reactionaries whose influence was on the rise, and it amounted to the most forthright defense of rationalism that any Muslim would ever write. One example usefully illustrates how different his views were from those of al-Ghazali. The Baghdadi mystic had used a homely example at one point to explain how human beings could misperceive underlying realities. When cotton came into contact with fire, he wrote, it only caught alight because God wanted that to happen. It might *seem* as though independent laws of cause and effect were at work, but the event was as direct a product of divine intervention as any more attention-grabbing miracle. Ibn Rushd, by contrast, insisted that it was mere sophistry to say that God was the immediate cause of every single instance of ignition. Human beings could more usefully say that fire caused cotton to burn—because creation had a pattern that they could discern.

When translation of Ibn Rushd's own work then began—at around the time that Spain's reconquest was sealed with the capture in 1236 of Córdoba—Latin clerics therefore found themselves in the middle of an intellectual dogfight. It was just the latest round of an argument that had been raging for four centuries among Muslims, but they were enthralled. Monks in Paris and Naples quickly set about reading Averroës (as they called Ibn Rushd) and another Córdoba-born scholar: an Arabic-speaking Jew named Musa bin Maimun (Maimonides). The study circles coalesced into universities, and though Ibn Rushd's impact was highly contentious—with conservative clerics at the Sorbonne soon clamping down on philosophy with some fervor (deploying arguments that were often derived directly from al-Ghazali)—it was also massive. The Dominican friar who did more than anyone to integrate Aristotelian thought into Catholic theology, Thomas Aquinas (1225–74), referred to the Andalusian at least 503 times, in arguments that were structured along lines that Cordobans had learned from the thinkers of ninth-century Baghdad. And the critics of the new learning did not condemn the proponents of rationalism as Aristotelians: they knew them simply as Averroists.

Ibn Rushd thereby stood at an intellectual pivot. Works he had written to challenge conservatism among Muslims inspired a radical rethink among Catholics. The extent of his contribution would eventually be forgotten, as Europeans of later centuries imagined themselves heirs of ancient Greece, but the rationalism he inspired moved inexorably from the theoretical to the practical. It led many Christian theologians to wonder whether God's ideas about right and wrong were as predictable as the connection between cause and effect, and to develop the notion of natural law—the belief that certain norms were so fundamental that God Himself observed them. The subsequent history of Western jurisprudence lies beyond the scope of this book, mercifully enough, but credit for its development belongs in part to Ibn Rushd. The Andalusian helped thirteenth-century clerics to conceptualize that all power—even if attributable ultimately to God—was defined and potentially limited by rules.

After the caliphate's fall in 1258—to bring this excursion to an end—Islamic jurisprudence might therefore have looked to rationalism to address the uncertainties that loomed. Terminal damage had been done to the institutionalized person of God's law, but the idea was in play that scholars themselves could ascertain its fundamentals and use reason to develop ideas about government and rules of general application. Shi'a jurists were already traveling down that path. The chance that Sunnis would argue from first principles was slim, however. They had collectively been distancing themselves from moral philosophy since the late ninth century, and al-Ghazali's critique was just the most erudite expression of their hostility. Ibn Rushd's own fortunes illustrated the point. His encyclopedic grasp of Sunni jurisprudence would never cease to be admired, but his philosophical endeavors put him in such bad odor that he was briefly exiled from Córdoba during the 1190s.

Islam's alternative source of legitimacy—the traditions that had been sanctified as *sunna*—was almost by definition more likely to underpin the majority's response. And that posed difficulties that went to the heart of the problem facing Sunnis in 1258. It was almost unthinkable for them to do what the Shi'a scholar Ibn Tawus had effectively done when summoned by Hülegü—profess obedience to abstract ideas of justice—but the degree of deference that they were used to paying the caliphate had been counterproductive. Although jurists had identified conditions from mental incapacity to blindness that could disqualify a caliph, none had ever dared delineate the powers of the caliphate as an institution. The one who came closest, a constitutional theorist named al-Mawardi (972–1058), had merely advised scholars to make sure that caliphs were not led astray by mischievous underlings. And the theoretical respect had often served to promote precisely the opposite. When Caliph al-Mutawakkil had been killed in 861, jurists had retroactively validated his murder with a fatwa. Eight years later, they had testified to the lawful abdication of a successor, after he had been dragged from a toilet, beaten unconscious, and thrown into a vault to die. By the middle of the tenth century, judges were solemnly confirming that the onset of blindness had disqualified a caliph, without mentioning that they had just been assembled to witness the gouging of his eyes. Such skulduggery was hardly unique to Islamic societies. Sunnis placed disproportionate reliance on the personal authority of each succeeding caliph, however, and that became very problematic now that Baghdad's last caliph had been killed, and all that remained was a tradition that he personified the authority of God.

That is not to say that there were no traditions out of which abstract ideas about government could be formulated. Centuries of legal development had regularized the behavior of lesser officials, and the Abbasids had institutionalized some significant checks and balances. Day-to-day governing powers were divided among judges, ministers, police officers, and a moral enforcer known as the *muhtasib** (reckoner), and anyone mistreated at their hands could seek redress from the caliph himself at the Court for the Review of Injustice. Al-Mawardi had laid down limits for each and made clear that the *muhtasib* in particular should never mistake suspicions for proof or investigate sins that occurred behind closed doors. Trial procedures were regulated by rules that dated back to the Qur'an, and an arrested person was at least sometimes accorded protections even in jail. A treatise written in Seville in the early twelfth century warned guards against unauthorized brutality and affirmed a right in prisoners to receive visitors and have their cases heard quickly. It also recorded what is arguably the first statement of due process in European history: "No agent of the state may imprison an individual without the authorization of a judge and governor." The vitality of such arrangements is confirmed by another glance toward Christendom. English common law was only just being hammered into shape, and certain scholars have argued that during this period, it incorporated at least two concepts of Islamic jurisprudence: actions for debt and the equitable trust. Sicily's King Roger II (r. 1130–54) meanwhile commandeered the Court for the Review of

---

*Among the *muhtasib*'s regular targets were shameless drunks and those who shirked fasts, crooked shopkeepers, people who avoided mosques too blatantly or slept in them too often, and any man who dyed his hair black, unless he could show that he was on the way to war and did not intend his new hair color to facilitate the seduction of women: al-Mawardi, *Ordinances*, pp. 260–80, esp. pp. 278–80. Similarly upstanding characters exist in modern Iran and Saudi Arabia, where they are respectively known as "guidance patrols" (sing.: *gasht e-ershad*) and "volunteers" (*mutawwin*).

Injustice, and it would form the nucleus for a system of administrative justice that his grandson Frederick II (1194–1250) would extend up through Italy after his coronation as Holy Roman emperor in 1220. Islamic civilization possessed undeniably complex legal and political tools. The question was how that historical reality was going to interact with theoretical traditions in the post-caliphal world.

It is sometimes tempting to cope with change by pressing on as though it has not occurred, but the futility of ignoring events in Baghdad very quickly became clear after the battle at Ain Jalut in September 1260. Old Mamluk rivalries quickly flared up again, to the extent that the sitting sultan was murdered within weeks. His heavily implicated successor, a tall and half-blind former slave by the name of Baybars, moved rapidly to consolidate his grip—only for an uncle of the murdered caliph al-Musta'sim then to emerge in Cairo in June 1261. Baybars expressed his undying allegiance and staged a grand ceremony to prove it. He then equipped the restored Commander of the Faithful with three hundred men and put him on the road back to Baghdad. When the party was annihilated by a Mongol force, as might have been anticipated, Baybars offered obeisance instead to a more distant relative, whose descendants would decorously receive visitors in Cairo palaces for the next two centuries. Historians disagree over whether the emasculation of the Abbasids was deliberate or just inevitable, but no one has ever claimed it was insignificant. A figurehead had been preserved, but the touchstone shattered by Hülegü was never to be pieced back together.

Baybars chose instead to fall back on the most fundamental source of legitimacy there was—the shari'a itself. As Muslims across the region steeled themselves for a Mongol return, aware that Hülegü's army had retreated only as far as northwestern Persia, he issued a series of edicts in the name of tradition. The unlawfulness of alcohol was reiterated, an unpopular tax was rescinded as unholy, and renovations were made to Jerusalem's al-Aqsa Mosque. But, as Caliph al-Mansur had realized at the beginning of the Abbasid era, political stability required more than a few pious acts—it needed the consistent application of rules—and Islamic law in the 1260s was incomparably more complex than it had been during the 760s. An authoritative thirteenth-century overview of Sunni doctrines, written by none other than Ibn Rushd, detailed literally hundreds of differences between the various schools of jurisprudence, and though many issues did not require the services of a judge—the question of how to bless a person who sneezed, for instance—there were vast numbers that might. An activity as apparently uncontentious as suckling on a breast created legal relationships that might later in life give rise to matrimonial and inheritance liabilities. Spiritual pitfalls surrounded commercial transactions ranging from forward contracts to the sale of horse manure. And someone's choice of doctrine was generally determined by accident and restricted by conscience alone.

Baybars rose to the challenge with a judicial reform of commensurate scope. Although Cairo's courts had been operated exclusively by Shafi'ites, the Mamluk sultan appointed chief judges from each of the four Sunni schools in 1265, and the measure was so popular that it was soon being rolled out across Syria and Palestine. A 1332 decree of appointment helps explain why:

> The people of Damascus are often in need of a judge from the Hanbalite school in most contracts of sale and lease, in certain sharecropping contracts, in assessing settlements when contracts are frustrated by natural disasters, in marrying off a male slave to a free woman with the permission of his master, in stipulating that a bride should not be re-located from her hometown, in dissolving the marriage of a husband who deserted his wife without maintenance, and in the sale of an irreparable and dilapidated endowment that is of no use to its beneficiaries.

The justification is a reminder of an aspect of Islamic law that should be obvious but is nowadays too often overlooked. It served for centuries to do what laws have always done, offering ordinary people relatively predictable solutions to straightforward problems. In a region that was awash with refugees from the Mongols, the empowerment of new judges helped to narrow the gap between the supply of judicial services and the demand for them. And yet the legal diversification had a darker aspect that reflected the inadequacies of relying on tradition alone. Although it made it easier than ever for people to combine the practicalities of daily life with pursuit of the straight and narrow, sinners who were brought to court unwillingly faced a procedure that could be capricious rather than flexible. There were risks even if they faced a fixed Qur'anic *hadd* penalty, and judges were also entitled to hand down discretionary punishments (*ta'zir*) for any sin, according to rules that differed markedly between the jurisprudential schools. Insolvent debtors were generally required to sell their goods, but Hanafites would send them to jail until their creditors were paid, for example. They, like the Shafi'ites, allowed a judge sometimes to rely on information personally acquired instead of independent testimony—even if a defendant faced death. And the dangers could be compounded by deliberate manipulation. Malikites were known for an expansive approach to capital punishment and a view that evidence could be beaten out of people with a bad reputation, and by the fourteenth century judges adhering to other doctrines were often choosing to send unlucky defendants in their direction.

Within just a few years of the caliphate's destruction, a new legal and political order therefore began to emerge. Its shape, however, was as yet impossible to discern. It claimed to rest on tradition, and most of its supporters would have insisted that Islam knew no distinction between government and religion, but that was as meaningless a piety then as it is today. A great tension between politics and law was in fact in play. The effort to co-opt jurists was continuing under the Mamluks, but the autonomy inherent in Islamic scholarship had been greatly boosted by the fall of the dynasty that had helped give it shape. Many scholars remained resolutely on the sidelines, more reluctant than ever to engage with the murk of government and the burden of judgment. And one approach to the shari'a that had always looked beyond conceptions of state power was about to come to the fore. It was the one that had so exercised al-Ghazali: the Sufi focus on the individual relationship with God.

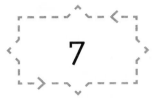

7

The Reinvention of Tradition: Salafism

The threat from the Mongols did not decline as the thirteenth century proceeded. Hülegü himself died in 1265, but three generations of his descendants would maintain the pressure out of northwest Persia, and the country that blocked their path to Egypt—Syria—turned into a permanent war zone. Expeditionary forces regularly tested its defenses, and when the Mamluks razed northern farmlands to deny them to invaders, famine was added to its woes. Uprooted residents fled south to Damascus, and a city that had been eclipsed by Baghdad for five centuries moved from the backwaters to the front line. Every Mongol mobilization sent crowds surging into the Umayyad Mosque to pray for deliverance. Anxious believers superstitiously held Qur'ans over the heads of holy men until carrier pigeons were able to confirm that the latest threat had passed. Local legend had long foretold that Jesus would one day manifest himself at the southern minaret to slaughter a pig, destroy a crucifix, and battle the Antichrist. There had been false alarms, but few Damascenes could have much doubted in the last decades of the thirteenth century that the Hour of Judgment was close.

Anyone looking for confirmation of the worst could have spotted many additional signs on the ground. Having developed apocalyptic assumptions very similar to those of Jews and Christians, Islamic tradition anticipated a great upsurge in abnormality at the end of time, and the thousands of refugees who were now streaming toward Damascus included some whose deviations from the norm were striking. There were the enraptured of God, who smeared themselves in mud, lived in garbage dumps, and babbled with the Almighty instead of praying to Him. The Qalandariyya flouted the Prophet's reported preference for luxuriant beards so comprehensively that they shaved not just their cheeks and chins but their heads and eyebrows. The Haydariyya preferred handlebar mustaches, which they accessorized with iron collars and chains, and they manifested their collective commitment to chastity by exposing their pierced penises. The mortification was complemented by a fondness for hashish—which was just beginning to make its way west from Persia—and a belief that cemeteries were magical gateways to a great beyond. As a consequence, intoxicated hermits established entire colonies in the extensive graveyards to the south and west of Damascus, where they sang and drummed up a storm.

Self-denial on such a scale is not easy to distinguish from self-gratification, and it elicited both controversy and hostility. There were complaints about drug abuse and sexual misconduct that sound almost modern in their outrage, and even Hülegü made time to quiz and execute a band of Qalandariyya after being told by his Assassin astrologer that the hairless mystics were superfluous to worldly order—"the scum of the earth," to use an approximation of his exact words. But though there was no denying the strangeness of the new sects, they reflected many entrenched aspects of Islamic mysticism. Itinerant ascetics known as *darvish*es had for centuries been combining the quest for God with talents for jugglery and acrobatics. The newcomers' exhibitionism went further—often by several steps—but their very distance from dusty book learning paid additional homage to Islam's past. It honored the belief, so common among early Arabs, that truth was most reliably transmitted through verbal lessons and personal example. The best-known mystical discipline of them all, Sufism, was steeped in that idea. Until the groundbreaking work of al-Ghazali, many contemplatives had considered it almost axiomatic that wisdom could not be found until books were lost. Early Sufi legends invariably celebrated literature's destruction rather than its production—eighteen cartloads, in the case of one especially wise ninth-century ascetic.

The reality is that the flamboyant faith of groups such as the Qalandariyya and Haydariyya was symptomatic of social dynamism rather than corruption. An eclectic ideology was coalescing—a kind of neo-Sufism—that rested on long-standing Islamic traditions. It exemplified the independent-mindedness popularized by al-Ghazali and derived support from respectable Sufi fraternities that had been proliferating across the Middle East ever since his death in 1111. Most important of all, it was able to draw on an intellectual inspiration all its own: the teachings of an Andalusia-born Sufi named Ibn Arabi (1165–1240), who had settled in Damascus during the 1220s.

Although Ibn Arabi had been conversant with rationalism—to the extent that he met the philosopher Ibn Rushd during his youth—he had been convinced that reason was inadequate to comprehend reality. Like al-Ghazali, he had valued literature, however, and he had produced the most ambitious written attempt that any Islamic mystic would ever make to circumscribe the universe. It was as elliptical as one might expect of a theologian who opposed logic, and the Andalusian mysteriously warned on occasion that his words ought not to be confused with their meaning, but the vision that it tried to convey differed fundamentally from that of conservative Muslims. Ibn Arabi's concern was not to isolate causes and effects but to comprehend the link that unified them—namely, God—and he imagined a Creator who existed within His creations as well as beyond them. Human beings, for their part, were lit by a spark of the divine, and even someone as damned as Pharaoh was so perfectible that he might yet partake in the greatness of God. Such ideas are not easily encapsulated, but their scope is mirrored by one of Ibn Arabi's better-known admirers, Jalal al-Din Rumi (1207–73). Rumi shared the Andalusian's concern to rise above temporal tribulations—not least because, as a refugee from the Mongols, he experienced them firsthand—and was inspired as a consequence to verse so transcendental that his anthologies of poetry are still bestsellers in the United States. His perspective harked back to a past when, "before garden, vine and grape were in the world, our soul was drunk with immortal wine" and it appealed to the future with self-evident success. His epitaph was particularly memorable. "When we are dead," he wrote, "seek not our tomb in the earth, but find it in the hearts of men."

The expansive religious vision of the neo-Sufis has been affecting the trajectory of Islam ever since it first appeared, and from the outset, it was promoting some very distinctive views about the shari'a. Exhibiting a bibliophobia typical of his sect, the founder of the Qalandariyya was celebrated for issuing fatwas without referring to any written texts at all. Other mystics imagined themselves to be so close to God that His law had fallen away, giving them license to indulge in otherwise forbidden activities: a sense of privilege that underpinned the smearing, shaving, and piercing activities so popular in thirteenth-century Damascus. Conventional Sufis were never comfortable with claims that extreme, but they agreed wholeheartedly that fear would not guide humanity to salvation: the path of the shari'a was delineated by love. God was almost painfully bound up with the fate of His creatures—"closer to [man] than his jugular vein" in the words of the famous Qur'anic verse—and the intimacy was matched by an empathy that could not but undermine authoritarian concepts of divine vengefulness. That was well conveyed by a story Sufis told about an eleventh-century mystic whose prayers had once been interrupted by a familiar voice. "Oh, Abu al-Hasan!" God had boomed. "Do you want me to tell people what I know about your sins, so that they stone you to death?" "Oh, Lord," he had whispered back. "Do you want me to tell people what I know about your mercy, so that none will ever feel obliged to bow down to you again?" "Keep your secret," came God's conspiratorial reply. "And I will keep mine."

So subtle an approach to commands and prohibitions was never going to be shared by anyone who equated the shari'a with coercion alone. And yet, by the end of the thirteenth century, Ibn Arabi's doctrines were making great headway even within the expanding Mamluk judiciary. Lower-level mystics were meanwhile encouraged to challenge any legal scholar more narrow-minded than they thought right. According to a Damascene poet named Afif al-Din Tilimsani (d. 1291): "Between the spiritual Muslims and the jurists there is an unceasing struggle, and battles which will not end until . . . the Day of Judgment." With apocalypse so close and conventional ideas of the shari'a under such threat, conservatism was crying out for a champion. And as God, luck, or cause and effect would have it, just the hero was at hand— Ahmad ibn Taymiyya (1263–1328).

Ibn Taymiyya looms so large in Islamic legal history that as he steps onto the stage, a few murmured words to introduce his role become appropriate. His struggle with the Sufis of Damascus has helped to define the modern face of Islam, and he did more than any other individual to rally resistance to the last great Mongol assault on Mamluk Egypt—with immense consequences for the jurisprudence of jihad that are set out in the next chapter. As a result, he has the dubious distinction of a twenty-first-century media profile. Quoted in the only two fatwas that Osama bin Laden ever wrote and mentioned twice by the 9/11 Commission, he is revered and reviled across the world. His aura has effects so palpable that even a liberal historian of Islam has favorably compared him to Saint Augustine for his "influence in shaping Muslim ideology." And though the exaltation risks substituting pious myth for reality, there can be no doubt that Ibn Taymiyya was several cuts above the average reactionary. He was as familiar with Aristotelian logic as he was skilled in disputing the Torah and the Bible, and his arguments were as dense as they were fierce. His truest legacy was a focus on commands and punishments that was unrepresentative even during his lifetime, however—and theories about the shari'a that are contested more bitterly today than at any time since his death.

Ibn Taymiyya reached Damascus, like so many people, as a refugee. In 1269, at the age of six, he and his family fled the ancient Anatolian city of Harran as the Mongols and Mamluks marched and burned the surrounding region into a wasteland. But whereas displacement inspired thousands of other Muslims to spiritual experimentation, his instinct was never to transcend divisions; it was to mark the dividing lines. That first became clear in 1293, when, barely thirty years old, he led a protest against a decision by the authorities not to punish a Christian for insulting the Prophet Muhammad.* The official leniency was more

---

*The large and boisterous Christian minorities of Syria and Egypt always bore a disproportionate share of Ibn Taymiyya's acrimony. He was less outspoken against Jews

noteworthy than Ibn Taymiyya's stance, at a time when memories of the Crusades and Christian collaboration with Hülegü were still fresh. But more remarkable than both was the young man's response. After being lashed and sent to jail, he wrote a closely argued and rancorous treatise to reiterate that the crime had demanded execution. Death would have been obligatory, he argued, even if the culprit had been a Muslim and his blasphemy had been directed at a prophet other than Muhammad. The opinion was cogent, controversial, and uncompromisingly punitive, setting the tone that would define Ibn Taymiyya for the rest of his life.

Ibn Taymiyya's approach to the shari'a would be as idiosyncratic as his willingness to clash with the authorities suggests. Sunni jurists were all agreed by the thirteenth century that God's law had to be ascertained by reference to four sources of knowledge—the Qur'an, hadiths, analogical argument, and a scholarly consensus—but Ibn Taymiyya now took it on himself to add a crucial gloss to that formula. An old approach toward tradition known as Salafism held that the most reliable way of understanding Islam was to look at the reported practices of the first three generations of Muslims—the Ancestors, or *salaf*s. Ibn Taymiyya turned that into a legal theory. The *salaf*s' collective viewpoint, he argued, was far more valuable than a scholarly consensus could ever be. And an example illustrates just how much reinterpretation that could facilitate. In 1299, Hülegü's great-grandson launched one last great push to subdue Syria, and over the course of his four-year campaign Egypt's panic-stricken rulers imposed a series of emergency measures. As well as purging non-Muslims from the government and ordering Peoples of the Book to color-code their turbans (blue for Christians, yellow for Jews, and red for the Samaritan sect), they ordered that churches should close for a year. Although the first two steps had several precedents, the closure order was unprecedented, and it violated a six-hundred-year-old covenant of toleration attributed to Caliph

---

and even seemed sometimes grudgingly respectful of the Torah's legalism. Jews merely clung to outdated revelations, whereas Christians garbled their Gospels and followed monks who were always changing their ideas about God. "That is why the Christians have not succeeded in formulating a permanent shari'a," he explained: Memon, *Ibn Taimīya's Struggle*, pp. 209–11.

Umar II. Ibn Taymiyya was able to justify it nevertheless. That covenant was of no legal effect, he explained, because it had been drawn up after the time of the Ancestors. The Muslim conqueror of a country might once have *chosen* to protect Christian places of worship, but he had never been obliged by the shari'a to do so. And it was therefore open to his successors to prefer closure—or even destruction.

Ibn Taymiyya doubtless assumed that the use of Salafism as a legal tool served to uncover ancient truths about God's law rather than to invent them. The doctrine was highly susceptible to manipulation, however. It offered arguments that were as malleable as they were morally unassailable, because no one could conclusively rebut a claim made on behalf of a consensus of the sacred dead. The only theoretical limit was imposed by reports of what the early Muslims had actually done, and the Hanbalite jurisprudence preferred by Ibn Taymiyya acknowledged the veracity of thousands of hadiths. Salafism also allowed a jurist to borrow from any of the other established schools of Sunni law, and Ibn Taymiyya once contradicted all four of them, in a controversy over the status of oaths in divorce proceedings. And though he happened to conclude in that particular situation that oath breaking was a new problem that did not merit a punitive response, he did not consider silence on the part of the *salaf*s to require forbearance in principle. The question was what they *would have* done, and his answers often sounded very intuitive indeed. Considering the lawfulness of hashish, for example, Ibn Taymiyya proposed that the new drug was analogous to wine (as feces to urine, to paraphrase his precise comparison) and that users therefore merited the eighty lashes due to drunks. Anyone who disagreed was an apostate, he added, whose corpse ought not to be washed or given a decent burial.

Ibn Taymiyya's ideas about the shari'a had a haphazard practical impact. Spiritual authority among Sunnis has always depended primarily on public acclaim, and he opposed many popular ideas about religion while pandering to none. At the same time, he was never afraid to make his views felt, and mystics at the exotic end of the spectrum were among those he targeted most often. He had no objection in principle to the love of God, as long as it was subordinated to obedience, and he associated with a reputable contemplative fraternity known as the Qadiriyya. He was appalled by the extent to which the neo-Sufis were abandoning the supposed practices of the *salafs*, however, and in 1305 he led followers in giving effect to his legal theories. He began in February by humiliating a hashish-addled Sufi—shaving his long hair, clipping his fingernails, and cutting up his multicolored robe—and he went on to supervise the destruction of a rock that several of his compatriots had taken to venerating. In late spring, he attended to another adversary—Lebanese Shi'a villagers suspected of collaboration with the Mongols*—and he was back in Damascus by November, when he achieved the greatest of all his practical victories. It involved a band of wild-haired dervishes known as the Rifa'iya, who were renowned for supposedly miraculous powers to ride lions, eat snakes, and withstand fire. On the basis that neither the Prophet nor his companions had done such things, Ibn Taymiyya organized a protest. A confrontation ensued on the capital's streets, and in the presence of the Mamluks' governor the scholar alleged that it was not God who was making the mystics inflammable. It was frog fat, orange peel oil, and talcum powder, and if he was wrong, he contended, they would have a wash before taking their next fire walk. After a tense standoff, the Rifa'iya apparently confessed that their powers worked "before the [Mongols], not before the shari'a"—whereupon Damascus's governor stripped them of their iron collars and warned them to keep out of trouble, on pain of having their heads chopped off.

Emboldened by his success, Ibn Taymiyya then decided to escalate his struggle. There was one man whom he blamed more than anyone else for the decline of the times—Ibn Arabi—and the Andalusian's teachings owed a great deal of their popularity to the influence they enjoyed among senior Mamluk officials. Temperamentally inclined as Ibn Taymiyya was to make enemies in high places, he chose at some point during 1305 to mail a letter of complaint to one of Cairo's most influential Sufis. An indication of its tone emerges from two of his most

---

*Ibn Taymiyya personally led posses into the mountains, and his expeditions were accompanied with diatribes that were forceful even by his standards. Ignoring the convention that Muslims do not question each other's good faith, Ibn Taymiyya characterized his least favorite sects as irredeemable apostates. They had to be shunned or killed on sight, and readers who doubted that opinion were heretics themselves: Michel, *Muslim Theologian's Response*, p. 59; see also Nadwi, *Life*, pp. 32, 37–39.

specific charges. He alleged that Ibn Arabi's claim to find God every-where had blinded Rumi so completely to the difference between Creator and creations that he had perceived the divine in "a dog, a pig, urine and excrement." His assertion of an underlying unity to existence had meanwhile led Afif al-Din Tilimsani to declare himself authorized to have sex with his mother and his sister. And though those particular men were unable to respond to the libel because they were dead, Ibn Taymiyya's audacity all but guaranteed a response, which came with a summons to Cairo from Egypt's most prominent jurists in March 1306. They chose to focus on another arcane theological controversy he had resuscitated, about the precise nature of God's body, and his insistence on its metaphysical massiveness earned him seventeen months in jail. He would not be allowed to return to Syria for almost seven years, and an ideological contest commenced that would see him repeatedly condemned and punished for the rest of his life.

Many details of the conflict are lost to history, and it is only possible to speculate about the political motivations that might have motivated the clampdown. It certainly suggests that the Mamluk authorities were not as confident as they pretended about their own religious stances, and it is conceivable that they feared a backlash from religious conservatives. But the issue over which the two sides sparred most often illustrates that Ibn Taymiyya was very much in the minority. It concerned his views about the rightfulness of visiting tombs. Cairo's vast cemeteries were famous across the Muslim world. Saintly birthdays and death days punctuated the year, each one an occasion for miraculists and hucksters to come out in force. Graveyards were so popular that there were guidebooks and tours to help strangers find the illustrious dead. But to Ibn Taymiyya, such traditions were simply unholy. Setting out to a cemetery with the intention of praying was an innovation unknown to the *salafs*, he warned, and it elevated the dead into pseudo-deities. A Muslim ought never to do more at a tomb than contemplate the afterlife, and even that was permissible only if he just happened to be passing. In any event, he observed, even the best-attested tomb miracle had a rational explanation. A Cairo shrine famous for curing horses of constipation was a case in point. It had been the scene of some uncanny equine bowel movements, he accepted, but they owed nothing to the intercession of the dead. All that happened was that the animals

supernaturally saw tortures being visited on the Shiʻa heretics buried
beneath and defecated out of shock.

Such arguments typified an aspect of Ibn Taymiyya's approach to
the shariʻa that would have ramifications far beyond their own peculiar
parameters. As had been true of several other scholars at earlier periods
of Islamic history, he was discounting actual custom insofar as it contradicted theoretical traditions. The fact that Muslims drew solace
from a practice did not reveal truths about Islam to him; it proved
that those Muslims were wrong. Ibn Taymiyya's vision of faith thereby
set real believers against an idealized version of their beliefs—and
nothing would illustrate the futility of that stance as memorably as
the scholar's own eventual fate. A court was convoked in October 1326
specifically to condemn his opposition to tomb visitation, and, as usual,
the hearing ended badly for the scholar. An order for his incarceration
at Damascus's citadel was augmented by an edict depriving him of pen
and paper, and though he defiantly scribbled a few final fatwas—with a
lump of charcoal, if the hagiographers are to be believed—he died after
an illness in September 1328. His affiliation with the Qadiriyya mystical order then earned him burial in the capital's Sufi cemetery. That
was an ironic twist, and what followed was a cosmic joke. Tens of thousands of people jostled for a view of his shrouded body. His personal
effects were in such demand that bidders for his lice-killing camphor
necklace pushed its price up to 150 dirhams; his skullcap fetched a full
500. A few eager mourners even got to drink the water used for bathing his corpse. And once underground, the erstwhile scourge of tomb
visitors was destined to receive pilgrims and sightseers for another six
centuries.

As the outpouring of grief shows, Ibn Taymiyya did not lack for
influence by the time of his death. Conflicted though some of his
supporters might have been, they represented a significant slice of
fourteenth-century Damascus. And the qualities that inspired the admiration are easy enough to state. His writings were grounded in serious efforts to comprehend the arguments of his adversaries. He was the
first Sunni since al-Ghazali to read Aristotle before disagreeing with
him, and his critique of logic—essentially, that its propositions were
bogus truths, justifiable only by their own formal standards—might
in another world have made him a great logician. He wrangled no less

energetically with Christian, Jewish, and Shi'a texts, and his assaults on Sufism were those of a man who knew his enemies inside out. But thinkers can usefully be divided between those who analyze and those who empathize, and Ibn Taymiyya's intellectual engagement was not matched by any appreciation of the emotional component of faith. Sufis were right to love their Creator, he believed, but adoration could not substitute for obedience. The deity he worshipped had an urge to punish that Muslims simply had to accept, with an existence so self-contained that it was necessarily untouched by human longing. All that could be known about God's relationship with humanity was that He had given it an unerring shari'a to follow. That ignored the riddle that was implicit in Sufi mysticism—why a loving God would force His creatures toward salvation with threats of hellfire—but Ibn Taymiyya considered the very question to be out of bounds.

Although that assessment of Ibn Taymiyya is necessarily subjective, developments in the wider Muslim world confirm how misaligned his views were with prevailing attitudes. By the time he was laid to rest in 1328, those regions once conquered by the Mongols were fragmenting, and Islam was reasserting itself with force, but it was not his ideas about God that were winning out. It was mysticism—and often, the wilder variety. A younger son of Hülegü's had adopted Islam as early as the 1280s, inspired by a wonder-working dervish with a taste for drugs, and by the 1320s horn-clutching, pelt-wearing Sufis were picking up converts from Anatolia to the steppes of central Asia. Regional warlords had also begun to strike deals with the charismatic leaders of organized mystic brotherhoods, and the tactical alliances were growing into politically ambitious societies. A Turkish-Mongol-Sufi warrior named Timur Leng (Timur the Lame, or Tamerlane, 1336–1405) commanded the first of them, and three other coalitions would evolve into states and transform the world. A Sufi-dominated tribe of Anatolian Turks known as the Ottomans succeeded in 1453 in capturing Constantinople, a prize that had been eluding Islam for almost eight hundred years, and their expansive energy would famously take them to the gates of Vienna in 1529. Warriors associated with the mystical Safavid order seized control of Persia in 1501, establishing a dynasty that would become a byword for Oriental sophistication as far away as Tudor England. And a Sunni member of their clan, descended from Timur and Genghis Khan, then conquered Delhi twenty-five years later in the name of the Mongols—or, as Persians pronounced the word, Mughals.

The ascent of Islamic mysticism was no guarantee of Muslim unity. Not for the only time in human history, the belief in cosmic unity co-existed with fury against its enemies on earth. Relations between the Ottomans and the Safavids were so prickly that the Persians adopted Shi'ism specifically to differentiate themselves from their pushy neighbors, whereupon Sultan Selim I destroyed their armies on the battle-field in 1514 and sacked the capital of Tabriz—sealing an animosity that has shadowed Turkish-Iranian relations ever since.* Selim was no friendlier toward the Sunni empire to his south, and he followed up by marching on Egypt and hanging the last Mamluk sultan from Cairo's Zuweila gate. Delhi's sultans then made sure to plow a very distinct furrow of their own. Although Selim staked an unequivocal claim to Sunni supremacy in 1517 by taking the figurehead Abbasid caliph into Ottoman custody while in Cairo, the founder of the Mughal dynasty ignored it. He pledged allegiance to his Shi'a Safavid kinsmen instead, ensuring that Persian influence would permeate Indian Islam for centuries. His descendants then rubbed in the snub by claiming to be caliphs themselves.

The to-and-fro was confusing in every sense, but as cultures churned, artistic energies were also released by the turmoil. The Khorasani city of Herat, adopted as a capital by Tamerlane's son in the early fifteenth century, became a particular vortex of creativity. Although the Timurid dynasty endured there for less than a hundred years, its scientists and artisans formulated models of beauty that would inspire their successors for centuries. Painters, heeding conventions of Chinese portraiture rather than warnings against graven images, immortalized Muslim faces in ink and watercolor for the first time. Bookbinders supervised the production of illuminated manuscripts that were canvases as much as they were literature, combining the emerging figurative skills of miniaturists with ancient calligraphic ones. The impact of Herat would be

---

*Attempts by the Turkish government after 2009 to broker compromise over Iran's nuclear ambitions marked an apparent break from the traditional rivalry—unless the eagerness to intervene was a very subtle expression of it.

most manifest of all in the architectural field. Designers developed an entirely new aesthetic, using cobalt and turquoise tiling that had become popular under the Seljuks to express in microcosm the order that God imposed at every other level. In cities from Istanbul to Agra, geometricians and craftsmen would create mosques of hypnotic elegance and shimmering mausoleums that still welcome venerators of the dead by the thousands.

Had Ibn Taymiyya lived to witness the changes, he might have persuaded himself that the Muslim rivalries departed from a fictitious seventh-century harmony. He would certainly have found the art appreciation, funerary architecture, and respect for foreign cultures to be terribly innovative idolatries. But the capacity of believers to recover from the collapse of the caliphate and organize empires signified strength rather than weakness. Open-mindedness and a willingness to accommodate alien traditions restored equilibrium to the Muslim world after more than a century of crisis. Innovation was not a sin that weakened Islam's fiber. It was a process that enabled the faith to escape extinction and helped create civilizations as vibrant as any the world has ever seen.

Ibn Taymiyya's legal ideas had predictably little impact in the three great empires of the post-caliphal era. It was not resuscitated ancestral wisdom and an eternal seventh century that they sought to institutionalize; it was a set of reliable arrangements that could deal with the day-to-day challenges of government. The Safavids turned to Shi'a clerics, while Ottoman and Mughal sultans followed in the footsteps of the Abbasids by relying on the tried-and-trusted theories of Hanafite jurists. The pragmatism went further. At around the time that he conquered Constantinople in 1453, Sultan Mehmed II enacted a code of law to give effect to the shari'a. The move was unprecedented. A proposal to draft a summary of God's laws had been so controversial back in the eighth century that an adviser to Caliph al-Mansur who suggested it had had his limbs cooked in an oven. It was, however, an idea whose time had come. Shari'a-influenced codes became an entrenched aspect of Ottoman practice, and the innovation was then emulated by the Mughals. Attempts to express God's law in writing subsequently became so unremarkable that even conservative Muslims became liable to forget the blasphemous origins of religious statutes. More than a few nowadays campaign for their enactment.

There was one particularly telling detail of the Ottoman reform. An ordinance personal to a ruler was known in Arabic as a *qanun*—from the same Greek root that gives English "canon"—but the Turks also had another way of describing the laws enacted by their sultans. The statutes were often called *yasa*s, a term Turks had been using to mean "sacred custom" since their days as warriors on central Asia's steppes, and that word had an almost precise Mongol equivalent. It was another reminder of the ties that now bound Islam to its erstwhile adversaries, and one story illustrates with some poignancy how close those ties became. In 1401, almost three-quarters of a century after Ibn Taymiyya's death, Tamerlane launched a devastating assault on Damascus. The onslaught reduced the Syrian capital to a blanket of ash and a few walls around the Umayyad Mosque, and in its aftermath refugees staged widespread protests against the Mamluk failure to defend the city. The authorities made up for their previous inactivity with a domestic clampdown, which included the establishment of drumhead tribunals to dispense summary punishments. Popular anger only increased, and a contemporary writer named al-Maqrizi (1364–1442) attributed the government's heavy-handedness to Genghis Khan's customary law code: his *yasa*. After reciting some particularly un-Islamic aspects of that code—its imposition of the death penalty even for unmarried adulterers, for example, and a rule obliging people to slaughter animals by dismembering their limbs and pulling out their hearts—he claimed that earlier generations of Mamluk rulers had corruptly promoted Mongol prisoners of war to senior positions. That had caused them to prefer Mongol law to the shari'a, and injustice had been the result.

Al-Maqrizi was mistaken. His selective description of Genghis Khan's *yasa* was based on someone else's verbal summary of a copy once seen, and no independent evidence exists to support his statement that Mamluk officials were relying on it. They did not need a *yasa*, because they already had the *siyasa*—the sweeping discretion that rulers had enjoyed since the time of Caliph Umar to override individual interests for the sake of the greater good—and that power owed nothing to

Mongol tradition.* The fears that al-Maqrizi expressed were telling nonetheless. The Mamluks had been asserting greater legal authority than ever before, just as he claimed. Insofar as that could be characterized as a corruption of Islamic law, it was not the descendants of Genghis Khan who were to blame, however. Avowedly conservative jurists had taken a lead in justifying such changes—and one of the most influential had been none other than Ibn Taymiyya.

The sense that that there was something un-Islamic about repression was not unique to al-Maqrizi. Islamic jurists had been unsure for centuries whether the *siyasa* could properly be categorized as an aspect of divine law. An influential early Hanbalite jurist named Ibn Aqil (1040–1119) had argued that a Muslim ruler could resort to the power whenever it seemed useful to bring Muslims "closer to righteousness and away from corruption." At the same time, however, he had implicitly recognized the ungodliness of a discretion that pragmatic: one that authorized practices "even if the Prophet had not himself performed them, or they were not prescribed by revelation." But Ibn Taymiyya had been far bolder. The *siyasa*, he claimed, was an integral part of the shari'a. In works that extolled the Prophet's governance of Medina and the rule of the first four "Rightly Guided Caliphs," he argued that the age-old Islamic duty to promote good and forbid evil applied to every state functionary with charge over other Muslims, "[from] the caliph [to] the schoolmaster in charge of assessing children's handwriting exercises." And whereas powers traditionally attributed to religious judges were hedged by evidential rules and procedural limits, Ibn Taymiyya's account of the *siyasa* focused only on duties and punishments. He justified the indefinite detention and lashing of suspected highway robbers who would not give up accomplices or loot, for example. He also allowed for the two legal procedures that were most central to al-Maqrizi's complaint—the whipping of imprisoned debtors, and a procedure that the Mamluks called "trials of suspicion"

*Although al-Maqrizi theorized otherwise, the similarity between the two words was coincidental. The *siyasa* was actually an old Arabic word connoting horsemanship: Bernard Lewis, *Political Words and Ideas*, pp. 31–32. Whereas European kings steered ships of state, Islamic rulers rode stately horses.

(*da'awi al-tuham*), which allowed military tribunals to convict defendants without witnesses or documentary proof.

Ibn Taymiyya's support for broad powers in the state might seem paradoxical, given his own persecution at the hands of Mamluk judges. It had a straightforward enough explanation, however. Like many radical idealists, he did not see a repressive government as a good reason to limit powers. It simply made it more important that the repression be righteous. His most influential student, Ibn Qayyim (1292–1350), then took that premise to even more far-reaching conclusions. He argued, for example, that it was often right to punish someone of lowly status who alleged improper behavior by someone more respectable. He also formulated evidential theories that made judges less reliant than ever before on the oral testimony of eyewitnesses. They could establish paternity by having experts scrutinize the faces of a child and its alleged father for similarities, for example. If a woman sought a marital dissolution on grounds of impotence and her claim was resisted, a judge might usefully procure a sample of the husband's ejaculate—because, Ibn Qayyim assured readers, only genuine semen left a white residue when boiled. And the quest for truth did not have to stop there. The majority of Islamic jurists had always acknowledged that alleged sinners were entitled to remain silent if accused, and Hanafites had gone so far as to propose that a judge who extorted a confession in a capital case was himself liable to execution. But Ibn Qayyim was of a different view. Testimony could be beaten out of disreputable suspects, he argued. That was, he claimed, no less than the Prophet Muhammad, the Rightly Guided Caliphs, and other noble Companions would have done.

It was legal Salafism at its most dynamic. As a matter of straightforward history, torture had originally been forbidden by Islamic jurisprudence. It was first justified during the ninth century by just one law school—the Malikites—and though a willingness to countenance judicial violence had subsequently spread, it remained very much a minority viewpoint until the crisis years following the caliphate's fall. Ibn Qayyim's selective citation of hadiths enabled him, however, to leapfrog centuries of actual legal doctrine. A religious outlook that considered it impossible to know truth through logic thereby ended up justifying its discovery by force. And there was a notable coincidence. At exactly the same time as Ibn Taymiyya and Ibn Qayyim were picking through texts to promote inquisitorial fact-finding and compelled testimony, the jurists of Latin Europe were reforming the trial process in a very similar way. The parallels are so close, in fact, that one historian has suggested there may have been direct contact between the canonists of Spain and Sicily and the Malikites of Andalusia and North Africa. That hypothesis has not been proved, but one verdict is inescapable. There was nothing divine about expediency. A pious Muslim jurist was as capable as any Christian inquisitor of pursuing an ideal legal order through brutality.

The Salafi arguments for torture advanced by Ibn Taymiyya and Ibn Qayyim gained no more of a foothold in the post-caliphal civilizations than any of their other ideas about the shari'a. That owed little to principle, however. Ottoman Hanafite jurists, to take the most prominent example, did not claim that early Muslims had inflicted violence on criminal defendants, but that was only because they resorted to another fiction—which relied, again, on the *siyasa*. Unlike Ibn Taymiyya, they differentiated between emergency legislation and God's law, but they recognized a power to authorize repression all the same. Forceful interrogations were impermissible if someone faced a sacred penalty such as amputation for theft, for example, but if it was merely proposed to execute a suspected thief pursuant to a sultan's powers, torture was permissible. And as that implies, there was a conflict in play. Hanafites felt that a religiously righteous state ought to hold wrongdoers accountable for their acts, but they retained a nagging sense that it was somehow ungodly to inflict vicious violence on the basis of suspicion alone. That reflected a tension between purity and necessity that was as old as politics itself. And as states grew more complex, it was only going to increase.

A tangential consequence is that Ibn Taymiyya's limited impact in the years after his death has not put a lid on his legacy. His reputation continued to smolder, particularly among Hanbalite scholars, and during the mid-eighteenth century it erupted back into fiery life. Islam's post-Mongol empires were by then succumbing to internal dissension and external economic and military challenges. The Safavid dynasty collapsed in 1736, and Ottoman authority in Arabia was coming under pressure. The sultans of Istanbul governed the region as protectors of the two holy sanctuaries, Mecca and Medina, and their custody of both cities was giving rise to mounting criticism that they were failing to fulfill the old Qur'anic obligation to do good and prevent evil. Ottoman officials allegedly indulged in innovations of a cardinal sort, from the wearing of silk to the smoking of tobacco, and pilgrims on hajj were supposedly getting away with sins that ranged from lust to graveside prayers. An admirer of Ibn Taymiyya, Muhammad al-Wahhab (1703–92), then tapped into the anxieties with eloquent sermons warning that the debaucheries were not isolated events. They were symptomatic of a general slippage into paganism across the Hijaz. And in the early 1740s, he took a stand that managed to be both symbolic and very straight-forward. After felling a much-venerated tree and taking a sledgeham-mer to the tomb of Caliph Umar's brother, he unilaterally assumed the most solemn duty of a *qadi* under Islamic law: the obligation to enforce one of God's own rights. To be more specific, he judged a woman for adultery and had her stoned to death.

It was an even more remarkable assumption of power than is immediately apparent. One of the lesser-known facts of Islamic legal practice—a substantial category of lesser-known facts, admittedly—is that, as far as five centuries of documentation can prove, Ottoman courts imposed a stoning to death just once in all of their history. Al-Wahhab's neighbors were commensurately appalled and hounded him out of town, but at least one man was impressed. Muhammad ibn Saud (d. 1765), the leader of a clan based some thirty miles to the south, saw in the fugitive a reformer who meant what he said, and he was soon persuaded by al-Wahhab's preaching to put his people at God's disposal. The fortunes of the Saudis would be bound up with the religious teach-ings of al-Wahhab forevermore.* The ensuing civil war culminated in 1806 with the fall of Mecca and Medina to Ibn Saud's grandson. Saudi forces were soon desecrating tombs and stamping out frivolities across their new realm, and though Ottoman sovereignty was reasserted in 1818, they had by then established themselves as a permanent politi-

---

*Muslims who subscribe to al-Wahhab's views are sometimes nicknamed Wahhabis, but they often resent the term and argue that it humanizes an allegiance that belongs to God alone. They prefer simply to be known as monotheists (*muwahhidun*). Like believers who admire Ibn Taymiyya, they can be neutrally characterized as Salafis.

cal presence on the peninsula. And during the 1920s and 1930s, they returned—thanks in part to British political backing and logistical support—to establish the hold over the holy sanctuaries that they have maintained ever since.

Al-Wahhab's debt to Ibn Taymiyya, which was repeatedly acknowledged and amplified by his own later supporters, has lent the Damascene a reputation for unquestionable orthodoxy. It is an impressive turnaround for someone who died a convicted heretic, but his rising stock is significant for reasons beyond his posthumous services to Saudi Arabia. As the next chapter will show, it illuminates the rise of violent Muslim extremism, before and since 9/11. It is also central to a more general aspect of modern Islamic jurisprudence that is going to dominate the rest of this book: efforts among some radicals to yoke selected features of Islamic legal theory to the power of the modern state. Ibn Taymiyya's resurgence comes with contradictions and ironies. Vociferous Muslim critics of Western policy hold him up as a champion of justice, unaware or unconcerned that his quasi-totalitarian vision has served in the past to justify torture and military tribunals. The legal Salafism he popularized, and its insistence that God's laws are permanently open to reinterpretation, have simultaneously made him the scholar of choice for any radical Sunni with a grudge to legitimize. His writings are consequently inspiring ideas of big government at the same time as they are promoting dreams of root-and-branch revolution. And that has placed them at the eye of a very tumultuous storm indeed.

8

Jihad: A Law-Torn World

Over the course of 1295, important events unfolded in and around the northwest Iranian city of Tabriz. It was still less than half a century since Hülegü's destruction of the caliphate, and his descendants had been regularly threatening to finish the westward campaign that he had started. As the years passed, growing factionalism had seemed to be dimming the prospects for a renewed assault on Egypt's Mamluk dynasty, but a flurry of activity now reinvigorated the Mongol cause. The sitting ruler was strangled with a bowstring in April 1295, his successor was executed by army officers six months later, and a great-grandson of Hülegü's then assumed power. Ghazan was just twenty-four years old, but the sense of a new beginning that he brought was already manifest. Although a baptized Christian, a sometime Buddhist, and a student of shamanism, he had supposedly just seen the brightest light of them all—because on June 17, 1295, he had embraced Islam.

Ghazan's decision was a triumph for Sufi missionaries within his entourage, but his submission to God was also a shrewd political move. It put him in the same camp as most of his Persian subjects, and in an age when communal identities were still defined by faith, it gave him a potential claim to govern believers beyond his realm. The Qur'an obliged them to obey "those charged with authority among you," after all, and Sunni jurists such as al-Ghazali had made clear the importance of submission to an established Muslim ruler. Ghazan accordingly sent a message to the citizens of Damascus and Cairo to inform them of the good news. Any animosity that his forefathers might once have shown them now lay in the past, he explained, and an era of prosperity and unhindered commerce lay ahead. There was one more thing: "Be assured that all countries owe us obedience, and particularly Egypt, where the throne has passed from kings to slaves, and where there is no longer any difference between masters and servants!"

The message would have had more appeal than might be immediately apparent. The Mamluks were a rancorous clique, and an Islamic realm unified under a zealous convert would have been considerably more to the taste of many conservatives. The problem was that no one was very sure just how zealous Ghazan's conversion was. It was troubling enough that his great-grandfather had destroyed the caliphate. He himself was displaying an attitude toward the shari'a that looked almost lackadaisical at times. Soon after acceding to the throne, he determined on marrying his father's widow and threatened to revert to Buddhism when told that such unions were disallowed by the Qur'an. Apostasy was averted when a court scholar pronounced the earlier marriage invalid, but his subsequent reforms had done little to allay the suspicions. He proclaimed his continuing loyalty to Genghis Khan's customary laws, for example, and cited the alleged ineffectiveness of prohibition under the Prophet Muhammad as a reason not to ban alcohol. "Even if we forbid [intoxication] absolutely," he observed, "it will not go away." Instead of prescribing the eighty-lash penalty laid down by the earliest caliphs, he therefore ordered "this much: anyone who comes into cities and marketplaces drunk will be arrested, stripped naked and tied to a tree." It was law—but it was not the shari'a as most Muslims knew it.

The uncertainties then became acute in the autumn of 1298, when Ghazan finally mustered troops to undertake the long-anticipated westward invasion. The first mobilization ended in a false start, after a lightning storm electrocuted several armored soldiers and spread panic in the ranks, but the Mongol army assembled again a year later, and luck this time was very much on its side. It was Mamluk soldiers who now fell victim to a flood and a plague of locusts, if chroniclers are to be believed, and at the end of December 1299 the Mongols batted aside the heavily outnumbered defenders of Damascus. Worshippers at the Umayyad Mosque were immediately reassured of Ghazan's peacefully Islamic intentions, but events on the ground soon told a different story. Haphazard exactions escalated into a pattern of looting and murder, and the violent occupation came to an end—three months later—only because Ghazan needed armed manpower to deal with a crisis closer to home. Within a year, he sent an army back into Syria, and though it abruptly reversed in its turn, a third incursion followed in early 1303. The conflict then, at last, found its resolution. A Mamluk contingent confronted the invaders at the southern outskirts of Damascus and won a victory so decisive that sixteen hundred Mongol captives were soon paraded through Cairo, each one with the head of a fallen comrade strung around his neck.

The Mamluk victory of April 1303 was not quite as significant as the one at Ain Jalut in 1260, simply because Islam's survival was no longer at stake, but it was far-reaching enough. Ghazan succumbed to a fatal illness and died without a son just a year later, and when Persia passed into the hands of his less confrontational Shi'a brother, the existential menace that had stalked the Middle East for more than eighty years finally dwindled into a merely political threat. But the trouncing of the Mongols on the battlefield was never a foregone conclusion. Ghazan's claim to be a righteous Muslim ruler stymied resistance, and the large number of Muslims in his army caused widespread confusion. Theologians and jurists, far from clarifying matters, fled in large numbers for Cairo, and most of those who stayed behind counseled prevarication or capitulation. But there was one very noteworthy exception—Ahmad ibn Taymiyya. Within days of the Mongols' arrival, he led a delegation to Ghazan's tent to challenge him about the conduct of his forces. A year later, he rode to Cairo to demand a Mamluk defense against Ghazan's expected return, and in the spring of 1303 he was at the front line—authorizing soldiers to skip their Ramadan fasts so as to fight more effectively, according to one popular tale. The scholar's conduct—characteristically single-minded and undeniably brave—would become the stuff of legend. And his practical efforts were complemented by three legal opinions that have reverberated down the centuries.

Ibn Taymiyya's fatwas aimed specifically to deal with the lawfulness of resistance to Ghazan's invading force, but the scholar tackled the question of Mongol legitimacy at its roots. He undermined the Mongol claim to theological respectability by warning that they paid heed to scholars of all types—"ascetics, priests, rabbis, astrologers, [and] magicians"—and the assault on their magpie spirituality was complemented by a reminder of the origins they customarily claimed for themselves. Referring probably to his own audience with Ghazan, Ibn Taymiyya observed that "the greatest of [the Mongol] leaders" had once told "Muslim envoys" that Genghis Khan was a sign from God comparable to the Prophet Muhammad. In case anyone failed to recoil at the blasphemy, he then amplified it.

> They believe that [Genghis Khan] is the son of God, as the Christians do about the Messiah. The sun, they say, impregnated his mother. She was lying in a tent; the sun descended through an aperture and penetrated her, and she thereby became pregnant. It is obvious to any religious person that this is a lie. And it is proof that he was a bastard. His mother slept with someone and made that story up to avoid the shame of her adultery.

It was a harsh critique—potentially even counterproductive, given the Qur'an's assurance that Jesus was born of a virgin—and its tone was matched by the gravity of Ibn Taymiyya's conclusions. Although he would be having no shortage of run-ins with the Mamluks in years to come, he contended in this context that the sultan merited unequivocal allegiance and that his enemies were therefore legitimate targets in war. Analogizing from seventh-century illustrations, as befitted his Salafi outlook, he argued that anyone who claimed to be a Muslim while expressing loyalty to Ghazan was on a par with the Kharijite rebels who had conspired to assassinate Caliph Ali—apostates worthy of death. It was even permissible to kill those troops in the Mongol's service who were genuine believers, because those who were righteous would be received by God as martyrs.

Ibn Taymiyya's conclusion broke new legal ground. No jurist had ever before issued a general authorization for the use of lethal force against Muslims in battle. But its pronouncement turned it into a precedent, and as the rest of this chapter will show, that precedent has been revived in modern times and extended to deadly effect. Radicals have built on his anti-Mongol fatwas to justify violence against people for being bad Muslims—or even, sometimes, for their failure to be Muslims in the first place. They have used them to legitimize tactical innovations such as suicide bombing. And they have claimed them as the inspiration for murders without number.

Whatever else might be said about that legacy, it makes for a formidable historical footprint. When in June 2009 I found myself on a bus in southern Turkey, just thirty miles away from the scholar's birthplace, it seemed sensible to make the requisite detour. The town of Harran had been sacked by the Mongols soon after Ibn Taymiyya had fled with his parents in 1269, and according to my guidebook there was not much left to see—just a few ruins and some odd beehive-shaped mud houses. Historical sites are always thought provoking, however, and they do not get much more historical than Harran. The town is named in the book of Genesis, and an academy for which it used to be famous was ancient even in the 820s, when Caliph al-Ma'mun asked its scholars to help staff his new House of Wisdom. I also hoped that a visit might give me some perspective on the Mongols. Although Genghis Khan and his offspring had killed millions and reduced civilizations to rubble, their territorial conquests had flourished so successfully that it was easy to discount their violence. Just a few days earlier I had been in the Iranian village of Soltaniyeh, where Ghazan's brother had built his own mausoleum—an immense aquamarine dome of a sort that would soon be emulated across Persia—and I had caught myself wondering if a people capable of such elegance could really be as bad as they were painted. I wondered now if Harran might serve to recalibrate my ideas.

It did. Ibn Taymiyya's birthplace had not merely failed to rise from the rubble; it still was rubble. The half-mile mound on which a young prophet Abraham is said to have walked looked almost untouched since the Mongols had passed through. A once magnificent mosque had been reduced to an orphaned minaret and a skeletal arch, while the courtyard in which Ibn Taymiyya's father used to memorize hadiths was a grassy wilderness. Toppled pillars and blocks of stone marked out spectral lanes, houses, and a church, and cisterns and heaped graves pitted the landscape to the horizons. There was a farming settlement about a mile away, complete with beehive-shaped mud houses, but the only sign of life among the ruins was a teeming colony of beige lizards. They basked on the mossy rocks, streaking into occasional motion as I collected glazed pottery fragments, which glittered on the ground like tiny blue jewels.

The afternoon impressed upon me, more than any other experience I had while writing this book, that theories are rooted in history. I had by then spent months plowing through critical analyses of Ibn Taymiyya's contribution to the *sunna*, but it was only in Harran that I began to realize just how much effect a person's background might have on his understanding of a hadith or Qur'anic verse. The threat from the Mongols felt tangible even on a summer's day in 2009—those blue fragments were once good pots, after all—and its effect on Ibn Taymiyya, forced uncomprehendingly to flee for his life at the age of six, was barely imaginable. Among the ruins, it seemed incontestably true that promises made by Mongol invaders merited skepticism. It also seemed beyond dispute that Ibn Taymiyya's seven-hundred-year-old legal opinions were the product of a particular time and place. And the irony of reviving those opinions in the twenty-first century would come to seem particularly stark. His fatwas against the Mongols were intended to warn people that lip service to Islam is no proof of religious sincerity and peaceful intentions. They are mouthed today to validate murder after murder in Islam's name.

The Qur'an, taken as a whole, displayed a distinctly equivocal approach to war and peace. God had explicitly permitted His followers during the early 620s to take up arms against their enemies in Mecca, and He had taken an even more bellicose line after the city's surrender. "Fight and slay the [impenitent] pagans wherever you find them," urged the Verse of the Sword. "Seize them, beleaguer them, and lie in wait for them." Other verses hostile to polytheists were similarly concerned to encourage "fighting" (*qital*), and one even urged Muslims to fight Peoples of the Book if they refused to pay tribute. But such revelations were hardly representative of the Qur'an's tone. Calls for violence were greatly outnumbered by recommendations of harmony, and even aggressively minded interpreters of God's words were bound to recognize

how often He had spoken of peace. One ninth-century theologian identified 124 verses that seemed inconsistent with the Verse of the Sword.
There were no fewer than 140, if a calculation made a couple of centuries later was to be credited.

Scholars were undaunted. Toward the end of the eighth century,
at a time when attempts to make sense of the shari'a were gathering
considerable momentum, a renewal of hostilities against Byzantium led
jurists to consider for the first time what place warfare should possess
in the Islamic body politic. In order to resolve the Qur'an's ambiguities,
they turned to the emerging theory of abrogation (*naskh*)—the idea
that God had gradually improved His revelations over the course of the
Prophet Muhammad's mission—and argued that the confrontational
verses of later years took precedence. They went further. Although campaigns to extend Muslim control beyond the Hijaz had not begun until
after the Prophet's death, they explained that the conquest of Mecca had
divided the whole world into an Abode of Islam and an Abode of War.
A state of hostility would continue to separate them until the Hour of
Judgment, and non-Muslims everywhere had become liable meanwhile
to choose among God, punitive taxation (*jizya*), or death. And there
was a third strand of their thinking, the most important one of them
all. The Qur'an's clearest calls for violence all referred to "fighting," but
scholars now linked them to verses that encouraged Muslims to exert
themselves in pursuit of faith—the struggle known as jihad. They
recognized that there were many ways in which that duty might be
discharged—by striving through the heart, for example, or by the hand
or tongue—and later generations would identify several other sacred
battles, such as the speaking of truth to an unjust ruler and the suppression of egotism. But scholars in the ninth century made very clear that
one spiritual exertion lay at its core—struggles of the sword.

The theory was subject to a crucial caveat, however. No one had forgotten the Kharijites—the extremists who took it on themselves to judge
and kill Caliph Ali for his sins—or that they had claimed their lethal
campaign to be a jihad binding on all Muslims. The jurists made clear,
therefore, that the obligation to struggle by the sword was not a personal
obligation (*fard ayn*) but a collective one (*fard al-kifaya*), which had
to be discharged "in the way of God" (*fi sabil Allah*). It could only be
directed by the caliph, whose discretion over its conduct was all but

absolute. The world might forever be split, but the Commander of the Faithful could confront the infidel as he chose—delaying the confrontations when convenient, or negotiating truces for up to ten years at a time.

That legal model was eminently suited to the political interests of the early Abbasid caliphate. It obliged Muslims to fight but imposed no corresponding duties on the state, creating an engine of holy war that could be used in any way that jurists might deem fit. Non-Muslims were eligible to help with the logistics, and during the ninth century infidels were even appointed, twice, to serve as ministers of jihad. As the caliphate fragmented, however, its utility declined. Emirs began increasingly to dignify their regional conflicts as holy wars, while compelling arguments to declare jihad were ignored—most remarkably, when twelfth-century caliphs found themselves powerless to rally resistance against Crusaders in the Holy Land. Destruction of the caliphate made the decentralization of authority permanent, and the response to Mongol encroachments then confirmed just how far from its origins the concept of jihad had traveled. A mere jurist—Ibn Taymiyya—asserted an authority for the Mamluks that they barely dared claim for themselves, in order to instruct believers to fight a war in God's name.

The precedent that Ibn Taymiyya thereby established was capable of being understood in an even more expansive sense. That first became apparent during the eighteenth-century Saudi uprising in the Hijaz. Muhammad al-Wahhab was as sure as his Damascene predecessor that many Muslims had abandoned the practices of their seventh-century ancestors—the *salafs*—but whereas Ibn Taymiyya had campaigned against religious innovations through written legal opinions, al-Wahhab turned his grievance into a justification for war. The failure of Ottoman officials to forbid such evils put them on a par with the pseudo-Muslim followers of Ghazan, he argued, and they could therefore be confronted under the banner of jihad. That was enough to inspire the first Saudi uprising, but it also redefined centuries of jurisprudence. A legal concept that had been developed to consolidate Abbasid government and deployed to defend the Mamluk regime was used to promote a rebellion against the Istanbul sultanate—then the oldest Muslim dynasty in the world. And though al-Wahhab's followers were knocked back after 1818, their use of Ibn Taymiyya's teachings would have lasting effects. The temporary control they established over Mecca and Medina introduced pilgrims from across the world to the concept that violent revolution might be a pious jihad. At a time when Islamic states were on the decline and Western colonialism was on the rise, the idea was a potent one.

The emerging link between political and religious struggle then found its most receptive audience yet, as a consequence of events in India. The rise there of a number of Islamic dynasties—most famously, the Mughals—had historically encouraged its Muslim jurists to accommodate outsiders, despite their own status as members of a minority faith. Far from imagining a world forever split on religious lines, they had always theorized that India's polytheists were Peoples of the Book, eligible to worship freely. That had not only spared rulers the obligation of having to convert or kill the subcontinent but also allowed for the creation of ostensibly Islamic legal systems that accommodated much local custom and religious diversity. Over the course of the eighteenth century, however, the legal fictions were overtaken by events. The Honourable East India Company engaged and defeated the Muslim ruler of Bengal in battle at Plassey in 1757, and as that suggests, the Company was no mere trading enterprise. It was effectively a commercial arm of the British state, with ambitions to match, and it very quickly set about creating a business environment suited to its interests. As well as monopolizing opium production with a view to facilitating exports to China, officials assumed control of tax collection and civil administration and then turned their attention to other aspects of Indian life. And one matter troubled them in particular. The Islamic laws of Bengal, they felt, were badly in need of revision.

The concern reflected a simple political truth—that the interpreter of a people's laws is better able to control popular behavior—but it was also heavily tinged by moral assumptions. Over the course of the eighteenth century, England had become one of the most punitive legal systems in the world, with some two hundred separate capital offenses on its statute books, and Company officials found Islamic law to be both arbitrary and unduly lenient by comparison. Two of their most immediate objections concerned the practice among Muslim judges of leaving a murderer's fate for a victim's next of kin to decide and their reluctance to impose capital sentences in the case of nonlethal robberies. A regulation was accordingly promulgated on August 21, 1772, making it mandatory to execute highway robbers in their home villages "for a terror and example to others" and to enslave a hanged person's family "for the general benefit and convenience of the people, according to the discretion of the government." The process then accelerated after 1786, when the British government stepped up its own involvement in India by dispatching a governor-general to Calcutta. He established an entirely new set of criminal courts across Bengal, staffed by British magistrates, and officials were soon formulating a program of root-and-branch legal reform. Somewhat perplexed by Islamic jurisprudence and convinced that Muslims were not even applying their own laws efficiently, they simplified and translated certain Hanafite texts, published collections of precedents, and invited a few cooperative muftis to assist the British magistrates as they sat in judgment. They called the newly rationalized system Anglo-Muhammadan law.

The legal activity inspired a degree of resentment that few of the reformers would have comprehended, let alone anticipated. It was already widely believed in Delhi that India's ascendant rulers were the offspring of apes, pigs, and Sri Lankan prostitutes, and British claims to rewrite the laws of God transformed the contempt to fury. Ever since the fall of Toledo in 1085, there had been jurists who insisted that Muslims should emigrate whenever they could not follow the shari'a, just as the Prophet had done when confronted by Meccan oppression. Ibn Taymiyya had similarly advised Muslims to stay in areas under Mongol suzerainty only if they remained free to worship God. The idea that believers should emigrate en masse from India was almost unthinkable, but Anglo-Muhammadan law threatened to deprive them of their path toward salvation, and India's scholars were soon being driven toward a confrontational conclusion. Shah Abdul Aziz (1746–1824), an influential Delhi-based admirer of the Saudi revival, issued a fatwa in 1803 that set out how dire the situation had become. Even within the capital, he observed, the Mughal emperor "wields no authority while the decrees of the Christian leaders are obeyed without fear . . . [T]hey demolish mosques without the least hesitation, and no Muslim or [infidel] can enter the city or suburbs except with their permission." He acknowledged that they did not interfere with basic rituals such as prayer—"but that is of no account."

The opinion was elliptical, and it called for no specific action, but

India's Muslims spent many years debating its meaning, and during the early 1820s a charismatic religious reformer named Sayyid Ahmed (1786–1831) was driven at last to an unequivocal conclusion. Islamic rule had been so eviscerated, he decided, that India had slipped back from the Abode of Islam into the Abode of War. Paradoxically mindful of Islam's traditional hostility toward rebellion, he declined to confront the British within India, however, and led followers instead toward Afghanistan with a view to liberating his homeland from a Muslim base. "There were many who advised me to carry on jihad in India, promising to provide me with whatever was necessary by way of material, treasure and weapons," he explained. "But I could not agree to this, for jihad must be in accordance with [holy tradition]. Mere rebellion was not intended." Sayyid Ahmed's convoluted principles were his undoing, for Pathans were as hostile to outsiders in 1826 as they are today, and he and his six hundred men vanished into the valleys beyond Peshawar. But his presumed martyrdom inspired a new generation of Indian Muslims, and they would have far fewer scruples about characterizing a revolt as a jihad.

Their turn came in 1857. By then, British attempts to rewrite the shari'a had been given an overtly religious tinge by a rash of Christian evangelism among senior British officers. Economic grievances were also festering, for the Honourable East India Company was now augmenting its opium-running operations with landgrabs, having enacted a statute that allowed it to confiscate entire principalities if a ruler failed to produce a natural heir. The atmosphere was charged, and in the spring of 1857 it exploded. A rumor was circulating among Company troops that their gunpowder cartridges, which had to be bitten open prior to loading, were lubricated with tallow and lard. The claim offended cow-venerating Hindus and swine-averse Muslims alike, and when eighty-five infantrymen were court-martialed and given ten-year prison terms at Meerut for refusing to use the ammunition, the garrison rose in revolt. Almost fifty Europeans were killed, around a third of them women and children. The mutineers then marched on Delhi, and a rebellion spread across northern India that would take more than a year to suppress.

Although the most militant early rebels were Hindus, the struggle for Delhi—on which the fate of the uprising would pivot—soon came to assume a stridently Islamic character. Several of the city's scholars proclaimed a jihad to be under way, and over the scorching summer of 1857 many of the city's defenders began very self-consciously to act like Islamic warriors of yore. Bearded and clad in black, they banged drums on the ramparts, clutching their burial shrouds and calling for martyrdom. Artillery fire ensured that many got their wish, and the reoccupation of the city led to thousands of civilian deaths, often by way of cold-blooded retribution, but the British were in no doubt where ultimate blame for the slaughter lay. At the trial of the Mughal emperor Bahadur Shah II (1775–1862), the military prosecutor emphasized his role as a Muslim leader and the Islamic character of the uprising. "The known restless spirit of Mahomeddan fanaticism has been the first aggressor, the vindictive intolerance of that peculiar faith has been struggling for mastery, seditious conspiracy has been its means, the prisoner its active accomplice, and every possible crime the frightful result."

In fact, the 1857 rebellion illustrated even more clearly than that of the Saudis just how protean the supposedly eternal concept of jihad had become. The most basic element of a jihad in classical doctrine—its declaration by a Muslim ruler—was not merely lacking. Bahadur Shah II refused point-blank to issue such a statement, far more concerned not to offend Hindu sensibilities than he was to indulge the pieties of a handful of Muslims. It was scholars who unashamedly seized the lead role in defining opposition to the British as a struggle for God. And that illustrated another aspect of the changing face of jihad. The men most eager for martyrdom had been motivated by their hatred of intruders in their homeland. Calls for holy war had been put to the service of anti-imperial sentiment. In the face of colonialism, religious loyalties were fusing with a national identity.

The British victory led to the imposition of direct rule from London, and hopes of Indian independence were set back decades. The immediate impact on Muslims of India was devastating. Delhi's congregational mosque was requisitioned and locked until 1862, and a penal code came into force that same year eradicating any last traces of Islamic jurisprudence from Indian criminal law. Islamic legal scholars, struggling to make sense of God's refusal to support their cause, began teaching that duties to resist infidelity by force had been suspended—or even overruled altogether, in the view of some daring heretics—while secular intellectuals penned essays to reassure English readers that jihad had always been essentially spiritual in nature anyway. And the ramifications of 1857 were soon reaching far beyond India's borders. Advocates of imperialism were encouraged throughout Europe, and although they would leave their mark on the entire nonwhite world, Muslims were regularly at the sharp end. The French extended their political influence in North Africa through a series of invasions, and the British seized control of ancient Arab trading routes across the east of the continent. The ambitions that both powers had for Egypt also found a resolution of sorts during the early 1880s, when the Royal Navy bombarded Alexandria and sent in forty thousand marines—the outriders of an occupation that would last for the better part of a century.

Western expansionism challenged Islamic assumptions wherever it occurred, and the effects were personified by a Persian traveler named Jamal al-Din al-Afghani (1838–97). As a visitor to Bombay in 1857 and a resident in Egypt during the late 1870s, he saw firsthand the destabilizing impact of imperialism. He quickly recognized, however, that the West's capacity to exploit hugely superior technology posed problems that were as moral as they were military, and his outspokenness made him only too aware of the institutional failings of the Islamic world. His regular calls for political and educational reform earned him deportations from Istanbul, Cairo, and Iran—on the last occasion, in chains—whereas he traveled easily through Europe and spent several months publishing a journal in Paris. As a consequence, he wrestled throughout his life with contradictions that would soon become commonplace among Muslims. He was enthralled by Europe's freedoms but appalled by its swagger. He thundered in Arabic against European adventurism while engaging with French intellectuals on the decline of Islamic rationalist thought. And he harbored ideas of progress that were almost defiantly uninventive. The problems afflicting the Muslim world would be solved, he told coreligionists, if they simply united and returned to a purer past. "[Its] schisms and divisions . . . originate only from the failure of rulers who deviate from the solid principles upon which the Islamic faith is built and stray from the road followed by their earlier ancestors."

The notion that a more correct understanding of Islamic tradition might resolve otherwise baffling disagreements was itself ancient, and hopes of finding a traditional basis for renewal now led some Muslims to look to the oldest Islamic institution of them all—the caliphate. Pretenders to the Abbasid legacy had been living in Istanbul since 1517, when the Ottoman sultan Selim I persuaded the family to leave Cairo—by hanging Egypt's last Mamluk ruler—and though they had been mere figureheads for centuries, they were regaining a profile of sorts. One of Selim's successors had decided during the 1870s to assert their presence as the basis for a right to speak for the world's Muslims. He was only trying to counter the bullying of European powers, which were advancing claims to defend Christian minorities as pretexts to gnaw at his territories, but the effect was to remind many ordinary believers of a time when Islam stood unequivocally tall among the powers of the world. Rival candidates for the caliphate emerged in Sudan and the Hijaz, and some believers dared to imagine that the faith was at last on the verge of a political renaissance. But the promise was false, and the hopes then came to an apparently conclusive end.

The immediate cause was World War I. The Ottoman Empire entered the conflict on Germany's side (once the sultan made sure to have his senior mufti certify it a jihad) and consequently emerged from the other end in a sorrier state than ever. The deathblow came when the sultan signed up to a viciously punitive peace. A popular war hero named Mustafa Kemal (also known as Atatürk; 1881–1938) denounced his submission as treachery, rallied an army to depose him, and ousted foreign occupiers so effectively that the terms of the Turkish peace were renegotiated from scratch. Admirers around the Muslim world were electrified—until, in early 1924, with that battle won and the Republic of Turkey proclaimed, Atatürk swiveled his sights toward the caliphate. It now turned out that, for all his opposition to Western imperialism, he was also a committed secularist. The legislature voted on March 2, 1924, to abolish the institution, and a couple of days later the last officeholder was bundled at 5:00 a.m. onto the Orient Express, along with three servants, two wives, a couple of daughters, and £2,000 in used British banknotes.

Although Caliph Abdülmecid II was personally displeased by his

ouster, his inability to discharge his sacred functions made little practical difference.* But the abolition of an institution that had done nothing since the fall of Baghdad managed paradoxically to turn it into a
symbol of just how far the Islamic world had sunk. Anti-imperial sentiment among Muslims in far-off India swirled into a movement to restore
the caliphate, and when an Egyptian scholar named Ali Abd al-Raziq
cautiously proposed that the Turkish decision was unimportant because
the Prophet's role had been to reveal truths rather than wield power,
twenty-five scholars at Cairo's al-Azhar University staged a formal hearing to declare him a heretic. Others were yet more forceful. An Egyptian
primary school teacher named Hasan al-Banna (1906–49), convinced
that jurists were collectively failing to acknowledge the enormity of the
caliphate's abolition, embarked on a course of religious study himself.
In 1928, he founded a movement known as the Muslim Brotherhood to
encourage his co-religionists to rise to the challenges of modernity, and
he began to publish polemics to a wider audience. In one such work,
written toward the end of the 1930s, he became the first influential
scholar since the 1857 India uprising to call for a holy war. In *On Jihad*,
he warned readers against the "widespread belief among many Muslims"
that struggles of the heart were more demanding than struggles with a
sword. After reciting a number of truculent hadiths, he insisted that
colonial rule in Egypt proved exactly the opposite:

> Muslims . . . are compelled to humble themselves before non-Muslims,
> and are ruled by unbelievers. Their lands have been trampled over, and
> their honor besmirched. Their adversaries are in charge of their affairs,
> and the rites of their religion have fallen into abeyance within their
> own domains . . . Hence it has become an individual obligation, which
> there is no evading, on every Muslim to prepare his equipment, to

*The last caliph rescinded his resignation as soon as the train left Turkish territory
but found to his chagrin that no one much cared whether or not he was still God's
shadow on earth. He soon came to terms with his fate, however, and comfortably
spent the next two decades honing his considerable talents as a painter in Paris and
the south of France. According to a report in *Time* magazine on February 22, 1937,
"Almost any sunny day he may be seen strolling with . . . great dignity along the beach
near Nice, attired in swimming trunks only and carrying a large parasol." See also
Mango, *Atatürk*, p. 406.

make up his mind to engage in *jihad*, and to get ready for it until the opportunity is ripe and God decrees [it].

Hasan al-Banna's prescriptions had no timetable. The Muslim Brotherhood was committed to the thorough moral reform of its members—a gradualist approach toward change that is still prevalent within the organization today—and it had made no plans for a violent takeover of Egypt. But his claims, and the link between anticolonialism and Islam more generally, were then tested by one of the most contentious events of the twentieth century: the 1948 partition of Palestine and creation of the state of Israel.

Ever since Ottoman control over the region had crumbled during World War I, a campaign among European Jews to have part of the territory recognized as a Jewish state had been gathering momentum. The movement, known as Zionism, was encouraging thousands of immigrants to settle, and by the 1930s, with the territory under British administration, Arab protests against the newcomers were at least as violent as the opposition to colonial rule in Egypt. When Nazi repression in Germany then escalated into systematic murder, Jews around the world—including many non-Zionists—made desperate calls for the territory's partition. The pleas were ignored. Some six million Jews died in Europe's extermination camps before that changed. But on November 29, 1947, two and a half years after the war's end, thirty-three of the United Nations' fifty-six members acceded to the demand. Arabs across the region reacted with outrage. Palestine had been governed by Muslims for thirteen centuries, they pointed out. After atrocious crimes committed by Europeans in Europe, the states making up the UN majority— all of them historically Christian—were proposing that the one-third of Palestine's inhabitants who were Jewish should be granted sovereignty over 55 percent of its territory. In the eyes of many Muslims, it was a landgrab without precedent since the Crusades—the work of a Zionist-Crusader alliance, to use a term that gained currency for the first time.

The immediate consequences were predictable. Just three days after the United Nations vote, the scholars of Cairo's al-Azhar University declared a "worldwide jihad in defense of Arab Palestine." Ferocious fighting broke out, and up to eight thousand foreign volunteers, including several hundred members of Hasan al-Banna's Muslim Brotherhood, poured into the contested territory. The fatwa was renewed in April 1948, and when Jewish leaders proclaimed Israel into existence on May 14, Egyptian aircraft and five Arab armies threw themselves into the civil war. They were resoundingly defeated, but the moral implications of Israel's victory were as disputed as the military outcome was certain. Jews overwhelmingly took the view that they had repulsed another genocidal conspiracy, just three years on from the Holocaust. For Palestinians, well over half of whom were displaced forever from their homes and communities, it was an unparalleled tragedy—the *nakba*, or catastrophe. In their view, it was not Israel that had been invaded, but Palestine.

The grievances that erupted in 1948 have never ceased to flow, and the impact on the theoretical foundations of jihad was no less seismic. Hasan al-Banna's demand for Muslims brave enough to challenge peaceful interpretations of jihad had inspired individuals to wage freelance warfare for the first time. And although al-Azhar's scholars had firmly reiterated in their April 1948 fatwa that governments were in charge ("it is obligatory for anyone personally participating in jihad to submit to the rules that the states . . . lay down"), the credibility of both the scholars and the governments plummeted as the extent of the Palestinian defeat became apparent. Spiraling recriminations saw the Muslim Brotherhood banned in Egypt in December 1948, and when members of the organization responded by assassinating the prime minister, Hasan al-Banna was gunned down in revenge on a Cairo street. Classical doctrines upholding a ruler's prerogative to run a war were more vulnerable than ever, and the rules were then rewritten, literally, in the form of a manifesto called *Milestones* that was penned in a prison cell during the early 1960s by a jailed Brotherhood activist named Sayyid Qutb.

Qutb was another student of religion who was largely self-taught, with a professional background as an educational inspector, but the scope of his work did not lack for ambition. With the selective approach to Islamic scholarship characteristic of Salafism, he relied heavily on Ibn Taymiyya's student Ibn Qayyim and described a state of affairs that was cosmic in scale and grim in aspect. A shadow loomed over the world, he claimed, as profound as the *jahiliyya* that had enveloped

Arabia before the coming of the Prophet. Only jihad could lift the gloom, and it was both meaningless and defeatist to differentiate among "spiritual," "defensive," and "offensive" struggles. People everywhere had to be allowed to recognize Islam's truth, and a righteous vanguard (*tali'a*) was obliged to lead humanity toward its liberation. Any person or institution that stood in the way of spiritual freedom would therefore have to be eliminated. "No political system or material power should put hindrances in the way of preaching Islam . . . If someone does this, then it is the duty of Islam to fight him until either he is killed or until he declares his submission."

Qutb's work, though tethered to hadiths and anchored in fourteenth-century scholarship, reflected a political stance that was going to become one of the most distinctive characteristics of modern Islamic radicalism: an intense hostility toward Muslim secularists. When *Milestones* was written, during the couple of years preceding Qutb's release from jail in 1964, Egypt was led by Gamal Nasser, the fiery nationalist who had become a hero across the developing world for resisting a Franco-British-Israeli attack at Suez in 1956. Qutb warned, however, that it was a "distortion of history" to imagine that imperialism even existed as a distinct phenomenon. The reality, which "Christendom" was trying to conceal, was that it was just a "mask for the crusading spirit." The world was as divided as it had always been between the Abode of Islam and the Abode of War. And yet for all that Qutb distanced himself from anticolonial thought, his work was steeped in the left-wing theories that underpinned it. The idea that people should be forced to be free had originated with Rousseau, not the Prophet Muhammad. The specter haunting *Milestones* looked a lot more like Marx's capitalist alienation than the *jahiliyya*. And Qutb's belief in a righteous vanguard came straight from Lenin: for all the talk of God, salvation for the masses would come from a dedicated band of revolutionaries with a rigor sufficient to overcome the laxness of the age.

Qutb himself would not live to see the impact of his work. The publication of *Milestones* in November 1964 led to his rearrest, a summary trial, and a swift death sentence. The authorities then realized that they had a potential martyr on their hands, and senior government figures anxiously enlisted his sister to persuade him to appeal his conviction, but Qutb refused. "My words will be stronger if they kill me," he told her. An epitaph that portentous is just asking to be forgotten, but it was correct.

Qutb went to the gallows on August 29, 1966, and less than a year later the unresolved claims of Israel and Palestine reasserted themselves more violently than at any time since 1948. After several months of Arab saber rattling, the Israeli government launched a preemptive strike against Egypt on June 5, 1967. Within days, it had annihilated that country's armed forces along with those of several other states, and it was in control of territories belonging to Egypt and Syria as well as all those parts of Palestine that it had not seized in 1948. Settlers were soon establishing outposts in the occupied territories. Another war in 1973 paved the way for a peace agreement with Egypt, but Israel's grip over its other acquisitions steadily tightened. The expropriation of Palestinian homes and businesses accelerated, especially on the west bank of the river Jordan, and during the 1980s amendments to Israeli planning law would facilitate the expansion of several settlements into well-appointed and heavily guarded towns.

The psychological impact of 1967 was no less significant than the territorial shifts it promoted. Already squalid Palestinian displacement camps took in several hundred thousand more refugees, and opposition to Israel generated a more general contempt for Jews. Arab polemicists became even fonder of Western anti-Semitic myths that had first gained traction after 1948—medieval tales of ritual murder and nineteenth-century fantasies about global Jewish cabals—and Israel became the apotheosis of the conspiratorial fears: a protean entity that had spawned itself into existence by abolishing the caliphate and hoodwinking the Christian United Nations. A few ninth-century hadiths had identified the Antichrist as a Jew. The twentieth-century apocalyptists now realized that he would in fact be Zionism personified.

As seventh-century grudges from the Hijaz were yoked to sinister modern antagonisms, the country that had cradled and killed Qutb simultaneously incubated a pernicious and self-destructive Islamic radicalism. A shadowy Egyptian organization called Takfir wa al-Hijra began to argue during the early 1970s that any truly religious person should withdraw from the world because so many sinful Muslims had abandoned their faith. That sounds like an unremarkably cultish thing to say, but it transgressed a very important line in Islamic law and theology: the principle that one believer should never call another an infidel (*kafir*). That practice, known as *takfir*, had been taboo ever since Kharijite dissidents had murdered Caliph Ali as a sinner, and the sect drew an appropriately blistering condemnation from the scholars of al-Azhar. But although Takfir wa al-Hijra then imploded, a victim of its own exclusivity, the heresy that infidelities might be amenable to earthly judgment took root, and it was not to be so soon eradicated.

That would be proved in the context of an alleged infidelity with a very political character—a peace treaty with Israel. In September 1978, President Anwar al-Sadat and Prime Minister Menachem Begin signed the Camp David Accords, under which the Jewish state withdrew from the Sinai desert while Egypt rescinded its declaration of war of 1948. The peace put Sadat's country at odds with the rest of the Arab world, and in the face of mounting anger the president sought confirmation from the jurists of al-Azhar that his actions accorded with the shari'a. They duly provided it, citing the Prophet's example and relevant jurisprudence to show that a Muslim leader could reach an armistice whenever he deemed peace to be in Islam's interests. But while the scholars were squeezing Sadat's truce into lawful trappings, an electrical engineer named Abd al-Salam Faraj was undertaking some legal research of his own—based on the fourteenth-century work of Ibn Taymiyya.

Faraj, having carefully studied the Syrian scholar's opinions about how to handle the Mongols, had grown convinced that Muslims had forgotten the true meaning of jihad, and in his tract—*The Neglected Duty*—he set out to remind them. As well as reiterating Ibn Taymiyya's general ideas about warfare, Faraj drew from an opinion that the Damascene had handed down to a group of Anatolians who were worried that it was sinful to live under a Muslim emir who paid tribute to the Mongols. He had told them that their home was neither in the Abode of Islam nor in the Abode of War—it was a "composite" (*murakkab*)—and that they should emigrate if they could not practice their Islam freely. Faraj thought the fatwa spot-on. The extinction of the caliphate had left Egyptian Muslims in an equivalent state of limbo, he wrote. The rulers who now held sway over them were no more worthy of allegiance than a tributary of the Mongols: they were apostates whose Muslim names and avowals of faith were a sham. But he had no plans to emigrate anywhere. Instead, he argued that the extermination of such rulers was a sacred duty that personally bound every able-bodied Muslim man.

That conclusion went considerably further than Ibn Taymiyya ever had in challenging the mainstream principle that Muslims have no business calling each other infidels. The Damascene's justification for war against Ghazan, all those centuries ago, had been predicated on the claim that the Mongol was leading a rebellion against the Mamluk regime and that Egypt's rulers were right to put it down. His characterization of the conflict had been imaginative, but it lay a long way from the claims of Kharijite or Assassin extremists that Muslim rulers might themselves be characterized as rebels worthy of death. But Faraj was part of a clandestine organization—the Society of Struggle, or Jama'at al-Jihad—which was committed to the age-old notion that individual Muslims were duty-bound to actively promote good and forbid evil. Its members found his theories compelling. On October 6, 1981, at a military parade to commemorate the eighth anniversary of Egypt's 1973 war with Israel, four soldiers associated with Faraj broke ranks and hurled grenades toward the reviewing stand. As the dignitaries dived for cover, twenty-six-year-old Khalid Islambouli strafed Anwar al-Sadat with Kalashnikov fire. "I have killed Pharaoh and I do not fear death!" he yelled.

The murder of the Egyptian president had consequences that have cascaded down to the present. Faraj and the killers themselves were hanged within months, but police dragnets sent out by Sadat's deputy and successor, Hosni Mubarak, picked up thousands of suspected activists. A large number were members of the Muslim Brotherhood, guilty of nothing more than association, but in their frantic search for accomplices, the authorities subjected many to electric shocks and sexual humiliation, establishing hatreds that would fester for years. Some 280 men were then produced for trial in December 1982, displayed to the world's media in the cages of an improvised courtroom in Cairo's Exhibition Grounds. The most vocal defendant, who shouted avowals of faith and complaints about torture through the bars, was a bespectacled physician with a commitment to armed struggle that was already setting him apart from the reform-minded mainstream of the Muslim Brotherhood. His name was Ayman al-Zawahiri, and the world was destined to hear from him again.

But that is to jump ahead of the story—which in itself calls for a pause, and a reflection. Events since 9/11 have proceeded so rapidly and unpredictably that it is easy to forget just how recent a phenomenon the revival of ideas about violent jihad has been, but a succession of crises took place over a few short years in the late 1970s that would transform the political shape of the Muslim world. Over in Saudi Arabia, a brief and bloody siege in Mecca on November 20, 1979, saw hundreds of armed militants take thousands of hostages: one of the first signs that widespread Western assumptions about the kingdom's slow evolution toward liberalism might be off the mark.* A series of apparently random events farther east were by then settling into an unexpected pattern as well. In Pakistan, a general named Zia ul-Haq had overthrown the civilian government in July 1977, and though he was just the latest in a line of military dictators, he surprised everyone by announcing plans to "Islamicize" the country. Iranian revolutionaries meanwhile overthrew the Shah in early 1979, only for an exiled cleric named Ruhollah Khomeini to fly back and proclaim a Shi'a theocracy. And the third point of a newly volatile triangle then appeared in the country next door—Afghanistan. A revolutionary clique of the Afghan army had installed a Marxist government in Kabul on April 27, 1978, but as the West settled in for Christmas in the winter of 1979, news emerged that the Asian nation had succumbed to one of the lethal tiffs to which second-tier Communist states used to be so prone. Russian tanks were reportedly rumbling to the assistance of their favored faction. It was the kind of fratricidal assistance that the Soviet Union had provided neighbors many times before, but the decadelong occupation that ensued was going to transform the world.

Resistance to the invasion of Afghanistan took time to rally. Although several Muslim governments funded refugee relief efforts, their primary concern was to avoid causing offense to the Soviet Union, and none

---

*The Saudis requested foreign assistance during the crisis, and three French commandos tried (and failed) to end the siege by filling the mosque's underground chambers with narcotic gas. In order to avoid defiling the site, they formally converted to Islam first. Wright, *Looming Tower*, pp. 88–94, 397.

characterized the Afghan crisis as a jihad. The Shi'a revolutionaries of Iran preferred to posture against Western depredations, actual and imagined.* The Sunni regime of Saudi Arabia, keenly aware since the Mecca siege of its vulnerability to homegrown hard-liners and fixated on the religious challenge posed by the ayatollahs, focused its diplomatic energies on rallying support for the decision of Iraq's president, Saddam Hussein, in October 1980 to invade Iran. The effect was to virtually orphan Afghan opponents of the Soviet invasion, and their isolation was exemplified by a Saudi-brokered meeting of Muslim heads of state in January 1981. Baggy-trousered fighters, forlornly wandering the marble corridors, found that no one would talk to them except for the occasional journalist. Delegates concluded the powwow with a fiery demand for Jerusalem's liberation, but their only comment on Soviet misdemeanors was a polite call on Muslim states to help the UN's secretary-general resolve a situation that was "prejudicial to the Afghan people."

A state's preference for pragmatism over principle is never very surprising, but the failure of Muslim rulers to speak out could only alienate popular sentiment, and regimes that already lacked for democratic legitimacy were soon reminded that there were individuals ready to seize the initiative. It was Palestinian anger, once again, that provided the impetus. Abdullah Azzam had been born in the West Bank city of Jenin, which Israel had been occupying since 1967, and he knew better than most not to rely on the selflessness of Islamic states. With hopes for international assistance that spoke as much of his homeland as they did of Afghanistan, he sounded a clarion to wagers of jihad—mujahideen—around the world. In *Defense of the Muslim Lands*, a book prefaced by Ibn Taymiyya's demand that invaders be ejected from the Abode of Islam, he contended that Muslims everywhere were personally bound to take up arms on behalf of their Afghan coreligionists. The claim was all but unprecedented. There were fatwas going back to the Crusades that urged Muslims to defend one another against an invasion, but no one before Azzam had globalized that obligation.

---

*Although the Afghans were Sunnis, Twelver doctrine potentially allowed for military assistance. It holds that no one can lead a full-scale holy war except the missing imam but that struggles to defend Islam are permissible before his return. See generally Kohlberg, "Development," esp. pp. 78–86.

In the light of NATO's own experiences with international mujahideen in Afghanistan and elsewhere, the progress of his idea is worth briefly recalling. Though bold, it found a correspondingly adventurous audience. In one of the odder couplings of a tale filled with strange bedfellows, the charismatic Palestinian came to be embraced by anti-Communists in Reagan-era America. Over the course of more than twenty visits to the United States, he regularly enchanted listeners with tales from the killing fields—accounts of Soviet helicopters snared by angels, for example, and descriptions of the fragrance that would shroud a martyr's soul as it soared to paradise—and if his non-Muslim admirers were skeptical, it did not show. The struggles against infidelity and Communism merged so fruitfully that Afghanistan's freedom fighters were granted one more miracle in 1987: Stinger missiles. Thanks to cold warriors in Congress and the CIA, the Taliban's predecessors were empowered to wage the jihad that Islamic governments had refused to declare.

As the Afghanistan conflict radicalized thousands of fighters through the 1980s, the decentralization of jihad turned it into something of a mass movement, and another theater of conflict, this one even more directly related to the Israel-Palestine conflict, would do even more in its own way to promote the individualization of holy war. The region concerned was Lebanon, where Israel attempted in the summer of 1982 to rid itself of the threat of Palestinian fighters to its north by securing a strip of border territory and bombarding their bases in Beirut. Once those aims had been achieved, a United States–brokered peacekeeping force inserted itself into a conflict that was already kaleidoscopically complex, and on October 23, 1983, members of a Shi'a militia drove two explosive-laden trucks into its Beirut barracks. Some three hundred American and French troops were killed. It was the first of a series of spectacular suicide attacks, which some Western commentators quickly linked to the Shi'a admiration for martyrs such as Ali and Hussein. But though there had been one extremist Sevener sect that had notoriously been willing to die in order to kill—the eleventh-century Assassins—suicide bombing was not a routine expression of Shi'a spirituality. It was the tactic's absolute novelty that made it remarkable. There is no better evidence of that than observations made in February 1985 by Israel's defense minister, Yitzhak Rabin:

I believe that among the many surprises that came out of the war in
Lebanon, the most dangerous is that the war let the Shi'ites out of the
bottle. No one predicted that but if as a result we replace P[alestine]
L[iberation] O[rganization] terrorism in southern Lebanon with Shi'ite
terrorism, we have done the worst thing in our struggle against terrorism. In twenty years of PLO terrorism, no one PLO terrorist ever made
himself into a live bomb.

In an age when Muslim suicide bombers have become frighteningly unremarkable, Rabin's words offer a useful reality check. They
did not exist before 1983, and for more than a decade after that suicidal
attacks remained the specialty of certain Lebanese Shi'a factions—most
notoriously, the one known as Hezbollah (Party of God). The tactic's
only other practitioners during that period were Sri Lanka's Tamil
Tigers—a secular guerrilla group that was Hindu by background—
who invented the explosives-packed vest to assassinate the onetime
Indian prime minister Rajiv Gandhi in May 1991. And the dearth of suicidal Muslims was not a coincidence but the consequence of centuries-
old doctrines. The timing of a person's death had always been for God
alone to know, and several passages of the Qur'an made clear that suicide was a sin. Hadiths presented even greater theological obstacles:
not only was punishment by fire reserved to God, but those who took
their lives were warned to expect torture with the instrument of their
death on the day of resurrection.

The prospect of entering a hell filled with exploding sinners did not
prevent some jurists from legitimizing the tactic, however. Ayatollah
Khomeini personally authorized the Beirut blasts of October 1983, and
other Shi'a scholars were soon following his lead. Lebanon's Ayatollah
Fadlallah initially withheld his support for suicidal warfare, but he then
argued that the discrepancy of force made it permissible for the weak
to use their bodies as weapons against the strong. Sheikh Naim Qassem,
second-in-command at Hezbollah, observed in addition that a person
did not subvert predestination merely by choosing to die on a day that
God had always had in mind anyway. It was a legal achievement as lethally inventive as the assassination fatwa of Abd al-Salam Faraj in
1979. The idea that fighters might heroically lay down their lives for the
communal good was neither new nor unique to Islam. But the need to

circumvent an explicit prohibition in the Qur'an had inspired Shi'a jurists to prove the virtue of committing suicide non-suicidally.

As the 1980s proceeded, fighters in Afghanistan battled the Soviet Union toward a stalemate, and when the provision of Stinger missiles coincided with the rise to power of General Secretary Mikhail Gorbachev, the balance tipped. On February 8, 1988, Gorbachev finally announced plans for a pullout. The Soviets had lost close to fifteen thousand men and left at least a million Afghans dead. Six months later, with the withdrawal well under way, a core group of mujahideen convened in Peshawar under Abdullah Azzam's auspices to think about their next move. All were by now familiar with Sayyid Qutb's 1964 argument that a vanguard of righteous men should wage Islam's struggle globally, but there was little agreement over what that meant. Some began to contemplate taking the battle back to their homelands: North Africa, for example, or Kashmir. Azzam himself was eyeing Palestine, where his compatriots had recently begun for the first time to confront the Israeli occupation in large numbers, using rocks and gasoline bombs. He had recently helped establish a religious movement to channel the resistance—Hamas—and its charter was published just two days before the Peshawar meeting, on August 18, 1988. The hope was to tap political energy that had previously found an outlet in secular groups such as the PLO, and though Azzam's own struggle then came to a very sudden end—when on November 24, 1989, he was blown up by assailants unknown on the way to Friday prayers—there was no shortage of followers ready to take up the cause.

The most senior of them was Ayman al-Zawahiri, the Cairo-born physician whose tirade against Egyptian torture had briefly made the news during the 1982 mass trial that followed President Sadat's assassination. He first went to Afghanistan before his prosecution to treat the sick, but three years in the jails of Egypt had switched his focus firmly from life to death and his leadership of al-Jihad, a successor to the group that had killed Sadat, would cause havoc over the following decade. Another member of Azzam's circle was due to gain an even higher profile. Osama bin Laden (1957–2011) was the son of a Saudi construction magnate whose business trips to northern Pakistan during the early 1980s had instilled in him a deep admiration for the fighters who were standing up to a superpower. He had moved to

Peshawar in 1984 to participate in the war more directly, and he now emerged at the head of a loose organization known as "the base"— *al-qaʿeda*.

The two men made a good match, combining resilience, experience, and wealth, but their interests were still distinct. Bin Laden remained focused on events in his Saudi homeland. Al-Zawahiri was steeped in Egyptian radicalism—he was the grandson of one of the caliphate's greatest champions during the 1920s and had admired Sayyid Qutb since childhood—and his primary concern was to combat dangerous tendencies toward moderation that he had begun to detect in the Muslim Brotherhood. But both men had a reason to take an interest in the crisis that began in August 1990, when the armies of Saddam Hussein invaded Kuwait. The senior muftis of both Saudi Arabia and Egypt were prevailed upon to proclaim resistance to the invasion a holy struggle, and an American-led force began gathering on the Arabian Peninsula to restore the emirate's independence. Iraqi forces were then expelled, and a triumphant president George H. W. Bush declared on March 6, 1991, that a "new world order" was at hand.

Coming at a time when the joyless certainties of the Cold War were collapsing, the phrase sounded innocuous enough to many Western ears—optimistic even. But Muslims of a traditionalist outlook were far more suspicious. Events quickly offered up reasons to wonder at the new order's shape—a decision by Algeria's Western-backed army to annul an Islamic party's electoral victory in December, for example, and the beginnings of outright genocide against Muslims in Bosnia—and bin Laden was particularly concerned by developments in the Hijaz. A hadith claimed that the Prophet Muhammad had told followers from his deathbed, "Let not two religions be left in the Arabian Peninsula," and Muslim historians recorded that Caliph Umar had obediently expelled all non-Muslims from the region. The rulers of Saudi Arabia, however, were making apparently permanent arrangements for the United States to operate military bases in the country. Osama bin Laden was driven to a momentous conclusion. Whatever the Americans might have been up to in Afghanistan, they now stood revealed as enemies of Islam, and the new world order they and their lackeys planned to impose stood in direct opposition to the shariʿa.

The next few years were hectic but productive. Bin Laden and al-Zawahiri, shuttling between temporary refuges, acted independently but pursued agendas that became ever more likely to target U.S. interests. Although anti-Shi'a attitudes thrived among their followers, they also managed briefly to suppress the sectarianism—to the extent that the early 1990s saw some joint military training with Lebanese Shi'a groups such as Hezbollah. But as the two groups expanded their operations and moved toward merger, one problem became pressing. Neither man believed that the pursuit of violent jihad should be unrestrained. Each knew it to be a sacred duty with definite legal limits, and that called for jurisprudential skills they were not yet ready to assert. Bin Laden, for all his piety, seems to have considered himself lacking in the requisite scholarship. Ayman al-Zawahiri, though better read, remained unwilling to put out a fatwa in his own name. The Saudi therefore delegated the task of investigating the legal position to one of his followers: a communications engineer named Mamdouh Salim, whose familiarity with religious texts had won him considerable respect from other members of al-Qa'eda. And in the autumn of 1992, by which time the coalescing organization had abandoned a fracturing Afghanistan for Sudan, Salim set out his conclusions. Addressing some three dozen men at bin Laden's Khartoum villa, he explained that Islamic law allowed not only for the forcible expulsion of American invaders from the Hijaz but also, in certain situations, for the killing of innocent Muslims. The most detailed account of his words comes from the later courtroom testimony of a Sudanese al-Qa'eda member turned FBI informant. His truthfulness in general terms is as suspect as his English, but the specific evidence he gave about Salim's advice has a definite ring of truth. And it very plausibly conveys the reality, as opposed to the theory, of the legal limits that are observed by the modern exponents of violent jihad:

> [Salim] said that our time now is similar like in that time, and he say Ibn al-Taymiyya, when a Mongol come to Arabic war, Arabic countries that time, he say some Muslims, they help them. And he says Ibn al-Taymiyya, he make a fatwa. He said anybody around the Mongol, he buy something from them and he sell them something, you should kill him. And also, if when you attack the Mongol, if anybody around

them, anything, or he's not military or that—if you kill him, you don't
have to worry about that. If he's a good person, he go to paradise and
if he's a bad person, he go to hell.

It is said of frogs that if they are placed in a pot of water that is
heated gradually enough, their biological thermostats adjust so that
they boil alive rather than jump free, and something similar was happening to jihadi jurisprudence. Incremental changes of legal doctrine
were normalizing the previously unthinkable. And just as had been the
case with Abd al-Salam Faraj, Salim's restatement went considerably
further than Ibn Taymiyya had ever gone himself. The fourteenth-
century jurist was no milquetoast, but the only good Muslims whose
murders he had ever countenanced were those who were on the battlefield as part of an enemy army. In his more general writings about jihad,
he had contended that noncombatants should be spared, and that was
in reference to infidels. But Salim's fatwa, along with similar efforts
elsewhere, was creating its own reality. A veteran of al-Qaʻeda's training
camps set off an explosives-filled van under New York's World Trade
Center on February 26, 1993, killing six people and injuring hundreds
more. Palestinian violence moved up several notches on April 16, when
a Hamas operative emulated Lebanese Shiʻa groups to become the
first Sunni suicide bomb at a Jewish West Bank settlement. Ayman
al-Zawahiri was meanwhile taking notes, and four months later two
motorcycle-borne members of his al-Jihad organization detonated
themselves in a failed bid to assassinate Egypt's interior minister.

Al-Zawahiri then had cause to enter the legal fray in person. An attack that he orchestrated on Egypt's embassy in Pakistan in November
1995, in which the drivers of a jeep and a pickup truck killed themselves and seventeen people, drew scathing criticism in the Egyptian
media. At a time when he still imagined his group to be a viable alternative to the Muslim Brotherhood in the struggle for his compatriots'
hearts and minds, al-Zawahiri was sufficiently stung to formulate one
of the first-ever Sunni justifications for suicide attacks. It explained
that the homicides were not murders but "martyrdom operations" and
that the people dying to commit them were not killing themselves at
all. Some oppressed early converts to Islam had willingly suffered fatal
tortures, he pointed out, and no Islamic jurist had ever called *that* suicide.

And though it was regrettably inevitable that some innocent Muslims would be killed, it was a well-known principle of Islamic law that exceptional threats to the faith allowed for the validation of otherwise forbidden acts.

At around the same time, Osama bin Laden also began to engage personally in the legal debate. His first tentative effort came in the form of a fax that he sent King Fahd in August 1995 to protest Saudi Arabia's accession to a regional trading bloc called the Gulf Cooperation Council. The monarch's submission to the organization's "constitution, international law and norms, and the principles of Islamic law" was a "mockery," complained bin Laden—because "you have put the Islamic law only at the end." It was not the most sophisticated of arguments, but bin Laden was to prove a quick learner. He returned in May 1996 to Afghanistan, where the ultra-traditionalist Taliban were asserting control over factions that had been battling each other since the Soviet withdrawal, and by August he was ready to issue his inaugural fatwa. It was a confident debut. After enumerating countless impieties that were being committed in infidel-occupied Saudi Arabia, it alerted believers, seven times, to the evils of the Zionist-Crusader alliance. Despite the taboo surrounding *takfir*—accusations of religious infidelity against a fellow Muslim—bin Laden accused the kingdom's rulers of idolizing man-made laws instead of obeying the shari'a. And, invoking Ibn Taymiyya, he proclaimed the presence of foreign forces in the Hijaz to be an invasion, imposing an obligation on all Muslims to wage war on the United States.

All the legal activity then culminated in a joint fatwa issued by Osama bin Laden and Ayman al-Zawahiri in February 1998. It opened with the Qur'an's most bellicose passage—the Verse of the Sword, in which God had commanded a final assault against unrepentant pagans in the Hijaz—and after another diatribe against the Zionist-Crusader alliance, it proclaimed its conclusion: "The [requirement] to kill the Americans and their allies—civilians and military—is an individual duty for every Muslim who can do it in any country in which it is possible to do it." The document justified itself in terms of self-defense, but an event three months earlier offered grim clues as to what that might mean in practice. In the hope of sabotaging Egypt's Nonviolence Initiative—an agreement by the government to release thousands of imprisoned radicals in return for their formal disavowal of violent activity—al-Zawahiri's group had massacred fifty-eight tourists and four locals at the ancient temple of Luxor. And the fatwa of February 1998 soon proved its own worth. At 10:30 a.m. on Friday, August 7, 1998, car bombs tore through the U.S. embassies in Dar es Salaam and Nairobi. The time had been chosen on the basis that good Muslims would be at prayer, and the explosions managed to kill 12 American infidels. The other 212 dead and almost all of the several thousand injured were Africans. The ancient notion that an Abode of Islam was pitted permanently against an Abode of War had reached its most extreme conclusion. Self-styled mujahideen were no longer merely assassinating leaders and exploding themselves into kingdom come. Al-Qaʿeda's jihad was against the world.

Subsequent events are too well-known to need much recapitulation. Almost three thousand people were killed in the attacks against the United States on September 11, 2001, and NATO retaliation against al-Qaʿeda camps in Afghanistan began a so-called war on terror that led to a presidential decision to invade Iraq. In the inferno that opened, tens of thousands, perhaps hundreds of thousands, died. The violence perpetrated by Muslim insurgents and sectarians came to dwarf that of the occupiers, but any significance that might possess was obscured as Operation Iraqi Freedom morphed into the torture of Abu Ghraib and phosphorus shells over Fallujah. And twelve hundred years after Islamic jurists had first split the world into two abodes, millions bought into a modern rhetoric of polarization. Some believed President George W. Bush's announcement on September 20 that "every nation [is] either . . . with us or . . . with the terrorists." Others preferred Osama bin Laden's observation a couple of weeks later that "these events have divided the whole world into two sides: the side of believers and the side of infidels."

The splits were rather less clear-cut, of course. If any single lesson can be said to have emerged out of the coalitions and compromises that were struck in the decade after 9/11, it was that communities were not unequivocally with or against anyone. Millions of people were simultaneously hostile to the conduct of the war on terror and opposed to al-Qaʿeda. Most devout Muslims had little time for coreligionists who ignored the mercy of the Prophet and the love of God, while violent ones showed no affiliation at all to the believers whose murders they justified and perpetrated. Nor were the conflicts as timeless as the confrontational slogans implied. Attempts to destroy international infidelity by force after 2001 were the work of recently emerged free-lancers, whereas no Muslim state had pursued such a policy for centuries. The very idea that Muslims might blow themselves up for God was unheard-of before 1983, and it was not until the early 1990s that anyone anywhere had tried to justify killing innocent Muslims who were not on a battlefield. The arguments for violence are recent.

A sense of perspective on events since 9/11 calls for recognition of one other very important fact, however. Of late, Muslims claiming to interpret God's law have been justifying aggression more readily than ever before. And though reasons for the change can be easily stated—economic injustice, political repression, and the humiliations of foreign occupation, for example—such grievances can only motivate radical-ization. Its direction and speed have been determined by the malleabil-ity of Islamic jurisprudence itself. Countless examples could serve to prove the point. Certain foreign scholars after 9/11 urged American believers to battle their own government, but others within the United States found legal justifications for war against al-Qaʻeda. While the senior mufti of Saudi Arabia condemned Sunni sectarian attacks in Iraq during 2005, another well-known sheikh let it be known soon after-ward that the Shiʻa bore "all the characteristics of infidels." In the con-text of suicidal violence, the disagreements have been particularly cacophonous. Certain scholars have bravely reiterated its sinfulness, and in countries such as Afghanistan and Pakistan some have even been killed for speaking out. But others have equivocated, and in the context of Israel the concern to accommodate Palestinian desperation has skewed perspectives to an extent that can look distinctly peculiar. After a twenty-seven-year-old woman killed herself and an eighty-one-year-old Jewish man outside a shoe shop on Jerusalem's Jaffa Road in January 2002, for example, the only moral qualms expressed by the Egyptian jurist Yusuf al-Qaradawi concerned the propriety of a female martyr traveling to her death unchaperoned.

The theological controversy has its upside. It is no easy task to dis-abuse fanatics of their dreams—tougher still to deter someone set on suicide—and inconsistent warnings of hellfire are better than none at all. In a very tangential way, the disputes also reflect the legal flexibility that has lent Muslim communities their resilience over the centuries. When a juristic disagreement concerns the legitimacy of lethal violence, however, adaptability is better characterized as arbitrariness, and the disputes signify not the strength of legal doctrines but their fragmentation. The arguments are the tail end of a process that has seen Islamic institutions hemorrhaging legitimacy for more than a century, discredited by their response to foreign intrusions and domestic corruption. The terms of the debate pay backhanded tribute to the rise of maverick scholars and the legal doctrine that has stood them in such good stead—Salafism. Respect for the *salaf*s, the first generations of Muslims, is perfectly conventional among believers, but the legal exploitation of their authority, as pioneered by Ibn Taymiyya, has proved extremely potent. It has allowed freelance jihadis to devalue the importance that Sunnis traditionally accord consensus, through claims that are tricky to contest and impossible to disprove. Schoolteachers, engineers, and doctors have thereby been able to reverse the classic orthodoxy about holy war—that its pace and direction are for governments to decide—and justify legal innovations in fields from sectarian violence to suicide bombing. And more than a few respectable jurists have simply played catch-up to their agenda.

Anyone of peaceful inclinations who surveys the harrowed landscape covered in this chapter cannot but be pessimistic. The hierarchical restructuring of the last few decades looks profound, and the deaths of individuals—even ones as important as Osama bin Laden—have only ever had transitory effects on jihadi morale and funding. It is always important to accentuate positives, however, and the revolutionary cyclone that began sweeping through North Africa during the spring of 2011 may yet do more than just shake up the institutions of the Arab world. Insofar as new regimes are able to entrench themselves and accommodate popular expectations, they will be better positioned to assert a Muslim ruler's traditional prerogatives—including the right to restrain individuals from waging war on their own account. But that comes with a crucial qualification. Representative governments do not control the sentiments of their citizens—they channel them—and one particular issue has to be addressed if governments are to recover their lost authority. That issue is the Palestinian question. Every significant doctrinal escalation of the last three-quarters of a century, from the validation of assassination to the redefinition of suicide, has been catalyzed by the dislocations set off during the dismemberment of Palestine in 1948. Vast refugee camps still distort the demographics of the Middle East, and Israel's slow-motion annexation of the West Bank since 1967 causes fury to seethe unabated. It is no coincidence that the regional group best placed to benefit from fair elections is one that is steeped in anti-Israeli sentiment—the Muslim Brotherhood—and the democratically proven popularity of another grassroots movement, Hamas, is a reminder that enfranchisement can simply allow anger to be vented more efficiently. Even if new governments acquire greater credibility and use it to pragmatic effect, the consequence could be simply that scholars dare acknowledge the minimal truth that jihad is given a bad name by certain brutalities—the murder of octogenarians, for example. Uninventing the modern theories that legitimized the brutalities is going to take work. It demands imaginative leaders and urgent policy shifts on Arab and Israeli sides alike. But the prize is great, and the alternative is dire.

In the face of geopolitical stakes that high, a quiet prayer cannot go amiss, and when the journey that had taken me to Ibn Taymiyya's desolate birthplace of Harran in June 2009 ended in the city of his death, Damascus, I decided to round off my stay with a visit to his tomb. The Sufi cemetery in which he was buried was long ago built over, but research revealed that his specific grave had been preserved in the grounds of one or another of the city's hospitals. Establishing its precise location was not easy. The regime of Bashar al-Assad was jumpy enough even then, and my wanderings quickly attracted the attention of *mukhabarat* intelligence officers—though they were so baffled by my claim to be looking for a long-deceased Sunni sectarian in a medical facility that after several hours of interrogation, they let me go. I eventually found the scholar in the parking lot of a maternity ward. His forlorn slab and broken headstone had seen better days, but the existence of any memorial at all was proof of his complex legacy. He had spent a lifetime objecting to tomb veneration, only to cast a more powerful posthumous spell than any of his Sufi contemporaries. The French colonial authorities of Damascus had been able to raze acres of surrounding burial grounds during the 1920s in the name of redevelopment, but Arab demolition teams had insisted that Ibn Taymiyya's resting place—uniquely—was too holy to touch.

Standing next to a scraggly acacia that had pushed its way out of the marble, I struggled to formulate a coherent assessment of the scholar. His contempt for popular Sufism and Peoples of the Book contradicted my understanding of Islam as an inclusive faith, but I was not sure how useful it was to apply modern assumptions about tolerance to an era of religious rough-and-tumble. The ease with which he justified war was alien to me, but his opposition to the terrors of Mongol occupation made eminently good sense, and in a battlefield scenario he certainly seemed someone whom it would be better to be with than against. Any fair appraisal of Ibn Taymiyya also had to give due weight to the terribly dark views of his modern acolytes. Although Algerian activists of the early 1990s quoted him to justify their electoral struggles, extremists have more often relied on his ideas about idolatry to argue that democracy is a false god. In the hope of inflaming civil war in Iraq in 2004, an al-Qa'eda associate named Abu Musab al-Zarqawi had invoked his seven-hundred-year-old anger against Shi'a collaborators to explain why it was necessary for Sunnis to murder members of the rival sect: "They stop Muslims on the border roads and rob them . . . their heart is full of vinegar." The most vicious among his admirers have taught teenagers to believe that it is holy to turn their bodies to shrapnel and to machine-gun their coreligionists at prayer. No one can know if that legacy would have made Ibn Taymiyya more proud or ashamed. It must at least be presumed, however, that he accepted one of the Qur'an's better-known verses. "Whoever kills a human being," God had warned, "shall be deemed to have killed all mankind."

Part Two

The Present

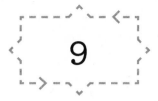

9

Innovation and Its Discontents: Islamic Law and the Challenge of Change

The no-man's-land separating believers and unbelievers allows prejudice to take deep root, and a couple of assumptions have always been common on the skeptical side. Atheists who take pride in their clear-mindedness often imagine that anyone who follows a sacred text is committed to an outdated perspective on the world and that revealed religion more generally is essentially irrational. To credit literature with such power is itself a little magical-minded, however—simply because words are given meaning by the present as much as the past— and the belief in God has never excluded a respect for logic and consistency. Among Muslims in particular, the contest between the claims of revelation and those of reason has often been unequal, and it is a good nine centuries since rationality could last plausibly claim to have had the upper hand, but truly blind faith has never come close to delivering a knockout blow. Even the most devout Muslim will justify his or her belief in terms of evidence—even where a skeptic might see assumptions alone.

One relatively recent incident that crystallized the shifting status of Islam's revealed truths was the publication in 1988 of Salman Rushdie's *Satanic Verses*. The novel contained a number of controversial passages— fantasies of a parody prophet surrounded by harlots, drunks, and charlatans—and they were enough to inspire Ayatollah Khomeini's notorious call for the author's death on February 14, 1989. The passages were undeniably offensive to many people, albeit that those offended were never very likely to read them. Rushdie's book raised hackles for reasons other than its contents, however. Its title echoed a legend, known in Arabic as "the story of the cranes" (*al-qissat al-gharanik*), that claims to describe a moment during the early 620s when the Prophet briefly faltered in his mission. Worn down by pagan hostility, he supposedly became convinced that his adversaries' three favorite goddesses were worthy of prayer. He even led a congregation in worship with an observation that the deities were as heavenly as soaring cranes. Only then, faced with his followers' incredulity and pagan triumphalism, did the angel Gabriel disclose to Muhammad the extent of his mistake. The supposed revelations were not divine. They were the whisperings of a demon (*shaitan*): satanic verses.

The story has been contentious for centuries. Some indication of the sensitivities in play can be gleaned from the fact that the term "satanic verses" is liable to offend on linguistic grounds alone. The Arabic word that is represented in English by "verse"—*ayat*—specifically connotes a token of divinity. It is used to describe the holiest of heavenly gifts: revelations above all, but also those Shi'a men known in Farsi as signs of God—*ayatollah*s. The notion that a demon might even pretend to utter such a miracle has aroused intense passions. A religious seminar that convened in Cairo in 1966 to consider the story's historicity concluded by simply declaring it a forgery—"a fabricated tale which [dissembling heretics] have concocted against the great Qur'an"—and one participant suggested that all classical texts in print be reviewed in order to censor it out of modern existence. The historical arguments never rested on mere assertion, however. Theologians typically backed their claims about the incident with analyses of the literary sources. They observed, for example, that the oldest written evidence of the Prophet's supposed lapse relies ultimately on the testimony of Abdullah ibn Abbas (ca. 619–78), who was about three when his cousin Muhammad left Mecca for Medina. Some fair-minded critics also acknowledged the other side of the balance. They recognized that Ibn Abbas has an otherwise stellar reputation among both Sunni and Shi'a Muslims, for example; and that his account, which is repeated or reflected by about thirty other hadith transmitters, lends meaning to three extant verses of the Qur'an that are highly elliptical. Most remarkably, several scholars of great standing actually accepted the story's truth. They include the chronicler Muhammad al-Tabari (839–923), the hugely admired Sufi mystic Abd al-Qadir al-Jilani (ca. 1077–1166), and the eminent Shafi'ite hadith scholar Ibn Hajar al-Asqalani (1372–1448)—as well as no less a figure than Ibn Taymiyya himself. In the course of a treatise that examined why God had caused Jonah to be swallowed by a whale, the Damascene jurist had pondered the subject of tribulation more generally and concluded that the demonic ploy against the Prophet had been a test. And Muhammad's retraction was incontrovertible evidence that he had passed it with flying colors: "Do you not think the person who seeks his own aggrandizement through falsehood would want to back up everything he says, even if it is wrong? So the Prophet's [proclamation] is a yet greater proof of his striving for veracity and his innocence from lying."

Having grown up associating the term "satanic verses" with book burnings, I learned about such theorizing with some surprise. The scholars who once accepted the tale of a tempted Prophet covered so broad a range that no believer can fail to credit at least one of them. When I traveled to the Indian subcontinent in the spring of 2009, I thought therefore that it might be interesting to find out how their modern counterparts accommodated their predecessors' insights. And the responses were proof of how much had changed—in the name of immutable tradition. A leading Sufi in my father's hometown and a lecturer on jurisprudence in a Lucknow madrasa simply denied point-blank that any learned Muslim had ever accepted the legend. I then took to equipping myself with photocopies of the texts and eventually got a more meaningful response during an interview with a highly respected religious jurist in Karachi. And though terse, it was also telling. After unhappily leafing through the relevant eleventh-century work of Abd al-Qadir al-Jilani, Mufti Munib ur-Rehman made a vague complaint about the Urdu translation and referred me to a scholarly refutation of the legend. When I pressed him on what he himself thought, he impatiently explained that the story undermined the concept of divine revelation (*wahy*). If a demon had once expressed itself through the mouth of the Prophet, it would be impossible to rule out repetition of the incident. That contradicted the Qur'an's own evidence that Muhammad was divinely inspired, and it was therefore absurd.

The mufti's concerns were comprehensible enough. Every moment of the Prophet's life is considered by the pious to be not merely exemplary but incontrovertible proof of the shari'a. Muslims have always believed that Muhammad could not persist in a mistake, and a stronger version of that opinion—an assumption that Muhammad was incapable of making mistakes in the first place—was already commonplace during Ibn Taymiyya's lifetime. But Munib ur-Rehman's rationalism had a circular quality, which exemplified an unresolved aspect of the broader tension between reason and revealed truths. Scholarly attempts to rely on evidence have often rested on notions of proof that are themselves contested. That has made many religious arguments somewhat sterile—in that they are acceptable to the devout only insofar as they confirm existing assumptions—and that has had an important practical consequence. The absence of self-scrutiny can so eviscerate faith that it ends up opposed to demonstrable realities.

The point is vividly illustrated by another story, which this time is indubitably historical. Half a century after the Mongols' final attempt to reach the Mediterranean, the Middle East suffered an invasion that was significantly more successful. Sailors brought the Black Death to Alexandria in the autumn of 1347, and it was soon laying waste to Egypt and radiating across the Levant and North Africa. The pestilence was pneumonic as well as bubonic, transmissible by both breath and touch, and by the time it had consumed itself a year and a half later, up to a third of the Muslim world lay dead. Men and women were known to expire within minutes of noticing their symptoms, torn apart by internal bleeding "as if . . . slain without a knife." Burglars who entered victims' houses were sometimes struck down with such rapidity that their bodies were found at the scene. And as mosques turned to mortuaries, stacked with so many corpses that funeral rites had to be abandoned, those believers who survived were faced with an age-old riddle: What was God up to?

Many theologians thought they knew the answer. Quoting well-sourced hadiths, they explained that the plague was a curse if it afflicted

infidels but a great blessing when caught by a Muslim. There were disagreements over the details—whether the sickness was transmitted by
corrupt vapors or the poisoned arrows of invisible jinns, for example—
but the overwhelming majority of hadith scholars agreed that any
believer whom God chose to infect would go straight to paradise. And
yet, although the hadiths were flawless and the arguments venerable,
few people seemed to agree with them. Indeed, far from welcoming
martyrdom, many Muslims did their utmost to avoid it. Peasants abandoned their villages, leaving behind silent minarets and stilled waterwheels that would intrigue travelers for decades. The elders of Cairo
and Damascus led barefoot processions and called for penitential fasts,
and anxious citizens tried to protect themselves by wearing ruby charms
or daubing themselves in mud. It was even suggested that the plague
seemed less like a gift than a punishment.

The boldest dissent was heard in Granada, the last outpost of Islamic rule in Andalusia. A politician and scholar named Ibn al-Khatib
(d. 1374) took careful notes of the disease's progress during 1348, and
by the time he wrote up his observations more than a decade later, he
had reached a daring conclusion—that it naturally passed from person
to person. "The existence of contagion is established by experience," he
claimed, "[and] by trustworthy reports on transmission by garments,
vessels, ear-rings; by the spread of it by persons from one house, by
infection of a healthy sea-port by an arrival from an infected land
[and] by the immunity of isolated individuals." It was true, he recognized,
that the Prophet was sometimes said to have suggested otherwise, but
"a proof taken from the traditions has to undergo modification when
in manifest contradiction with the evidence of the perception of the
senses."

Ibn al-Khatib's willingness to ignore the clear meaning of un-
contested hadiths was fairly remarkable. It might even have cost him
his life. A few years down the line he would be strangled in a jail cell,
and though he had been incarcerated pursuant to a private vendetta,
the charge laid against him was heresy. But his respect for the scientific
method put him in some eminent historical company. The Persian physician al-Razi (865–925) had pioneered a diagnostic approach toward
disease more than four centuries earlier, while Arab polymaths such
as Ibn al-Haytham (965–1040) and Ibn Zuhr (1091–1161) had based

groundbreaking advances in optics and surgery on experimental observations. Their views reflected a more general theory about knowledge that had been around for just as long: the view that people could
form ideas without having been told them. The philosophers Ibn
Sina (980–1037) and Ibn Tufayl (ca. 1110–85) had each contemplated
how human beings would think if left to their own ruminations—
postulating the idea of being born rational but afloat in a dark silence,
or raised on a desert island by animals—and both had concluded that
humanity would realize God's existence without His help.

Muslim scholars had long been sensitive therefore to the obvious
risk, that religion would be discredited if too wide a gulf opened between reason and revelation, and the pandemic simply made the point
rather more urgent. Even Ibn Qayyim (1292–1350), the jurist who did
most to build on the work of Ibn Taymiyya, was concerned enough
to contextualize and explain away the plague hadiths in a medical
law text that he published during this period. One writer was particularly perspicacious: the Tunis-born Ibn Khaldun (1332–1406), whose
Muqaddimah—a magisterial account of humanity's place in the world,
combining history, philosophy, and sociology—would one day be
called by Arnold Toynbee "the greatest work of its kind that has ever
yet been created by any mind in any time or place." The North African
expressed no doubt at all that prophecy had a real meaning: a prophet
was the most inspired of individuals, capable of traveling beyond the
veil of appearances and handing down laws that reflected eternal and
transcendent truths. But his writing was simultaneously suffused with
an awareness of human frailty, and he had personal reasons to doubt
that the plague had any moral meaning. He had been in his mid-teens
when the disease struck Tunis, and by the time it had finished with his
homeland, "rolling up the carpet with all there was on it," his own parents were among the dead. Despite his beliefs about prophetic wisdom, he had no time for anyone who confused Islam's spiritual value
with the medical ideas that had attended its emergence:

> The medicine mentioned in religious tradition . . . is in no way part of
> the divine revelation. [It was] merely [part of] Arab custom and hap-
> pened to be mentioned in connection with the circumstances of
> the Prophet, like other things that were customary in his generation.

[It was] not mentioned in order to imply that [it] is stipulated by the religious law. Muhammad was sent to teach us the religious law. He was not sent to teach us medicine or any other ordinary matter.

Ibn Khaldun's words stand as eloquent expression of a premodern willingness among Muslims to acknowledge that religious convention might set a believer at odds with the real world. And yet, six hundred years on from his death, a definitive distinction between religious law and ordinary matters remains elusive. Even the most headstrong hadith scholar would think twice nowadays before declaring it un-Islamic to believe in germs, but certain jurists still cite hadiths to contest the lawfulness of toothbrushes and mustaches. And such disputes form part of a far bigger controversy over the correct approach toward innovation (*bid'a*) in general. A well-known hadith insists that "every innovation is heresy, every heresy is error, and every error leads to hell"—and matters have never been that simple. Scholars long ago acknowledged that some novelties were "good," and attempts to exclude only the bad ones have made for the kind of inquiry that gives split hairs a bad name. Eighth-century jurists transformed loopholes (*hiyal*) into an entire branch of legal science, and they openly departed from the Qur'an by inventing a way of ending marriages that is still known as "innovatory divorce" (*talaq al-bid'a*).* Ninth-century traditionists such as Ibn Hanbal considered human literature to be an unholy innovation, while the ultraconservative Ibn Taymiyya wrote books by the dozen and railed against mathematics instead. By the beginning of the twentieth century, most Muslim revivalists were unashamed men of letters and technophiles whose neophobia frequently focused on Western fripperies such as ties and top hats. Contemporary views about change are liable still to be both arbitrary and imaginative. In

---

*The Qur'an allowed a man to divorce simply by saying so three times, but it sought to discourage impulsive splits. As well as forbidding parties to reunite until a wife consummated and ended another marriage with someone else, it required that each of the three pronouncements be separated by a month: 2:229–30. Early Hanafites instituted a new rule that men could say "I divorce you" (*talaq*) three times on a single occasion and established that the process was effective even if the words were uttered while drunk or under duress. See Ibn Rushd, *Distinguished Jurist's Primer*, 2:88–93, 97–98, 103–104.

November 2008, Malaysia's National Fatwa Council warned, for example, that yoga was a forbidden pagan activity—a year after it had published guidelines for the first Muslim astronaut, explaining how he ought to pray while orbiting the earth in zero gravity.

Assessing the optimal degree of flexibility for Islam would be as difficult as it would be arrogant. Its certainties were a crucial aspect of its early appeal, and resilience has enabled it to resist pressures that would have floored a flimsier faith. But its capacity to accommodate variety and local custom has been no less important, and the only true constant over the years has been flux. Conservatives sometimes even admitted as much. The Cairo-based author of one fourteenth-century tract against innovation, which condemned newfangledness in matters ranging from the recitation of stories to bathing in the Nile, was driven to conclude that "each age is distinguished by its own customs and habits." Al-Ghazali, who viewed the foibles of his fellow Muslims with an eye more acute than most, appreciated the inevitability of cultural development. He observed that all sorts of phenomena which his age thought legally unobjectionable, from mosque carpets to a passage in the call to prayer, had once been innovations. "Strange as it may seem, accepted practices of today are the taboos of a day gone by," he wrote. "And the taboos of today are the accepted practices of a day yet to come."

Islam's evolving ideas about change are hard enough to pin down when they are expressed in the form of ancient texts. Approaches to the past among the living are even more dynamic, and understandings of the shari'a that prevail among the modern world's 1.6 billion Muslims are particularly fluid. There are fifty states in which Muslims are demographically dominant and many others where they make up significant minorities, and they acknowledge the shari'a in correspondingly varied ways. Most treat it as an aspect of the individual's relationship with God, and though they give formal effect to Islamic jurisprudence in certain civil fields—family law, for example—the jurisdiction of religious judges is otherwise made subject to secular edicts. Almost a dozen state constitutions explicitly privilege Islam, however, and some have enacted statutes that authorize supposedly sacred criminal punishments. There are also two true theocracies—Iran and Saudi Arabia—that allow judges to act on the basis of almost any hadith or Qur'anic verse that they think suited to the case in hand.

When I began to think about making a journey to put flesh on the historical bones of this book, a degree of selectivity was therefore in order. There is no such thing as a typical Muslim state, and any assessment of contemporary attitudes toward the shari'a could easily have become unrepresentative—or tediously comprehensive. In my attempt to avoid either failing, I would spend some five months on the road—three of them traveling overland between India and Istanbul—and the trip gained a degree of coherence from a duality that became apparent at the outset. My father's Badaun birthplace was the obvious place to start this book, and its magical, musical, shrine-centered rituals have a sectarian rival. The Deobandis, named after the North Indian town where their movement coalesced, regard the Barelvi group with which Badaun is associated as hopelessly innovative. They see its respect for dead saints as proof of a preference for Hindu idolatry over monotheism and symptomatic of a more general crisis: a cultural drift away from the tenets of revealed Islam. The Deobandis and Barelvis each claim tens of millions of followers worldwide, and they cover both ends of Islam's most significant polarity: the interplay between believers who are relatively relaxed about the evolution of tradition and those who want to safeguard the future by recovering an idealized past.

The rivalry can be traced back to the failure of the 1857 uprising against colonial rule in India. As the British dismantled the last remnants of Mughal government, Muslims across the subcontinent tried to salvage a degree of autonomy by emphasizing those aspects of communal life they could still control. The larger group, which would later coalesce as the Barelvis, stressed the importance of continuity, but a number of better-educated scholars argued that it was crucial also to weed out inauthentic customs, and in 1866 they established a madrasa in the town of Deoband to promote that idea. One of its earliest and most distinctive features was an arbitration and fatwa service, which aimed to furnish believers with authoritative Hanafite rulings that could sideline the widely reviled British-run courts. The madrasa's muftis did not rule on matters other than belief, ritual, and personal status, however. Although many of the college's founders thought highly of Salafi-inspired radicals such as Ibn Taymiyya and Muhammad al-Wahhab, caution characterized their movement. Having just survived a disastrous war, they wanted to institutionalize stability, not legal adventurism.

The madrasa at Deoband became the nucleus of a phenomenally successful educational movement. It is the model for thousands of similar colleges all over the world, and graduates are often at the most visible end of Islam—in terms of proselytizing, protesting, and even, in a handful of cases, violence. But their contribution to the present has done nothing to change the Deobandi reverence for the past, and madrasa jurists formulate theoretical stances against innovation with a passion that would not have been out of place in the fourteenth century. That has produced some mystifying consequences. They have declared, for example, that the Prophet's reported opposition to figurative art proves watching television to be a mortal sin.* They nevertheless saw fit in September 2007 to launch a website that computerized their fatwa service. Deobandi warnings against innovations such as birthday parties and games of chess are consequently archived and downloadable in electronic form.

Such priorities seemed to call for scrutiny, and after visiting the shrines of my father's birthplace in April 2009, I therefore stopped off in Deoband on my way northeast toward Pakistan. As my train squealed to a halt in its two-platform station, I had almost no idea what to expect. The madrasa's relations with curious outsiders had been prickly since 2006, when an undercover Indian journalist had persuaded a mufti at the madrasa to write him a fatwa for a fee. The sting, rapidly nicknamed the Cash for Fatwas scandal, had led college elders to fulminate for months against a supposed media conspiracy against them.†

---

*The stance is unusually harsh. Saudi Arabia, considered a bastion of virtue by many Deobandis, launched a state television service in 1965 with a programming schedule that was leavened by *Mighty Mouse* cartoons and reruns of a sitcom called *The Wackiest Ship in the Army*. Notwithstanding deadly riots against the innovatory broadcasting machines, the channel is still going strong. See Lippman, *Inside the Mirage*, pp. 119–22.

†The dubious Deobandi fatwa condemned credit cards as un-Islamic. That was at least plausible, given the Qur'an's disapproval of usury, but another madrasa issued two opinions that were jointly far harder to justify, even in religious theory. The first

Barely had that fear ebbed when, in December 2008, a squad of armed Muslim militants went on a citywide killing spree in Bombay. India had been on edge in the months since, and the country's shriller media commentators had been regularly asserting that the mass murders were somehow linked to madrasas in general. An attempt on my part to make contact with the college authorities had not even earned a reply, and though breakdowns in communication often signify nothing worse than inefficiency in India, there was reason to wonder whether the arrival of an unannounced visitor claiming to be a writer would be welcome.

If tensions on the ground were high, however, it was not apparent. A cycle rickshaw juddered uneventfully from the railway station through a bustling market town and deposited me at the madrasa's crumbling archway. Teenage boys in white cotton uniforms were laughing and loafing in the early morning cool, and even if their wakefulness was not typical of Western undergraduates, they seemed no more militant than students anywhere else. In search of friends, I entered the central courtyard. Having read a couple of historical accounts of Deoband that mentioned a pomegranate tree around which the first students were taught, I ostentatiously contemplated the surrounding vegetation. It was not long before a skullcap-wearing student in his early twenties beckoned me into an arcade with a smile. When I explained what I was looking for, however, the welcome tightened into a frown. That pomegranate tree had been chopped down a couple of years ago, he told me. The faculty had decided that Muslims were venerating it at God's expense—which was, in case I did not know, a forbidden innovation.

It was a mixed start. An attempt to break the ice had marked me out as a tree worshipper. But it gave me a new acquaintance, and Abdussalam quickly turned out to be a forgiving sort. He was a postgraduate English student, considerably keener to explore the difference between a proverb and an idiom than to dwell on the dangers of idolatry, and even after he learned that my father had been born a Barelvi, he was more interested in my geographical home than my spiritual roots. It was not long before he insisted that I meet the four classmates

---

declared televisions to be forbidden, while the second stated the opposite. See generally Aravind Adiga, "India's Cash-for-Fatwa Scandal," *Time*, September 21, 2006.

with whom he shared a dormitory. All were from poor South Indian families, and as soon as I arrived, they excitedly spread a thick shawl over a thin mattress and set a kettle boiling on their gas ring. None had ever met a foreigner before, and by the time the shudderingly sweet tea was ready to pour, they were bombarding me with more linguistic queries.

The enthusiasm at Deoband for English as a language seemed impressive, but the unfamiliarity with the culture that had produced it then became equally clear. It emerged that the faculty member who taught Abdussalam and his friends had recently visited England, and his experiences had made a great impression. The teacher had apparently been touched by the politeness of the country's people, pleased by the cool weather, and impressed by its public transportation facilities, but one of his observations had disturbed them all. He had claimed that all the women wore short dresses. Could that be true? When I assured them that it was not, a barrage of supplementary questions forced me into an admission that my mother and sister wandered the streets unveiled. A stressful silence ended only when someone suggested, with attempted kindness, that the British government had no business forcing women to lead such shameful lives. Were men also prevented from following the shari'a? More specifically, were they forbidden to wear beards long enough to be grasped within a fist and cotton pants cut off at the calves?

The questions were less surprising than they might sound. They echoed hadiths that claimed to describe how the Prophet expected Muslim men of his time to carry themselves, and Deobandis have been paying them keen heed since at least the 1880s, when one of the school's founders issued a fatwa urging his students to avoid Hindu haircuts. It was an unwelcome conversational turn, all the same. My own heresies, a beard more fungal than fist-sized and heel-length jeans, were all too apparent. In the interests of communal harmony, I tried to switch the focus of attention to a more controllable distraction. Although the room contained not much more than five mattresses and a few fragile books, I disingenuously wondered whether they thought that television was a useful way of learning English. Expressions flickered between suspicion and shock. Abdussalam gently expressed surprise that I did not know the forbidden status of televisions under

Islamic law. Whereas the Internet offered a useful way of propagating the faith, he explained, broadcast networks were responsible for *"too much"* immorality. When I pointed out that there was plenty of immorality to be found online as well, Abdussalam bit his tongue and shook his head with distaste, as though I were describing pornography instead of alluding to it. The question had been considered by scholars who understood the shari'a, he explained—a put-down as pointed as it was tactful.

Still mindful of my tree-venerating faux pas, I did not pursue the subject. Deoband's founders were committed to the notion that the most fundamental principles of jurisprudence were fixed into place about eight hundred years ago, when "the gate of interpretation" closed, and madrasa rules replicate that hierarchical assumption. Students are obliged to assume that previous and current generations of teachers are possessed of greater wisdom than themselves. Abdussalam and his friends were simply falling into line with two fatwas: an acknowledgment by the faculty in 1996 that computers could promote Islamic virtues, and an opinion issued during the summer of 2004 that declared television to be "principally a means for [frivolous] entertainment." As far as they were concerned, any doubts that remained were their own fault. Rhyme and reason were beyond their remit, and it was sinful to give rein to curiosity. Years of scholarship might change that, but a truly devout Deobandi student would be at least as likely to abandon uncertainties as to explore them.

After tea, Abdussalam introduced me to his English teacher, an amiable mufti named Obaidullah, who was eager to discuss his recent trip to England. The subject of female immodesty did not come up, but as we strolled through the cloisters, we covered topics ranging from the war on terror to the Punjabi restaurants of Whitechapel. Classes were in full swing, and heaps of slippers lay outside the rooms, where graybeards could be seen through lattice-screen windows intoning hadiths and parsing revelations while rows of cross-legged students rocked and fidgeted. Obaidullah then invited me to address his class on a topic of my choice, and I delivered a short homily on the pleasures and pitfalls of multiculturalism, which elicited a flurry of questions—all of them, dispiritingly enough, about the sartorial preferences of Muslims in London. As evening approached and the time came for me to head back to the railway station, Abdussalam escorted me to a stall just outside the college gates so that I could buy a souvenir skullcap. He refused to venture farther into the market, however. "I do not usually come this far even," he explained. "There is a danger of seeing things that will lead me into sin."

It was a suitable end to a thought-provoking day. About two-thirds of Deoband's population are Muslims—a proportion that probably rises close to totality in the crowded alleys around the madrasa—and though it was certainly possible that Abdussalam would glimpse a DVD or sense womanly flesh, his fear said far more about his awareness of corruptibility than it did about corruption itself. His predicament was simultaneously affecting, however. When I typed up my diary that evening, I characterized his parting remark as a simple reluctance to confront reality. The longer I reflected, however, the less fair that seemed. In a country like India, where countless millions still perch just one rung above insolvency, the education to literacy of a single child can keep a family from destitution. It is hardly irrational for a responsible student to believe that temptations are better avoided than confronted. And the freedom to wander a marketplace must be even less appealing when salvation itself seems to be at stake.

Sympathy is a poor reason to overlook the limitations of the Deobandi madrasa system, all the same. Its core curriculum was formalized in Baghdad during the viziership of Nizam al-Mulk, three decades before his murder by an Assassin in 1092, and although English has been taught since the late twentieth century, other intellectual innovations—philosophy, for example—are mentioned only to be vilified. The educational template has been successful, in the sense that thousands of madrasas around the world now emulate its example, but self-perpetuation is not the same as fruitfulness. Academic rigor has doubtless improved since the days when Deoband's founders would grade exams by intuition alone, but students around the world graduate on the fringes of national educational and employment structures. And the cultural perspectives available to students are woefully narrow. The Nadwa college at Lucknow, considered an intellectual powerhouse by Deobandis around the world, contained some intriguingly unorthodox entries in its library catalog—a 1910 work on syphilis, prewar English children's adventure stories, and *Lady Chatterley's Lover*, for example—but its bookshop contained not a single secular text. Although the Deobandis I encountered in India were almost always personable and very often charming, their collective approach toward education was resolutely unadventurous. They had no expectation that fresh ideas might resolve contemporary problems. Any new answers that might emerge would flow only from redoubled contemplation of what was already known.

My exposure to Deobandi thought did not end in India. I went on to spend the rest of April 2009 in Pakistan, and though that country figures prominently in the next two chapters, its Deobandis have carved out so distinctive a status that a few preliminary observations are in order. They have been present in Pakistan ever since its creation in 1947, but the movement truly took off only during the 1980s, when it also began to rapidly mutate. As the war against the Soviets in neighboring Afghanistan intensified and Zia ul-Haq spoke of Islamicizing Pakistan, several leading scholars dropped the suspicion of government that had long been integral to the movement. Whereas their Indian brethren remained as resistant to governmental interference as they had been under British rule, Pakistan's Deobandis took to thinking that a powerful state, in the hands of righteous Muslim men, might serve to promote the faith.

Intensifying communal conflict promoted the movement's politicization, and few parts of the country have been affected quite as profoundly as the port city where I spent the most time—Karachi. Three decades of war in Afghanistan have left it awash in refugees, drugs, and guns, and at least eighteen million people now jostle for social position on its reclaimed shorelines and in its mangrove swamps. Stability is in correspondingly short supply. While the rich shuttle between high-walled villas and gated clubs, fearful of kidnappings and carjackings, the poor are sunk in a squalor that is hard to exaggerate. I spent several days in a heroin- and disease-ridden district called Lyari: a slum divided by junk-strewn sewers so cluttered that children regularly drown trying to walk them and ethno-political rivalries so bloody that government departments no longer compile fatality statistics. I was able to visit only because a community-worker friend offered to put three

armed men at my disposal, and their presence was a permanent reminder of the tension rather than any guarantee of peace. One hard-
won interview with an elusive mufti from the doctrinaire Jamia Farooqia
madrasa came to a sudden end when my guards received text messages
to say that there had just been a number of drive-by shootings in the
neighborhood, and we left to find the streets crackling with Kalashnikov
fire, and a driver who was almost as keen to make a getaway as me. The
go-between who had facilitated that rendezvous, a baby-faced gangster
with relatives at the madrasa, would himself be gunned down by police
four months later. The most disconcerting news came in August 2009, a
couple of months after my return to London, when my Lyari friend reported that one of his guards had gone missing. I remembered Zeeshan
for his shy smile and the way he would reassuringly pat his pistol pocket
whenever trouble loomed, but the police were now identifying him as a
covert al-Qaʻeda operative.

One tangential consequence of the violence has been a sporadic demand among Westerners of a gung ho tendency that Pakistan's government should somehow close down its thousands of madrasas. That is
to confuse cause and symptom, however, and no Pakistani with sense
would ever propose the same. Islamic colleges are even more integral to
the country's economy of poverty than they are to that of India. Absent
an educational Marshall Plan, the hope of educating a literate bread-
winner is about as bright a future as millions of families will ever
get. Another promise that they hold, though less tangible, is equally potent: to the sons of the lower middle class, and even a few of the daughters, they typically offer shelter from the social storm. The school day is
structured. Classrooms offer camaraderie instead of chaos. And though
their walls might not exclude the stench of diesel or the noise of gun-
fire, they enclose a space where more than a thousand years of scholarly
certainty still seem to hold sway.

Everything I saw of Pakistan's madrasas left me convinced, however,
that they were manifestations of a malaise rather than a signpost toward
solutions. Their scholars focus unduly on moral controversies rather
than social and economic problems—as the next couple of chapters
will show—and they often seem to acknowledge the outside world only
on their own very rigid terms. One vignette rather perfectly illustrates the intransigence. Soon after my arrival in Pakistan, somewhat

jittery before my first madrasa appointment, I set off with the intention of arriving a few minutes early but was surprised to find myself arriving with a full hour in hand. When the next interview came round, I was less anxious but somehow managed to do the same again. The mystery was then resolved. Pakistan's madrasas had refused on religious principle to put their clocks forward for the summer, because the muftis in charge considered daylight saving time to be an unholy innovation.

There is a third religious tradition that no survey of Islamic legal practice can overlook. The Barelvis and the Deobandis jointly cover a very considerable part of the Sunni spectrum, but Shi'ism has its own very distinct history. At the beginning of May 2009, I therefore flew from Karachi into the world's most dynamic Shi'a culture: Iran. By then, several Deobandis had warned me against the country's impieties and innovations, and my curiosity was piqued. The objection I heard most often—that the Shi'a worship at shrines—was not that intriguing, given the number of tomb aficionados I had already encountered at my father's birthplace. But the attitudes of Iranian jurists posed a greater mystery. I knew that Twelvers had differentiated themselves from Sunnis about a thousand years ago, when they had accepted the Mu'tazilite argument that the human intellect could illuminate God's law. That had encouraged their scholars to interpret religious texts with relative confidence, at least by comparison to those ultracautious conservatives who considered rationalizing the shari'a to be a sin. The contemporary consequences of the Twelver stance were difficult to conceptualize, however. Iran's ideas about law and order have come to be represented in the global media by stonings, fist-shaking demonstrators, and assassination fatwas, and though there was doubtless more to the story, the contribution of human intellect was not obvious.

The very notion of a Shi'a republic constituted another puzzle. Although Iran is now synonymous with politicized religion, Islamic government has been a controversial concept among Twelver jurists for longer than a millennium. Ever since the disappearance of their last imam, they have accorded earthly rulers no more than conditional legitimacy; and despite the pragmatic decisions of certain scholars over the centuries to assume political roles, it was universally accepted for most of the modern era that God's spiritual authority was distinct from earthly power. The first signs of a change appeared during 1970. At a time when Iran's dictatorial ruler, Shah Reza Pahlavi, was ruthlessly suppressing both political dissent and expressions of religious tradition, a senior cleric named Ruhollah Khomeini (1902–89), exiled in Iraq, decided that it was time for a more hands-on approach. Ayatollah Khomeini was a firm believer in rethinking the shari'a to take account of changing circumstances, and in a series of lectures delivered at the Shi'a seminary in Najaf, he daringly urged clerics to be not only the moral guardians of society but also its governors. The political model he proposed, known as the Rulership of Jurists (*velayat e-faqih*), was as influential as it was unorthodox. When the shah was ousted by Tehran's revolutionaries in early 1979, Khomeini returned to persuade his fellow divines that God wanted them to take control. Iran's revolution was steered toward theocracy, and the ayatollah became the first Supreme Leader of a clergy-dominated political structure that remains in place to this day.

History alone therefore suggested that surprises were in store, and Tehran still managed to be startling. Friends of friends repeatedly apologized for its shabbiness during my first days, but it looked a model of prosperous efficiency compared with Pakistan. And it was a treat just to watch the Iranian world go by. Although the state had firm views about what people should wear—and enforced them by law in the case of women—plenty of citizens had fashion senses that were very much their own. After weeks during which beards had loomed large in my consciousness, spiky mullets and razored sideburns were everywhere. Tightly tailored coats did the work that a miniskirt would in the West, and I felt renewed sympathy for Deoband's students as I caught myself gazing at highlights and fringes that seemed always to be tumbling out of loose head scarves. But the individualism, for all its appeal, was also a reminder that the capital is not where you go to learn about Shi'a jurisprudence in Iran. You head for a very different place: the seminary town of Qom.

Qom is Iran's Ivy League and Vatican City combined, a vital symbol of clerical power that counts not just Ayatollah Khomeini but much of the nation's current religious elite among its alumni. My guidebook, along with a fair number of Iranians, warned that it is a place of stifling conformity, and it was not hard to see their point. The people of Qom possessed their own brand of ostentation, but it could hardly have differed more from the skinny jeans and fancy haircuts of Tehran. City life revolved around death—more specifically, around a gold-domed mausoleum at the town center—and though its occupant had slipped away peacefully back in 816, the sister of the eighth imam was mourned as though she had just been cut down by a NATO missile strike. Under immense chandeliers and dazzling mirrored shards, crowds of robed and shrouded visitors gazed incredulously at her silver tomb. Marshaled by stewards wielding rainbow-colored dusters, they shuffled into queues and slapped their foreheads inconsolably. The agonies intensified as they neared the sarcophagus—until, with a caress and a condolence, catharsis descended and they moved on, the latest lamenters in a line that has not stopped snaking by for twelve hundred years.

But sorrow was only part of the story. The pilgrims were out-of-towners from as far afield as Afghanistan and Zanzibar, and though deathly devotions certainly mattered, the mood was jaunty. Qom's market heaved with shoppers, fingering rosaries and biting veils in place as they sniffed, licked, and stroked the goods on offer. Men gathered at the city's main newsstand, absorbing information from the dozens of front pages that permanently covered the sidewalk. And after evening prayers, as juice blenders whizzed and chickens rotated, its main drag turned into the Shi'a equivalent of the boardwalk at Coney Island. Giggling hijabis swayed in not-so-dumb show past rapt seminary boys, money changers riffled bricks of banknotes, and brown-cloaked clerics bickered with their wives and shared downtime and mushroom pizza with their children.

The vibrancy was initially as frustrating as it was exhilarating. Although I had come to Qom in the hope of learning about Shi'a attitudes toward modernity and the shari'a, it was risky to begin a conversation with anyone. Even in ordinary times, Iran's government is so sensitive about what the seminary's clerics might be saying to each other that foreign diplomats have to obtain prior authorization to travel to the city at all. I had arrived just a month before the nationwide presidential elections, and overfriendliness on my part might easily have been mistaken for espionage. The British have a reputation for political dabbling—not least because in 1952 Winston Churchill's government successfully instigated the United States to engineer a putsch against the country's elected prime minister, Mohammad Mossadeq—and it lives on. With a certainty that even the most blinkered English patriot might nowadays be embarrassed to assert, many Iranians assume that London still runs an empire devoted to global mischief and that the United States of America is a mere puppet in its hands. Two of Qom's hotels turned me away after seeing my passport, and even the humorous responses to my presence were barbed. "British?" a market stallholder had mused wryly as he scrutinized my features and wrapped a pistachio-embedded chunk of caramel. "The British control the world." Another customer, clicking his teeth with disapproval, reminded him that God did that. The confectioner wagged his finger in emphatic denial. "God controls the *universe*," he explained. "The British control the world."

Not for the last time on my trip, however, hospitality trumped suspicion. Through a series of serendipitous encounters, I learned that one of the more modern additions to Qom's educational scene—Mofid University, founded in 1988 by one of the country's most senior ayatollahs— was staging a two-day conference titled "Peace, Human Rights, and Religion." The event's theme was vaguely expressed, but it also promised views very different from those I had encountered at places such as Deoband. Sunni scholars, even of the relatively radical Pakistani variety, are ambivalent about the extent to which Muslims are entitled to rethink God's law for themselves. Shi'a clerics, by contrast, assume that until the return of their occulted imam, they are collectively obliged to keep it under permanent review. It takes some time to master the skill—a couple of decades, on average—but a diligent seminarian will then emerge as a fully qualified interpreter of God's will: a *mujtahid*. Whatever peace, human rights, and religion might mean to a Twelver scholar, it seemed unlikely therefore that there would be any shortage of opinions.

On the morning of the conference, I found Mofid's glass-and-concrete campus at the parched desert perimeter of the city. Abandoned by a taxi at its main gate, I had to trudge the long approach road on foot, and it shimmered in the distance like a functionalist mirage. Turbaned scholars in SUVs spat dust as they shot past, and I cursed anticlerically. It made me wonder again what lay ahead. Publicity for the conference claimed that participants were going to pool their experience and promote "dignity, justice, security, flourishing, tolerance, cooperation, and self-determination." It was an impressive goal, but the aspirations sounded potentially meaningless—even propagandistic. And then, at the very first session, the doubts crystallized. The speaker was not Iranian but Irish, and her subject was a 2005 case in which the European Court of Human Rights had considered a Muslim medical student's complaint that governments violated religious freedom if they excluded a woman from a state university for wearing an Islamic head scarf (*hijab*). The Strasbourg tribunal had ruled against her, holding that the infringement could be justified by a state's interest in upholding secularism. No case was more likely to spark denunciations of Western double standards, and though I personally despaired of the court's decision, my heart sank at the presentation's conclusion, when a cleric who had been scribbling intently raised his hand. He was wearing the black turban distinctive to *sayyid*s (descendants of Hussein), and I steeled myself for a righteous diatribe. It came, but the target was entirely unexpected. With some charity, he observed that Strasbourg's judges might have been unaware of the importance of modesty in Islam. But, he insisted, their decision recalled another issue closer to home, and in that context legal officials could not claim ignorance as an excuse. It was as offensive to force women to cover up as it was to forbid it. And yet the Iranian state threatened to fine or imprison women if they wore "improper *hijab*." What concern was it of a government, he demanded, to police a woman's relationship with God? It might as well oblige citizens to pray!

Having just spent a month among many Muslims who would have found few propositions more agreeable, I was taken aback, and I would remain wrong-footed for much of the next two days. When I spoke to the questioner after the session, he turned out to be a senior professor at Qom's main seminary whose views were well-known and publicized on his website. No government, he explained, could transform people into good Muslims against their will, and Iran should not be in the business of trying. Equally unexpected ideas were expressed at subsequent sessions by dozens of other clerics and students. Conference participants, women as well as men, took conservative theologians to task by quoting Western thinkers such as Immanuel Kant and Jürgen Habermas. Ayatollahs and academics proposed that the Qur'an's disapproval of economic speculation ought to be expanded to address other forms of exploitation so that Iran was better placed to meet its international obligations to tackle child trafficking and forced prostitution. Proceedings concluded with a debate about harmony between a Jew, a Catholic, a Zoroastrian, a humanist, and a grand ayatollah, and though none delivered a punch line as good as the setup, the very thought of their argument would have seemed a joke before I got to Qom.

The focus on rationalism at Mofid was not representative of Iranian society at large. Qom's own mausoleum was evidence that passion retained its traditionally important place in Shi'a thought, and shrines elsewhere pulled in vast crowds each night. On the evening I visited the airport-sized mosque of Jamkaran, for example, there were at least fifty thousand people present—most of whom were staring tearfully at the eastern horizon, because the Twelfth Imam had supposedly manifested himself on-site in 984 with a promise to come back on a Tuesday. Spirituality had its hold among even apparently secularized Iranians. Although my random conversations were dominated by mundane Western mysteries (soccer transfer fees, dating etiquette, and the like), quite a few casual acquaintances grew suddenly misty-eyed if the subject of Caliph Ali's murder or Hussein's martyrdom arose—which, in the interests of curious research, it quite often did.

The open-minded theology prevalent at Mofid was the tip of an iceberg, all the same. Over the course of my month in Iran, the country seemed sometimes to be bubbling with religious ideas. I spoke to many admirers of Mohammad Shabestari, for example: a scholar who has proposed that the act of reading a text contributes to its meaning, that interpretations change over time, and that Muslims should acknowledge that wisdom can arise from nonreligious sources. Others pointed me toward Abdolkarim Soroush, who has challenged conventional notions of the Qur'an; its shape, he has argued, was affected by the Prophet Muhammad's personality, through revelations that reached him like "an ocean poured into a jar." And though such ideas might sound abstruse, they had great political significance. They staked out an intellectual space from which Iran's government was excluded, and in a republic which asserted theological omniscience, that was subversive almost by definition.

It is never possible to predict when thoughts will spark deeds, and my own feeling after a month in the country was that expectations of change were as minimal as dissatisfaction was widespread. But then, just three weeks after my departure, the tensions burst into the open. On June 12, 2009, presidential elections produced a resounding victory for the incumbent, Mahmoud Ahmadinejad—and protests nationwide. It was widely assumed that the president's backers had over-rigged or stolen the ballot, and anger mounted when an official recount confirmed the result rather too well, by crediting Ahmadinejad with more votes in fifty cities than there were voters. Fraud can disfigure elections anywhere, but any state truly guided by God would presumably have eradicated incipient corruption with dexterity. Iranians got ham-fisted manipulation and an iron hand instead. Demonstrators were arrested by the hundreds, some were fatally shot, and several were raped or beaten to death in police custody. The man at the apex of Iran's secular and spiritual hierarchies, Grand Ayatollah Ali Khamenei, meanwhile declared the result a "divine assessment"—and let it be known that he had always supported Ahmadinejad anyway.

The regime shored itself up within a couple of months. A show trial of about a hundred defendants in August 2009 claimed to identify and shatter a treacherous cabal behind the unrest, and prosecutors described a vast conspiracy that extended all the way to Jürgen Habermas himself. Dissent more generally was asphyxiated by threats of dismissal, suspension, or expulsion from college. But though the crackdown was temporarily effective, the haste with which Khamenei re-anointed Ahmadinejad was destructive in a way that the repression could not properly repair. In the short term, it reignited jibes that had always plagued the Supreme Leader's reputation. As far as Twelver Shi'a are concerned, the several dozen grand ayatollahs scattered about the Middle East are paragons—Sources of Emulation, or *maraji al-taqlid*—who are closer to God than anyone except the Twelfth Imam himself. Khamenei, however, had not even reached ayatollah status when a dying Khomeini shoved him forward as a compromise candidate for the succession in 1989, and it took five more years for the clergy to recognize its nominally Supreme Leader as a grand ayatollah—"from corporal to field marshal in two easy fatwas," in the words of one underwhelmed Iranian I met. But events in June 2009 did more than recall Khamenei's personal inadequacies. His effort to characterize a palpably flawed election as the work of God exposed just how hollow the Iranian state's claim to enshrine Shi'a Islam had become. There was considerable popular support for Ahmadinejad himself, to an extent that was sometimes underestimated in the West. But attitudes toward the supposedly Supreme Leader were fundamentally split. Although he had his conservative supporters, there were countless others who agreed instead with an open letter that Abdolkarim Soroush sent him in September 2009—accusing "Mr. Khamenei" of being ready to disgrace the name of God rather than face up to his own shame.

The ferment among intellectuals and clerics had deep roots. Ayatollah Khomeini, for all that his theories served to institutionalize clerical intransigence, also revitalized the historically dynamic Shi'a approach toward legal interpretation; and thoughtful Twelvers are inherently sensitive to the dangers of overmighty government—because their predecessors have been despising despots ever since Caliph Yazid ordered the murder of Hussein at Karbala. They are also well placed to recall more recent traditions that complacent supporters of the current theocracy would prefer erased: the ideas of the popular religious reformist Ali Shariati, for example, who presciently warned during the 1970s that clerical power would corrupt individual faith as much as it could ever enhance it. But for precisely the same reasons that a degree of opposition might have been predictable, it poses a particular threat to a governing system that purports to reflect God's eternal will. Nothing exemplified that better than the stance of Grand Ayatollah Hossein-Ali Montazeri, one of the opposition's most authoritative voices before his death in December 2009. He had cowritten the revolutionary constitution of 1979 and was Ayatollah Khomeini's designated successor until cut off for protesting a secret massacre of several thousand political prisoners that took place toward the end of 1988. Though he has been officially reviled ever since, Montazeri's grand ayatollah status meant that he could not be silenced and his spiritual authority could not be challenged. And two months after Khamenei validated the elections of

June 2009, Montazeri issued a fatwa to explain what God's law had to say about Iran's government:

> A political system based on force, oppression, changing people's votes, killing, closure [of civil institutions], arresting [people] and using Stalinist and medieval torture, creating repression, censorship of newspapers, interruption of the means of mass communications, jailing the enlightened and the elite of society for false reasons, and forcing them to make false confessions in jail, is condemned and illegitimate.

The challenge came to nought, and two years later the apparent failure to hold Iran's government to account was underscored by dramatic images of triumphant Arab revolutionaries in Tunisia and Tahrir Square. And yet the legitimacy of the Rulership of Jurists is looking more fragile than ever. In mid-2011, a gulf opened between Grand Ayatollah Khamenei and Mahmoud Ahmadinejad, and conservative theologians rallied to the Supreme Leader's side. Their efforts were not a sign of strength. Every move they made to discredit the man returned to power in 2009 knocked more bricks from Iran's theocratic foundations, because Khamenei could hardly withdraw his earlier claim that Ahmadinejad's reelection was a miracle. It is impossible to say how the crisis will be resolved and easy to predict how it could worsen. Iran's nuclear program is the improbable source of deep nationalist pride among ordinary people, and such passions are easily inflamed or exploited. Ongoing agitation by the long-suppressed Twelver majority in nearby Bahrain inspires similarly volatile emotions, and it could serve several distinct interests to fan sectarian sentiment against the Gulf state's Sunni rulers. Whatever the future may hold, however, the questions opened up in the summer of 2009 are not going to close down anytime soon, and though the Western media tends to focus on young secularists when covering opposition in Iran, it is clerics who pose the most fundamental challenge to the status quo. Many have become convinced that politics is a dirty game and that the institutions created after 1979 are theologically dubious at best and blasphemous at worst.*

---

*Similar concerns outside Iran have further eroded support for Khomeini's concept of a Rulership of Jurists. Grand Ayatollah Mohammad Fadlallah of Lebanon stated in

It does not take many weeks of traveling the Islamic world to realize that there is no single Muslim approach to reason, revelation, or modernity. Groups of believers have developed numerous strategies to distinguish between aspects of religion they consider fundamental and others they think fake. Their efforts to come to terms with the twenty-first century have been defined by imagination at least as much as they have been limited by God. That gives rise to a basic question, however. Any given stance might or might not be sacred, but who has the authority to decide?

There is no simple answer. Islam recognizes no figure equivalent to the pope, capable of resolving earthly disputes with presumed infallibility, and though arguments about religion continue to have tremendous political ramifications, the sacred struggle to understand the shari‘a—*ijtihad*—has always been proper to scholars rather than state officials. Rulers since the Abbasids have draped the trappings of holiness about their regimes, but jurists have historically lent out only a small part of their authority. They always retained exclusive powers to pronounce on most aspects of etiquette, ritual, and morality, and though they argued incessantly among themselves, they did their best collectively to ensure that their prerogatives were never damaged by legal friction. The Malikites of eighth-century Medina proposed and all Sunnis later accepted that a consensual wisdom (*ijma*) could disclose God's will. Muslims loyal to the memory of Ali and Hussein were never keen on that notion—which looked to them like majority rule—but they came to accept, like Sunnis, that honest disagreement (*ikhtilaf*) was blessed. Everyone agreed that they could look beyond the terms of a rule to give effect to the common good (*maslaha*). And scholars laid down a very important bottom line. Admirable though it always was to think about God, they encouraged ordinary believers to leave *ijtihad* to the experts—themselves.

The equilibrium inherent in such ideas evolved over centuries of Islamic expansion, however, and it has largely broken down in the

the spring of 2009 that it had "no role" in his country, for example: Robert L. Pollock, "A Dialogue with Lebanon's Ayatollah," *Wall Street Journal*, March 14, 2009.

modern era. The relationship between scholars and states was tested to the breaking point by the collapse of Islam's last empires. Emigration, partitions, and war have reshuffled believers around the world since then, and Islamic ideas and aspirations are more diverse today than at any time in history. And the trust that scholars once enjoyed among believers has begun to crumble in the fractious new world of nation-states. Even in relatively flexible Twelver communities, where dissatisfied believers are always at liberty to switch their allegiance from one grand ayatollah to another, their authority has been damaged. Among Sunnis, there are millions who think theologians and jurists to be irrelevant or out of touch. The idea has spread that people should work out problems for themselves—simply by reading the Qur'an, perhaps, or by thinking hard about what the Prophet, his companions, and the *salafs* of seventh-century Arabia would have done.

The impact on ideas about deciphering the shari'a has been dramatic. Taking a public stand on God's law was once so great a responsibility that hadiths promised believers a great spiritual reward even if they misconstrued the law (and two spiritual rewards if they didn't). It was so challenging that inadequate pretenders to authority were warned that resolving competing claims was like being slaughtered without a knife. Scholars would turn the awe to their advantage and thereby create their near monopoly over *ijtihad*. But the mystique has been evaporating. Individuals have become proactive in their efforts to find out what God expects of them. Scholars have amplified their own expertise in response. And the consequences have been erratic, to say the least.

The phenomenon is illustrated most clearly by the spread of Islamic legal activity across the electronic media. Activists have been exploiting communications technology since the late 1980s, when taped sermons first began to circulate. Radio, cable, and satellite channels are now noisy with televangelist sermons and chat shows, and anyone with an Internet connection can access an e-Qur'an and a hadith database. But the 1997 launch of IslamQA.com by a protégé of Saudi Arabia's then grand mufti marked the beginning of an online fightback by traditionalists. Almost any Islamic authority with a reputation to maintain was soon asserting itself online; Deoband's scholars alone, as if to compensate for their television boycott, were uploading edicts at a rate of about ten a day by mid-2010. And though many are still new-bies, concentrating on the ritualistic concerns that lie at the shariʿa's core, they are increasingly alert to the complexities of the world in which they have begun to move. Some advise correspondents on how to handle the dangers of virtual blasphemy, for example, while others are analyzing the dangers of electronic intimacy with members of the opposite sex. When a correspondent contacted IslamQA in March 2010 to ask whether it was acceptable to update his Facebook account, the site's cyber muftis ruminated over several ancient hadiths before concluding that it would be a positive sin to do anything else: "It is not permissible for [a person] to write about himself that he is outside or in school, for example, when in fact he is at home, because this is lying. If he forgets to change his status (by typing or writing), he should change it whenever he can. And God knows best."

In certain ways, the explosion of online *ijtihad* today parallels the creation of the madrasa at Deoband in the nineteenth century. Schol-ars, faced with a potentially destabilizing situation, are asserting their traditional power to keep Muslims on the straight and narrow. But the websites are not simply doing more efficiently what muftis have always done. Opinions handed down in person at a madrasa are part of a pro-cess that is relatively confidential and conditioned by customs familiar to both parties. Online fatwa factories, by contrast, have no preexisting connection to their perplexed users. Scholars from Cairo and the Hijaz are resolving the dilemmas of a world where only around one Muslim in eight is Arab, and madrasas such as Deoband are exporting regional perspectives to computer terminals around the planet. As correspon-dents struggle with their consciences and keyboards, curious believers from Chicago to Kuala Lumpur are reading about their problems, and it is impossible to know whether they are learning more about Islam or the sins to which Muslims internationally are prone.

The globalization of confusion might one day homogenize inter-pretations of Islamic law—or curdle them—but whether it does more ultimately to promote harmony or disharmony, the consequence so far has been a moral maelstrom. The muftis often attempt empathy, but their typical response to a cry for help does not exactly meet the ques-tioner halfway. Two Muslim mothers who have fallen in love with each other after being abandoned by their husbands are told that "the solution to this disastrous situation is total separation." An Arab resident in the United States whose American husband has turned against Islam is advised to seek an annulment and immediately leave "that doomed land." A newcomer to the faith, struggling against a penchant for pornography, is urged to "conjure up images of hellfire" and to contemplate what it would be like to die addicted to masturbation. Perversities of all sorts are meanwhile addressed without fear, and though expertise among the muftis must be assumed, inconsistencies abound. It does no one much good to dwell on the details, but the general point is illustrated by the divisions over the lawfulness of oral sex. Whereas the Egyptians at IslamOnline.net told a Belgian correspondent in 2004 that "it is permissible for a husband and a wife to practice cunnilingus and fellatio," the Saudis of Fatwa-Online.com and AskImam.org have repeatedly forbidden both, taking particular pains to prove the impropriety of consuming semen.

It would be conceited, if not downright Salafi, to second-guess the rights and wrongs of such rulings. But the very fact that they exist possesses a great cultural significance. Although any particular opinion might conceivably reflect the settled wisdom of generations, their public proliferation on so immense a scale is generating a confessional culture out of a jurisprudence that has historically stressed the need for discretion. Expanding electronic archives are allowing believers to contemplate previously unimagined dilemmas and temptations. Technological changes to the organization, retrieval, and distribution of religious knowledge stand to alter ideas about faith at least as much as the shift to a written culture once did. It was futile in the ninth century for traditionists to complain that books were an innovation. It is peculiar that the modern heirs of their traditionist legacy act as though online Islam raises no novel moral questions at all.

In order for one to appreciate the significance of that omission, it becomes important to focus on what modern hard-liners *have* considered important. And one of their priorities demands attention above all others. Faced with challenges to their authority, many have championed the enforcement of Islam's ancient criminal penalties, and though they have characterized their cause as traditional, it has been capricious in the extreme. The penalties were first revived by revolutionaries in 1920s Saudi Arabia, and they spread no farther until the 1970s, when military officers in Libya and Pakistan and radical theoreticians in Iran resuscitated them anew. The process was erratic from the outset, and while some scholars were only too eager to grasp the levers of power, the hard-liners have turned out to be singularly uninterested in developing novel ways to control their use. The consequences are set out in the next two chapters.

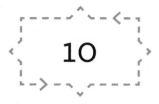

10

Punishment and Pity: The Modern Revival of Islamic Criminal Law

Pakistan is so endemically chaotic that its crises do not conclude—
they mutate—but if any year of the post-9/11 decade could be said to
mark a watershed, it would be 2007. Springtime saw an attempt by the
country's military dictator, Pervez Musharraf, to destroy its last relatively independent organ of government by dismissing the chief justice.
Summer was marked by a military assault on a radical mosque in Islamabad, which killed more than a hundred people holed up within
and set off a nationwide wave of suicide attacks. Burgeoning political
protests by Pakistan's lawyers then led Musharraf to declare a state of
emergency, and the terrible year shuddered to a tragic conclusion on
December 27 with the assassination of the country's best-known civilian politician, Benazir Bhutto.

The tensions were made worse by a steady escalation of military
conflict. Hostilities had been intensifying in neighboring Afghanistan
since mid-2006, and as NATO forces attempted to establish control
over previously stable regions in that country, violence spilled over
into border provinces in northern and eastern Pakistan. The Pakistani
army steadily lost ground, and by the middle of 2008 homegrown insurrectionists associated with the Taliban were entrenched in several
previously peaceful swaths of territory. One of them was the Swat Valley,

a ski resort of mountainous beauty, which the rebels turned into a test-
ing ground for their ideas about the shari'a. Dozens of health centers
and girls' schools were burned down on the basis that polio vaccines and
female education were un-Islamic innovations. Alleged sinners were
simultaneously required to account for themselves at show trials. Every
Friday morning saw an unlucky few produced in the squares and play-
grounds of three of the district's market towns. Anyone found in sufficient violation of the guerrillas' conceptions of Islamic law was liable
to be flogged, beheaded, or shot dead.

It was hard to imagine how Swat's agony could worsen, and imagination then became unnecessary. In the spring of 2009, the insurgents
negotiated a cease-fire with the feeble civilian government that had
taken over from Pervez Musharraf the previous August, and the two
sides agreed to a deal that made it suddenly possible that the lynchings of Swat would be formally recognized as the law of the land. A
proposed administration of justice ordinance delegated to the insurrectionists a right to impose their interpretations of the shari'a across
the several thousand square miles of land that they controlled. And
although secular and religious politicians solemnly predicted that an
era of great tranquillity was at hand, evidence then emerged of what
the administration of justice, Swat-style, might look like. Shortly before my arrival in the Indian subcontinent in April 2009, Pakistani
television stations aired a mobile phone video clip that showed a wail-
ing woman encircled by dozens of men. She was being held down and
beaten with a leather lash. It was said that she was seventeen years old,
and her alleged crime was to have spent time in the company of her
father-in-law without a chaperone.

The footage showed a girl in clear distress, but by comparison to
weekly playground executions it was merely repulsive. Since I was
anticipating that criminal justice would be a contentious topic in the
madrasas I was due to visit, it therefore seemed to offer an almost
tactful way of raising the subject of religious punishment. But when I
first tried to discuss the whipping a few days later, sitting cross-legged
in the rug-strewn computer room of Lucknow's Nadwa madrasa, the
college's chief law lecturer was amazed that I saw fit even to mention
the video. As a clutch of fascinated students watched him, he glowered

at me. "Fake!" he announced. "It is creation of Western media." That view turned out to be widespread, and by the time I reached Pakistan, the only issue of interest to many theologians was which foreign intelligence agency had staged the hoax. When I suggested to a Lahore scholar that a malevolent camera crew would surely have produced more effective propaganda—a full-on decapitation, say—he seemed unsure whether I was deeply sinister or hopelessly naive. My attempt to discuss the underlying issue at Karachi's Jamia Binoria madrasa was no more successful. The director of fatwas, invited to consider whether punishment would have been justified *if* a seventeen-year-old girl had been lashed, would only grin through his vast black beard and offer me a sip of his warm milk. "A mufti," he claimed, "does not deal in hypotheticals."

I had already been around enough muftis to know that there were plenty who dealt in little else. The reticence owed nothing to circumspection. It arose out of the fact that since the Soviet occupation of Afghanistan during the 1980s, Deobandi madrasas have been ubiquitous in the border regions of Pakistan. The sense is widespread that the battles being fought there today are a continuation of that jihad, but such sympathies cannot easily be vocalized, because the quietist traditions of Deoband acknowledge that justice is the prerogative of established rulers alone. And the contradictions then intensified. In mid-April, Swat's rebels not only disavowed their cease-fire; they declared that it was un-Islamic to obey Pakistan's government in any way at all. It was one act of defiance too many. A delegation of senior Deobandi muftis headed for Swat to have words. That was probably good for the movement, but it made it harder than ever to find someone capable of explaining to me the complexities of Islamic criminal justice.

Fortunately, the Deobandis were not the only scholars in town. Their Barelvi rivals command the loyalties of far more Pakistanis, and a friend put me in contact with one of the sect's most highly esteemed jurists, Mufti Munib ur-Rehman. The scholar's expertise extends from Islamic finance to the law of moon sighting—a much-prized competence in a faith that structures many rituals around a lunar calendar—and he expressed himself willing to clarify any uncertainties I might have about Islamic law. We met at a Karachi bank, where he helps to square insurance products with the theological implications of pre-destination, and as teas were poured into porcelain cups, he readily confirmed that Pakistan's Deobandis were in some disarray. They were divided, he explained. Extremists were ascendant among the rank and file, and leaders needed to make very clear that it was *haram* (forbidden) to take up arms against a government. Neither Islam nor Pakistan could tolerate terrorists in its midst.

But when the subject of the video arose, Munib ur-Rehman's urbane appraisal of his rivals suddenly sharpened into a critique of my questions. He was as suspicious of the film's provenance as any Deobandi, and though he maintained that no Muslim should take the law into his own hands, he seemed to find my arguments in favor of a girl that I did not know almost distasteful. He suggested that no lawyer of any caliber would ever try to defend a guilty person and, after revealing that he had studied law himself, observed somewhat uncharitably that certain barristers turn to writing because they are career failures. Apropos of no direct question, he then moved on from sexual immoralities in general to fornication (*zina*) in particular. As and when a married person was properly convicted of the crime, he explained, stoning to death was mandatory. It was one of the fixed-penalty *hadd* transgressions that arose out of duties owed to God; and whereas offenses against the person could be remedied by retaliation, compensation, or forgiveness, offenses against God allowed a judge no discretion. In such cases, so-called human rights had to give way to divine rights. It was sinful even to pity a convict who had committed a *hadd* crime.

The discussion was a reminder that the Barelvi community, for all its syncretism, is capable of accommodating some very uncompromising views. But the fact that Munib ur-Rehman was almost as keen as the guerrillas of Swat to assert the holiness of violent punishment reassured me on at least one point. When this book began, I had worried that an extended examination of criminal justice might encourage those people, of all faiths and none, who falsely equate Islam with every brutality that is inflicted in its name. There are many non-Muslims who imagine that any harsh punishment inflicted by Muslims is essentially Islamic, discounting or ignoring the possibility that it could be motivated by, say, a sympathy for victims or irreligious cynicism. Some radicals are just as eager to embrace punitive violence, as long as the person inflicting it claims to be Islamically inspired. Making sense of the relationship between religious belief and penal law presents a corresponding challenge. But my conversation over tea in Karachi convinced me that it was important to make the effort. Pitiless punishments may not be characteristic of the shari'a, but anyone who insists that they have no place in the Muslim world is ignoring those places where they do.

At the same time as it settled one uncertainty, the dialogue with Munib ur-Rehman opened up others. When I asked him why, in his opinion, God was so eager to kill adulterers, he began by explaining that the suppression of one crime could deter many future criminals. But he then ruminated at considerably greater length about Ma'iz ibn Malik, the young man whose case is described in the first chapter of this book. He pointed out that the Prophet had tried repeatedly to ignore the youth's confession and had put a number of excuses into his mouth. Ma'iz himself had insisted on his guilt, four times, and asked to be purified through stoning. Even then, the Prophet did not try to trace his partner in crime. I wondered why not. Had he not just told me that a person guilty of a *hadd* offense was unworthy of pity? Doubt, explained the mufti, was always a reason to avoid punishment for a crime laid down by the Qur'an. The answer seemed oblique to the point of irrelevance, and when my confusion showed, Munib ur-Rehman tried again to explain his point. His clarification involved another self-confessed seventh-century fornicator. This one was a pregnant woman, and she was spared execution entirely—until her baby had been weaned and found a new home.

There was a cryptic quality to Munib ur-Rehman's responses. I had asked him to justify the punishment for adultery, and he had spent at least as long describing reasons to avoid punishment. And while the hadiths he cited were hardly accounts of innocence vindicated, they were far less bloodcurdling than some stories I had come across. Ahmad ibn Hanbal reported, for example, that the prophet Isa (Jesus) once faced down a crowd that was baying for an adulterer's blood with the words "Let no man stone him who has done what he has done." In a twist on the familiar Gospel tale, all the assembled sinners dropped their rocks—except for John the Baptist (Yahya ibn Zakariya), who impeccably dashed out the sinner's brains. Munib ur-Rehman, by contrast, was upholding violence in principle while setting out all sorts of reasons to avoid it in practice. It was as though a penalty's existence was somehow more important than its use, and as I was to find out, his view reflected an equivocation that is common across the Muslim world.

The standoff in Swat reached a bloody denouement a few weeks after my meeting with Munib ur-Rehman. The rebels' disavowal of democracy led the government to belatedly acknowledge that it was dealing with an enemy rather than a partner, and the regional insurrection was crushed by a military invasion in May 2009. The turmoil then shifted elsewhere, as American drone attacks multiplied in the tribal areas bordering Afghanistan, and al-Qa'eda's leader, Osama bin Laden, continued for a couple more years to be one of the few people in Pakistan who enjoyed a tranquil life. But though the specific crisis informing our conversation became redundant, it raised issues that would stay with me for the rest of the writing of this book. I was left in no doubt that Munib ur-Rehman was inspired by some noble values, including a belief in fairness, and yet his insistence that a punishment might in itself be eternally just threatened to rob those values of any substance. He was right that classical jurisprudence does not make it easy to impose a *hadd*. Judges are advised to avoid such a penalty whenever they harbor doubt (*shubha*) about a defendant's guilt, for example. Repentance prior to arrest automatically precludes punishment for an offense against God, and even if the remorse comes after arrest, there are many situations in which sinners are supposed to be given a second chance. But the difficulty of applying a penalty hardly proves its perfection. And uncorroborated confessions have made for some notoriously unsafe convictions in recent times. Whatever might have been decided pursuant to divine inspiration fourteen hundred years ago, killing vulnerable defendants on the basis that they begged to die was a dangerous model for the twenty-first century.

Although it would sometimes be easy to assume from Western media coverage that Qur'anic penalties are integral to Muslim life, the reality is very different. They are theoretically applicable in fewer than a dozen of the fifty or so states with majority Muslim populations—most of which made them lawful less than thirty years ago—and their application in practice is exceptional. As a matter of history, they have been just as uncommon. Stonings are recorded just once in Ottoman legal history, for example, and they were even less frequent in Syria, where the only known case occurred three centuries *before* the Prophet Muhammad's birth, when a certain Elias was stoned according to Roman law for preaching Christianity. The dearth of courtroom records is no explanation. Muslim chroniclers and Christian travelers were typically fascinated by terrible punishments and tortures, and a penalty such as stoning would almost certainly have been memorialized by any writer who encountered it. Its rarity points to a fact that became increasingly apparent to me as I wrote this book. Islamic states have been capable of much violence in their time, but the *hadd* penalties laid down by the Qur'an have always had a symbolic value far in excess of their practical importance. Upholding them in theory has never been the same as their actual imposition.

That is not to downplay the importance of their resuscitation. It makes it all the more remarkable. The event that marked their revival exemplifies the point with some force. It occurred in the southern Iranian city of Kerman on July 3, 1980, soon after dawn prayers had come to an end. With Iran's revolution in full swing, clerically supervised hangmen and firing squads were working flat out to eliminate supposed drug dealers, perverts, and leftists, but a group of Kerman zealots had just decided that there was a holier way of dealing with enemies of the people. After sunrise, four prisoners were bathed, dressed in white shrouds, and buried in earth up to their chests. Two were said to be prostitutes, one a homosexual, and the fourth a rapist, but all had been convicted of the same crime—fornication. The presiding judge then took a rock from a pre-gathered collection—all of them chosen to ensure a diameter of one to six inches—and hurled it at the captive group. A hail of missiles followed, until all four convicts were dead. The journalist Robert Fisk, reporting on the event for *The Times* of London, was mystified. Iran's judiciary "seems to be possessed of an ever increasing passion of late to stress the rigours of Islamic justice," he observed. But "just why the local court should have visited so terrible a punishment is unclear."

Fisk had good reason to be bewildered. At the time, stonings were the stuff of biblical legend and musty history almost everywhere. The penalty was notionally in force only on the Arabian Peninsula, and though there had been occasional reports of its application—none officially confirmed—the penalty could only have seemed like an atavistic throwback. A fresh-faced army officer by the name of Muammar Qaddafi, who had usurped power in Libya in 1969, had more recently tried to outflank religious opponents by providing for two other Islamic penalties—amputations and whippings—but even they had never been used. Beyond the Arabian Peninsula, there had not been a single stoning officially imposed for around two centuries.

Revolutionary momentum meant, however, that the aberration at Kerman was not going to remain aberrant for long. The ideologue driving it forward, Ayatollah Khomeini, had already formulated legal principles that would make sure of that. He had laid down seven qualifications required to dispense justice in the newly established Islamic Republic. A judge had to be a legitimate postpubescent Muslim male who was versed in the Qur'an, justly inclined, and possessed of his mental faculties—in which case, he could handle any case that might come his way. "He can thus judge and dispose of twenty trials in a single day," explained Khomeini. "Western justice might take years to argue them out." As revolutionary norms were thereby married to ancient Shi'a jurisprudence, stonings proliferated, and by 1982 a penal code was regulating their operation. It stipulated, for example, that adulterers should be killed by stones "not so big that one or two of them may kill the convict, nor . . . so small that they may not be called stones." The same law addressed another procedure that had also been revived—amputations for theft. In honor of the tradition that Caliph Ali had been concerned that first offenders should not stop touching their earlobes during prayer, thieves of previous good character were permitted under the code to keep their palms and thumbs. Iran's Judicial Police designed a mini-guillotine to ensure a neat cut.

As the Shi'a clerics of Iran raced ahead, Sunni efforts to match their achievements began in earnest. Zia ul-Haq of Pakistan had deposed Prime Minister Zulfiqar Bhutto in the summer of 1977 and he initially invoked martial law powers to authorize corporal punishments, but in late 1978, with the Iranian revolution heating up next door, he turned to a higher authority. His authority of choice was Saudi Arabia—and the jurists of Mecca and Medina, concerned by the gathering momentum of radical Shi'ism, were only too willing to help. The result was the enactment in February 1979 of four Hudood Ordinances and the beginning of a new era in Pakistani history. Zia called it "Islamization," and though no one claims it has yet been achieved, there have been politicians and scholars promoting it within the country ever since.

The Saudis then embarked on some legal modernization of their own—by way of a step which illustrated a peculiarity that was beginning to attach to the reformist trend. Their move came in the field of crucifixion. Exposure from a cross is a punishment that the Qur'an authorizes for anyone who has "[made] war against God and His apostle" or "spread disorder in the land." It served historically to humiliate rather than kill, but it could be combined with execution, because the holy book acknowledged those crimes—uniquely—as capital offenses.*
Most classical jurists had construed their definition with commensurate care, establishing a thousand or so years ago that they referred specifically to banditry in the open country: a uniquely destabilizing threat to civil order in a premodern society. But in September 1981, senior Saudi scholars issued a fatwa to advise the kingdom's judges that the rules were changing. With Salafi certitude, they adapted a minority view associated with just one Sunni law school—the Malikites—and ruled that execution and crucifixion ought to be imposed in the case of all sexual abductions, armed robberies, and drug offenses, wherever committed. In another context, updating laws to keep pace with change would make unquestionably good sense. When it was being done by jurists who simultaneously claimed that crucifixion was at some level eternally valid, the legal revamp looked rather more incongruous.

The reality was that the revival of traditional punishments was being structured around modern moral concerns and assumptions. Both Libya and Pakistan had decided not to revive crucifixion at all, a decision that evinced a belief in public relations rather than in God, and their attempts to approximate seventh-century practice seemed sometimes more concerned to improve on tradition than to follow it.

---

*The Qur'an allows for the execution of homicides, but a killer's fate is in the hands not of a judge but of the victim's next of kin, who can elect either to avenge or to forgive: see p. 27. Insofar as several Muslim states punish murder by death, they are relying on extra-Qur'anic *ta'zir* penalties, discussed below.

Libyan thieves were only to be relieved of their hands under general anesthetic, for example, and doctors were given the mystifying instruction to hold off if amputation might "prove dangerous to [the offender's] health." Pakistan's adultery law went so far as to imply that modern weaponry might have made stones redundant. "Such of the witnesses who deposed against the convict as may be available shall start stoning him," it stated, "and, while stoning is being carried on, he may be shot dead, whereupon stoning and shooting shall be stopped." The very existence of written statutes to enshrine such provisions would once have been considered a blasphemous innovation, and yet the codes kept coming. By the end of the 1980s, Mauritania, Sudan, and the United Arab Emirates had also enacted laws to grant courts the power to hand down *hadd* penalties. Somalia, Yemen, Afghanistan, and northern Nigeria followed suit during the 1990s. Even the Iraqi president Saddam Hussein, who was always concerned to keep a tight lid on potentially destabilizing religious sentiment, saw fit to jump on the bandwagon in 1994 with a decree ordering that robbers and car thieves should lose their hands.

The arbitrariness of the reforms ran deeper, for, notwithstanding their pragmatism, they subverted some fundamental political assumptions about the modern state. That was most apparent in the field of retaliation (*qisas*) and blood money (*diyat*). The requirement that citizens choose among punishment, compensation, and forgiveness once served to limit violence—an eye for an eye rather than a life for one, the price of a tooth instead of an actual tooth—and it minimized the risk that anger or accident might spiral into lethal feuds. But as civilizations grew more complex, the idea spread that the public good would be better served by acknowledging a governmental monopoly over the right to use punitive force. In most of the world, that monopoly is nowadays considered an essential attribute of statehood, but in those countries that have revived seventh-century notions of legal order, the process has gone into reverse. Saudi Arabia facilitates the removal of eyes for eyes and teeth for teeth by way of forcible blindings and compulsory dental work at Medina's King Fahd Hospital. Judges there and in Iran have considered authorizing even more imaginative forms of retaliation: the removal of a spine and the dripping of acid into a defendant's eyes, for example. And though the opportunity to demand or waive such agonies is sometimes portrayed as a vindication of victims' rights, the claim is spurious. The rich are always liable to buy themselves impunity by paying blood money, and a Somalian case of May 2006 serves as a graphic reminder of why, in any event, the individual's desire for revenge can never convincingly be called justice. A militia known as the Islamic Courts Union liberated a war-torn Mogadishu in that month and announced that the shari'a was in force. Its judges gave sixteen-year-old Mohamed Moallim permission to avenge his murdered father, so long as he made sure to mirror the original crime. Hundreds of people turned out to watch the boy take a knife to forty-five-year-old Omar Hussein, who was tied to a post, and stab him repeatedly in the head and throat.

There is one more aspect of the revival of Islamic criminal justice, conceptually distinct from those mandatory penalties imposed for *hadd* crimes and the personal right of revenge enshrined in the Qur'an, that is in many ways the most significant of all. A jurisdiction to hand down discretionary penalties known as *ta'zir*, which developed in the seventh century as the judicial equivalent of the executive's *siyasa* power, allows for the punishment of any sin that carries no explicit sentence in the holy book. Having originated at a time of upheaval and military expansion, the right to impose a *ta'zir* was never counterbalanced by the safeguards that the Qur'an required for *hadd* punishments, and a judge can therefore take account of retracted confessions, vague suspicions, and his own personal knowledge about a case, among other things, and convict even if the evidence leaves room for doubt.

In the modern context, that has made for some fearsomely freewheeling powers. Modern Iran authorizes courts to order seventy-four strokes of the whip for breach of "any religious taboo" and ninety-nine for an offense against public morals—a category of crime that can cover attendance at a party. Saudi judges are even less constrained and can potentially impose all but unlimited corporal punishments if they feel that a religious norm has been violated. And hard-liners have used the legal discretion to give effect to some predictable prejudices. Whereas relics of paganism such as forced marriages and clitoridectomy are subject to no more than scholarly disapproval, the Qur'an's call for feminine modesty has been taken as a cue to punish women who are badly veiled (in Saudi Arabia), poorly head scarfed (in Iran), or trousered in any way at all (in Sudan).

Channeling modern state power through *ta'zir* penalties has had a particularly marked effect on the tradition, deeply rooted in Muslim history, that private sins lie beyond the reach of earthly judges. Whereas the ninth-century writer al-Jahiz merely mused on the intimacies that were left unregulated by *zina*'s focus on vaginal penetration ("How near is what God permits to what he forbids!"), moralists today are claiming to police the bedroom. On the strength of an ambiguous passage in the Qur'an, several Muslim countries punish lesbianism by whipping. At least six allow for male homosexuals to be sentenced to death. Privacy can even be a positively aggravating factor, due to a hadith that warns that the devil is always present when an unrelated man and woman are alone, and a shocking 2006 case illustrated where a diabolical threesome can lead in a twenty-first-century *ta'zir* jurisdiction. A married teenager and a male friend from the Saudi city of Qatif were given ninety lashes for sitting in a car unchaperoned—even though their assignation came to light only because both had been dragged from the vehicle and repeatedly raped by seven men. When the girl appealed, backed by her supportive husband and a tenacious defense attorney, her sentence was *increased* to two hundred lashes and six months in prison. An outcry finally caused King Abdullah to step in with a pardon. The lawyer, Abdul Rahman al-Lahem, had to spend several more weeks fending off a disciplinary complaint from a judge who thought him impertinent for challenging the sentence.

It is not easy to establish how *ta'zir* penalties are operating in practice to complement the emblematic *hadd* crimes. Secrecy rather than pride usually marks their imposition, and the Saudi judicial system specifically is characterized by deep but obscure divisions. There is perennial conflict between relatively liberal ministers and conservative judges, and its defense lawyers are, in any event, not helped by open association with Westerners. But there is one country where the judicial system is more accessible—Pakistan—and it contains lawyers who understand the realities of Islamic criminal law better than anyone else in the world. One of the most prominent, whom I met in Lahore on December 12, 2008, is Asma Jahangir. With her equally formidable sister

Hina Jilani, she has been at the forefront of efforts to counter the discriminatory impact of Zia ul-Haq's laws ever since 1980, when she established a women's legal aid center while still in her twenties. The Human Rights Commission that she later cofounded is widely regarded as one of Pakistan's most effective nongovernmental organizations, and conservative fury consequently falls on her as surely as lightning to a rod. Legislators have abused her on the floor of the national senate, and her career has been shadowed by violence. There have been regular public protests and murder threats, and just months before my visit a religious columnist for Lahore's *Din* newspaper had invited readers to consider whether Jahangir's activities might have made her "worthy of death."

I found her at a reassuringly anonymous office, amid the bougainvillea, ice-cream parlors, and retail precincts of a leafy Lahore suburb. A young Benazir Bhutto laughed out of a photograph behind her desk, and cartoon mullahs glared back at them both from a phalanx of picture frames on the opposite wall. Examining the doodles, all teeth and beards and skullcaps, I looked for some familiar faces. She smiled, lighting the first of countless cigarettes, and doubted that I would recognize anyone. "Maybe you will. But the fundies [fundamentalists] are not so easy to tell apart." Pleasantries exchanged, I explained that the realities of Islamic criminal justice were what interested me, and she had a very definite idea about where our discussion should begin. It was not with the provisions of Pakistani statutory law but in Swat. The regional insurrection was reaching its peak at the time of our meeting, and she had just learned that locals were being forced not just to accept whippings, shootings, and decapitations but also to attend them. The intimidation was proving effective. "Some of our human rights workers have psychologically surrendered," she told me. "They had no option. The military does not support them. The police do not protect them. They get killed if they are found to be even vaguely opposing the militants. The same people who once told me that 'the Taliban is barbaric' now say, 'They have their own form of justice because they give you three warnings before chopping your head off.'"

It was a good starting point. Events over the next few months would confirm Jahangir's account, but in late 2008 I was still entirely unsure how to understand the modern revival of Islamic criminal law, and her remarks touched off a question that had been playing on my mind since my arrival in Pakistan. The country's citizens have always had an unusual faith in the law. Ever since the 1950s, they have been challenging the legality of coups and emergency measures in courts, and in August 2008, just a few months before my visit, the dictatorship of Pervez Musharraf had been brought down as a consequence of protests that had been spearheaded by lawyers. Although beheadings on notice could hardly be considered a model of legality, it was at least arguable that the judicial violence in Swat was grounded in aspirations as well as intimidation. The original Taliban swept to power in Afghanistan on a wave of popular support, and the Qur'an-and-Kalashnikov-wielding judges of the Islamic Courts Union were seen as liberators by many Somalis after fifteen years of civil war in 2006. The peaceful introduction of ostensibly Islamic law in northern Nigeria was also extremely popular, with many locals jubilant that the authorities might at last be about to tackle social evils such as graft, drunkenness, and gambling. Fears shadow such enthusiasm and horrors have followed it, but might its appeal not reflect a simple longing for justice?

Jahangir would have none of it. "I'm not so sure that the violence has ever had any appeal at all," she replied firmly. "During Zia's regime there was a huge outcry against his penalties. The police were once made to round up people to watch a public hanging. Even in a city as vast as Lahore, they only got ten thousand people. Everyone else was sitting outside, horrified. There were no amputations or stonings—but not because Zia ul-Haq had any real inhibitions about imposing them, or any compassion. It's because he knew that they would create even greater outrage. And though there were some public whippings, my recollection is that people were absolutely horrified. There was a kind of deadly silence across the country."

She spoke with a wistfulness that, at the time, made me suspect she was being a tad nostalgic. A later trawl through newspaper records proved, however, that her memory was more reliable than my skepticism. Pakistan's first open-air whippings in late 1977 and early 1978, staged pursuant to martial law regulations, drew crowds of up to 100,000. But though the government strove to keep everyone entertained—going so far as to wire microphones to its flogging frames—its efforts were already losing hearts and minds on March 23, 1978, when *The Times* of London referred to the "many glum faces" who watched three hooded criminals swing from a public gallows in Lahore. Executions were soon being canceled for want of an audience, and by the time Zia enacted his Hudood Ordinances in February 1979, disenchantment had firmly set in. One last public lashing in November managed to draw 10,000 people, but the Islamization of martial law brutalities did not popularize them. Spectacular judicial punishments then vanished from Pakistan's streets entirely, never to return.

The genesis of General Zia's supposedly Islamic laws is a salutary reminder of the limits of politicized religion in Pakistan. Parties that directly credit God for their policies have only once polled in the double digits—after a cyclonic year of protests that followed the U.S.-led invasion of Afghanistan in late 2001—and their share of the vote has since fallen back to well under 5 percent. As Jahangir reminded me, the country's medical profession collectively refused to supervise amputations throughout the 1980s, and more than three decades of official Islamization have so far failed to produce a single actual stoning or amputation. And yet, as she also made clear, the secular sentiment that still holds sway in the country has coexisted with systematic injustices that often claim Islam as their justification. Thousands of people have been jailed on trumped-up adultery charges, the overwhelming majority of them women. Husbands have abandoned spouses, secure in their own religious right to polygamy, and reported them to the police if they then found a new partner. Daughters who marry without the permission of a possessive father have been jailed on the pretext that they were having sex out of wedlock. Women have even been murdered in the name of "honor" (*izzat*), on the basis of regional customs that are disguised as God's will.

The most egregious cases have involved rape complainants. Victims of sexual assaults everywhere run the risk that their supposedly loose character or a delay in coming forward will be held against them, but the worst outcome is usually that an assailant will go free. The consequences in Pakistan have sometimes been far harsher. One case can stand for dozens of others. It involved a pregnant fifteen-year-old orphan named Jehan Mina who told her uncle in September 1982 that his brother-in-law and her cousin had both forced themselves on her while she had been looking after his ill sister. He complained on her behalf to the police, and both men were charged with *zina-bi'l-jabr*—nonconsensual sexual intercourse outside marriage. The stringent evidentiary requirements laid down by the Qur'an—a confession or four male eyewitnesses to the act of penetration—ensured their acquittal. But that was not the end of the matter. The girl herself was now charged and convicted of fornication, and when she appealed, the court sidestepped the difficulties of proving the *hadd* crime by using its *ta'zir* powers. The defendant's "unexplained pregnancy coupled with the fact that she is not a married girl" was sufficient to prove guilt. Taking account of "her tender age . . . and the fact that her father was dead and her mother had contracted another marriage," the court decided to be lenient. She would be lashed ten times and serve three years of rigorous imprisonment, once her baby had reached the age of two.

It could have been worse. Sudan's courts have been known to rule that a rape complainant who fails to prove an accusation is guilty of falsely imputing unchastity to her assailant—the *hadd* crime of *qazf*, for which the Qur'an prescribes eighty lashes—and Iran's penal code contains an explicit provision to similar effect. But whatever may be inspiring such notions, it is not God. The crime of *qazf* became the subject of revelations specifically in order to *protect* women, after the slur of infidelity was leveled against Muhammad's wife A'isha. The Qur'an and hadiths frequently enjoin men to treat women with respect, and Islamic jurisprudence in all other contexts presumes innocence and acknowledges a right to silence. It was not God who decided to treat rape victims as capital offenders and pregnancies as confessions; it was men.

There are countless Pakistanis who, to their credit, have never failed to appreciate that claiming divine authority is not the same as possessing it, and the last few years have seen some important changes. In July 2006, about thirteen hundred alleged adulterers were released from custody on bail. A series of debates that a satellite television channel promoted under a suitably sensitive title—"Is the Hudood Ordinance (Man's Interpretation of Allah's Law) Islamic?"—then helped pave the way to a significant legal reform. The Protection of Women Act, passed in November 2006, returned rape cases to the jurisdiction of ordinary criminal courts and obliged police officers to obtain a warrant before arresting women for *zina*. As legislative overhauls go, it was fairly timid. It even left stoning on the statute books. But it caused pandemonium. Mosque leaders organized protests across the country, and religious parties boycotted the parliamentary vote on the basis that it was inaugurating an era of "free sex." Even Ayman al-Zawahiri, al-Qa'eda's then second-in-command, took time out from his other concerns to pander to the passions. He warned in a video that attempts to erode Pakistan's adultery law were part of a great "crusader" plot. Its sinister intent, he believed, was to portray Islam as a religion of "enlightened moderation."

The most influential critic of the reform was a high-profile Deobandi mufti named Muhammad Taqi Usmani. He had long argued that Pakistan's adultery laws were entirely gender neutral,* and he characterized the Protection of Women Act as an overreaction to a few instances of police abuse. The argument was rational, if not entirely plausible, but his response to one aspect of the reform showed the true reason for his opposition to the proposed law. It was that the Protection of Women Act authorized leniency for a crime that he thought unforgivable—literally. In relation to a clause that entitled convicted adulterers for the first time to petition provincial governors for clemency, he argued that the Prophet would have amputated his own daughter's hand had she ever committed a theft and that "no one has the right to reduce or forgive" a *hadd*. The theology was doubtless deeply felt, but it sat very uneasily with popular ideas about Islamic justice. Every good Sunni child learns how wise Caliph Umar was to suspend amputations for theft during a year of famine, and Ali's compassion for the wretched and downtrodden is proverbial. The Qur'an teaches that God values forgiveness ("if a man charitably forbears from retaliation, his remission

---

*See his "Islamization of Laws in Pakistan: The Case of Hudud Ordinances," published online via www.muftitaqiusmani.com. Taqi Usmani relied in part on a 1988 article by an American academic, and in view of the seriousness with which some people regard his scholarship, it is worth noting here that the most salient finding of that article is fundamentally flawed. According to Charles H. Kennedy, an assistant professor from North Carolina: "One may have legitimate quarrels with the implementation of [Pakistan's adultery statute], but gender bias against women is not one of them" ("Islamization in Pakistan," p. 313). Kennedy reached that mistaken view because he compared male and female conviction statistics as though they were alike, ignoring the fact that most men would have been rapists, whereas the women would all have been rape victims or alleged consenting adulterers. See also Jahangir and Jilani, *Hudood Ordinances*, pp. 137–38.

shall atone for him") and that the Prophet Muhammad was divinely recognized to be the bringer of mercy to the world. For Usmani, however, it was punitive traditions alone that merited emulation. Someone sentenced to a *hadd* was to be denied not only mercy but the right to beg for it.

A face-to-face discussion with Mufti Taqi Usmani would have been interesting, but it was not to be. At a time when Pakistan's Deobandis were in crisis over the situation in Swat, his schedule was permanently full. On the basis of an assurance from his secretary that the scholar's books and website would tell me all I needed to know, I read up on him instead, and it quickly became clear that he had been equally busy for the previous three decades. Alongside Arab colleagues, he has formulated influential new ways of redefining contractual transactions as profit-sharing operations, helping thereby to create a market in Islamic financial products that is today worth billions. He has diverged from the Deobandi mainstream on the vexed subject of televisions, drawing a distinction between frivolously watching broadcasts and piously appearing on them—and has found his own reasoning so persuasive that he regularly holds forth on Pakistan's satellite channels. But his concern to reconfigure Islamic jurisprudence also had a very definite limit, which was reflected in his fears about the Protection of Women Act—a view that it was impermissible to acknowledge any ideas about law or morality that do not derive directly and exclusively from an established Islamic source.

The concern has loomed large in Taqi Usmani's thought ever since he first emerged on the scholarly scene. He memorably gave it voice in 1984, at a religious conference attended by President Zia ul-Haq. At a time when most Pakistani theologians still had a very cautious view about reopening issues of Islamic law—because God had long ago closed "the gate of *ijtihad*"—the forty-one-year-old urged a more dynamic attitude. There was no shortage of fine minds capable of interpreting the shari'a, he averred, and it was "sheer propaganda" to argue otherwise. But there was a darker aspect to his optimism. Certain unqualified people were exploiting *ijtihad* in the hope of contaminating Islamic law with Western ideas, he said. It had even been suggested that the Qur'an's call to amputate thieves' hands could be read as a metaphor rather than a literal command. With a figure of speech that might have signified very dark humor in anyone else, he warned that *ijtihad* was therefore a "double-edged sword."

The speech, for all its bravado, reflected serious obstacles on the road toward Islamization that had first become apparent a couple of years earlier. In March 1981, the Federal Shariat [*sic*] Court set up by President Zia ul-Haq had gone rogue. Having been set up to strike down laws that were "repugnant to the injunctions of Islam," its judges had ruled in an adultery appeal that stoning people to death was itself repugnantly un-Islamic. An outraged Zia had swiftly packed the court with more like-minded judges, one of whom was Usmani himself, and it had duly overruled itself, but the incident was the first sign of a tendency that has dogged Islamization ever since. Although the Federal Shariat Court could never be called a force for liberalism, practicalities have required that lawyers make up a permanent majority of its members, and their professional training, based on English common-law principles, has always restrained its radical potential. Sacred language and spiritual exhortation figure in all its decisions, but they are invariably combined with a residual respect for ideas such as due process and international human rights norms. And one consequence has been that the court has found technical flaws in every stoning and amputation appeal that it has ever heard.

The upshot is that legal Islamization is, like so many other aspects of Pakistani life, a compromise and a battleground at the same time. Every court in Pakistan must strain for interpretations of the law that promote Islamic principles, but a colonial accident means that the professionals who argue and judge cases think in terms of Anglo-American common-law principles. The critical question has been whether the men with power perceive Islamic jurisprudence as a body of rules above international standards or one consistent with such standards. Muhammad Taqi Usmani's approach was clear enough. He was no longer on the bench, however, and in April 2009 the court's then chief justice, an erudite seventy-eight-year-old occasional playwright and poet, made clear in an interview with me that alternative perspectives still survived in Pakistan.

Haziq ul-Khairi graciously agreed to receive me at his Karachi residence: an elegant but fortified villa, identifiable by the sandbagged bunkers and machine-gun emplacements that mark professional distinction in modern Pakistan. As servants wheeled in trolleys of refreshments, he spoke about Islam's compatibility with international human rights norms and revealed that he had helped draft the Protection of Women Act—an achievement he considered to be the pinnacle of his career. Among several recent decisions we discussed was one in which the Federal Shariat Court had ruled that Pakistani women had the same right as men to pass on their nationality to spouses. Gender discrimination was "repugnant to the injunctions of Islam," his court had explained—citing reams of holy text and a verse of the Qur'an that supposedly required Pakistan's government to fulfill its treaty obligations under the Universal Declaration of Human Rights.

But when our chat then turned to the legal theories that had produced judgments such as the one against the fifteen-year-old rape victim Jehan Mina, a sudden despondency shadowed his face. He recalled the many evidential safeguards laid down in the Qur'an and classical jurisprudence but only shook his head when reminded that pregnancy had been proof enough to order a whipping in her case. And there was one matter into which he refused to be drawn at all. He thought it inappropriate to comment on the jurisprudential contributions of the court's former members, such as Muhammad Taqi Usmani. In respect to three religious judges who currently sat alongside the court's five trained lawyers, he was similarly discreet. The only clue to his thoughts came from his observation that they lacked expertise in certain fields—specifically, "the penal code, the criminal procedure code, and the law of evidence."

Haziq ul-Khairi cut a very sympathetic figure, and his decency is only enhanced in retrospect by the fact that after his retirement in the summer of 2009, his successor's court struck down four sections of the Protection of Women Act. But I left the meeting dispirited nonetheless. In the face of reactionaries who dare to deny that mercy has jurisprudential significance, it seemed almost as though he was smuggling leniency into the system. Another court ruling that he showed me illustrated the point well. It concerned three bank robbers whose amputation sentences were commuted to ten-year jail terms. The result seemed fair enough, but the court had reached it only by a very convoluted route. It had found that the trial judge had been mistaken to believe a witness who admitted to praying irregularly over one who claimed to be more observant. It certainly *might* have been the case that the more ostentatiously pious man gave more reliable evidence. Only the most credulous of believers can honestly argue, however, that people who go to mosques necessarily give more accurate testimony than anyone else, and it seemed very likely that the Federal Shariat Court's reasoning had been colored by its concern to avoid amputation.

The meeting with Haziq ul-Khairi thereby sensitized me to another of the many ambiguities that attaches to Islamic criminal justice. Although it had become all too clear that judges sometimes exploit religion in order to inflict violence, I had not previously taken on board the extent to which Islamic law facilitated the opposite phenomenon: the manipulation of mercy. Paradoxically enough, the punishment of the pregnant teenager Jehan Mina recalls a good example of the process at work. Classical jurists long ago developed fantastic presumptions to minimize the possibility that the pregnancy of a single woman would be considered reason to stone her to death. Hanafites mitigated the risks by ruling that gestation could last for as long as two years—which, in cultures where women were frequently divorced or bereaved, was often a lifeline. Shafi'ites then doubled that period, while Malikites estimated the maximum at five years, encouraged by their own founder's claim to have spent three years in the womb. The Hanbalites acknowledged that impregnation was no proof of illicit sex by way of a particularly memorable precedent: a claim that Caliph Umar once acquitted an expectant mother when she told him that she was a "heavy sleeper" who had undergone intercourse without realizing it. And such rules have come to the rescue of merciful modern judges in search of a rationale. In March 2002, an appellate court in the north Nigerian state of Sokoto overturned a stoning sentence for adultery on the basis that the divorced defendant, Safiyatu Hussaini, might have been carrying her baby for as long as five years. Eighteen months later, the Katsina state court of appeal assessed the upper limit at a full seven.

In themselves, legal fictions are neither remarkable nor objectionable. Assuming unproved matters to be true can help deal with situations where resolution is more important than accuracy, and it can be a useful way of addressing messy factual situations with minimal complexity. A false assumption that circumvents an otherwise mandatory death penalty raises some fairly fundamental questions about the utility of the underlying rule, however; and that points toward the most remarkable aspect of the modern revival of Islamic law. Just as the *hadd* penalties have been applied only exceptionally in history, those modern states that have so publicly enshrined them over the past few decades have gone to great lengths to avoid their imposition. Even Saudi Arabia managed no more than four stonings and forty-five amputations during the 1980s, and in those countries for which more recent statistics are available, the punishments are remarkable only for their infrequency. The courts of Pakistan have avoided enforcement of the *hadd* penalties entirely, extrajudicial lynchings and guerrilla activity notwithstanding. Colonel Qaddafi's Libya conducted just one official amputation, in a 2003 case involving a four-man robbery gang. Northern Nigeria has claimed about the same number of hands in total, and as a result of the ingenuity displayed in the two adultery appeals just mentioned, it has not carried out any stonings at all. Even the finger slicers of Iran have fallen into relative disuse in recent years, and adultery prosecutions have repeatedly fizzled out since the country's senior judicial official declared in December 2002 that stonings to death were in "suspension." A suspended punishment is not the same as an abolished one, especially in a country where jurists expect an invisible imam imminently to rematerialize and enforce God's law throughout the universe, but it is yet more evidence of the same basic point. Hard-liners everywhere are struggling to circumvent the penalties that they publicly declare to be the most sacred ones that any Muslim judge can enforce.

The contradiction is not new. Muslim jurists have always disagreed over the extent to which *ta'zir* penalties should be considered divine in nature, but *hadd*s symbolize the certainty with which God delivered humanity from injustice, chaos, and ignorance. At the same time, centuries of practice reflect a widespread sense that faith should not depend on controlling people by force. The consequence has been equivocation. Similar oppositions have existed in many other cultures, and many ancient Western laws, from blasphemy to capital treason, have lasted long past the world that brought them into being, thanks to a conservative respect for legal symbolism. But when a system of penalties is enforced only erratically in every country where it is found, the time has come for a candid debate about the social evils that it is seeking to control. It cannot be right that Muslim judges have to resort to scientific impossibilities to commute death sentences or that legal systems acknowledge mercy only through anesthetized amputations and shotgun-assisted stonings. Traditions of leniency, pity, and forgiveness are valued for reasons, and those reasons deserve to be elucidated with at least as much urgency as the hunger to punish is satisfied.

The revivalists who seek to promote Islam through corporal and capital punishment typically portray judicial rigor as a matter of cosmic significance. Whippings and amputations are seen as incentives to repentance, marking sins on earth and erasing them in heaven. Laxness in imposing such measures is thought meanwhile to involve a potentially disastrous confusion of the permissible (*halal*) and the forbidden (*haram*): it has become increasingly common to hear scholars argue in Iran and Pakistan that adultery can set off earthquakes, for example, and that stonings are an essential precaution against future seismic disturbance. One Shi'a cleric I met in Karachi believed that the Qur'an's balance of protections and punishments was a glimpse of paradise itself. Maulana Asghar Shaheedi acknowledged that it might seem irrational to introduce such perfection to an impure society—"like making a horse push a cart"—but he had no doubt that all would come right in the end. When I worried about inconsistencies—the possibility that a Sunni thief would have his hand chopped off while a Shi'a codefendant lost a mere four fingers, for example—he expressed confidence that such "modalities" could be resolved through debate, and he chided my suggestion that some miscarriages of justice would be irreversible. "That problem only arises when we think in terms of this world," he explained. "If we have only a worldly vision, you are right, there is no compensation. But if our vision is stronger, we have reason to hope that a wrongly convicted person will receive a reward in the hereafter."

The ethereal perspectives obscure some very mundane realities. In a world where power is necessarily vested in human beings, the perfect lash and the unerring amputation are fantasies. The criminal justice regimes that purport today to be eternally Islamic are creatures of modernity—innovations even—that originated in the aftermath of some thoroughly twentieth-century power grabs: the Saudi takeover of the

1920s, and coups and revolutions half a century later in Libya, Pakistan, and Iran. Their imposition of *hadd* penalties is entirely haphazard, and judges are immeasurably more likely to rely on *ta'zir* powers, which are not constrained even in theory by the procedural safeguards laid down in the Qur'an. And visions of faith have been at least as likely to inspire injustice as to restrain it. In January 2010, for example, two Iranian dissenters were hanged for organizing protests against the previous year's election results—a crime that prosecutors characterized as the "waging [of] war against God."

That is not, however, the last word. Punishments certainly do not become infallible just because a legislature or judge labels them Islamic, but any rational assessment of their use and abuse ought to look beyond the supernatural justifications advanced in their favor to the sociological factors underpinning their application. And that offers a reminder that the penalties are not quite as singularly Islamic as they sometimes appear. They offer swift and exemplary retribution, and the universal appeal of that promise was vividly illustrated by reactions to a Saudi court's decision in June 2009 to convict Muhammad Basheer al-Ramaly of "spreading disorder in the land." The twenty-two-year-old had kidnapped, raped, and sadistically murdered several young boys, and the court sentenced him to be not just executed but crucified. His day of reckoning on December 7 would actually be less exciting than it sounded—involving the display of his beheaded remains for a few hours on top of a pole—but as news of a Muslim "crucifixion" ricocheted through cyberspace, Western law-and-order enthusiasts found themselves on the horns of a dilemma. Though loath to acknowledge that Arabs could get anything right, they found it hard to formulate a meaningful objection. A few reconciled racism and bloodlust by proposing that a less primitive people would hang al-Ramaly by the neck or give him a lethal injection instead. But many simply took their hats off to the Saudis. The comments section of the British *Daily Mail* attracted some especially loquacious supporters. According to the most highly rated of 844 commentators: "A good punishment for a sick peado [*sic*]. Why can't we hand out this very appropriate sentence to UK offenders? Put it this way, he won't re-offend, or cost the taxpayer anything in the future."

Even if the pros and cons of crucifying pedophiles are left to one side, there are aspects of al-Ramaly's fate that merit emphasis. The Saudi resort to spectacular bloodshed tapped some mysterious forces, but they were not spiritual; they were visceral, and they are perennially exploited by lethally punitive regimes the world over. That is why Saudi Arabia (like Iran) appears year after year close to the top of global death penalty league tables, alongside several countries of a definitively un-Islamic nature—China and the United States, for example. And though its presence there might seem unremarkable, that is only because hard-liners have turned Islamic penal history on its head. The Qur'an allows for executions in just two situations—neither of them mandatory. At the time of the Abbasid caliphate's foundation, traditions of judicial restraint were so ingrained that scholars would weep in court rather than judge in God's name. Over the next millennium, Islamic legal systems were consistently and significantly less violent than their European counterparts, and ordinary Muslims were incomparably more likely to seek advice about the shari'a than to demand its enforcement. The truly remarkable fact is that hard-liners have managed in the space of less than forty years to make that history seem surprising—and that they have associated the shari'a in many people's minds with some of the deadliest legal systems on the planet.

Their practical successes are incontestable, however, and upheavals in the Arab world since early 2011 have opened up the possibility that a new wave of radicalization is imminent. Several of the factors underlying the original revival—anger at corruption, invasions, and foreign occupation—are at least as significant today as they were a generation ago. But though there are bound to be calls to realign legal systems along Islamic lines, the chances of a revolutionary restructuring of criminal laws are minimal. It is gradualism that characterizes successful Islamic political parties today, and the most dynamic one in the modern Middle East, the Muslim Brotherhood, has a distinctly ambivalent approach toward the *hadd* penalties prescribed by the Qur'an. The moral rigor that they symbolize makes them nonnegotiable in principle, but practical plans to put them into effect are given a very low priority. The prevailing view is similar to one that was expressed to me by the president of another avowedly reformist movement: Pakistan's Jamaat e-Islami. "Unless and until we get a just society," Syed Munawar Hassan said, "the question of punishment is just a footnote."

It might seem melancholy to think of violent penalties as a long-term goal, and bizarre to portray coercion as a consequence of justice, rather than a regrettable necessity. Some humanitarians find the outlook incredible and claim that the aspirations themselves must be challenged. But the equivocation is real, and it creates an important space for compromise. It accords due respect to the sacred status of the Qur'an and the symbolic power of its words, while honoring truths on which all sides can agree. Justice presents challenges that are bigger than a rock, a noose, or a whip. And though religion always has imperatives, whenever it starts to depend on compulsion rather than attraction to win followers, it destroys the faith that it is supposed to instill. Al-Ghazali once expressed the point pithily, with an insight he attributed to the Prophet Muhammad. "If men had been forbidden to make porridge out of camel's dung, they would have done it," he observed, "saying that [it] would not have been forbidden unless there had been some good in it."

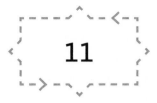

11

"No Compulsion in Religion"? Apostasy, Blasphemy, and Tolerance

As dawn broke on the morning of March 26, 922, an elderly man in a black woolen robe was escorted out of the police headquarters at the western end of Baghdad's bridge of boats. The prisoner was a well-known Sufi named Mansur al-Hallaj who had recently been found in possession of an incriminating document. It claimed that a truly pure Muslim might not need to make a physical pilgrimage to Mecca and that ritualized prayers in one's own house could in some circumstances please God just as much. The two judges called upon to consider the case had both found the opinion itself to be heretical, but they had disagreed over the legal consequences that flowed from al-Hallaj's ownership of the document. One of them, a Hanafite, had ruled that the mystic could escape punishment by disavowing any belief in the heresy. But the second, a Malikite, had found him to be incapable of sincere repentance and liable to execution. It had fallen to Caliph al-Muqtadir's vizier to choose between the two opinions. And driven by hopes of discrediting certain figures who had associated themselves with the Sufi, he had decided that al-Hallaj should die.

Al-Hallaj was no stranger to controversy. As a younger man he had trekked from Arabia to Kashmir with a troupe of disciples, and he had returned to Baghdad with a flamboyant approach to faith very different from the introverted asceticism characteristic of tenth-century Muslim mystics. Sufis of the time were expected to conceal their access to divine power, but it was said of al-Hallaj that he had lit four hundred oil lamps in Jerusalem's Church of the Holy Sepulchre with his finger and extinguished an eternal Zoroastrian flame with the tug of a sleeve. He was well-known for producing fish in the desert and fruits out of season, and his performances were so smooth that even the glitches were miraculous. After he once plucked an apple from the air, claiming to have pulled it out of paradise, a puzzled spectator found it to contain a worm. Thus, observed al-Hallaj, did the earth corrupt. He was just as showy about his intimacy with God. He predicted that heaven would crumble and hellfire cool in his presence, and it was scandalously rumored that he so valued his own purity that he fed admirers his excrement. He even declared himself to be "the Truth," one of the ninety-nine names attributed by tradition to the divinity. Other Sufis turned to God in the hope of annihilating their egos, but none before al-Hallaj had publicly claimed to become Him.

A man so colorful was always going to get a good send-off, and Baghdadis turned out to the banks of the Tigris in their thousands. Whether they came out of respect, curiosity, or bloodlust, no one would have been entirely sure what the day held in store. Al-Hallaj himself had long expressed an eagerness to suffer martyrdom, but there were strong indications that God might have other plans. A previous attempt to punish al-Hallaj had supposedly seen the flogger's hand wither when he raised his whip, and it was impossible to know what the mystic might pull off in extremis. The Sufi's verbal powers alone were causing the vizier concern. "Even if he says to you: I am going to make the Euphrates flow with gold and silver for you, don't listen to him," he warned the executioner. "Don't answer him, don't interrupt his punishment."

The vizier's fear was as unfounded as the hopes of al-Hallaj's followers. As the Sufi rose from his final prayer—a plea for God to forgive his killers, because "if You had revealed to them that which You have revealed to me, they would not do what they are doing"—the executioner smashed a fist into his face. The old man, streaming with blood, urged his tormentor to wait awhile because he had wisdom "as valuable as Constantinople," only to be lashed into unconsciousness. He was then decapitated, and after his head had been set on a spike at the center of the bridge with an accusatory note pinned to its ear, his hands and feet were cut off. Hoisted onto a gibbet, his body was then doused in oil and set alight. His acolytes would soon be putting it about that their master had been replaced at the moment of death by a sinful doppelgänger or, more mysteriously, by a mule. Others would detect his posthumous presence in a bursting of the Tigris's banks a month later. But al-Hallaj's physical being had come to a certain end. As dusk descended at the pontoon on the evening of his execution, all that met the eye was a solitary Sufi squatting over the pyre's embers, scratching at them with a stick, and asking them softly to speak the Truth.

In an age when Muslim beheaders are in the news only too often, it is easy to assume that al-Hallaj fell victim to a totalitarian belief system. But it was far from conventional to punish heresy in the tenth century. The Sufi's views were so acceptable that a cenotaph was quickly built on the site of his execution, and it drew pilgrims for a millennium, until swept away by one Tigris flood too many during the 1920s. To this day, he is considered a martyr by millions. Heretics were warned in the Qur'an of hellish terrors to come, but it was submission and repentance to which they were urged on earth. A couple of hadiths prescribed execution, but it was widely believed that backsliders who repented by articulating the *shahada*—the recitation of belief that God was unique and that Muhammad was His messenger—had to be forgiven. Any further measures were for God alone to impose. The Prophet had reportedly upheld the principle even in extreme situations. Upbraiding a follower for killing a raider who had uttered the *shahada*, Muhammad had been unimpressed by claims that the dead man had adopted Islam only for fear of death. "Who will absolve you, Usama," he asked repeatedly, "from ignoring the confession of faith?"

Al-Hallaj himself had benefited from the principle during an earlier brush with the law in 911, when his talk of being at one with God had led to a charge that he was exaggerating his own powers at divine expense. The accusation was enough to get him shaved, pilloried, beaten with the flat of a sword, and jailed, but a Shafi'ite judge had ruled that his words were no proof of disbelief. Indeed, conviction only seemed to enhance his reputation for sanctity. He was sought out in his jail cell by no less a figure than the caliph's son and heir, whose parrot he apparently raised from the dead, and admirers reported that he greeted visitors by swelling to vast proportions or shrinking to the size of a rat. And in 922, the notion of punishing someone for holding unusual religious opinions remained deeply problematic. The charge that al-Hallaj was devaluing the importance of the Muslim pilgrimage certainly offered a good pretext for action—because it served to associate him with the Qarmatian rebels, whose raids on Mecca-bound desert caravans were then at their height*—but there was solid authority for the view that anyone accused of heresy could simply avow his belief in God by pronouncing the *shahada*. Al-Hallaj had already done precisely that earlier in his trial, and when eighty-four respectable male Muslims were assembled to countersign his charge sheet (pursuant to courtroom procedures that were then standard in Baghdad), several made clear their opinion that punishment would be unjustified.

It became possible to execute al-Hallaj only because the vizier was able to exploit a very distinctive legal doctrine. The theories binding on the Malikite judge who finally sent him to his doom postulated, unlike other schools of jurisprudence at the time, that among those Muslims whose heresies amounted to apostasy (*ridda*)—the abandonment of faith—some were so perfidious that they were incapable of honest repentance. The decision whether to transform a disreputable heresy into a punishable apostasy therefore pivoted in 922 on the same simple question that it has been turning on ever since: Who was empowered to decide? The outcome had a significance no less timeless. Whether al-Hallaj was a charlatan or a saint—on which point the jury will be forever out—he died a victim.

The legal status of opposition to Islam first became controversial during the wars that followed the Prophet Muhammad's death in 632. The campaign against rebellious tribes in the Hijaz was an early sign that the tolerance of silent misbelief did not imply passivity in the face of misdeeds. As Arab armies then moved beyond the peninsula, scholars began to justify the use of force against foreigners who refused to submit to Islam. One of the most developed of the realms invaded, Persia, gave rise to a particular problem as efforts were made to pacify the native

*See p. 91.

population. Zoroastrians were generally extended the same protected status as Jews and Christians, but the country's Manichaeans excited great mistrust. Their view of the universe as a moral battleground, where evil sometimes prevailed against good, was easily perceived as diabolism. And as conversions to Islam accelerated among Persians, many Muslims—especially Arab ones—suspected that some newcomers to the faith remained sorcerers (*zindiqs*) at heart.

The cynics were doubtless right in some cases. The adoption of Islam carried significant privileges, and at least some of those making the switch would have thought it sensible to observe the conquerors' faith in public and the ancestral one in private. The truth behind the fear was less important than its consequence, however, for the problem of secret *zindiqs* gave rise to a fateful legal interpretation. Those who waged "war against God and His apostle" or spread "disorder in the land" faced the possibility of three very exemplary punishments under the Qur'an: if a judge chose not to exile them, he could impose any combination of double amputation, beheading, and crucifixion. This penal triad, Islam's equivalent of the hanging, drawing, and quartering that medieval Europeans inflicted on traitors, was the only capital penalty permitted rulers by the holy book, and it would be gradually narrowed to apply only to highway robbery in the open country. But during these early years, when enemies of the faith and political rebels often looked frighteningly similar, the crime had a far broader application, and it was soon being linked to emerging ideas about apostasy. Early Hanafites had no doubt that disloyal Muslims merited some kind of discretionary punishment. The jurists were concentrated in and around the town of Kufa, however, and by the second half of the eighth century they were sufficiently immersed in Persian culture to be unsure of the dividing line between permissible magic and unholy sorcery. Like the Shafi'ites who emerged in Baghdad a few decades later, they also allowed for repentance in all cases. But Malik ibn Anas, who was polishing and repolishing successive editions of his seminal *al-Muwatta* in distant Medina, took a far sterner line. As well as observing that scholars in his city customarily considered apostasy so serious that decapitation was mandatory, he made clear that in one situation, sinners had to be executed even if they claimed to be remorseful Muslims: "[*Zindiqs*] are killed without being called to repent because their repentance is not recognised. They were concealing their disbelief and making their Islam public, so I do not think that one should call such people to repent and one does not accept their word."

It was a creative theory, made all the more audacious by the Malikite claim to exclude human opinion from the shari'a, and it reflected dramatic events on the ground. The establishment of Baghdad in 762 was encouraging the suppression of *zandaqa* throughout Iraq and Persia, and Caliph al-Mahdi appointed an inquisitor after his accession in 775 specifically to detect and punish the crypto-Manichaeans in his realm. A thousand palm trees were reportedly cut down to be erected as gibbets, and allegedly false converts across the country were raised onto crossbeams while their sacred texts were slashed to ribbons below. And though the last sparks of non-Muslim rebellion had dwindled into insignificance by the end of the ninth century, *zandaqa* turned out to be too useful to vanish with the *zindiq*s themselves. The word was adopted by the Hanafites and Shafi'ites, whose jurisprudence always predominated in the caliphate, and it was used by jurists from all the schools to describe any deviation from Islam that was not openly expressed. Malikite judges simultaneously perfected the view, later adopted by Hanbalites as well, that the offense authorized the execution of any apostate who seemed too untrustworthy to re-embrace the faith. It was that legal history that allowed a Malikite judge to send al-Hallaj to his death in 922—because the theory had by then lost any connection to the enemies it was originally designed to eradicate.

As the years passed, Malikites would always be at the fore when apostates were suppressed. Their efforts are illustrated by the fate of an unfortunate Cairene named Fath al-Din. He was a long-standing troublemaker by all accounts who spent years flouting the fasting obligations of Ramadan and using the Qur'an as a footstool, but he got his comeuppance only after he chose in 1301 to insult the city's leading Malikite jurist in writing. Said Malikite swiftly commenced a *zandaqa* prosecution and sentenced him to death. Friends tried desperately to have the case reheard before a Shafi'ite judge, who would have acknowledged Fath al-Din's belated recitation of the *shahada*, but the order for execution stood. The Malikite approach was complemented by other state-friendly stances. They were the first jurists to countenance torture, for example, formulating ideas in the ninth century that were picked up by Hanbalites and amplified by Ibn Taymiyya and Ibn Qayyim. And their usefulness did not go unexploited. At least twenty-six more people are recorded as having faced apostasy charges in Egypt and Syria during the fourteenth century, and though both countries were dominated by Shafi'ites, eighteen of the judges who were chosen to try the defendants were Malikites. The precise circumstances of their selection are lost to history, but malign machinations must be presumed from the outcome. There were only four acquittals, and every one of the Malikites imposed a death sentence.

The mere fact that Malikites were prone to punish apostates is not very illuminating. By the fourteenth century, Christian inquisitors were staging heresy prosecutions that could send dozens to the stake at a time, and their efforts would escalate into a 250-year witch hunt that claimed tens of thousands of lives. More generally, Islam was hardly unique in possessing intolerant traditions. The Talmud envisioned a hell where God boiled high-ranking heretics eternally in semen and excrement, for example, while the Gospels repeatedly blamed Jews for Jesus's crucifixion. Many crusading Christians had taken an openly exterminatory approach to Islam: Bernard of Clairvaux had ruled out peaceful coexistence "until [the Muslim] religion or nation has been destroyed." The statistics are important, however, because they show how uniquely malleable apostasy becomes when it is defined by thoughts alone, and the lesson has become worth recalling of late. That is because apostasy, like other ancient penal concepts, has begun in the past three decades to be put to the service of supposedly Muslim states. And the first modern prosecution, pursued in Sudan at the beginning of 1985, showed that it remained as susceptible as ever to political and legal manipulation.

The defendant was a septuagenarian religious scholar named Mahmoud Muhammad Taha. He believed that Islam's ethical core was to be found in those passages revealed to the Prophet Muhammad in Mecca during the early years of his mission—focusing on equality and individual responsibility—rather than in the Medina revelations that dealt with the practicalities of government at a time of war. That view questioned long-standing assumptions about abrogation (naskh)—the theory that God had overruled many Qur'anic verses—and it had great practical significance in Sudan. President Jaafar al-Nimeiri, wanting to prove himself more devout than certain religious opponents, had enacted a battery of laws in September 1983 in supposed emulation of the Prophet's example that had almost overnight given Sudan one of the most violent legal systems in the world. Taha contended that the September Laws took the shariʿaʾs name in vain. To be more specific, he and his followers distributed leaflets on Khartoum's streets arguing that they unjustly discriminated against women and non-Muslims and allowed for corporal punishments without acknowledging traditional Islamic safeguards. At a time when newly empowered Islamic judges were amputating thieves' limbs at an average rate of more than one a week—an eighteen-month frenzy that paralleled the Saudi revolution of the 1920s and the more recent one in Iran—it was a bold move. The regime responded with an even bolder one. Taha was arrested for sedition on January 5, 1985, put on trial two days later, and convicted a day after that. He was sentenced to die unless he repented of his errors. The court of appeal then stepped in to "rectify" the verdict. Its concern was not the haste with which he had been convicted, however. It explained that Taha had committed not sedition but apostasy, that the penal code's failure to mention that offense was no reason not to convict him, and that—in a country where Malikite jurisprudence has historically predominated—he was too incorrigible to repent. The judges simultaneously denied him the benefit of a statute forbidding the execution of people over seventy, asserting that crimes against God were punishable at any age. Thirteen days after his arrest, the seventy-six-year-old was hanged in front of a two-thousand-strong crowd.

The judicial homicide was as exceptional as it was ruthless. President al-Nimeiri was deposed by a coup two months later, and though Khartoum's rulers still maintain their claim to be dispensing Islamic justice, no Sudanese citizen since Taha has ever faced the death penalty for apostasy. But a total of six Muslim countries now acknowledge the sin to be a capital crime, and though most have avoided the embarrassment of actual executions—a Yemeni convert to Christianity was allowed to "escape" to New Zealand in 2000, for example, while an Afghan apostate was freed in 2006 on the fiction that his abandonment of Islam proved him to be a lunatic—the one recent exception to that rule is salutary. The Salafi judges of Saudi Arabia, who have always been guided by the tough Hanbalite-Malikite line on criminal justice, decapitated an Egyptian pharmacist as a *zindiq* in November 2007 after finding him guilty of magically attempting to split up a married couple. Six months later, a charge of capital sorcery was leveled at a popular Lebanese television psychic named Ali Sibat, and it was one and a half years before a very tactful intervention by Lebanon's justice minister saw him freed from his condemned cell, absolved of the crime of fortune-telling. Such cases are a reminder that twenty-first-century apostasy, like other modern reincarnations of Islamic criminal law, does not need frequent enforcement to possess symbolic value. Its availability sends out the requisite message, and attendant menace hangs heavy in the Saudi air. When two Riyadh-based journalists proposed in March 2008 that it might be good to stop calling non-Muslims "infidels," a jurist named Abd al-Rahman al-Barrak asserted that merely to air that view was to renounce God and court death. "Anyone who claims this has refuted Islam and should be tried in order to take it back," he explained. "If not, he should be killed as an apostate."

The approach toward apostasy promoted by modern hard-liners raises wider issues of religious freedom, for it sits uneasily with some very explicit and apparently clear verses of the Qur'an. The decision to deny Islam, like the failure to adopt it in the first place, is said by several verses to carry unfortunate consequences—an eternity in hell with only molten brass to drink, for example—but a person's right to choose them is sacrosanct. Islam is the truth, observes God, but "let him who will, believe, and let him who will reject it." One particularly famous passage reaffirms the principle in terms as simple as they are persuasive: "Let there be no compulsion in religion. Truth stands out clearly from error."

The actual practice of Islamic states was similarly confident for most of the last fourteen hundred years. Minorities were never forced to abandon their faiths, and they frequently thrived. Non-Muslims served as senior government officials under Abbasid caliphs, whereas papal edicts of the twelfth and thirteenth centuries would pave the way in Europe for an era of humiliation and segregation: walled ghettos, permanent clothing restrictions, and penal laws that sometimes required Jewish convicts to be hanged upside down or wrapped in pigskins prior to execution. And yet premodern Islamic societies were never egalitarian.

Non-Muslims were occasionally subjected to sumptuary regulations like those later made permanent in Europe, and they were required to pay the onerous *jizya* tax. If they were killed, only Hanafites considered them to be worth the same as a Muslim for blood money purposes; the Malikites assessed them to be half as valuable, and a next of kin received just a third of the compensation due a Muslim if a Shafi'ite was doing the counting. Classical jurisprudence therefore struck a balance between accommodation and subjugation that was unequal but ahead of its time. The crucial question for modern interpreters of the shari'a is whether that is to be a foundation for religious freedom—or a ceiling.

A by-product of Islam's historical traditions of tolerance—diversity among Muslims themselves—means that there is no single answer. The conclusions to be drawn from a state such as Saudi Arabia, where infidels are denied residency rights and suffered only to serve, are very different from those that might be suggested by Malaysia, for example, where two-fifths of the population belong to faiths other than Islam. But even if no single country can precisely represent the meaning of Islamic tolerance, there is one that comes closer than most: the Islamic Republic of Iran. Indigenous minorities make up a relatively modest proportion of the population—perhaps 2 percent—but they include about twenty thousand Zoroastrians, a similar number of Jews (who trace their roots back to the Babylonian captivity), and a Christian community at least ten times as large, which has been around for almost as long as the faith itself. And they are surprisingly visible. Opponents of the Islamic Republic sometimes suggest that all minorities are obliged to worship in secrecy, but my own experience was of a country seething not just with faith but with faiths. At an Esfahan synagogue, I was invited in to watch children reciting from the Torah; there were active churches in every major town I visited; and at a Zoroastrian temple in the ancient city of Yazd, I was able to pay my respects to a goblet of fire that has been ablaze since the year 470.

At the same time, the atmosphere is very different from that characteristic of Western cities such as London and New York. Every society is part melting pot and part mosaic, but Iran stands far to one end of the continuum. Christians, Jews, and Zoroastrians vote for parliament on separate electoral rolls, and most live in city quarters that have housed their ancestors for centuries. Fraternizing across communal lines is entirely lawful—but virtually unthinkable. I once transgressed the taboo, with some embarrassment, while chatting with an Esfahani student about the difficulties he and his girlfriend faced when trying to find public places to spend time together. He meant that Iran's morality police were permanently liable to stop them for proof that they were siblings or spouses, but I misunderstood and suggested that they sneak off to a convivial pizza parlor I had just found in the Armenian Orthodox district. He looked shocked. "But we are Muslim," he said gently. I made a similar mistake when I tried to visit a north Tehran synagogue on the eve of Shabbat. My path had been blocked by a nightstick-twirling soldier in khaki, and I thought, unreflectively enough, that he was there to intimidate Jews. As he told me to go on my way and dozens of respectable families strode by, shooting disapproving looks in my direction, the truth dawned: his job was to keep out Muslim gate-crashers.

There are solid reasons of theology, history, and legal theory to explain the patterns of diversity in Iran. The Qur'an acknowledges that humanity is made up of many "nations and tribes," and Muslim theologians long ago concluded that an all-powerful God must have created other peoples for a purpose.* Twelver jurisprudence emerged after three centuries of anti-Alid activity by powerful majorities and rulers, and supporters of the Islamic Republic often claim that its laws honor that Shi'a legacy by safeguarding the rights of minorities. To an extent they are clearly right. Whereas the Saudi Arabian constitution does not even bother to specify what its citizens are entitled to expect from the state, Iran formally guarantees benefits that extend to housing and legal aid. It acknowledges that all Iranians are equal, and it stipulates that "the investigation of individuals' beliefs is forbidden, and no one may be molested or taken to task simply for holding a certain belief." Most notably of all, the country that hosted the first *zindiq* crucifixions does not explicitly acknowledge apostasy in its current (1991) penal code, and it has not officially executed Muslim-born citizens for abandoning the faith since the late 1980s.

The existence of laws is never the same as their observance, however,

---

*Two of the Qur'an's verses promise a reward in the afterlife to good Jews and Christians: 2:62, 5:69.

and there is at least one group for whom the freedom of conscience promised by the Qur'an and the Iranian constitution has proved entirely elusive. The Baha'is, followers of a man who declared himself a successor to the Prophet Muhammad during the 1860s, are as good as excluded from the body politic by a constitutional provision which states that "Zoroastrian, Jewish, and Christian Iranians are the only recognized religious minorities," and they have experienced terrible persecution as a consequence. The community claims to have suffered around a thousand jail terms and more than two hundred executions or extrajudicial killings. The government offers no official confirmation or denial of that figure—but its very silence testifies to a certain contradiction in the state's approach to religious freedom.

The closest I got to comprehending that contradiction came during a session at the May 2009 human rights conference that I attended at Qom's Mofid University. A mid-ranking cleric was giving a talk titled "The Prophet's Peaceful Coexistence with Non-Muslims," which was initially unremarkable: a string of pieties that reiterated how harmonious some tenth- and eleventh-century Shi'a writers had imagined the seventh century to be. Sacred stories make for law in Islamic jurisprudence, however, and even the apparently anodyne conclusion—a remark that Muhammad had always "stood up to states that did not allow religious freedom"—carried potent implications in Iran. When questions were invited from the floor, the four-hundred-strong auditorium crackled into life. Hands waved for attention, and the microphone found its way to a chador-clad law student, whose image then appeared on a large screen behind the rostrum. The Prophet had indeed fought valiantly for the freedom to convert to Islam, she acknowledged, her eyes flashing across the hall. "But what happens after that?" she demanded. "After a person becomes a Muslim, they cannot change their religion. How do you account for that?"

Even in May 2009, a liberal lull before the storm that followed Mahmoud Ahmadinejad's controversial reelection as president a month later, the question was dangerous. Iran had not officially executed anyone for abandoning Islam since 1989, but people who renounced the faith had been murdered in murky and unresolved circumstances during the decade that followed, and at least two converts to Christianity were languishing in jail cells as she spoke. But as the shadows fell, the speaker chose to let them linger. "So long as this individual does not attempt to fight Islam, the mere fact that he or she has changed religion is not ground for punishment," he replied blankly. The cleric who was chairing the session, a conservative ayatollah named Mohsen Araki, fixed him with a quizzical stare. The speaker responded by gazing dead-pan toward his questioner. As it became clear that he was not proposing to qualify his answer, the tension mounted—until Araki realized that any clarification was going to have to come from himself. "Sometimes someone *expresses* the change of religion," he announced tersely. "If an individual doubts Islam, he does not become the subject of punishment, but if the doubt is openly *expressed*, this is not permissible."

One possible explanation for Araki's intervention was a concern to register his views about a contentious debate in Iran—still unresolved three years later—over whether a much-postponed revision of the 1991 penal code should incorporate a new offense of capital apostasy. But the distinction that he drew between changes of religious belief and expressions of the change echoed a much more long-standing aspect of Islamic jurisprudence: its "don't ask, don't tell" attitude. The sense that wrongdoers compound transgressions against God by talking about them is ancient. Ever since the Prophet reportedly discouraged confessions for adultery, jurists have warned that flagrant sinning can corrode the social fabric and produce copycat crimes. They routinely advise sinners that God is cloaking undiscovered misdemeanors for a reason and that they should spend their time preparing in private for Judgment Day. As a few clicks on any good online fatwa site will show, a drug taker, homosexual, or serial masturbator will always be told to atone sincerely—but quietly.

Discretion is certainly preferable to confession in some situations. The white lie and the stiff upper lip have value even in the West, and only bores insist that it is always good to talk. But whatever value reserve might possess in other contexts, there was little to commend Araki's attempt to silence religious freedom. State officials could not punish an unmanifested belief even if they wanted to, and Iran is a nation where religious expression is central to social identities. Judaism and Christianity derive much of their meaning through practice and collective worship, while the five pillars of Islam—prayer, fasting, pilgrimage, almsgiving, and recitation of the *shahada*—are virtually defined by their expressiveness. To say that people are free to convert as long as they keep it secret drains religious freedom of almost all meaning.

And there was more—because Araki went on to add that the renunciation of Islam was not just an unprotected activity but an unprotectable one. "The fact that I believe in God and the Prophet is the foundation of all my rights," he explained. "Ignoring truth is itself the violation of a right." When the microphone returned to the audience, it promptly ended up with a student no less outspoken than the first, who wanted to know why Iranian law disadvantaged "those religions that are considered deviant for political reasons." As everyone would have understood, the question was a very cautious reference to the Baha'is, and though it was politely addressed to the cleric who had delivered the original presentation, Ayatollah Araki was by now in full flow. With the main speaker watching quietly from the lectern, Araki pronounced that all "concocted religions" were outside the scope of Islamic law. "A belief, in itself, is not sacred. The rights that flow from a belief are only guaranteed if the belief is founded on arguments that are acceptable to a large group of Islamic scholars."

The disdain for any religion unmentioned by the Qur'an ignored a legal history that had allowed Muslims to live alongside Hindus, Buddhists, and Sikhs for centuries, and a young cleric raised his arm next to ask the obvious question. "If it is only possible to accept beliefs that correspond with Islam, there is no freedom of belief," he said. "What you are really saying is that we tolerate religions inasmuch as they have features in common with Islam." If Araki recognized the irony, he did not acknowledge it. "We respect other believers, but we do not respect their beliefs," he replied. "That is why they must enter into agreements with us. Their beliefs may be dangerous. Their behavior is unpredictable. They need to be constrained through agreements."

That turned out to be Araki's final word on "the Prophet's peaceful coexistence with non-Muslims," and although he was speaking in a relatively personal capacity, it was the most coherent explanation I ever heard of Iran's constitutional commitment to religious freedom. It could also stand as its epitaph. The claim that the nation's 98 percent Muslim majority had to "constrain" the dangerously unpredictable Baha'is, along with everyone else, imagined religious dissent to be presumptive evidence of treason. It was permissible only insofar as it was unnoticeable.

Citizens could believe what they wanted as long as they acted like monotheists, while Muslims were obliged to do nothing that might evince religious doubt.

It seemed a far cry from the Qur'an's emphatic rejection of religious compulsion, and a conversation around the conference tea urn then threw up a fact that made Araki's argument look even more dubious. Chatting with a few of the students who had been asking him questions, I learned that the primary speaker had won his scholarly spurs with a thesis outlining the rights of transsexuals. Edgy though that sounds, it was uncontroversial in Iran. Ayatollah Khomeini, in a fatwa that was adventurous even by his standards, had opined as early as 1963 that hermaphrodites who felt trapped in the wrong sex were entitled under the shari'a to undergo corrective surgery and receive new identification documents.* After 1979, that had formed the basis for a national policy in favor of allowing sex changes, and there had been no looking back. Despite a penal code that allows for the execution of homosexuals, Iran now permits and partly finances seven times as many gender reassignment operations as the entire European Union. All the while, debates continue to rage over whether apostasy should be made a capital offense. In other words, Iran encourages unhappy Muslims to change sex but threatens to execute them if they change the way they pray.

I left Iran with great affection for many of its people, but my visit also disabused me comprehensively of a romanticized notion that I had been developing about Shi'ism: a view that the sect's historic tribulations had made it intrinsically tolerant. The minority has certainly taken some knocks in its time, and its acute sensitivity to its own suffering since Karbala has given it reason to empathize with the downtrodden. Iran has more recently produced some admirably open-minded theologians, and Ayatollah Araki's willingness to take on all comers was

---

*No Sunni jurist of note has ever come out in favor of sex changes, but many have countenanced discretionary surgery that interferes with God's handiwork in other ways. Nose jobs and breast enlargements are routinely approved, and the preponderance of scholarly opinion allows for organ transplants, unless the prospective donor is a pig: Birgit Krawietz, "*Darūra* in Modern Islamic Law," in Gleave and Kermeli, *Islamic Law*, p. 185; Fatwa 82240 (August 21, 2000), online at www.islamweb.net /emainpage.

itself some reflection of that dynamism. But the operation of the Islamic Republic manages all too often to make such aspects of the Shi'a
heritage look like an accident of history. The hard-liners who are grip-
ping the reins of power have learned to crack the whip as sharply as
any oppressive caliph of old.

Open threats and insults against Muslims are deplored by the Qur'an
just as much as apostasy, but as is the case with so many sins, the holy
book says nothing about their earthly punishment. Believers are urged
instead to shun perpetrators and assured of a time when their tormen-
tors will learn the error of their ways. Certain hadiths report that the
Prophet Muhammad ordered a number of enemies executed in the
hours after Mecca's fall, however, and early jurists postulated therefore
that *sabb al-nabi* (abuse of the Prophet) was a crime so heinous that
repentance was disallowed and summary execution was required. And
though actual prosecutions for blasphemy are vanishingly infrequent
in the historical record—with one of the few known cases ending in an
acquittal—Islam's penal resurrectionists have been increasingly likely
in recent decades to call for its punishment. Many of their arguments
have a familiar ring. Criminalizing hostility toward Islam is said to
safeguard communal cohesion. It supposedly protects the faith against
external subversives, just as apostasy defends against enemies within.
It is, in other words, another branch of religious high treason.

The sensitivity of some Muslims to abuses actual or perceived has
been bewildering Westerners ever since Ayatollah Khomeini's lethally
critical assessment of Salman Rushdie's *Satanic Verses* in 1989, but it is
within the Muslim world itself that the realities become clearest—and
nowhere more so than in Pakistan. When the country was partitioned
from India in August 1947, the notion that it might presume to protect
Islam with a criminal offense was unthinkable. The country had inherited a nondenominational blasphemy statute from the British, but its
first leaders were firm secularists. They had campaigned for a Muslim
state on the basis of a supposed need to avoid Hindu domination, and
all expressed confidence that Pakistan would not inflict on others the
oppression that they themselves had publicly feared. The nation's founding father, a London-trained barrister named Muhammad Ali Jinnah,

had personal reasons to value tolerance—he was Shi'a, with a Parsee wife—and he repeatedly hailed the central role that pluralism was going to play. According to a speech to the nascent Constituent Assembly on August 11, 1947, citizens would be able to "belong to any religion or caste or creed—that has nothing to do with the business of the state." Six months later, he reiterated the promise: "Pakistan is not going to be a theocratic state to be ruled by priests with a divine mission." But no country created to advance the interests of a specific faith can cherish equality alone, and when Jinnah then died, barely a year after his creature had been born, another part of the national psyche began to stir. In March 1949, the Constituent Assembly formulated a statement of goals known as the Objectives Resolution that has haunted Pakistani politics ever since. It observed that governance of the country was a "sacred trust" and that citizens would enjoy the right "to order their lives in the individual and collective spheres" according to the Qur'an and sacred tradition (*sunna*).

The practical significance of that commitment remained unclear for the next three decades. Power oscillated between secular politicians and army officers, and theologians made their mark only by stirring up unrest during occasional periods of crisis. One reason for their lack of influence, which now seems almost quaint, was that the most vocal religious movements, including the Deobandis and the Jamaat e-Islami, had positively opposed the creation of Pakistan. The Jamaat's founder, Abul Ala Maududi, had complained before 1947 that Islamic nationalism was "as contradictory a term as 'chaste prostitute.'" Conservatives had regularly vilified Jinnah himself as a hopeless sinner—the nation's Infidel-in-Chief, in the words of one provocative couplet. But the balance shifted decisively on the night of July 4, 1977, when the then-obscure general Zia ul-Haq overthrew Pakistan's elected prime minister, Zulfiqar Bhutto, in a coup that he called Operation Fairplay. Zia had been considered unimaginative by the few people who thought they knew him, but he would link nationalism and Islam to an extent that few Pakistanis had previously dreamed possible. And removing any equivocation about the national mission was fundamental to his program. Six years after his 1979 Hudood Ordinances harnessed the penal machinery of Pakistan to religious ends, Zia incorporated the Objectives Resolution into its constitution. "This country was created in the name of Islam," he explained. "You take away the ideology of an ideological state [and] nothing is left."

Zia would die in a mysterious plane crash in August 1988, but his concerns for Pakistan's ideological coherence would by then have been complemented by a series of crucially important amendments to the country's colonial-era blasphemy law. All of them privileged Islam above other faiths, and they culminated in 1986 with a provision that outlawed defilement of "the sacred name of the Holy Prophet Muhammad," regardless of intention, on pain of life imprisonment or death. Forty-four prosecutions over the period 1987–99 leaped to fifty-two in 2000 alone, and the total may now be more than a thousand. No death sentence has ever been upheld on appeal—and there are still enough brave judges around to ensure that some charges are dismissed—but the mere existence of a complaint has often been sufficient to cause a defendant to be lynched. And even a cursory survey of the cases is enough to give the lie to claims that they counter any real dangers. Those convicted have included several mentally ill defendants, thanks to provisions that make a person's intentions irrelevant. Tawdry land disputes and neighborhood quarrels have formed the background to countless allegations. The greatest practical threat to civil order in Pakistan has actually come not from blasphemers but from supporters of the blasphemy laws. That was illustrated soon after November 2010, when a Punjabi court condemned a forty-five-year-old Christian to die for a profanity that she allegedly uttered during arguments about a bowl of water. Governor Salmaan Taseer expressed the view that the mother of five did not deserve to hang. His bodyguard was so offended that on January 4, 2011, he shot the politician dead.

In the one instance where a genuinely ideological opposition does exist, the corrosive effects of attempting to win an argument of ideas through force have been immense. That instance concerns a group known as the Ahmadis. Like so many other Indian communal movements, they emerged from the wreckage of the 1857 challenge to British rule. At a time of great uncertainty, religious factions across the subcontinent were trying to prove their continued relevance by adopting distinctive stances on theological niceties—whether God could tell lies or the Prophet commit a sin, for example—and one argument was inspiring particular controversy. Islamic history had proceeded for more than twelve hundred years on the basis that Muhammad was the "seal of the Prophets" and the last of God's messengers. But though the finality of his mission was assumed, so too was God's power to do as He pleased. Poets and controversialists had long delighted in pondering what the apparent contradiction might mean, but some answers now crystallized—sharply. In 1863, the Iranian founder of the Baha'is announced that he was a successor to the Prophet Muhammad. The claim would fuel animosities that are still going strong, as shown by the comments of Ayatollah Araki above, and India then produced a home-grown pretender of its own. A Muslim preacher named Mirza Ghulam Ahmad (1835–1908) declared during the 1880s that, in fact, *he* was humanity's new savior. And whereas Baha'ullah (1817–92) admitted at least that he was leaving Islam behind, Ahmad—or the Promised Messiah, as his followers now began to call him—held himself out as the truest Muslim of them all.

The teachings that Mirza Ghulam Ahmad proceeded to dispense were controversial enough. He denied the ancient theory of abrogation, with its claim that one verse of the Qur'an might supersede another. He argued that God's hostility toward Mecca's pagans had not affected His general preference for peace—a view that, in a climate of simmering anticolonialism, led his many enemies to peg him as a pro-British sycophant. But it was not the substance of his words that caused anger so much as the capacity in which he claimed to speak them. As far as most Muslims were concerned, Ahmad's claim to be an emissary of God contradicted one of Islam's central tenets, and the antagonism against his followers reached a head as Pakistan was partitioned into existence. Within a year, the same Punjabi conservatives who had until recently opposed the country's creation were challenging the new government to prove its Islamic status by penalizing the Ahmadis. A campaign of arson and murder culminated in early 1953 with two weeks of riots and the imposition of martial law, and though that crisis passed, the underlying rivalries remained so strong that a renewed campaign of incitement and killing bore fruit twenty-one years later. Prime Minister Zulfiqar Bhutto then amended the constitution in September 1974 to declare that anyone who disbelieved in the "absolute and unqualified finality of the Prophethood of Muhammad" was no longer a Muslim "for the purposes of the Constitution or the law."

The immediate consequences of the redefinition were limited. Bhutto was as secular as all his predecessors, and his concession signified no more than the humdrum cowardice of politicians everywhere. But after he was overthrown by Zia ul-Haq, the reform gained teeth. It allowed Zia in 1985 to relegate Ahmadis alongside other non-Muslim minorities to separate and unequal electoral rolls, and although they constitute up to 2 percent of Pakistan's population, they are now collectively entitled to vote for just one out of 342 of the National Assembly's representatives. It made it easy to characterize Ahmadis as enemies of Islam's messenger—to the extent that over the next twenty years, they would be charged more than a hundred times under the 1986 capital statute forbidding abuse of the Prophet. And it also facilitated a 1984 amendment to the blasphemy law that specifically targeted the sect, making its members liable to three years of imprisonment if they proselytized, held themselves out as Muslims, or usurped an Islamic ritual or usage. Those offenses were as broad as they sound. Calling a place of worship a "mosque" became enough to earn a jail term. So did the publication of a wedding notice that quoted from the Qur'an. When I visited the Ahmadi town of Rabwah, community leaders showed me a warrant of December 15, 1989, that accused "the entire population" of unlawfully appropriating the greeting *salam alaikum* (peace be upon you). And by way of a law that is as obsessive as it is repressive, all Pakistanis who apply for a passport or register to vote are now required to affirm in writing that they do *not* accept the prophethood of the sect's founder. It was difficult to disagree with the assessment of one Ahmadi, delivered with a shake of the head as he talked me through hundreds of typed police complaints: "In Pakistan, the definition of a Muslim is not that he believes in God and the Prophet. The definition of a Muslim is someone who does not believe in the truthfulness of Mirza Ghulam Ahmad."

A community is always liable to affirm its beliefs by defining dissenters as outsiders. Heretics invariably establish barriers of their own, and the Ahmadis are as exclusive in their prayers and funerals as any body of Sunni or Shi'a believers. But dangers gather whenever a larger group is in a position to secure political or material advantages. Absent strong institutional restraints, majority rule quickly becomes oppressive, and the communal fabric is coarsened as bullies come to the fore.

Pakistan has been producing illustrations to prove the point for half a century, and they have been proliferating in recent years. When a television presenter named Aamir Liaquat Hussain proposed on air in September 2008 that Ahmadis were "worthy of death," three murders followed within the week. A gun-and-grenade attack on two Ahmadi mosques in Lahore in May 2010 took almost a hundred lives, and anyone complacent enough to hope that the miasma would confine itself to heretic deaths was disabused a month later, when two human bombs tore through dozens of worshippers at the city's most famous Sufi shrine. Violent victimization is simultaneously piling pressures onto the country's political culture. The killing of the Punjab governor Salmaan Taseer in January 2011 was followed two months later by the assassination of the Christian minister for minorities Shahbaz Bhatti on an Islamabad street. He had been one of just two federal politicians courageous enough to back reform of Pakistan's blasphemy laws. The other one was then obliged by Pakistan's prime minister to drop her attempt to pilot a repeal through the legislature.

Although there has never been an actual execution for blasphemy in Pakistan, the legal future looks as bleak as the multiplying murders suggest. The country can still boast many lawyers and judges of great integrity, but there are also others of a meaner spirit who are constantly plumbing new depths. The caliber of their jurisprudence is well represented by a couple of cases. The first of them saw the author of a self-published book tried in 2005 not only as a blasphemer but also as a "terrorist" for having observed that the Qur'an contained no written verse ordering that adulterers be stoned to death. Five years earlier, a doctor had been convicted for allegedly saying that the Prophet Muhammad had not followed all of Islam's rituals until God had told him what they were. No sane, literate, honest person could have contested either claim—because the first is a verifiable fact and the second a matter of logic—but religious scholars trooped through the witness box to avow that both defendants were blasphemers. The first of them had his life sentence affirmed on appeal in February 2011. The second languished in a condemned cell for three years until, freed on appeal, he was able to flee Pakistan forever. And it may only be a matter of time before the country actually carries out an execution. In April 2009, the Supreme Court upheld an argument that it was "repugnant to Islam" to allow

mere life sentences for abuse of the Prophet. As a consequence, hanging ceased to be an option; it became a requirement.

The chances of an imminent reversal are correspondingly slim. The
muftis I met during my visits to Pakistan all defended tolerance in
principle, but none was prepared to acknowledge that there might be
a connection between the country's mounting problems and legal attempts to punish people for wrongful beliefs. Most preferred to revile
Western propaganda or to wonder what made me so interested in blasphemers anyway. The only partial concession came from a judge who
groaned when asked how his colleagues had become so expert in assessing the secrets of a Muslim's heart. "It is better you do not ask me about
that," he said. "For me, anyone who recites the *shahada* is a Muslim."
That opinion, reflecting age-old hadiths and the understanding of centuries, should have been a truism. Its expression has become so dangerous in modern Pakistan that I had to promise to keep his tolerance
a secret.

The assertion of great truths can easily give rise to a belief that only
liars can oppose them. A well-known hadith warns that Muslims are
destined to split into seventy-three sects, only one of which will avoid
the fires of hell, and purists have been trying ever since to make sure
they are on the winning team. Communal strife has been the inevitable result, and as Jonathan Swift observed long ago, the scale of such
conflict always tends to bear an inverse relationship to the grievances
that exacerbate it. In *Gulliver's Travels*, he satirized two centuries of
Catholic-Protestant hostility as a protracted war between Little- and
Big-Endians—fought over which side of an egg should be cracked first—
and Islamic jurists have sometimes made Swiftian wit look like report-
age. While Mongols menaced the Middle East, the scholars of Mamluk
Cairo and Damascus actually did warn against the dangers of painting
Easter eggs. After India's thwarted anticolonial revolt of 1857, Deoband's
muftis urged disheartened believers to cleave to the faith by using copper Muslim pots instead of brass Hindu ones. And the first Ahmadi to
fall victim to a sectarian murder in Pakistan, an army officer lynched
on August 11, 1948, was identified not by his incendiary deeds or fighting words but by his distinctively trimmed beard.

Ideological squabbles that end in death are never simply ludicrous, and their legal validation is even less of a laughing matter. It remains possible to argue, however, that the monopoly over religious truth claimed by some Islamic legal systems is relatively insignificant. Although intolerant laws have been demonstrably proliferating for the last thirty years, official executions for heresy have occurred in just three countries—Saudi Arabia, Iran, and Sudan—and even there, they have been exceptional. Infringements of religious freedom in the West, though very different in nature, are meanwhile on the rise. Several European states have restricted the right of Muslim women to wear veils, sensitive only to their presumed desires to throw them off.* The status of Islam in the United States has become so tenuous that a nationwide furor greeted President Obama's insistence in August 2010 that Muslims who wanted to build a cultural center in lower Manhattan could rely on their constitutional freedom of worship. Darker fears about religion have often lurked in the background: a credophobia that is all the more pernicious because its proponents typically fail to recognize how many of its assumptions are just xenophobia and racism repackaged. Communities struggle with difficulties about which many people are both ignorant and contemptuous, but because they define themselves by faith rather than ethnicity, distaste toward them is rationalized and condoned.

The problems are serious ones, and yet an attempt to justify rules against apostasy and blasphemy by reference to the flaws of Western societies is not worth making. Islamic intolerance is objectionable because of its toxic effects on Islam's own traditions. It has led avowedly devout Muslims to treat modern statutes as totems, followed more closely than the words of the Qur'an itself. Heirs to a jurisprudential tradition that once put the bigotry of Christendom to shame are failing or victimizing non-Muslims and elevating doctrinal disagreements into Muslim thought crimes. In order to approximate a justice that religious judges are failing to achieve, embarrassed politicians and

---

*Supporters of such bans would do well, incidentally, to speak to a few Ahmadi women. They have always been disproportionately likely to wear veils, perhaps because they want to prove their piety to doubters. They also have more experience than most of being told how to manifest their faith.

merciful officials are sidelining and therefore corrupting regular legal procedures. And far from facilitating harmony, societies that used to be oceans of diversity are shrinking into sectarian swamps, consumed by meager talk of treachery and efforts to compel acceptance of an outlook that the Qur'an itself states to be self-evident.

There are important arguments to be had over the ideal balance between the interest of individuals to do as they desire and the interest of religious believers in having their faith respected. There are also good reasons why people should sometimes avoid saying things, even if laws recognize their right to speak. Any community worth that name needs a citizenry that can empathize with emotional pain it does not feel—other people's ideas about dignity, for example—and that calls for manners and taste as well as statutes and constitutions. The point is basic, but it bears constant reiteration. It was last forgotten on a grand scale in September 2005, when Denmark's *Jyllands-Posten* published twelve cartoons that were supposed to represent the Prophet Muhammad, several of which depicted a stereotypically menacing Arab accessorized by a large beard, veiled women, a scimitar, or a bomb. An organization calling itself the Arab European League soon responded by posting an online image of Anne Frank in bed with Adolf Hitler, and an Iranian newspaper then ran a competition to find the best cartoons about the Holocaust. Whatever one's views about the individual pictures, there was at least one level on which all three stunts were equally objectionable. Parodies of the Prophet Muhammad as an armed psychopath and cartoons that mock the innocent dead are appalling because there are many people whom they appall. Arguments about free speech and fair comment are beside the point when it comes to acknowledging sensitivities.

That comes with an important qualification, however. States have no business punishing every act of incivility. Efforts to characterize the "defamation of religion" as a breach of human rights law, like those made in recent years by an influential international body known as the Organisation of the Islamic Conference, acknowledge one side of a problem without paying any heed to the accompanying dangers. The recent history of apostasy and blasphemy shows that pluralism begins to wither whenever touchiness is allowed to become a measure of lawfulness. Social groups grow competitively sensitive, and cultures shrink into silence or explode into violence. The right not to be offended consumes the rights of people who are said to have caused offense. There are few incentives to take account of a defendant's intentions and mental capacity and, ultimately, whether the events alleged took place at all.

The suspicions and resentments covered in this chapter are so capricious that any conclusion is liable to raise more questions than it resolves. Contemporary Islamic scholarship is more likely to reflect repressive or dissenting attitudes than to explain them. Fortunately, there is one non-Muslim of suitable stature whose divisiveness makes his insights oddly appropriate: former president George W. Bush. The parting thought he has to offer formed part of a speech that he delivered on January 21, 2000, at a time when the West's long-standing Communist adversary had vanished and no obvious replacement was in sight. Events in September 2001 would notoriously fill the vacuum. They would even give rise to ominous speculation in radical circles, both Western and Muslim, that Bush and his neocon allies had planned it that way. That particular theory merits no analysis in this book, given the clear evidence that Islamic revivalism has been on the boil for almost half a century, but Bush's ruminations encapsulate how easily demons are conjured when identities are challenged. Addressing a group of Iowa students, he recalled: "When I was coming up, it was a dangerous world. You knew exactly who they were. It was us versus them, and it was clear who them was. Today, we are not so sure who they are. But we know they're there."

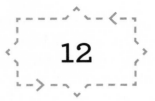

12

Heaven on Earth

Among the lesser-known marvels of Cairo are its ancient cemeteries. Sprawling across five square miles of the Egyptian capital, they are home to at least a million people. Ancestral plots are enclosed by walls of pink brick and gates of wrought iron, and once-abandoned slabs have been staked out and screened off by squatters. The descendants of pushy morticians and stonecutters now occupy entire mausoleums: palaces of decay, shaded by acacias and wreathed by tumbling trumpets of pink hibiscus. As one would expect of a district so filled with the deceased, a certain solemnity prevails, but the living are as vital as surface dwellers anywhere else in Cairo. Babies wail, muezzins chant, and everyone else sews and snips and hammers and nurses and bakes their days away—until their fleeting purchase ends, and it is time to make the trip downstairs to join the dead.

The necropolises are poorly integrated into Cairo in almost every sense. They make it onto city maps only as blank spaces. Municipal authorities have regarded them as slums for decades, and bureaucrats periodically propose ambitious corpse-relocation schemes to modernize them out of existence. They figure in the minds of most middle-class Cairenes as ghettos, glimpsed by car from the highways that vault and bisect them. And yet they occupy a central place in the history of

Egypt and Islam alike. The immense southernmost graveyard was already hallowed ground in the 630s, when Egypt's last Byzantine governor is said to have offered Islam's incoming commander a vast sum to retain ownership, and legend records that Caliph Umar himself turned down the money after learning how close the land stood to paradise. It became a major pilgrimage destination after Cairo's foundation in 969, when Fatimid rulers enshrined the supposed remains of various Shi'a luminaries. And its sanctity to Sunnis is symbolized by the dome at the cemetery's core, the largest in Egypt, which floats serene over its surroundings like a supernatural egg. It marks the resting place of the jurist who signposted the way to a hadith-based system of Islamic law—Muhammad al-Shafi'i (767–820).

I visited the shrine in July 2010 and found a scene that was by then familiar. The glass case that enclosed the tapestry-swaddled teak tomb, illuminated by strips of sickly neon, welcomed a steady trickle of supplicants—overwhelmingly poor and largely female. They had come for the divine blessing, or *baraka*, that all saints are thought to facilitate. Many were inviting it by reciting holy texts; some tried to capture it with their mobile phone cameras; and a fair number were absorbing it with a snooze. Scribbled notes, photographs, and airmail stationery had been posted through cracks in the vitrine's wooden frame, and though the correspondence was inaccessible, the strain on the petitioners' faces was more easily read. It suggested that hopes had not changed much since the 1960s, when a sociologist had leafed through a selection of the letters. Imam al-Shafi'i had been told then about problems ranging from long-term unemployment to troublesome neighbors—and asked to furnish remedies ranging from a wage increase to an assault and battery.

To my untrained eye, the devotions looked unremarkable. It did not take uncanny prescience to realize in the summer of 2010 that plenty of Egyptians thought justice elusive in Hosni Mubarak's Egypt. Nor was it surprising that downtrodden folk might turn to a legal saint for miracles. But there have always been people with a less laid-back outlook. The letters to al-Shafi'i used to be publicly burned in the 1980s (they are nowadays incinerated without ceremony), and the stern sheikh responsible could have cited much ancient authority in support of his actions. Fourteenth-century polemicists warned that customs that allowed men and women to mingle in Cairo's cemeteries were liable to produce gluttonous feasts and rampant orgies. Several Shafi'ites themselves came to believe that their teacher's domed memorial was a blasphemy. And Salafis had been sure since the time of Ahmad ibn Taymiyya that to approach any grave as a pilgrim or bereaved relative was fraught with risk, because permissible contemplation of the afterlife could all too easily turn into worship of the dead.

The spiritual dangers may or may not be real—on which point, it seems only right to let God be the judge—but the existence of the objections merits a couple of observations. Cairo's graveyards have been sacred for as long as Egypt has had mosques, and apparently pious Muslims have been honoring the memory of the dead for nearly a millennium. The man who gave al-Shafi'i his ornate tomb in the late 1170s was Saladin—the warrior who liberated Jerusalem from the Crusaders— and it was one of his nephews, a successor sultan and another renowned jihadi, who first surmounted it with a dome. At a time when Egypt's two-hundred-year experiment with Shi'ism had just come to an end, both men were engaged in a very orthodox attempt to bolster Sunni Islam, and their shrine was so immediately successful that the neighborhood has been inhabited ever since. City cemeteries more generally became so popular by the thirteenth century that pilgrims were able to choose from three tours each week, and by 1410 a guidebook to the tombs would be referring to thirty earlier works. And Cairenes were not alone. Two of the most cosmopolitan Muslims who ever lived, the late-twelfth-century Andalusian traveler Ibn Jubayr and his fourteenth-century Moroccan successor Ibn Battuta, considered the tearful prayers at Egyptian shrines both virtuous and entirely normal. In the country that gave the world mummies and pyramids, Muslims might possibly have pondered death with added seriousness, but there was nothing un-Islamic about their respect for it.

None of that would faze the objectors, whose hopes for heaven imply a very crowded hell, but the argument has ramifications that go far beyond the niceties of funerary etiquette. It reflects a fundamental gulf between the overwhelming majority of Muslims, whose faith cannot be separated from their communal history, and a minority who discount all traditions that contradict their beliefs about how Islam was originally practiced. The difference is illustrated by comparing the tenacity of prayers at the tomb of al-Shafi'i with the posthumous fate of his teacher Malik ibn Anas (718–96), the founder of Malikite jurisprudence. When the older man died in late-eighth-century Medina, he was buried in the city's Jannat al-Baqi (Garden of Paradise) cemetery alongside some indisputably honorable figures. They included several thousand of the Prophet's contemporaries, among whom were ten of his wives, the daughter who perpetuated his lineage, and his only infant son. An excursion to the tombs quickly became popular among pilgrims to Mecca, and by the time Ibn Jubayr passed through town, the graveyard was a forest of shrines, with Malik ibn Anas himself lying under a cupola. That changed for the first time in the early nineteenth century, when Saudi rebels seized the holy cities. Having been taught by the revivalist Muhammad al-Wahhab that overly ornate gravestones were epicenters of resurgent paganism, they defaced and damaged many of the memorials. During the more recent Saudi revolution, zealotry was allied to technology, and dynamite completed the job that pickaxes had begun. In April 1925, the Garden of Paradise was razed to the ground—or more precisely, about six inches above it—and it assumed its modern appearance: a pigeon-infested wasteland of stubbly boulders, hemmed in by highways and considerably less inviting than the average parking lot. Anyone who wants to do today what Muslims did for centuries—pay the graves a visit—faces locked gates, hostile guards, and perennial accusations of idolatry from Saudi Arabia's many arbiters of religious correctness.

The effect has been to wipe out tangible layers of history in favor of a theorized instant of purity, and such other relics of seventh-century Islam that survive in the Hijaz are faring equally badly. Only about twenty structures from the Prophet's lifetime remain, and speculators and scholars are conspiring to eradicate them forever. Even buildings directly associated with Muhammad are at risk. Hard-liners have spent decades contemplating whether the remnants of his birthplace constitute an invitation to idolatry, and although the authorities have balked at demolishing his tomb, guards at his graveside brandish sticks at visitors who mumble prayers or linger too long. Debates meanwhile rage as to whether the green dome that has stood overhead for some thirteen hundred years is an innovation that merits destruction.

Conservation Saudi-style is out of step with almost the entire Muslim world. The Sphinx still gazes contemplatively from Giza; the pre-Islamic cities of Palmyra and Persepolis survive replete with graven images in the deserts of Syria and Iran; and domed shrines are part of the municipal furniture in cities from Istanbul to Agra. Only the Taliban have displayed a similar aesthetic, when they restored two ancient sandstone statues of the Buddha to oblivion with rocket launchers in March 2001. And insofar as there is genuine theological anxiety underpinning the urge to destroy, it is unhinged from history. The revulsion for headstones stems from a Qur'anic prohibition of the graveside cairns at which Arab pagans once sacrificed animals to the dead, and the Arabic word for a dome—*qubba*—once referred to tents that were erected during those rituals. The opposition to funereal flamboyance is therefore a relic from a struggle that was won more than thirteen hundred years ago. And it coexists with a distinctly uncritical approach to some modern temptations. Citizens in search of a truly upmarket shrine—a Gucci store or Cartier showroom, say—can find a luxury mall less than a quarter of a mile from the Ka'ba. Rather than update its approach to idolatry, the Saudi state is making haphazard attempts to backdate the world.

Any society that claims to be traditionalist while ignoring actual traditions is at risk of forgetting why continuity matters in the first place, and the notion that history and politics have no effect on legal development is particularly corrosive. Far from disclosing pristine truths about Islam, it reveals that the supposed purists cannot even agree on which sins to repress. Saudi Arabia forces women to be veiled and forbids them to drive, while Iran allows females to show their faces behind wheels but threatens them with jail if they expose too much hair. Sunni rigorists insist that God hates men to be clean shaven, whereas Tehran's Ministry of Culture suggested in July 2010 that He was more perturbed by ponytails and mullets. Some extremists have even attached spiritual significance to customs that mandate physical violence, such as female genital mutilation and so-called honor killings, oblivious to the pagan roots of the first practice and the unequivocal hostility of the Qur'an and hadiths to the second one. Instead of acknowledging the one fact that is empirically certain—that their interpretations of Islam are not universal—the purists are falsely elevating cultural choices into sacred obligations.

The development of Islamic jurisprudence was an immense achievement. Formulated over the course of a few centuries, it took root across three continents and outshone Christendom for almost a millennium. As it adapted to local conditions and customs, it helped bind civilizations that were as diverse as any the world has seen. But four decades of legal revivalism have promoted theories that are eliminating space for fresh ideas and dissent wherever they gain ground. And though Muslim reformers and human rights activists are resisting the narrow-mindedness with some courage, they have their work cut out. Those states that have gone furthest in institutionalizing their interpretations of Islamic law trail the rest of the world when it comes to children's rights, gender equality, and religious freedom—and score highly only in terms of lethality.

No attempt to survey the modern state of the shari'a can ignore the controversy that its subject has been exciting in the West of late. Swiss voters, alarmed by the existence of four minarets within their cantons, voted in a referendum on November 29, 2009, to ban their construction outright. The governments of Belgium, France, the Netherlands, and Italy, ostensibly concerned to protect Muslim women from oppression, have introduced or enacted criminal laws to stop them wearing veils in public. The United States has seen some especially intense anxiety. In the decade since 9/11, websites with names such as Jihad Watch have sprung up to warn of Muslim fanatics in America's midst, and conservative commentators and politicians have heeded the cry. Energized by protests against a proposed Islamic cultural center in New York's Financial District, the Republican chairman of the House Homeland Security Committee even began in March 2011 to hold hearings devoted specifically to Islamic radicalization—the first time in history that federal legislators were scrutinizing American citizens by reference to their religious beliefs.

One aspect of the faith—or more precisely, one word—is inspiring particular dread. Hostility toward the shari'a has become contagious. The almost magical speed with which it can spread first struck me during the summer of 2008, in the unlikely surroundings of a Welsh literary festival. Listening to the British writer Martin Amis deliver one of his characteristically ruminative addresses on the state of the world, I was startled to hear him assert that the then up-and-coming senator Barack Obama faced execution under the shari'a if he ever reached the White House. An Internet search soon turned up his source: a recent *New York Times* op-ed, in which a certain Edward N. Luttwak had opined that the presidential candidate was an apostate under "Muslim law" because he ignored the faith into which his Kenyan father had been born. After asserting that "the recommended punishment is beheading at the hands of a cleric," the author had observed that "most citizens of the Islamic world" would be "horrified" (and possibly homicidal) once they learned of Obama's "conversion" to Christianity. Luttwak's most pertinent qualification was the expertise that he had garnered as a historian of Byzantium and a theoretician about war, and the only Muslim he bothered to consult had ridiculed his notion of hereditary apostasy (as the *Times*'s public editor later acknowledged), but his pseudo-fatwa was far from unique. Dozens of self-styled "counter-jihadis" are nowadays campaigning online against their own conceptions of the shari'a, cherry-picking from the Qur'an and hadiths to formulate theories about Islamic law that could give any Salafi a run for his money. They even have their own miniature cause célèbre: a June 2009 case in which a New Jersey family court judge denied a Muslim woman a restraining order against her ex-husband, partly on the ground that the man had believed himself divinely authorized to rape her during marriage; and though the bizarrely unjust decision was swiftly overturned on appeal, it regularly forms the centerpiece for claims that the American legal system is under attack. And those claims have found considerable support—most notably, in November 2010, when 70 percent of Oklahoma voters approved an amendment to their state constitution to ban local courts from ever "considering or using shari'a law." No Oklahoma court had ever given any indication that it might do so, admittedly, and the state's thirty thousand Muslims were to all outward appearances content with the status quo. Supporters of the amendment thought that irrelevant, however. The measure was, they explained, a "pre-emptive strike" against an imminent "onslaught."

The alarm is not entirely irrational. Several Muslim extremists have attempted or committed terrible acts of violence in recent years, and it would be disingenuous here to deny the trauma they have caused—not least because I have experienced it, as a resident of Manhattan on 9/11 and a commuter in London on the July 2005 day that its transportation system was multiply bombed. And though such atrocities call for deliberation rather than retaliation, worries of repeat attacks are not groundless. Within the United States itself, there have been more than three hundred successful prosecutions under the country's core terrorism statutes over the last decade, and law-enforcement agencies have claimed to break up dozens of serious conspiracies. A survey of opinions among American Muslims in May 2007, meanwhile, reported that 8 percent were willing in some circumstances to justify suicide bombing in defense of Islam. That finding is too ambiguous to merit much analysis—especially because a more recent poll shows that Muslims are less likely than any other faith community in the United States to justify military attacks on civilians—but it cannot be spun into insignificance either. In an age of online bomb recipes and exploding backpacks, a single extremist who has made his peace with violence is one too many.

At the risk of laboring a very well-worn point, however, the overwhelming majority of the United States' two and a half million Muslims are just as happy as anyone else to live and let live. And though opponents of radical Islam invariably portray their cause as rational, "Islamophobia" is an appropriate way of characterizing the climate they have helped to create. The American way of life is not succumbing to the scimitar, and a caliphate is not about to rise where the U.S. Constitution once stood. The reality is that Muslims are serving as a lightning rod for social tension, just as Communists and Jews and black people have done at other times, because a minority of Americans are still shell-shocked by 9/11 and concerned to oppose people who seem reminiscent of its assailants. Muslims in the United States are thereby facing vilification in some quarters as a foreign peril, even though a third of them are native-born and the remainder come from at least sixty-eight different countries. Whereas it would ordinarily be thought either offensive or stupid to blame vices on cultures—to attribute the high female infanticide rates of India and China to Hinduism or Confucian thought, for example—a spurious link between Islamic beliefs and extremists' deeds is being forged. Every Bosnian-, Bangladeshi-, and Arab-American is coming to look that much more like a wife beater, honor killer, or suicide bomber—smeared by association, pending confirmation of innocence.

The demonization is obviously objectionable on the basis that it is unfair, but its baleful consequences extend further. The atmosphere of menace makes it harder to focus on genuine threats; and American Muslims have disproportionately lost faith in the FBI, thereby denying law-enforcement agencies valuable linguistic expertise and actionable intelligence. Even the courtroom successes of recent years carry risks. Most of the serious conspiracies prosecuted over the last decade have been facilitated or promoted by police informants, with only a handful of agreements coming anywhere close to actual fruition. Nipping mischief in the bud is an excellent strategy in principle, but the pattern is one that bodes ill. Overreliance on sting operations is always prone to nurture complacency—because any system that rewards the creation of controllable crimes makes it that much less likely that officials will attend to uncontrollable ones.

The most serious danger is the least tangible of all. As the United States pursues domestic terrorists, the far greater global significance of non-terrorism is being obscured: the fact that Muslims are the most numerous victims of Islamic extremism, for example, and the fact that devout believers in countries such as Pakistan are dying to defeat the fanatics in greater numbers than anyone else. Instead of trying to accommodate such complexities, the counter-jihadis are drawing directly from their opponents' playbook to portray the world as a battle between Islam and the West. Many works could illustrate the point, but one that is convenient to mention—because I read it soon after visiting Cairo in July 2010—is a book written by an Oslo-based American named Bruce Bawer. The author personified the rapidly mutating nature of the anti-Muslim cause. Whereas some high-profile social conservatives such as Glenn Beck and Ann Coulter have based their contempt for Islam on "Judeo-Christian values," the openly gay Bawer was more concerned to stress the faith's supposed intolerance. And his polemic, *While Europe Slept: How Radical Islam Is Destroying the West from Within*, was as gloomy a prognosis as the title portended. In Bawer's eyes, Norway in particular and the Continent in general had brushed aside the enormity of 9/11. In thrall to pernicious ideas about multiculturalism, indigenous Europeans had lost their bearings and were straining to appease Islamic extremists, yielding up freedoms at every turn. Muslims were meanwhile breeding at a tremendous rate and threatening to reproduce "beyond the point of no return." Subservience or civil war lay on the horizon, warned Bawer, and it was not preposterous to imagine that Europeans would soon accept the right of Muslims to perpetrate mass murder against Jews. Deftly blurring the battle lines of World War II, the book concluded with a lament for a continent that once echoed to the speeches of Winston Churchill—which was now walking, "step by step, to the gallows."

Although Bawer's hyperbole was never likely to win me over, I read his book with genuine curiosity. Libertarian anger against Muslims is often more intriguing than straightforward bigotry, if only because of the relish with which its exponents tend to cast aside previous inhibitions, and it is always interesting to hear familiarities described by a stranger. But Bawer's Europe was a bleakly alien landscape, and the belligerently fertile Muslims scrounging across its surface were unlike anyone I knew. Only his tone was recognizable, and it was not comforting. Many children of immigrants learn early in life to be sensitive to gripes about multiculturalism, because they are often coded expressions of xenophobia, and the presentation of Islam in *While Europe Slept* seemed woefully one-sided. The book's deficiencies became even more apparent after a terrible event in July 2011 that had nothing to do with Bawer himself: the massacre perpetrated by Anders Breivik, the Norwegian neo-fascist who fancied himself the herald of an anti-Muslim crusade. Shortly before bombing and shooting dead more than seventy people, Breivik posted a rambling online justification in the hope of inspiring copycat murders, and it included twenty-two references to Bawer's writing. The citations were an understandably unwelcome surprise to Bawer, who expressed concern that his points about Islam's destructiveness might somehow be discredited, but though no book can properly be blamed for every act it inspires, the link cannot simply be discounted either. Tirades always generate more heat than light, and the same danger that attaches to the incendiary language of some Muslims—the risk of sparking violent rage—applies to non-Muslims. That is not to deny the value of opinionated argument but to recall the value of empathy. At a time when interfaith relations are fraught, even critiques can try to imagine opposing points of view, and if they do not, it is fair to wonder whether they might be promoting the very conflict that they claim to illuminate.

The importance of mutual comprehension is nowhere greater than the country of my birth. The United Kingdom's 1.65 million Muslims are disproportionately connected to the volatile regions of Pakistan and India, and they have gained an international reputation for extremism. The urban neighborhoods in which they live have come to be characterized as socially dysfunctional hotbeds of extremism, and in the years after 9/11 Muslims have frequently been blamed by right-wing commentators for a breakdown in the cohesiveness of Britain. And the hostility has often focused on a familiar theme. Oklahoma legislators justified their opposition to the shari'a by telling local reporters that Britain was succumbing, perhaps terminally, to its "cancer." Islam's critics more generally are prone to cite opinion polls that suggest that 30 to 40 percent of British Muslims want to live under the shari'a.

The meaning of such findings is far from self-evident, however. British Muslims are not known for their admiration of actual foreign legal systems, and supporters of the shari'a are a lot more likely to complain about its misrepresentation than to celebrate its application. The people responding to the pollsters are far from settled in their views, in any event. Self-identified champions of the shari'a tend to be young, with sixteen- to twenty-four-year-olds more than twice as favorable as those over fifty-five, according to one poll. The only study to explore what all the support might entail—a 2008 survey of Muslim students—implies meanwhile that many people are not at all sure. Fifty percent of respondents were unwilling or unable to express a view on the very basic question of whether Islam allowed legal interpretations to differ according to time and place. The shari'a undoubtedly has its adherents, but their backing does not make for a legal framework, still less a political manifesto.

Those comments are just another illustration of the same old truism—that assumptions are not the same as evidence—but they gain substance when set against the evolving structure of British Islam. Unlike American Muslims, who fairly representatively reflect the faith's global diversity, most British Muslims share a common South Asian cultural heritage. And whereas the United States has been built on a culture of mass immigration and rapid assimilation, Britain has historically received newcomers with a combination of curiosity, hostility, and indifference. The effect has been to foster self-absorption in immigrant communities, and historical factors made that particularly true of the Pakistani and Indian Muslims who surged into Britain's mills and factories between the late 1950s and the 1970s. Ever since their forefathers had failed to overthrow imperial rule in 1857, they had been unusually suspicious of British officials. But though that encouraged a degree of isolation and fortified social conservative views, it did not promote aggression. Introversion rather than pushiness typified Muslim interactions with the majority community.

That is not quite the whole story, however. A more assertive aspect to British Islam has been in evidence for more than two decades—at least since January 14, 1989, when Muslims in the northern English town of Bradford staged one of the world's first public burnings of *The Satanic Verses*—and it has grown exponentially as turmoil has intensified in South Asian hot spots such as Afghanistan and Kashmir. But factors other than faith have determined the pace and nature of radicalization, and the most important has been age. A small minority of young people have embraced revivalist doctrines that remain entirely alien to most of their parents. Bewildered community elders shake their heads at the ostentatious religiosity and outlandish styles of the rebellious subculture: its crazy calf-length pants, top-to-toe veils, and defiant facial hairstyles. Teenage hotheads impress their peers and confuse adults by quoting obscure religious texts and fiery online preachers. And though they move with more ease than older Muslims in wider British society, they have inherited a particularly malign variant of the community's traditional insularity. First-generation South Asian Muslims, steeped in a culture that had just ended two centuries of colonial rule in India, often identified politically with minorities such as Irish and black people, and it was natural for them to make common cause with Hindus and Sikhs. A few of their children and grandchildren, by contrast, are rejecting theories of equality and secularism outright.* Some envisage non-Muslims as simplistically as racists might regard

---

*One reason for the hostility, small but significant, is linguistic. "Secularism" is rendered in Urdu as *la-diniyat*, which translates roughly as "faithlessness" and carries connotations of unscrupulousness.

their targets—stereotypical infidels whose primary concerns are to binge drink, copulate, and kick sand in Islam's face.

The generation gap has been reflected by the expansion in recent years of Hizb ut-Tahrir, or the Party of Liberation: a group that owes much to the recent revival of radical Islam but very little to the historical concerns of British Muslims. Originating from the 1948 partition of Palestine and Israel, it campaigns in more than forty countries for restoration of Islam's ancient caliphate, and though the British branch has no more than a couple thousand supporters, activists are young and highly motivated, with an influence on campuses that is out of proportion to their number. Trading on discontent, the group enjoys a particularly loyal following among the Bengalis of east London—one of the United Kingdom's poorest, least employed, and worst-educated Muslim communities—which comes with multiple ironies. The district is close to the capital's former docks, and though the opium dens and Huguenot chapels that memorialized some earlier disembarkations are gone, several synagogues remain from the great influx of eastern European Jewry that began to reach London in the 1880s. The buildings stand as mute rebuke to Hizb ut-Tahrir, which has always had difficulty distinguishing between sympathy for Palestinians and malice toward Jews, but they could also usefully give pause to critics of Islam who think that anti-Muslim sentiment is always rational or that the term "Judeo-Christian values" speaks for itself. Turn-of-the-century Russian immigrants were regularly beaten up and sometimes killed for wearing beards and distinctive clothing. Social reformers used to lament the newcomers' equivocal attitudes toward integration, almost as though they were congregating in tuberculosis-ridden tenements by choice, rather than fear and necessity. And populist newspapers vilified them for decades—a campaign that reached its nadir in August 1938, when the right-wing *Daily Mail* demanded that British ports turn away stateless foreigners, because political asylum rules were being "outrage[ously]" abused by Jewish refugees from Nazi Germany.

As is true of any dynamic political movement, Hizb ut-Tahrir tailors its messages to its audiences, and its global affiliates speak in many tongues. In Western states, the organization condemns democracy as a false idol. In Muslim countries, it favors political freedom—because autocrats and dictators have accused it of insurrectionist ambitions and forced it underground. Although it is collectively careful to avoid the advocacy of violence, its calls to overhaul the existing moral and political order are fluent in double-talk—swift to champion righteous resistance, and slow to condemn armed attacks. But even if many aspects of its message are fuzzy, its ultimate goal is clear. According to the draft constitution that it hopes will one day form the basis for a revived caliphate, Muslims should look forward to a world in which apostates are executed, women and infidels are put in their proper place, and slavery is restored as a category of citizenship.

That is an eccentric wish list—especially because it is based on a legal manual about eleventh-century Baghdad rather than idealized claims about the Prophet's governance over Medina—and back in August 2008, I made an effort to comprehend its appeal. The occasion was a conference that the group holds annually to prepare for the caliphate's return. Held at an Art Deco movie theater called the Troxy, deep in its east London stronghold, it was a somewhat surreal experience. Sharp-suited bouncers marshaled queues of adolescents and young families past the popcorn machines into a glittering auditorium, illuminated by a silent slide show of grisly images from nameless wars. As children scurried in the aisles, the stills gave way to a slick documentary about the caliphate's rise and fall, in which galloping warriors, chin-stroking astronomers, perfidious popes, and callous imperialists enacted centuries of Islamic magnificence and Western treachery. To the sound of a drumbeat, scrolling facts and figures then revealed just how formidable Muslims would be once again, if they only got their act together, fading to black with one final statistic. The Islamic world apparently contained "4.7 million armed personnel—more than the USA, Europe and India combined."

The hint of doom came out of left field, and with the skittish emotional energy of all good cults it was instantly followed by an ebullient welcome. The organization's chairman strode onto the stage like a pro, jovially wondering why the British government was so frightened of Muslims, and as cries of "Allahu akbar" arose among the audience, he introduced the main event. A foreign affairs specialist soon took to the rostrum to outline how the caliphate was likely to revive: the world's so-called Islamic states were so rotten that one would soon "fall" and set others tumbling like dominoes. A legal scholar followed up with confirmation that imposition of the shari'a would bring about universal justice, and an economics expert flicked through PowerPoint pie charts to show how everyone would be guaranteed free health care, education, and an end to hunger. Proceedings eventually concluded with a celebration of Islam's intellectual achievements, which identified the pinnacle of Muslim scholarship as al-Ghazali's "refutation of Greek philosophy."

It was difficult then to credit those assessments with much force, and today, with the Arab Spring of 2011 fading into memory and fresh points of conflict popping up across the Islamic world, the group's predictions are harder than ever to evaluate. Although Hizb ut-Tahrir confirms via its website that world events are continuing to unfold as expected, only the blindly faithful and the very fearful could be sure that each crisis is another step on the road toward a caliphate. And whatever might be said about the delegates' foresight, their hindsight was certainly not worth much. The Abbasid and Ottoman caliphate had been ignored or opposed by five of the civilizations they seemed to think it had governed.* The same speaker who admired al-Ghazali for refuting Greek philosophy lionized Ibn Sina, a prolific philosopher whose work on Aristotle had been the target of al-Ghazali's refutation. And though historical generalizations abounded, the one that is most cogent was studiously ignored. Hyper-Sunni dogmas like those of Hizb ut-Tahrir had numbed creativity whenever they had been ascendant, while cultural achievements had repeatedly flourished under open-minded rulers whom the group would consider heretical: the Mu'tazilite caliphs and Shi'a sultans of ninth- and tenth-century Baghdad, for example, and the eclectic emperors who emerged out of Anatolia, Persia, and central Asia after the Mongol invasions.

The accuracy of the arguments is beside the point, however. Hizb ut-Tahrir is in the business of radicalism, not rational discourse, and its leaders invoke wonders lost and glories to come in order to override history rather than describe it. And by that measure, the group's gobbledygook is not only adequate but potent. It reinvents the past, portraying Hizb ut-Tahrir as Islam's true custodian in a world of exploitative,

---

*Namely, Umayyad Andalusia, Fatimid Egypt, Safavid Persia, Timurid Khorasan, and Mughal India.

neocolonialist, brainwashing warmongers. Like the scholars who condemn Muslim tombs as pagan ones and deny the authenticity of thousand-year-old customs, the vision is neoconservative rather than conservative—determined not to preserve actual traditions but to uphold theoretical ones. And not for the first time in history, the idealism is driving youthful enthusiasts to fanaticism. As zealous in their jilbabs and dishdashas as an earlier generation might have been in overalls and Che Guevara T-shirts, they think themselves right and the world wrong—and totalitarianism a solution. If Hizb ut-Tahrir's draft constitution is any guide, they want to deny non-Muslims any political influence in their ideal state (Articles 21, 26, 28, 33, 42, 49, 67, 87, 105, and others). They propose to outlaw Muslims who oppose the caliph's interpretations of Islam by word, deed, or thought (Article 3). And they believe judges should have an unquestionable discretion—to hand down a death sentence, say, or to order the return of a runaway slave—with no right of appeal (Article 74).

It is always possible to comprehend the enthusiasm of revolutionaries, even if Hizb ut-Tahrir's utopia might make the blood run a little cold. Adherents are made to feel part of a very important and complicated moral endeavor and enabled to anticipate a time when day-to-day problems end and tables are turned on oppressors everywhere. But though Hizb ut-Tahrir's appeals to vanity and justice clearly have an audience, the market is niche, and three years on from my trip to the Troxy it shows few signs of expansion. Traditional social and family structures have asserted themselves against the radicals with some force, while surveys suggest that British Muslims in the twenty-first century are actually more trusting of government agencies than the population at large. Although leafleteers put in hundreds of man-hours to warn mosque-goers that hell awaited anyone who voted in the United Kingdom's 2010 elections, believers braved the risks to the extent that female Muslim legislators were returned to Parliament for the first time—three of them, in fact. And while Hizb ut-Tahrir still holds annual conferences in the East End, its heartland looks no more prepared for a caliphate than it has ever been. The last time I passed the Troxy, the cinema was hosting a gay nightclub—called, with eerie suitability, Salvation.

The fault line between the neoconservatism of Hizb ut-Tahrir and the conservatism of many ordinary believers is of correspondingly fundamental importance. Were a pollster one day to ask British Muslims not simply if they have faith in the shariʻa but also what they mean by that faith, the point would be proved. Some disaffected youths would undoubtedly hanker for the destruction of television sets, the concealment of women, and compulsory beards. A disturbed handful might even thrill at the thought of mutilated shoplifters, brained adulterers, and open-air crucifixions. But the maniacs are exceptional. Most British Muslims would not be able to tell a *taʻzir* punishment from a *hadd* if they tried. Insofar as they express enthusiasm for life under "the shariʻa," they are saying that they believe in doing God's will. They doubtless hope that He will help them out in return, but the overwhelming majority want nothing more sinister than those intangibles that are missed in their absence: things like solidarity, status, and dignity.

The aspirational appeal of the shariʻa has a significance that extends far beyond the United Kingdom, and it has particular resonance in the United States. Radicals who adhere to groups such as Hizb ut-Tahrir have even less of a toehold in North America than they do in Britain, and though some Muslims might espouse views that others will find unpalatable or controversial, the mere belief in the shariʻa is not a call for justice red in tooth and claw. The overwhelming majority of immigrants to the West have made their peace with secularism, and the remedies they expect from Islamic law are correspondingly minimal. A woman whose husband has abandoned her without speaking the words of release required by the Qurʼan might approach a mufti in search of an annulment. Senior figures in a community will pay visits to the homes of disruptive teenagers to remind them of their religious roots. Muslims who are prudent as well as pious might ask scholars to tell them which mortgage and insurance products are consistent with Islamic jurisprudence. Every faith community in the United States, from the Amish to the Zoroastrians, has equivalent ways of doing right by God. The only difference is that Muslims call their quest "the shariʻa."

Although that would have been a very unremarkable observation just a few years ago, it has become notoriously contentious in recent times. In 2011, there were attempts to formally delegitimize the shariʻa in more than a dozen states—among them Alaska, South Dakota, and Wyoming, where it would take considerable effort to find any Muslims in the first place—and the Oklahoma effort that set the ball rolling, as previously noted, was led by politicians who were convinced that "shari'a law" threatened Britain with extinction. That in its turn reflected jitters dating back to a decision in August 2007 by Deobandi muftis based near the English city of Birmingham to set up a so-called Muslim Arbitration Tribunal to offer consenting parties the right to have their commercial and family disputes resolved according to Islamic law, for a small fee. Counter-jihadis had been warning ever since of slippery slopes, thin ends of wedges, and political correctness gone mad. Several talked darkly of treason, linking the tribunal's emergence to the unique alienation of British Muslims. It was yet more confirmation, to those who sought it, that Europe was sleepwalking to the gallows.

It was also a storm in a teacup. Observant British Jews had been taking their quarrels to a similar body known as the Beth Din for more than a century, and the Muslim Arbitration Tribunal had no jurisdiction over criminal matters or cases involving children. A U.K.-trained lawyer sat on all its panels, and every decision was subject to judicial review—meaning that it was subject to reversal if it disclosed unfair procedures, human rights violations, or any other step that ordinary courts considered contrary to the public interest. But the moral panic was even less rational than such things are by their nature—because of one remarkable but under-acknowledged fact. Attempts to curtail judicial recognition of the shari'a in the United States were already several decades too late. There has been a federal arbitration law since 1925, and U.S. courts have been positively encouraging its use since the 1980s. Among the bodies that have thereby been legitimized are religious tribunals, and the judgments that result are given force of law by state and federal courts. Churchgoers are allowed to take their arguments to Christian conciliators, for example, and once they have agreed to do so, a ruling will be legally binding on both parties. The Beth Din of America does not merely decide the legal rights of devout Jews; it formally forbids believers to pursue complaints through the secular judicial system without prior authority from a rabbi. And Muslims can also have their inheritance, business, and matrimonial disputes sorted out by Islamic scholars, who attempt to decide them according to the shari'a. The precepts of Islamic law, like those of other religious codes, therefore have judicial force in the United States already. That

would change only if Congress overruled itself, because the 1925 statute preempts inconsistent state legislation, and the chances of that
happening are almost zero. Any reform would have to impact equally
on all faith communities, and it is not only Muslims who would object
if federal legislators presumed to do that.

Some people would be upset, were they to discover the truth. Die-
hard Islamophobes, having warned for years of barbarians at the gates,
are likely to take it hard that American courts have been upholding
Muslim arbitrations so uneventfully for so long. Even people of a more
tolerant disposition might feel residual unease at the thought of a U.S.
court treating Islam just like any other faith. But though perplexity in
the face of uncertainty is natural enough, antagonism toward the shariʻa
is no good answer to confusion. There are sound reasons to worry
about extreme interpretations of Islamic law, but the fact that American
Muslims profess to believe in a path ordained by God bears no relation
to that problem. And the Constitution is not so fragile that legalized
discrimination is necessary to ensure its survival.

The prosaic legal reality is that the United States, like any other secular democracy, is institutionally obliged to balance popular fears of
clerical domination and official respect for freedom of worship. A legal
thicket has always awaited government officials who upset that equilibrium by telling believers how to conduct their affairs, and the anti-
shariʻa cause is so clearly hostile to one particular religion that it is all
but certain to sink without legal trace. Oklahoma's amendment stalled
almost as soon as it was passed, when a local Muslim persuaded a
federal judge that it threatened his First Amendment rights—not least
because he hoped one day to be buried according to the shariʻa—and
state legislators have already abandoned attempts to draft a replacement. Efforts are continuing elsewhere to enact more durable laws, to
be sure, but no matter how cunningly they might disguise their intent,
any measure that targets people by reference to the shariʻa is never
going to pass constitutional muster.

None of that is intended to suggest that decisions made in the United
States under color of Islamic jurisprudence should ever be immune
from scrutiny or criticism. Muslim theologians are at least as likely as
anyone else to abuse their authority, and no immigrant ever came to
the West expecting to find an Islamic government, whereas a large

number came to escape one. But acknowledging the basic right of American Muslims to regulate their religious affairs is a constitutional necessity, not a capitulation to extremism. And if muftis in the United States are ready to square their interpretations of the shariʿa with the Bill of Rights, only a fool would stand in their way.

On a Friday evening toward the end of my stay in Cairo, I took one final stroll through the southern City of the Dead. It was as tranquil as usual. Away from the main tracks, cemetery dogs were stirring, and pumpkin and toadstool domes were casting ever longer and weirder shadows as the sun went down. Earthenware jars hung outside several sepulchres, honoring hadiths in which the Prophet commends gifts of water to the thirsty, and televisions flickered out of some of the better-appointed tombs. A group of chador-clad women giggled for snapshots in front of a pillbox shrine, and the courtyard beneath the great cupola of Imam al-Shafiʿi's mausoleum was alive with activity. Boys played soccer on its polished flagstones, and younger children squealed on a tin gondola that had been stranded there since the saint's recent birthday festivities. At a neighboring teahouse, white-turbaned Sufis gurgled on hubble-bubbles and clacked away at games of backgammon. Someone's mobile phone chanted a tinny verse of the Qur'an, but it was squelched and gave way to the "Lambada," blaring from a passing scooter.

As I sat among the Sufis, I fell to contemplating what Imam al-Shafiʿi would have made of it all. Actual communications from beyond the grave are reserved to the blessed in Islamic tradition, but fantasizing them is no sin, and I wondered whether he would have been more impressed by the continuities or appalled by the innovations. If, by the grace of God, his spirit had wandered forth to join me for a lemon tea, there was certainly a chance that he would have thought a few fatwas in order. He reportedly feared frivolities so much that he ruled musicians and board gamers to be unworthy of giving courtroom testimony. His followers later became vocally opposed to the presence of women in cemeteries, and some of them claimed that al-Shafiʿi would have condemned his own tomb. Many Shafiʿites today revile satellite televisions, digital cameras, and *shisha* pipes, and one of the most eminent— the grand mufti of Egypt—issued a fatwa in 2010 to warn Muslims that no good could ever come of Qur'anic ring tones. But it is at least conceivable that al-Shafi'i's soul would have taken a more easygoing approach. As a young man in the Palestinian town of Asqalan (Ashkelon), he had been more interested in the pleasures of archery than the rigors of law. He was the author of melancholy poetry that can still be recited by some Arabs today, and popular repute credits him with considerably more respect for female piety than some of his followers. When the time came to lay him to rest in 820, the person who conducted prayers over his grave was a woman named Nafisa—so respected by al-Shafi'i for her hadith scholarship that, according to local legend, he still pays intangible nocturnal visits to her own nearby shrine.

Speculations about what Muhammad al-Shafi'i would have thought about the evening of July 25, 2010, are in one sense pointless. It is of course impossible to know. But they help to illustrate that ideas about the shari'a have been demonstrably changing for at least twelve hundred years. Tens of thousands of reports about the Prophet were enshrined or disregarded by hadith scholars in the century that followed al-Shafi'i's death. Jurists went on to produce hundreds of thousands of pages of text. When those hadiths and legal opinions are interpreted today in the light of modern understandings of the Qur'an, the permutations become almost limitless. And whether a conclusion derived from the texts is best characterized as harmonious, violent, misogynistic, or liberal, it is a choice rather than a command.

No one understood the need for dynamic interpretation of the shari'a better than al-Shafi'i himself. He acknowledged that his teacher Malik ibn Anas had been too parochial in suggesting that disputes should be resolved by reference to the views prevalent in Medina alone. He was also the first scholar to consider in written detail what was implied by the sacred struggle to comprehend the shari'a—*ijtihad*—and he made clear that jurists were obliged to discount sacred texts almost as often as they had to apply them. Across the range from Salafi to Shi'a, Muslims nowadays do no less, and *ijtihad* has in recent years produced some notably fluid approaches to the shari'a. The American female scholar Amina Wadud drew on tenth-century scholarship to lead a mixed congregation in worship in New York in March 2005, for example, while Tariq Ramadan has worked to develop a theory of secular citizenship

out of Islamic principles of coexistence. Academics elsewhere are retrieving Islamic arguments to limit government intrusiveness and promote international human rights, on the eminently sensible basis that
Islamic states should not be the countries that most often deny liberties
to Muslims. Even the legal bureaucrats of Saudi Arabia have occasionally recognized the need for reform, and though it could never be said
of Saudi *ijtihad* that it was ahead of the curve, the kingdom went so far
in 2001 as to abandon Hanbalite-based laws allowing for the use of
torture in custody.

As that indicates, however, the path forward is by no means clear,
and there is one particularly formidable stumbling block. No matter
how overwhelming the call for change and no matter how brilliant a
scholarly insight may seem, it is often said that neither consensus nor
ijtihad can ever override an explicit textual provision (*nass*) set down
by the Qur'an or a sound hadith. And that has fortified some very uncompromising views indeed. Ayatollah Mohammad Taqi Mesbah-Yazdi,
a stalwart believer in the sacred character of the Islamic Republic of
Iran, has had occasion in recent years to consider the modern approach
of Islamic law toward slavery, for example, and he made clear his view
that the institution was alive and well. "If there's a war between us and
the infidels, we'll take slaves," was his opinion. "The ruling on slavery
hasn't expired and is eternal . . . We'll guide them, make them Muslims
and then return them to their countries."

It is fairly easy to piece together the thinking behind his argument.
Slavery was acknowledged by the Qur'an. Jurists at the end of the eighth
century laid down rules to regulate the purchase and sale of non-
Muslim prisoners of war and made clear that any who failed to embrace Islam would pass on captive status to their children. But though
Mesbah-Yazdi's reasoning *can* be justified, it has been publicly renounced
by every Muslim state in the world, through domestic reforms and international human rights treaties. Mesbah-Yazdi may believe in a God
who prefers servitude to emancipation, but his country quite rightly
acknowledges that the time for enslaving prisoners of war has passed.
And the reason for that is clear. Some aspects of Islamic jurisprudence
ought not to be applied today, whatever might have been the case a
thousand and more years ago. That is not to question the inviolability

of a *nass*. It would be futile to argue that slavery does not at some level form part of the shari‘a, because no one has the authority to erase revelations from the Qur'an. It is entirely proper, however, to consider that verses justifying manumission point the way to behavior more in accordance with God's long-term aims. And what is true of slavery might also be true of other aspects of the divine law.

The diffuse nature of the Islamic community means that changes to legal interpretation, however and whenever they come, are invariably gradual. But there is one final development worth acknowledging, which might yet transform its pace exponentially. Rank-and-file believers once had to undertake much contemplative prayer, at the very least, to resolve their legal uncertainties, and they often had no choice but to turn to a scholar. But communications technology has augmented their options. Local interpretations of the shari‘a have gone global, and countless thousands of Muslims are daily cutting, pasting, and instant messaging centuries of legal scholarship across the blogs and social networks of cyberspace. The workings of online *ijtihad* are utterly uncontrollable. Its practitioners vary in experience and intelligence as much as they differ in age and sex. Some want to do no more than flame heretics and troll infidels, and others are inspired most by the virtual sound of their virtual voice. But many must be thinking more deeply about how twenty-first-century humanity stands in relation to God, and in ways as yet unknowable the Islamic community's structure is being transformed.

Any decent journey should transform the person who undertakes it, and three years of exposure to cumin-scented bazaars, twilit mosques, and ancient scholarship certainly breathed life into the intellectual curiosity that sparked this book. Wrestling with jurisprudential concepts so different from those with which I was familiar from England and the United States also made me reassess some basic assumptions about the meaning of law. It was in my barristerial blood to think of legal order in simple terms—as a structure of court-enforced rules— but Islamic jurists had always imagined its dimensions more expansively. The shari‘a was the touchstone of right and wrong, and its guidance

enabled humanity to enjoy God's bounty without guilt. The failure
to differentiate the permissible from the prohibited, by contrast, was
shorthand for desolation: the fate of misguided cults, a fantasy with
which demons tempted holy men, and the manifesto of licentious ty-
rants. The only people who ever dared proclaim that the shari'a had
become redundant were false prophets, prematurely heralding a salvation that was not in their gift. Modern revivalists shared the sweeping
perspectives, and even the most thoughtful among those I met seemed
unable to comprehend how a truth so self-evident could be rationally
opposed. When I asked a Karachi scholar why, in his opinion, Pakistan's judicial authorities had never actually seen a stoning or amputation sentence through to enforcement, he was genuinely flummoxed.
"No one ever says that 100 legislators, or 120 lawyers, are perfect, and yet
we place our destiny in their hands," Maulana Asghar Shaheedi observed sadly. "It's always been a question to me as well why people who
say 'Obey a country's laws, right or wrong' do not submit themselves to
the laws of Allah. Can't the God who has created us do what He wants
to do?"

As the perplexity implicit in that question suggests, however, the
faith is nowadays shadowed by despair. The societies most receptive to
radical Islamic reordering over the last few decades have been those in
which disorder was previously most rife. In the aftermath of wars and
coups and revolutions, the shari'a has been shrunk to meet the needs
of the moment, and though punitive clampdowns have often brought
temporary relief, they have had about as much nobility as shotgun justice possessed in the Wild West. Revivalists have meanwhile spoken
of God as if He loves nothing so much as a thief's severed hand or the
blood of an apostate, disparaging criticism as blasphemy and reducing
Islam's genuine traditions of tolerance into platitudes. It was in Pakistan,
yet again, that the bleakness became most apparent, when I first heard
articulated the view that it was sinful to pity or pardon a person convicted of a Qur'anic offense. That theory turned out to be not a psycho-
pathic aberration but an opinion common among inflexible muftis and
clerics. They claimed that God obliged humanity forever to flog, amputate, and stone convicts, reserving for Himself alone the power to extend
mercy. In a country not lacking for injustice, they dreamed of a world

in which judges were required to punish but forbidden to forgive. Although I was no theologian, that did not look to me like an earthly paradise. It looked like a living hell.

The ruthlessness, though shocking, was not exactly a surprise. No one has ever said that Islamic scholars are infallible—except, perhaps, a few of those scholars themselves—and the claim to be doing God's work has never been the same as actually doing it. As the radicals would do well to ponder, it was in religion's name that Muslim judges meted out punishment to hard-liners such as Ibn Hanbal and Ibn Taymiyya during earlier eras of turmoil. The predictability of their views does not make them representative, however. Harsh approaches to justice exist in all cultures, and Western ways of handling matters such as criminal justice and war have many deficiencies of their own. And from a historical perspective, the narrow-mindedness is even more aberrant. No interpretation of the shari'a has ever been timeless, and Islam has never been doomed to insist otherwise. Muslims were experimenting with systems of jury trial and courts of appeal at a time when the tribes-people of Europe were requiring defendants to prove their innocence through ordeals. Innovative Islamic jurists institutionalized cultural diversity centuries before the canonists of Christendom came up with their best alternative—the ghetto. Such solutions evolved then as dynamically as did the problems, and Muslims today are no less capable of accommodating new expectations of fairness and compassion. Islamic jurisprudence has not spent the past fourteen hundred years opposed to change; it has been defined by it.

Perhaps the most important message that Islam's past offers the present comes in the repeated recognition among believers that confidence should not harden into arrogance. If any single assumption beyond Islam's core beliefs can be said to have united the community throughout its long history, it is the view that sins are ultimately for God to judge. That was why the Prophet Muhammad and early jurists preferred repentance to compulsion. It is the reason that thousands of scholars have distanced themselves from the temptations of worldly power. It explains the perennial reluctance of Muslim states to enforce the emblematic *hadd* penalties—just a single stoning during the five-hundred-year existence of the Ottoman Empire, for example. And it remains an excellent basis for social harmony today. The belief in a route toward salvation, winding ethereally from creation toward paradise, has always sought to transcend sins more than suppress them. It is onto that shari'a that believers are born, off its path that some will stray, and down its road that all will die. Earthly justice does not stand as still, however, and though humanity is bound to aim at rectitude, it has no business anticipating the terrors of the hereafter. Heaven and hell are beyond its jurisdiction, and whatever they may hold in store, mortals can only fail when they play God in the here and now.

Notes

Prologue: Infinite Justice

6 *A tenth-century writer*: El-Zein, *Islam, Arabs, and the Intelligent World of the Jinn*, pp. 105–107.

6 *At least eleven*: The countries are Afghanistan, Egypt, Iran, Iraq, the Maldives, Pakistan, Qatar, Saudi Arabia, Sudan, Syria, and Yemen. Libya's interim government indicated after October 2011 that it planned to acknowledge Islamic norms in a future fundamental law. Somalia and several northern Nigerian states also enforce provisions of the shari'a, though the former country lacks a constitutional framework, and the Nigerian constitution outlaws the establishment of any state religion. See also chapter 9, pp. 188–89, and chapter 10, pp. 216–20.

7 *fatally impaled himself*: Elliot, *History of India*, 5:91; see also Lane-Poole, *Mediaeval India*, pp. 70–71.

7 *they accentuated similarities*: On Sufism in thirteenth-century India, see Nizami, *Religion and Politics*, esp. pp. 58–61, 301–307, 311–12, 337–38; Frembgen, *Journey to God*, pp. 19–20.

11 *It was now to be known*: On the background to the name change, see Leonard, "American Muslims and Authority," p. 15.

12 *"[It] is the absolute cure"*: Abou El Fadl, *Great Theft*, p. 40, citing Ibn Qayyim's *A'lam al-muwaqqi'in*, 3:3.

13 *a dead shipmate, a pig, and a flask of wine*: Milani, *Lost Wisdom*, p. 34; see also Birgit Krawietz, "*Darūra* in Modern Islamic Law," in Gleave and Kermeli, *Islamic Law*, pp. 189–90.

13 *"Let none of you"*: Farah, *Marriage and Sexuality*, p. 106.

14 *The chief law lecturer*: Interview with Mufti Muhammad Yusuf Afshani, April 24, 2009. My conversation with the president of Jamaat e-Islami, Syed Munawar Hassan, took place in Lahore on April 13, 2009; the interview in Lucknow was with Maulana Ateeq Ahmad Qasmi Bastari of the Nadwa college, and it occurred on April 6, 2009.

15 *once demanded full credit*: Al-Jahiz, *Book of Misers*, p. 7.

15 *"If no one could write"*: Al-Mas'udi, *Meadows*, pp. 428–29.

1. Laying Down the Law

19 *"Recite!" The disembodied*: Qur'an 96. The narrative draws on the oldest detailed literary account of the Prophet's life, composed in the mid-eighth century but preserved only in the later edition by Ibn Hisham (d. 834): see Ibn Ishaq, *Life of Muhammad*, pp. 104–107 (hereafter cited as Ibn Ishaq). See also Ruthven, *Islam in the World*, pp. 36–37, where the author notes that the first revelation had antecedents in Arabic poetry; Nicholson, *Literary History of the Arabs*, pp. 150–80.

20 *"O Muhammad!" it boomed*: Al-Tabari, *History*, 6:71 (hereafter cited as al-Tabari).

20 *Waraqa bin Nawfal's response*: Ibn Ishaq, p. 107.

21 *Even the jinns*: Ibid., pp. 90–91, 194, and Qur'an 46:28–32 and 72:1.

21 *(hadiths)*: The word "hadith" literally means report, but it long ago came to mean a narration about the life of Muhammad specifically. A story about an early Muslim other than the Prophet is properly known as an *athar*.

21 *he is also supposed*: Al-Bukhari, 8.81.772; Abu Dawud, 38.4461. There is no standard way of citing hadiths, but these notes draw primarily on the online collection at www.usc.edu/schools/college/crcc/engagement/resources/texts/muslim.

22 *A coherent picture*: See Ibn Sa'd, *Tabaqat*, esp. 1:421–598; and see generally Ibn Ishaq.

22 *Khadija quickly accepted*: Ibn Ishaq, p. 111.

22 *"even though their fathers"*: Qur'an 2:170.

22 *They should pray*: On the obligation of prayer, see ibid., 50:39; Ibn Ishaq, p. 112; Goldziher, *Muslim Studies*, 1:43. On its direction, see Ibn Ishaq, pp. 135, 202.

22 *"nearer to [man]"*: Qur'an 50:16.

22 *Rumors rapidly spread*: See Ibn Ishaq, pp. 121–34; Qur'an 37:36, 21:5, 52:30; for God's ripostes, see Qur'an 69:41, 26:22. The accusation that Muhammad is possessed by jinns is referred to seven times in the Qur'an: Dols, *Majnūn*, pp. 217–23.

22 *In his telling, God*: See Qur'an 75, 77–79, 81–84, 88.

23 *women were chattels*: See Levy, *Social Structure*, pp. 94–95; but cf. Leila Ahmed, "Women and the Advent," who marshals an argument that the *jahiliyya* was a time of relatively egalitarian marriage customs, which began to succumb to patriarchal assumptions during the Prophet's lifetime.

23 *slaves bore a shameful*: See Goldziher, *Muslim Studies*, 1:115–25.

23 *Vengeance was as valued*: See Nicholson, *Literary History of the Arabs*, pp. 92–99.

23 *the birth of an actual girl*: Qur'an 6:137, 6:140, 6:150, 16:59, 17:31, 43:18, 81:8; see also Levy, *Social Structure*, pp. 91–92.

23 *Against that backdrop, Muhammad*: See Qur'an 49:10–11, 13.

23 *to teach that clemency*: See Goldziher, *Muslim Studies*, 1:24–27.

23 *The killing of a single*: Qur'an 5:32. The solemnity of the general prohibition is underscored by its single exception: the conclusion of a capital trial. Cf. 4:92–93, which deals with the killing of Muslims.

23 *every baby girl*: Ibid., 81:1–14.

23 *Penitents might yet spend*: Ibid., 56:15–38.

23 *The attitudes of many*: Ibn Ishaq, pp. 134, 136, 162–63, 180–81; Qur'an 6:8, 68:15, 25:6, 83:13, 44:14.

23 *Muhammad responded by challenging*: Qur'an 2:23–24, 10:38, 11:13, 17:88.

23 *He brushed aside charges*: Ibid., 2:106, 16:101.

23 *Specific circumstances had required*: Ibid., 29:47–51, 17:88–99, 26:4–68, 3:49; for affirmations of the non-miraculous nature of the Prophet's mission, see ibid., 2:118, 7:188, 17:59, 25:7–9.

23 *Many prominent Meccans thought not*: Ibn Ishaq, pp. 117–21, cf. pp. 79, 114.

24 *Abu Bakr had his beard tugged*: Ibid., pp. 131, 191; cf. p. 135.

24 *a group of Muslims fled*: Ibid., pp. 146–50.

24 *six visitors from Yathrib*: Ibid., pp. 197–98.

24 *"The apostle had not been given"*: Ibid., p. 212.

25 *After reportedly receiving*: Ibid., pp. 221–24.

26 *clitoridectomy*: See ibid., p. 375. Hadiths that later purported to authorize the practice are collected in Sami A. Abu-Sahlieh, "To Mutilate in the Name of Jehovah or Allah: Legitimization of Male and Female Circumcision," *Medicine and Law* 13, nos. 7–8 (1994), pp. 575–622, www.cirp.org/library/cultural/aldeebl/. Female genital mutilation is still endemic in Egypt, though the country's then-senior muftis, Ali Goma'a and Muhammad Sayyid Tantawi, declared it contrary to the shari'a at a conference on November 22–23, 2006. It was subsequently outlawed in June 2007.

26 *The custom of fasting*: Qur'an 2:183–87.

26 *God was requiring*: Compare ibid., 50:39 (two), and ibid., 17:79 and 52:49 (three). On the uncertain question of whether pagan Arabs prayed, see Goldziher, *Muslim Studies*, 1:39–44.

26 *Provisions in the Qur'an show*: The Qur'an's condemnations of *riba* are in 30:39, 4:161, 3:130, 2:275–80. The sin is often understood to mean usury, but it was understood more broadly: see Amedroz, "Hisba Jurisdiction," pp. 299–314. Almsgiving is commended throughout the Qur'an and would come to be assessed at 2.5 percent: Kremer, *Orient*, pp. 56–66. On inheritance, see Qur'an 2:180, 4:8–12, 4:176; Levy, *Social Structure*, pp. 96–97, 144–49.

26 *a relatively egalitarian outlook*: See discussions in Goldziher, *Muslim Studies*, 1:54–87; Levy, *Social Structure*, pp. 55–57.

26 *Muslims remained eligible*: Qur'an 4:92, 5:89, 24:33–34, 58:3, 90:10. Cf. discussion in Levy, *Social Structure*, pp. 73–81. It should also be noted that Islamic law would permit Christians and Jews to own Muslim slaves: Mez, *Renaissance*, p. 203.

26 *The criminal justice provisions*: The potentially capital offenses are known respectively as *hiraba* and *fasad fi'l-ard*: Qur'an 5:33–34. On the others, see ibid., 5:38–39 (theft/*sariqa*); 17:32, 24:2, 25:68–69 (fornication/*zina*); 24:4–5 (sexual slander/*qazf*).

27 *"a life for a life"*: Ibid., 5:45. On retaliation (*qisas*), see also ibid., 2:178, 2:194.

27 *Two additional measures*: Peters, *Crime and Punishment*, pp. 60–61, 64.

27 *a nonfatal means of humiliation*: Al-Mawardi, *Ordinances*, p. 259. The eleventh-century jurist states that a crucified person must be given food and water and permitted to pray and should not spend more than three days on the cross.

27 *Repentance was often reason enough*: See, for example, Qur'an 4:15–16, 5:34; cf. 5:39, 24:5.

27 *victims were urged*: Ibid., 17:33 ("If a man is slain unjustly, his heir is entitled to satisfaction. But let him not carry his vengeance too far, for his victim will in turn be assisted and avenged"). On blood money (*diyat*), see ibid., 4:92.

28 *The penalty itself had been known*: Lerner, *Creation of Patriarchy*, p. 63; Deuteronomy 13:10, 17:2–7, 21:18–21, 23:24; Leviticus 20:27.

28 *Islamic procedures were novel*: For the detailed rules that would later come to define the scope of this offense, see Peters, *Crime and Punishment*, pp. 59–62; Levy, *Social Structure*, pp. 119–20; al-Mawardi, *Ordinances*, pp. 257, 270–71.

28 *categorical answer*: Malik ibn Anas, *al-Muwatta*, p. 345.

28 *"Calling a spade a spade"*: Awdah, *al-Tashri*, 2:433–34, citing the hadith credited to Ibn Abbas in al-Bukhari, 8.82.813; cf. Peters, *Crime and Punishment*, p. 55. The English translation of Awdah's work contains a bowdlerized translation: see Oudah [*sic*], *Criminal Law of Islam*, 4:357.

29 *One of them states that*: Abu Dawud, 38.4405; cf. 38.4364. On the incident's divisiveness, see Muslim, 17.4205.

29 *One contemporary was heard*: See Abu Dawud, 38.4420.

29 *A second recalled that*: Ibid., 38.4414, 4428; cf. Hamid, *Moral Teachings*, p. 86.

30 *God was waiving the limits*: Qur'an 33:50; cf. 4:3.

30 *the dozen or so*: Ibn Sa'd gives the number as fourteen: *Women of Madina*, pp. 151–55; cf. alternative estimates in al-Tabari, 9:126–27.

30 *The teenager rode home*: See Ibn Ishaq, pp. 493–99; al-Bukhari, 3.48.829, 5.59.462, 6.60.274.

31 *The fault lay with*: Qur'an 24:4–5; cf. 24:11–16, 23–25; al-Bukhari, 3.48.829. The wording of the Qur'anic prohibition of *qazf*, which specifically protects "women," was later extended to include men as well: see Levy, *Social Structure*, p. 119. For a narrative account of the Affair of the Lie, see Abbot, *A'ishah*, pp. 29–38.

31 *At a series of debates*: See Ibn Ishaq, pp. 258–61, 270–77. For passages of the Qur'an dealing with the status of Jesus, the Trinity, and the crucifixion, see 2:116, 9:30, 10:68, 18:4–5, 19:88–89, 43:82, 5:73, and 4:156.

31 *"Now, Muhammad," they asked*: Ibn Ishaq, p. 270; cf. Qur'an 39:67. Evidence of deteriorating relations with the Jews is scattered across the Qur'an, but the relevant passages are concentrated in suras 2–5.

31 *Muhammad instructed his followers*: Ibn Ishaq, p. 258; cf. pp. 202, 289.

32 *A prankster then hitched*: Ibid., pp. 751n568, 363. For the Qur'an's injunction about veils (which applies only to the Prophet's wives), see 33:59; for a discussion, see Leila Ahmed, "Women and the Advent," pp. 681–84.

32 *one such force killed*: Ibn Ishaq, pp. 461–69; al-Baladhuri, *Origins*, 1:40; Qur'an 33:26. On Jewish participation at Uhud, see Ibn Ishaq, p. 384; cf. p. 372.

32 *As Muhammad returned in triumph*: Ibn Ishaq, p. 552; cf. al-Baladhuri, *Origins*, 1:66.

32 *"no compulsion in religion"*: Qur'an 2:256.

32 *Most Meccans were given*: Ibn Ishaq, pp. 550–55; al-Tabari, 8:178–92; al-Baladhuri, *Origins*, 1:66–68.

32 *"fight and slay the pagans"*: Qur'an 9:5; on the circumstances in which this verse was revealed, see Ibn Ishaq, pp. 618–19.

33 *Muhammad died*: Ibn Sa'd, *Tabaqat*, 2:324–29.

33 *"My legs would not bear me"*: Ibn Ishaq, pp. 682–83; see also Ibn Sa'd, *Tabaqat*, 2:332–39; cf. Qur'an 3:144.

33 *There are two versions*: Ibn Ishaq, pp. 683–87; al-Tabari, 9:189–206; see also discussions in Madelung, *Succession to Muhammad*, pp. 28–56; Ayoub, *Crisis of Muslim History*, pp. 8–25. According to Ali's supporters, the Prophet formally anointed his son-in-law as his successor shortly after the last pilgrimage near a pool called Ghadir Khumm and commended his followers to hold fast to the Book of God and the members of his household (the *ahl al-beit*).

34 *she never spoke to him again*: Al-Baladhuri, *Origins*, 1:52; al-Tabari, 9:196.

35 *A well-known story records*: Al-Bukhari, 1.9.486, and associated hadiths.

35 *"I feel," she told him*: Al-Bukhari, 6.60.311; see also Ibn Sa'd, *Women of Madina*, p. 113.

2. From Revelations to Revolution

37 *A particularly formidable challenge*: On Musaylima and the battle at Yamama, see Al-Baladhuri, *Origins*, 1:132–40; al-Tabari, *History*, 10:105–34 (hereafter cited as al-Tabari); Ibn Ishaq, *Life of Muhammad*, pp. 636–37, 648–49 (hereafter cited as Ibn Ishaq).

37 *A late revelation*: See Qur'an 9:29.

38 *Heraclius was stricken one night*: Ibn Ishaq, pp. 654–57; cf. al-Bukhari, 1.1.6.

38 *a particularly tenacious anecdote*: Abu al-Faraj [Bar Hebraeus], *Historia compendiosa dynastiarum*, 1:114 (Arabic text at 2:181). For a rumination on the library's fate, see Bagnall, "Alexandria: Library of Dreams," pp. 356–60; he notes at p. 357 that attempts to pin its destruction on Muslims "originate centuries after the fact and are surely fiction." Bernard Lewis has given the legend even shorter shrift: see *New York Review of Books*, September 27, 1990 (letters). For other correspondence

between Amr ibn al-Asi and Caliph Umar, see Butler, *Arab Conquest*, pp. 433, 456–60.

39 *"[it] is a great creature"*: Ibn Khaldun, *Muqaddimah*, 2:39; cf. al-Tabari, 15:26–27.

39 *"from parchments, scapula"*: Al-Bukhari, 6.60.201.

40 *Several injunctions address Muhammad's*: Qur'an 33:28–34, 53–54.

40 *hints abound of more substantial disputes*: The absence of documentary evidence from this period of Muslim history has given rise since the 1970s to a small but radical strand of historical revisionism in the West, according to which the Qur'an was actually compiled up to two centuries after the events it describes. The claim obscures considerably more than it explains, but a good overview can be found in Donner, *Narratives*, esp. pp. 22–30, 39–63; see also Reynolds, *Qur'ān in Its Historical Context*, esp. pp. 8–17.

40 *revelations that are unknown*: See Muslim, 8.3421; Ibn Ishaq, p. 684; Malik ibn Anas, *al-Muwatta*, p. 345; al-Tabari, 9:190–91; see also Burton, *Collection*, esp. pp. 117–59.

40 *Some supporters of Ali*: See discussion in Arjomand, "Consolation of Theology," p. 554.

40 *A minority of Alids claimed*: For a modern Shi'a polemic that nods at the goat theory, see Ali, *Commentary*, pp. 20–21; cf. Ibn Ishaq, p. 685n2. A'isha is the prime target of Shi'a conspiracy theorists, but Umar's daughter Hafsa, another wife of the Prophet, is not far behind.

41 *always more onerous*: See, for example, Kremer, *Orient*, p. 64, and Hugh Kennedy, *Muslim Spain and Portugal*, p. 51. On the development of taxation rules more generally, see Kremer, *Orient*, pp. 56–72; Tritton, *Caliphs and Their Non-Muslim Subjects*, pp. 197–228; Khadduri, *War and Peace*, pp. 187–93; Aghnides, *Mohammedan Theories*, pp. 397–406.

41 *Umar then resolved*: Kremer, *Orient*, pp. 72–73.

41 *Islam thereby became*: On the complexities of early taxation and conversion policies, see generally Dennett, *Conversion*.

41 *Occupying armies constructed*: Al-Baladhuri, *Origins*, 1:434–48, 2:60–66.

42 *"as tempting as a prostitute"*: Al-Tabari, 14:5.

42 *Another appointee took*: Ibn Ishaq, p. 529.

42 *A famous speech*: Tritton, *Caliphs and Their Non-Muslim Subjects*, p. 137.

42 *"If I had prayed"*: Eutychius, *Eutychii patriarchae Alexandrini annales*, 2:284–85, in Migne, *Patrologiae*, 111:1109. Eutychius was a Christian cleric writing with a self-serving agenda more than two centuries after the event, but the legend has been so often repeated by Muslims that it might as well be Islamic.

42 *When Damascus was occupied*: Al-Baladhuri, *Origins*, 1:191–93; Kremer, *Orient*, pp. 143–47; Tritton, *Caliphs and Their Non-Muslim Subjects*, pp. 40–42.

42 *they were being expelled*: Roth, *Short History*, p. 147.

43 *even as war ministers*: Mez, *Renaissance*, p. 66. Jurists would later lay down that non-Muslims could also hold the post of vizier, as long as they were not invested with absolute powers: ibid., p. 68. On the significant but often controversial role

that non-Muslims played as government officials and professionals, see Tritton, *Caliphs and Their Non-Muslim Subjects*, pp. 18–36; see also Tritton, "Islam and the Protected Religions," p. 338.

43 *he had found four*: Adler, *Itinerary*, p. 22n22. The text that Adler translates gives the figure as 200, but an accompanying note explains that the number 4, which appears in another manuscript of Benjamin of Tudela's work, looks the same in Hebrew and better conforms with the account of another rabbi "who passed through Palestine some ten or twenty years after R. Benjamin, and found but one Jew there." Cf. Mez, *Renaissance*, p. 46.

43 *Umar was mortally stabbed*: Al-Tabari, 14:89–93.

43 *Umar summoned six eminent colleagues*: Ibid., pp. 143–47.

43 *Escalating anger in the garrisons*: The killing is analyzed in some detail in Hinds, "Murder of the Caliph 'Uthman."

44 *that challenge petered out*: Al-Tabari, 16:122–72.

44 *He instructed his troops*: Ibid., 17:78.

44 *one of their number set upon him*: Ibid., 17:213–18. On the Kharijites generally, see Watt, *Formative Period*, pp. 9–37.

45 *he nominated his son*: Al-Tabari, 18:184–86.

45 *The denouement came*: Ibid., 19:91–183.

45 *obliged to curse Ali during prayers*: The practice was abolished by Umar II (r. 717–20)—see Ibn al-Tiqtaqa, *al-Fakhri*, p. 125—though it would be sporadically restored by later caliphs.

45 *Sind and Punjab*: Al-Baladhuri, *Origins*, 2:209–33.

46 *"interpretation of the Koran"*: Gibbon, *Decline and Fall*, 5:409 (book 51); see also Vasiliev, *History of the Byzantine Empire*, 1:236.

46 *Mu'awiya became Islam's proto-outlaw*: See, for example, Ibn al-Tiqtaqa, *al-Fakhri*, pp. 106–109.

46 *Yazid's crimes were even more enormous*: See Kremer, *Orient*, pp. 162–64.

46 *Salons opened in Mecca and Medina*: Ibid., pp. 39–53, 162; Hitti, *History of the Arabs*, pp. 236–39.

46 *"Since God, may He remain"*: Hitti, *History of the Arabs*, p. 239.

46 *Some libertines even ignored*: Rowson, "Effeminates of Early Medina," p. 683; Qur'an 24:31; cf. the book of Isaiah 3:16, 18.

47 *castrated by force*: Rowson, "Effeminates of Early Medina," pp. 688–92.

47 *he gave substance*: Tritton, *Caliphs and Their Non-Muslim Subjects*, pp. 104, 116–17, 230–31. The author observes that a covenant of toleration anachronistically attributed by Muslim historians to Umar I is likely to be based on Umar II's measures: see p. 233.

47 *Later legal manuals*: See, for example, the procedure detailed in Shayzari, *Book of the Islamic Market Inspector*, pp. 122–23 (in which a twelfth-century Syrian jurist instructs a *muhtasib* to "stand the *dhimmi* in front of him, slap him on the side of the neck and say 'Pay the *jizya*, unbeliever'"); see also Aghnides, *Mohammedan Theories*, pp. 405–406; Tritton, *Caliphs and Their Non-Muslim Subjects*, p. 227.

47 *End-time scenarios multiplied*: On the *mahdi* and *al-Dajjal*, see generally David
   Cook, *Studies in Muslim Apocalyptic Literature*; David Cook, *Contemporary
   Muslim Apocalyptic Literature*.
48 *Thousands died*: Al-Tabari, 26:36–55, 254–63; Ibn al-Tiqtaqa, *al-Fakhri*, pp. 128–32.
48 *a wine-filled swimming pool*: Hitti, *History of the Arabs*, p. 228; cf. Kremer, *Orient*, pp. 174–82.
48 *some very practical grievances*: Shaban, *'Abbāsid Revolution*, pp. 114–37; Dennett, *Conversion and the Poll Tax*, pp. 116–28; see also Elton L. Daniel, *Political
   and Social History of Khurasan*, esp. pp. 189–99.
48 *There was no agreement*: See Patricia Crone, "On the Meaning of the 'Abbasid
   Call to *al-Ridā*," in Bosworth, *Islamic World*, pp. 95–111.
49 *al-Saffah—"the Slaughterer"*: Al-Tabari, 27:154. Al-Mas'udi seems to have been
   first to use the title: see Bernard Lewis, *Political Words and Ideas*, pp. 89–97.
49 *done to death*: Al-Tabari, 27:184. The killing was publicly blamed on Kharijite
   extremists.
49 *Several Umayyads were exhumed*: Ibn al-Tiqtaqa, *al-Fakhri*, pp. 142, 145; Hugh
   Kennedy, *Early Abbasid Caliphate*, p. 48.
50 *"Spare me to battle"*: This account summarizes al-Tabari, 28:29–40; cf. Ibn
   al-Tiqtaqa, *al-Fakhri*, pp. 162–65.
50 *about two hundred*: See the breakdown in Kamali, *Principles*, pp. 26–27.
50 *to eat pork*: Qur'an 2:173, 5:3, 6:145, and 16:115. In an era of dietary obsessions, it
   should additionally be noted that Muslims are permitted kosher food and all
   Christian comestibles that are not explicitly forbidden: ibid., 5:5.
51 *indiscretion was simply repugnant*: On sartorial respectability, see ibid., 24:31; on
   male lechery, see ibid., 24:30; on the sin of backbiting (*gheeba*), see ibid., 49:12.
51 *the injunctions against exploitation*: on usury, see ibid., 2:275–80, 3:130, 4:161,
   and 30:39.
51 *Their power to improve*: See, for example, al-Bukhari, 3.32.227.
51 *a few iron rings*: Malik ibn Anas, *al-Muwatta*, p. 353.
51 *Umar had refused to punish*: Malik ibn Anas, *al-Muwatta*, p. 353.
51 *Ali's supporters admiringly recalled*: Ibn Khallikan, *Biographical Dictionary*, 2:125.
52 *intoxication*: The Qur'an's observations on alcohol are at 2:219, 4:43, and 5:90.
52 *That number was then doubled*: See Malik ibn Anas, *al-Muwatta*, p. 355; Muslim,
   17.4226; cf. al-Bukhari, 8.81.770. Scholars subscribing to Shafi'ite jurisprudence
   would later hold that the forty-lash penalty remained appropriate, and all jurists
   held that the applicable figure was halved for slaves.
52 *Arab scholars had begun*: On scholarly activity under the Umayyads, see Gutas,
   Greek Thought, pp. 20–27.

3. The Formation of the Law Schools
53 *a full-scale revolt*: For a brief account, see Nöldeke, *Sketches*, pp. 120–28.
54 *a capital to call his own*: On the foundation of Baghdad, see al-Tabari, *History*,
   28:237–50, 29:3–11 (hereafter cited as al-Tabari); Le Strange, *Baghdad During the*

Abbasid Caliphate, pp. 1–14; Lassner, *Topography*, pp. 121–37; Wendell, "Baghdād: *Imago Mundi*"; Lassner, "Some Speculative Thoughts."

54 *"poured into a mould and cast"*: Al-Jahiz, quoted in Irwin, *Arabian Nights*, p. 123.

55 *Ibn al-Muqaffa*: Charles Sourdel, "La biographie d'Ibn al-Muqaffa'," pp. 312–23; see also Zaman, "Caliphs, the 'Ulamā, and the Law," pp. 4–7; Bernard Lewis, *Political Words and Ideas*, pp. 36–37.

55 *even if such correspondence existed*: Questions over the letter's authenticity are discussed in Serjeant, "Caliph 'Umar's Letters." For the traditional view, see al-Mawardi, *Ordinances*, pp. 80–81; Ibn Khaldun, *Muqaddimah*, 1:453–56. It would also be widely recorded in later years that the Prophet authorized a follower named Mu'adh ibn Jabal to exercise discretionary judicial powers: see, for example, Ibn Sa'd, *Tabaqat*, 2:448–49.

56 *Even then, he cried so much*: Coulson, "Doctrine and Practice," p. 211. On the reluctance to serve, see also Mez, *Renaissance*, pp. 283–85; Amedroz, "Office of Kādi," pp. 773–75; A. J. Wensinck, "The Refused Dignity," in Arnold and Nicholson, *Volume of Oriental Studies*, pp. 497–99; Dols, *Majnūn*, pp. 446, 449.

56 *the Postponers (Murji'a)*: See Watt, *Formative Period*, pp. 119–28.

56 *bore fruit in 771*: Tyan, *Histoire de l'organisation judiciaire*, pp. 121–22; Coulson, "Doctrine and Practice," pp. 215–16.

57 *a minor civil suit*: Goldziher, *Muslim Studies*, 2:63; for other accounts of rulers subjecting themselves to the rule of religious scholars, see Coulson, "Doctrine and Practice," pp. 217–18 (the author observes that the "ideal . . . seldom found expression in practice").

57 *Most day-to-day disputes continued*: Levy, *Social Structure*, p. 342.

57 *Court for the Review of Injustice*: On this institution's disputed origins, which have been traced to the Umayyad caliphs Umar II and Abd al-Malik and the Sassanid kings of Persia, among others, see al-Mawardi, *Ordinances*, pp. 87–88, and Tyan, *Histoire de l'organisation judiciaire*, pp. 512–21. Both authors also discuss its historical operation in considerable detail; see also Levy, *Social Structure*, pp. 347–51.

58 *"You have not committed"*: Quoted in Peters, *Crime and Punishment*, p. 68. On the origins and evolution of the *siyasa*, see Bernard Lewis, *Political Words and Ideas*, pp. 31–46; Fauzi M. Najjar, "Islamic Political Philosophy," in Marmura, *Islamic Theology and Philosophy*, pp. 92–110; Tyan, *Histoire de l'organisation judiciaire*, pp. 446–53. The *siyasa* came to describe the use of force by rulers in pursuit of utility, convenience, or public order. Although the power impacted people's legal interests, it differed from *ta'zir* punishments in that it could be exercised whether or not persons affected were at fault: see Peters, *Crime and Punishment*, pp. 67–68.

58 *dark robes and long caps*: Mez, *Renaissance*, p. 294. On the office more generally, see ibid., pp. 280–304; Levy, *Social Structure*, pp. 340–50.

58 *deposited in a random pit*: Al-Tabari, 29:166–67; Ibn al-Tiqtaqa, *al-Fakhri*, p. 168.

59 *"mangled by beasts of prey"*: Qur'an 5:3; Ahsan, *Social Life*, pp. 239, 241; see also Ibn Rushd, *Distinguished Jurist's Primer*, 1:548–59.

59 *His construction of a hippodrome*: Ahsan, *Social Life*, pp. 244–46, 263.

60 *kill his entire stock*: Goldziher, *Muslim Studies*, 2:74–75; Ahsan, *Social Life*, p. 252.

60 fiqh: Although *fiqh* has come to mean Islamic legal science, it originally connoted something closer to the English word "understanding": see Abdul-Jabbar, *Bukhari*, p. 23, and al-Ghazali, *Book of Knowledge*, p. 75.

60 *One of the earliest fruits*: On the *hila*, see Schacht, *Introduction*, pp. 78–84. For examples in the financial sphere, see Horii, "Reconsideration of Legal Devices," pp. 332–33, 338–43; Siadat Ali Khan, "Mohammedan Laws Against Usury," esp. pp. 241–44. On economic inventiveness under the Abbasids more generally, see Fischel, "Origin of Banking in Mediaeval Islam," esp. pp. 574–78.

61 *Intoxication could therefore be*: Oudah, *Criminal Law of Islam*, 4:359.

61 *"When there is a clear practice"*: Abdul-Jabbar, *Bukhari*, p. 67.

62 *traded insults*: The dispute is summarized in Aghnides, *Mohammedan Theories*, pp. 66–70.

62 *Malikites condemned their rivals*: Melchert, *Formation of the Sunni Schools*, p. 10.

62 *Hanafites responded*: Goldziher, *Muslim Studies*, 2:82n2; Robson, *Tracts*, p. 34n1.

62 *"Why do they not scourge"*: The words quoted were said about Meccans by al-Jahiz (Pellat, *Life and Works*, p. 53), but Abu Hanifa reportedly expressed the same thought with respect to Medina scholars: Peters, *Crime and Punishment*, p. 15.

62 *Some Malikites had even begun*: Horii, "Reconsideration of Legal Devices," esp. pp. 352–57.

62 *a story told about Malik's*: Abdul-Jabbar, *Bukhari*, p. 38.

63 *The Qur'an observed*: Qur'an 33:21, 59:7.

63 *"never so ready to lie"*: Goldziher, *Muslim Studies*, 2:55.

63 *a Kufan was executed*: Kremer, *Orient*, p. 383.

63 *tips of their noses*: Goldziher, *Muslim Studies*, 2:154.

63 *no demon could impersonate*: For a later expression of this consensus, see al-Bukhari, 9.87.123, and associated hadiths.

63 *"Stay away from unusual hadiths"*: Abdul-Jabbar, *Bukhari*, p. 76.

63 *seventeen hundred times*: Goldziher, *Muslim Studies*, 2:202n7 ("around 1720").

63 *obligatory to decapitate*: Malik ibn Anas, *al-Muwatta*, pp. 303–304; see also discussion in Goldziher, *Muslim Studies*, 2:200–201.

64 *could simply be ignored*: Abdul-Jabbar, *Bukhari*, p. 69.

64 *He accepted the distinctively*: Al-Shafi'i, *Risāla*, pp. 32, 285–87.

64 *Islam's first theory of judgment*: For his ideas on analogy, *ijtihad*, and juristic preference, see ibid., pp. 31–32, 288–332.

65 *As long as a report could*: Ibid., pp. 31, 239–84. On the origin of the *isnad*, see Donner, *Narratives*, p. 121; on the increasingly rigorous rules by which a hadith's authenticity came to be assessed, see Aghnides, *Mohammedan Theories*, pp. 39–57; Abdul-Jabbar, *Bukhari*, pp. 110–17.

65 *the heavier punishment reflected*: Al-Shafi'i, *Risāla*, pp. 137–40, 197–99; discussion in Burton, *Sources of Islamic Law*, pp. 136–58.

65 *replaced by "better" ones*: See Qur'an 2:106; cf. 16:101.

65 *gave that analysis a legal spin*: Al-Shafi'i, *Risāla*, esp. pp. 29–30, 36, 123–30, 141–45, 181, 184–85, 195–202. For the status of al-Shafi'i's ideas about abrogation in the light of subsequent jurisprudence, see Kamali, *Principles*, chap. 7, esp. pp. 213–15. On the theory of abrogation, see generally Burton, *Sources of Islamic Law*.

65 *They thought it was wrong*: See, for example, Ibn Sa'd, *Men of Madina*, 1:123, referring to the bibliophobia of the celebrated traditionist and dream interpreter Muhammad ibn Sirin (653–728); Michael Cook, "Opponents," p. 437. The opposition to writing, though prevalent, was not universal: see Sprenger, "On the Origin and Progress of Writing"; Goldziher, *Muslim Studies*, 2:181–88; see generally Pedersen, *Arabic Book*.

66 *similarly dire predictions*: See Blair, "Reading Strategies."

66 *a fable that Plato*: Plato, *Phaedrus*, 274c–275c.

66 *a marvelous secret*: Al-Tha'alibi, *Book of Curious and Entertaining Information*, p. 140; Robert I. Burns, "Paper Comes to the West, 800–1400," in Lindgren, *Europäische Technik*, pp. 413–22; Gibb et al., *Encyclopaedia of Islam* ("Kāghad").

67 *famously victorious campaign*: Al-Tabari, 29:220–21; cf. Vasiliev, *History of the Byzantine Empire*, 1:238.

67 *a palace intrigue*: Ibn al-Tiqtaqa, *al-Fakhri*, p. 187. The death may have been facilitated by poison: see Clot, *Harun al-Rashid*, pp. 23–30.

67 *the digging of his own grave*: Al-Tabari, 30:299–301; al-Mas'udi, *Meadows*, p. 98.

67 *A postal service, modeled*: Hitti, *History of the Arabs*, pp. 322–25; Levy, *Baghdad Chronicle*, p. 208.

67 *A former slave*: Al-Makkari, *History of the Mohammedan Dynasties*, 2:116–21.

68 *three demons murmuring*: Al-Mas'udi, *Meadows*, p. 133.

68 *slave girls in disguise*: Ibid., pp. 390–91.

68 *The deal was sealed*: Al-Tabari, 30:179–95.

68 *violence spiraled for six years*: On the civil war, see al-Mas'udi, *Meadows*, pp. 149–72; Lapidus, "Separation of State and Religion," pp. 370–75.

69 *Arabic terms that translate*: Among the words used most often were *ayyarun* and *sifla*. Writers also drew on older insults that Mu'tazilites such as al-Jahiz had deployed to abuse the supposed ignorance of their enemies, especially the terms *hashwiyya* and *nabita* (or *nawabit*): see Hurvitz, "Mihna as Self-Defense," esp. pp. 97–102; Wesley Williams, "Aspects of the Creed," p. 450.

69 *they had become associated*: Lapidus, "Separation of State and Religion," pp. 372, 376; Michael Cook, *Commanding Right and Forbidding Wrong*, p. 13.

4. Commanding the Faithful

71 *Chinese junks began*: Levy, *Baghdad Chronicle*, p. 44.

72 *Disquisitions on the usefulness*: On sticks and the superiority of black skin, see Pellat, *Life and Works*, pp. 106–108, 195–98. On sexuality in the holy cities, see his *Kitab mufakharat il-jawari wa'l ghilman*, translated in Colville, *Sobriety and Mirth*, pp. 202–30, and Hutchins, *Nine Essays*, pp. 139–66. On sailors and sea monsters, see Pellat, *Life and Works*, pp. 182–83; on baby rhinoceroses, see Levy,

Social Structure, p. 468; on camels' testicles, see Grunebaum, *Medieval Islam*, p. 333. The claim about rhinos so intrigued al-Mas'udi that he investigated it half a century after al-Jahiz's death, while traveling Oman and southern Iran, and he reported that they actually gave birth just like cows and buffalo: al-Mas'udi, *Les prairies d'or*, 1:387–88.

72 *When he visited Egypt's*: See Vyse, *Operations*, 2:116, 117, 179–80, 209; the various accounts translated at pp. 333–34, 340–41, 347–52, 356–57. Cf. pp. 303, 329–30, where the author considers a passage of al-Mas'udi's *Akhbar al-zaman* that claims that it was actually Harun al-Rashid who broke open the Great Pyramid, using fire and vinegar.

72 *to test Greek theories*: See al-Biruni's account in Rosenthal, *Classical Heritage*, pp. 215–16; Ibn Khallikan, *Biographical Dictionary*, 3:315–16. On al-Ma'mun's astronomical activities, see Sayili, *Observatory*, pp. 50–87, 92, 391–93.

72 *The caliph's great innovation*: On the House of Wisdom and the translation movement, see Dodge, *Fihrist*, 2:583–90; Lyons, *House of Wisdom*, pp. 63–66. For a good overview, see generally Gutas, *Greek Thought*. For a list of lost ancient manuscripts that were bequeathed to Latin via Arabic, see Rosenthal, *Classical Heritage*, pp. 11–12.

73 *"with ruddy complexion"*: This paraphrases the translation in Dodge, *Fihrist*, 2:583.

73 *Al-Ma'mun was motivated*: The Arab translators' indifference to foreign prose and poetry has been characterized by some Western scholars as remarkably barbaric: "chilling[ly] insensitive to the range and richness of Greek literature," to paraphrase one offended Hellenist (Lamberton, *Homer the Theologian*, p. 238). In fact, their focus on practical wisdom was entirely typical of the premodern world. Late-medieval Christians would also ignore Arabic and Persian belles lettres and poetry while devouring the work of Muslim philosophers and scientists, and though Homer found a Latin translator during the fourteenth century, Athenian tragedy had to wait another two hundred years: Walton, *Found in Translation*, pp. 26–42. Some Westerners are unfamiliar even today with classical Islamic literature. See generally Bernard Lewis, "Translation from Arabic."

74 *"beliefs and opinions"*: Rosenthal, *Classical Heritage*, p. 27, quoting Hunain ibn Ishaq (808–73).

74 *Caliph al-Ma'mun's observatory*: Sayili, *Observatory*, p. 85.

74 *One of the earliest arguments*: The great mathematician Muhammad al-Khwarizmi introduced his seminal work on algebra by identifying legal activities that it could facilitate. They included "inheritances, bequests, tax assessments, land surveying [and] water rights": Cooperson, *Al-Ma'mun*, p. 99; cf. Gutas, *Greek Thought*, p. 113.

74 *the Mu'tazilites*: On the movement generally, see Watt, *Formative Period*, pp. 209–50; Fakhry, *History of Islamic Philosophy*, pp. 44–65; Mez, *Renaissance*, pp. 261–66.

74 *"without [knowing] how"*: On this verbal formula, which would play an important

role in theological arguments for centuries, see Wesley Williams, "Aspects of the Creed," pp. 448–49. Cf. Qur'an 3:7 ("No one knows its interpretation [*ta'wil*] except God").

75 *because it said so*: Qur'an 85:22.

75 *he mailed letters*: Al-Tabari, *History*, 32:199–204 (hereafter cited as al-Tabari); Patton, *Hanbal and the Mihna*, pp. 57–61.

75 *No one knows why*: For a discussion of the dispute, see Wilferd Madelung, "The Origins of the Controversy Concerning the Creation of the Koran," in Barral, *Orientalia Hispanica*, pp. 506–25. An old strand of Western historiography associated with Martin Hinds portrays the *mihna* as a philosophical tipping point—the moment when Islam repudiated the Middle East's Hellenistic traditions. Modern scholars often stress al-Ma'mun's attempt to defend scholarly inquiry against popular ignorance: see, for example, Hurvitz, "Mihna as Self-Defense." Its political utility as a means of asserting supremacy over an uppity ulema is emphasized by, for example, Nawas, "Reexamination," pp. 623–24, while Dominique Sourdel has argued that it was a crypto-Shi'a attempt to lead the faithful toward higher religious truths: see his "La politique religieuse," pp. 43–46. See also Lucas, *Constructive Critics*, pp. 192–202; Cooperson, *Classical Arabic Biography*, pp. 34–40.

75 *palace physicians had recently*: Sayili, *Observatory*, p. 66.

76 *he had sided with*: Cooperson, *Classical Arabic Biography*, pp. 28–32. On his accommodation with the Shi'a, see also Dominique Sourdel, "La politique religieuse," esp. pp. 33–37.

76 *"All it means is a whipping"*: Patton, *Hanbal and the Mihna*, pp. 63, 87. The quoted text is a paraphrase.

76 *Seven of them abandoned*: Al-Tabari, 32:205; Patton, *Hanbal and the Mihna*, p. 64.

76 *"If they do not then recant"*: Patton, *Hanbal and the Mihna*, pp. 65–82; see also al-Tabari, 32:214–25. It should be noted that al-Tabari was not a neutral source. He had a notoriously frosty relationship with the followers of one of the captives, Ibn Hanbal, and his work deliberately downplays the ordeal that he was about to suffer.

76 *There were contradictory accounts*: compare Al-Mas'udi, *Meadows*, pp. 219–20; al-Tabari, 32:224–25.

77 *fortified by two hairs*: Patton, *Hanbal and the Mihna*, p. 107.

77 *By the time he was cut down*: On Hanbal's trial and punishment, see ibid., pp. 93–111; Hurvitz, *Formation of Hanbalism*, pp. 132–34.

77 *Hagiographers affirmed*: See accounts cited in Patton, *Hanbal and the Mihna*, pp. 109–11.

78 *"The [traditionists] have been crushed"*: Pellat, *Life and Works*, p. 51; see also Wesley Williams, "Aspects of the Creed," pp. 452–53. The quoted passage refers specifically to "anthropomorphists" (*mushabihha*), because this was the theological stance most often associated with the scholars subjected to the inquisition.

78 *when he imported four thousand*: Al-Mas'udi, *Meadows*, p. 228.

78 *the caliph personally decapitated*: Al-Tabari, 34:27–34, 39–40; Cooperson, *Al-Ma'mun*, p. 124.

78 *The brother who succeeded*: On al-Mutawakkil's reign, see al-Tabari, 34:65–73, 89–95, 110–11; Ibn al-Tiqtaqa, *al-Fakhri*, p. 235; see also Tritton, *Caliphs and Their Non-Muslim Subjects*, pp. 23, 50, 107, 118–19, 231. For a relatively favorable appraisal of the caliph's cheerful disposition and convivial manner, see al-Mas'udi, *Meadows*, pp. 239, 241.

79 *rent his clothes in anguish*: Melchert, *Ahmad ibn Hanbal*, pp. 7, 15; cf. Hurvitz, *Formation of Hanbalism*, pp. 145–49.

79 *Eight hundred thousand men*: Ibn Khallikan, *Biographical Dictionary*, 1:45.

79 *he contemplated a move*: Hugh Kennedy, *Court of the Caliphs*, pp. 241, 263.

79 *Late one night in December*: Al-Mas'udi, *Meadows*, pp. 258–63. The author notes that there are several other versions of the murder (p. 269), and cf. al-Tabari, 34:171–84.

81 *were putting it about*: See, for example, the hadith later recorded by Abu Dawud, 24.3579.

81 *"In my community"*: Goldziher, *Muslim Studies*, 2:142. On the Hanafite accommodation of hadiths more generally, see Melchert, *Formation of the Sunni Schools of Law*, pp. 48–53.

81 *a round million*: Ibn Khallikan, *Biographical Dictionary*, 1:44.

81 *"There will be forgers"*: Goldziher, *Muslim Studies*, 2:127; cf. 2:56. Ignaz Goldziher (1850–1921) was the first Western scholar who systematically examined Islam's hadith collections, and he argued that even those acknowledged as "sound" were often anachronistic and unreliable reflections of later controversies. See the cited work in general; see also Donner, *Narratives*, pp. 13–15, 40–60.

81 *a core group of 2,762*: Gibb et al., *Encyclopaedia of Islam* ("Bukhari").

82 *Even one of Muhammad's*: Hitti, *History of the Arabs*, p. 243, citing Ibn Sa'd.

82 *"I may say something now"*: Quoted in Melchert, *Ahmad ibn Hanbal*, p. 66.

82 *"Whenever a [jurist] comes along"*: Ibid., p. 65. The observation may have been a traditionist commonplace: see Aghnides, *Mohammedan Theories*, p. 67, who records a similar quotation by the greatest early commentator on the Qur'an, Abu al-Hajjaj Mujahid (642–722/3). Al-Ghazali later claimed that Ibn Hanbal had condemned Malik's *al-Muwatta* as an innovation, and he observed that books of traditions "are a recent novelty": *Book of Knowledge*, pp. 203, 210.

82 *Al-Bukhari certainly worried*: Abdul-Jabbar, *Bukhari*, p. 91; Ibn Khallikan, *Biographical Dictionary*, 2:596.

82 *five similar collections appeared*: They were compiled by Muslim (ca. 821–75), Abu Dawud (d. 888), al-Tirmidhi (d. 892), al-Nasa'i (d. 915), and Ibn Maja (d. 886) and they moved from exalted to canonical status during the eleventh and twelfth centuries: Goldziher, *Muslim Studies*, 2:240.

83 *he had acceded to the calls*: Al-Bukhari, 5.58.208; cf. Qur'an 54:1, which merely notes that the moon was in fact cleft in two at one point. For the Qur'an's denial of miraculous powers, see chapter 1, pp. 23, 83.

83 *he had been known*: On water from fingers, see al-Bukhari, 1.4.170, 4.56.779, and associated hadiths. On the *istisqa* prayer for rain, see ibid., 2.17.119, and subsequent hadiths.

83 *a visit to God's throne*: See the various versions of the hadith at ibid., 1.8.345, 4.54.429, 5.58.227, 9.93.608. The passages of the Qur'an that are conventionally said to refer to the Night Journey, or *mir'aj*, are contained in its seventeenth sura: see esp. 17:1 and 17:60; cf. Ibn Ishaq, *Life of Muhammad*, pp. 181–87 and xx (hereafter cited as Ibn Ishaq).

83 *They had gathered*: See David Cook, *Studies in Muslim Apocalyptic Literature*, p. 326.

83 *The compilations sourced*: On the youthfulness of some transmitters, see Melchert, *Ahmad ibn Hanbal*, p. 24; on the inclusion of men who had succumbed to the *mihna*, see Lucas, *Constructive Critics*, pp. 198–99.

84 *so too were his meditations*: On the toothpick (*miswak*), see Muslim, 2.487; Malik ibn Anas, *al-Muwatta*, p. 23; Ibn Sa'd, *Tabaqat*, 1:573–74; al-Ghazali, *Imam Gazzali's Ihya Ulum id-Din*, pp. 154–55 (quoting the recollection of one of the Prophet's companions that he "so repeatedly commanded us to use tooth stick that we thought that soon a revelation would come for its use"). On facial hair, see, for example, al-Bukhari, 7.72.780, and Muslim, 2.501. For the Prophet's verification that the Antichrist (*al-Dajjal*) was chained on an island to the east of Arabia, see Muslim, 41.7028.

84 *"God has uttered the truth"*: Al-Bukhari, 7.71.614. Another hadith states that he was given honey again and cured: 7.71.588. On incense, see 7.71.611; on cumin, see 7.71.591, 592.

85 *They had also developed five categories*: Kamali, *Principles*, pp. 413–31; Aghnides, *Mohammedan Theories*, pp. 105–11. On the origins and moral significance of this model, see Carney, "Some Aspects of Islamic Ethics," esp. pp. 160–68.

85 *a word originally meaning*: Khaddduri, *War and Peace*, p. 29; cf. Goldziher, *Muslim Studies*, 2:24–25. The word for customs in general is *ada*; another word, *urf*, is used to describe practice, in the sense of "what is commonly known and expected": see Levy, *Social Structure*, pp. 242–70.

85 *The Prophet's first biographer*: Ibn Ishaq, pp. 552, 774; al-Mas'udi, *Les prairies d'or*, 1:317–18.

85 *"angels do not enter"*: See al-Bukhari, 7.72.833; for other iconophobic hadiths, see ibid., 9.93.646–47; Muslim, 24:5246–76; Malik ibn Anas, *al-Muwatta*, p. 407.

85 *"Among those who profess"*: This follows the translation in Pellat, *Life and Works*, pp. 269–71, restoring words that are there expurgated. The original passage appears in *Kitab mufakharat il-jawari wa'l ghilman*, paras. 3 and 4. There are alternative translations in Colville, *Sobriety and Mirth*, p. 203, and Hutchins, *Nine Essays*, p. 139.

86 *viewpoints that rested on alternative ideas*: See Ibn Rushd, *Distinguished Jurist's Primer*, 1:161; al-Mawardi, *Ordinances*, p. 72. See also Tyan, *Histoire de l'organisation judiciaire*, pp. 161–63, where the author states that many classical

Hanafites were relatively liberal, at least in theory, holding that women were competent to make any judicial ruling except one imposing a Qur'anic criminal penalty.

5. The Sunni Challenge and the Shi'a Response

87 *a lavish reception*: Ibn al-Zubair, *Book of Gifts*, pp. 148–55; Amedroz and Margoliouth, *Eclipse*, 4:56–60; Lassner, *Topography*, pp. 86–91, 268–71nn10–18; Le Strange, "Greek Embassy." The remainder of the material on Muqtadir's reign in the text comes from Amedroz and Margoliouth, *Eclipse*; Massignon, *Passion*; Ibn al-Tiqtaqa, *al-Fakhri*, pp. 260–71.

88 *an unassuming figure*: See Michael Cook, *Commanding Right and Forbidding Wrong*, pp. 87–113, esp. pp. 94–101, 105–106.

88 *a doctrinal controversy*: See Allard, *Le problème des attributs divins*, pp. 98–113; Wesley Williams, "Aspects of the Creed," p. 454. For the "throne verse," see Qur'an 2:255. The arguments crystallized around the teachings of a highly influential theologian named al-Ash'ari: see that author's *al-Ibānah*, translated in Allard, esp. pp. 31, 50, 83–94; cf. discussion at pp. 173–285. The claims of the anthropomorphists (*mushabihha*) would grow increasingly daring, as was vividly described by Ibn Khaldun, *Muqaddimah*, 3:65–69. On the *bi-la kayfa* formula, see chapter 4, p. 74.

89 *hadiths by the thousands*: Hurvitz, *Formation of Hanbalism*, pp. 3–5; Melchert, *Formation of the Sunni Law Schools*, pp. 137–55.

89 *"God does not accept"*: Robson, *Tracts*, p. 33 (the quoted words are a paraphrase of a hadith that is expressed in the singular); for the other complaints referred to in this paragraph, see ibid., pp. 19–40.

90 *Hanbalite vigilantes began*: Michael Cook, *Commanding Right and Forbidding Wrong*, pp. 116–18.

90 *"even if the ears"*: Quoted in Melchert, *Ahmad ibn Hanbal*, p. 99.

90 *A preacher who claimed Ali*: Al-Tabari's lengthy account of the Zanj rebellion runs from *History*, 36:29 to 37:139 (hereafter cited as al-Tabari); cf. al-Mas'udi, *Meadows*, pp. 317–18. See also Shaban, *Islamic History*, 2:100–102.

90 *the Twelvers concluded*: See this chapter, p. 94.

91 *an assault on Mecca itself*: Amedroz and Margoliouth, *Eclipse*, 4:226.

91 *Lesser acts of defiance*: Fierro, *'Abd al-Rahman III*, pp. 53–60; Wasserstein, *Caliphate in the West*, pp. 10–12; Clancy-Smith, *North Africa, Islam*, pp. 40–41.

92 *the regime's vizier*: Amedroz and Margoliouth, *Eclipse*, 4:438–39.

92 *Power devolved*: Ibid., p. 395.

92 *Caliph al-Mustakfi proffered*: Ibid., 5:90; Ibn al-Tiqtaqa, *al-Fakhri*, p. 280; al-Mas'udi, *Meadows*, pp. 422–23.

92 *That provoked sectarian riots*: Mez, *Renaissance*, pp. 89–91.

93 *the sect's leader arrived*: O'Leary, *Short History*, p. 110.

93 *would always express contempt*: The rivalry is well illustrated by an excitable correspondence between Caliph al-Mu'izz and Caliph Abd al-Rahman III al-Nasir

of Córdoba. The record is the work of a Fatimid partisan, but the insults and accusations of illegitimacy he memorializes present neither side in a very exalted light. For a discussion, see Wasserstein, *Caliphate in the West*, pp. 13–15; for extracts from the letters themselves, see Yalaoui, "Controverse."

93 *By the 980s*: See Mez, *Renaissance*, pp. 90–91; cf. al-Muqaddasi, *Best Divisions*, p. 48.

93 *in 981 Karbala also gained*: Mez, *Renaissance*, p. 92.

93 *Among the many writers*: On Abu'l-'Ala al-Ma'arri, see Nicholson, *Literary History of the Arabs*, pp. 313–34, 375; regarding the Qur'an's literary challenge, see 2:23–24, 10:38, 17:88. On the cultural vitality of this period in general, see Kraemer, *Humanism in the Renaissance of Islam*.

94 *an Andalusian visitor reported*: Sklare, *Samuel ben Hofni Gaon*, pp. 100–101.

94 *his followers entered a period*: See Modarressi, *Crisis and Consolidation*, esp. pp. 77–80, 86–91, 95–102; see generally Kohlberg, "From Imāmiyya to Ithnā-'ashariyya."

94 *"a man whose birth"*: Arjomand, "Consolation of Theology," p. 561.

94 *They contended that a twelfth imam*: Ibid., pp. 553–59; see also Wilferd Madelung, "Authority in Twelver Shiism in the Absence of the Imam," in George Makdisi, *La notion d'autorité*, pp. 165–68.

94 *scholars got to work*: On al-Kulayni's (*Usul*) *al-Kafi*, see Arjomand, "Consolation of Theology," pp. 551–52. The second compilation was the work of the Qom scholar Ibn Babuya (d. 991), and two others were then written by Muhammad al-Tusi (d. in Najaf, 1067). Sermons and writings credited to Ali were collected in ca. 1009 in a volume called the *Nahj al-balagha* (*Peak of Eloquence*) by Al-Sharif al-Radi (970–1015).

95 *Under Mu'tazilite influence*: On the development of Shi'a legal theory, see Calder, "Doubt and Prerogative," esp. pp. 62–64; see generally Gleave, "Between *Hadīth* and *Fiqh*."

95 *a Muslim version of Plato's* Republic: Al-Farabi's work on ideas in "the virtuous city" (*al-madina[t] al-fadila*) has been translated by Richard Walzer as *Al-Farabi on the Perfect State*. On Ayatollah Khomeini's admiration, see Martin, *Creating an Islamic State*, pp. 34–35, 172; on the philosopher generally, see Fakhry, *History of Islamic Philosophy*, pp. 107–28.

96 *moved swiftly to reassert*: George Makdisi, *History and Politics*, p. 158.

96 *unleashed its violent potential*: Ibn al-Athir, *Annals*, pp. 79–81, 88–89, 98, 103, 183–84, 193, 207; see also Michael Cook, *Commanding Right and Forbidding Wrong*, pp. 118–21.

97 *a bedraggled figure approached*: Ibn al-Athir, *Annals*, pp. 253–55.

97 *he had been following*: Bernard Lewis, *Assassins*, p. 47.

98 *the Venetian claimed*: Polo, *Book of Ser Marco Polo*, pp. 132–35.

98 *contemporary suggestions of drug use*: See discussion in Bernard Lewis, *Assassins*, pp. 6–12.

99 *the aftermath of that murder*: Ibn al-Athir, *Annals*, pp. 262–63.

99 *a closely argued condemnation*: See Mitha, *Al-Ghazālī and the Ismailis*, esp. pp. 50–70.

100 *"It is known that to feed on"*: U. M. Salih, "The Political Thought of Ibn Taymiyya" (Ph.D. diss., University of Edinburgh, 1980), p. 219, quoting from al-Ghazali's *al-Iqtisad fi al-i'tiqad*.

100 *"To kill [the Assassins]"*: Bernard Lewis, *Assassins*, pp. 47–48, 150.

100 *"that disillusionment bordering"*: Grunebaum, *Medieval Islam*, p. 168.

100 *"on the brink of a crumbling bank"*: Watt, *Faith and Practice*, p. 56, translating al-Ghazali's *Deliverance from Error* (*al-Munqidh min al-dalal*).

100 *The discipline sought to carry*: For discussions of Sufism in general, see Fakhry, *History of Islamic Philosophy*, pp. 234–56; Nicholson, *Literary History of the Arabs*, pp. 224–35, 383–404; Arnold and Guillaume, *Legacy of Islam*, pp. 210–38.

100 *He made surreptitious financial*: Watt, *Faith and Practice*, pp. 58–59.

101 *the heaviest criticisms of all*: A hostility toward jurists characterizes the entire first book of the *Revival*, but the quotations given can be found in al-Ghazali, *Book of Knowledge*, pp. 43, 142.

101 *"no harm"*: Quasem, *Al-Ghazali on Islamic Guidance*, p. 46 (a translation of Ghazali's *Beginning of Guidance*).

101 *It contains a long section*: Farah, *Marriage and Sexuality*, pp. 107–13.

101 *The companion work*: Quasem, *Al-Ghazali on Islamic Guidance*, pp. 25–27, 54–57.

102 *Christian accounts of what happened*: Raymond of Aguilers, quoted in Krey, *First Crusade*, p. 261; Fulcher of Chartres, *History of the Expedition*, p. 122.

103 *He never once mentioned*: Hourani, "Revised Chronology of Ghazālī's Writings," p. 291.

103 *a "lesser struggle"*: Al-Ghazali, *Marvels*, p. 19. See generally pp. 13–20, 91–115. The earlier and more orthodox textbook referred to in the text is his (*Kitab*) *al-Wajiz fi fiqh madhab al-imam al-Shafi'i*.

104 *Caliph al-Mustadhir's inactivity*: Ibn al-Athir, *Chronicle*, 1:154–55.

104 *Hanbalites took particular issue*: The criticisms were such that they even got to al-Ghazali's foremost biographer, al-Subki (1304–69). He felt obliged to admit his subject's inadequate scholarship, and a third of his biography was taken up with a list of inadequately sourced traditions that had been included in the *Revival*: George Makdisi, *History and Politics*, p. 162.

104 *jurists of a bellicose bent*: For a good discussion of the lesser/greater jihad debate, see David Cook, *Understanding Jihad*, pp. 32–48. The author notes that the notion of spiritual warfare is absent from all the canonical Sunni collections except that of al-Tirmidhi, who includes a hadith to the effect that "the fighter is one who fights his passions." See also Renard, "*Al-Jihad al-Akbar.*"

104 *a mujaddid, or "renovator"*: Hallaq, "Was the Gate of Ijtihad Closed?" p. 17; Landau-Tasseron, " 'Cyclical Reform,' " p. 86. It should probably be observed that al-Ghazali was first to record that others thought him worthy of the title.

104 *a claim that would become famous*: Hallaq, "Was the Gate of Ijtihad Closed?" pp. 20–22. On the eschatological assumptions underpinning the debate over the closure of *ijtihad*'s gate, see also Hallaq, "On the Origins of the Controversy," esp. pp. 137–41; for an overview of modern scholarship, see Ali-Karamali and Dunne, "Ijtihad Controversy."

106 *"deems it lawful"*: Ibn Jubayr, *Travels*, p. 60.

106 *one resident lyrically described it*: See the extract from Ibn Aqil's (*Kitab*) *al-Funun* translated in "Remembrance of Things Past," published in *Al-Ahram*'s weekly online English edition, April 17–23, 2003.

106 *"Most of its traces"*: Ibn Jubayr, *Travels*, p. 226.

6. The Caliphate Destroyed: A Shadowless God

107 *The warlord's response*: On the 1218–21 war, see Juvaini, *History*, 1:77–178; Minhaj al-Siraj Juzjani, *Tabakat*, 1:966–1077; Ibn al-Athir, *Chronicle*, 3:204–30; and see generally al-Nasawi, *Histoire du sultan*. For a secondary account that carefully examines the sources, see Barthold, *Turkestan*, pp. 393–462.

108 *Genghis Khan is said*: Al-Nasawi, *Histoire du sultan*, 2:63.

108 *Kublai was told*: Rashid al-Din, *Compendium*, 2:479.

108 *Chinese engineers*: Juvaini, *History*, 2:608–609.

109 *a Twelver Shiʿa contingent*: Howorth, *History*, 3:125, 127, 139.

109 *He audaciously announced*: Boyle, "Death," pp. 151–52; Howorth, *History*, 3:101.

109 *"He and his followers"*: Juvaini, *History*, 2:724–25.

109 *expressed greater optimism*: Rashid al-Din, *Compendium*, 2:492 (he "was apprehensive and thought it was some sort of test. 'None of these things will happen,' he said . . . 'Hulagu [*sic*] Khan will take the caliph's place'").

109 *a confidential communication*: It should be noted that Shiʿa writers have always considered Ibn al-Alqami an innocent scapegoat. See references and discussion in Howorth, *History*, 3:114–15, 137; Browne, *Literary History of Persia*, 2:464–65.

110 *Saddam Hussein invoked it*: Brian Whitaker, "Full-Text: The Saddam Hussein 'Letter,'" *Guardian*, April 30, 2003.

110 *warned that attempts*: Howorth, *History*, 3:114–15, 117.

110 *Clashes across the Tigris*: Minhaj al-Siraj Juzjani, *Tabakat*, 1:1237–42; Howorth, *History*, 3:122.

110 *The first glimpse*: Ibn al-Tiqtaqa, *al-Fakhri*, p. 323.

110 *Engines of war*: On the fall of Baghdad, see Rashid al-Din, *Compendium*, 2:493–99; Minhaj al-Siraj Juzjani, *Tabakat*, 1:1242–48; Howorth, *History*, 3:121–37.

111 *"Then why did you keep it"*: Boyle, "Death," pp. 148–49, 159.

111 *Writers would later memorialize*: On scented palaces, see Howorth, *History*, 3:131; cf. 3:127 (the precise distance asserted by the Chinese source is one hundred *li*). On books in the Tigris, see the unsourced quotation in Wiet, *Baghdad*, p. 167. Ibn Khaldun claimed in the mid-fourteenth century that the Mongols threw many scientific books into the river: see *Muqaddimah*, 2:219, 3:114n587.

111 *The caliph's end*: Boyle, "Death," pp. 149–50, 159–60; Rashid al-Din, *Compendium*, 2:498–99; Minhaj al-Siraj Juzjani, *Tabakat*, 1:1252–55.

111 *"the most awful catastrophe"*: Ibn al-Athir, quoted by W. M. Thackston in his preface to Rashid al-Din, *Compendium*, 1:xi.

111 *"Things happened which"*: Ibn al-Tiqtaqa, *al-Fakhri*, p. 323.

111 *he avoided any mention*: For a discussion of this aspect of Juvaini's *History of the World Conqueror*, see Ayalon, "Great Yāsa (B)," pp. 160–61.

112 *Cairo's sultans had recently*: See Jackson, *Islamic Law and the State*, pp. 42–46.

112 *"You have heard"*: Al-Maqrizi, *Histoire des sultans mamlouks*, 1:261–62 (marginal numbers).

112 *battle was joined*: Ibid., 1:103–106 (marginal numbers); Howorth, *History*, 3:167–69.

113 *The only half-relevant advice*: See Qur'an 4:59, 3:159, and 42:38.

113 *Al-Ghazali had famously urged*: See Binder, "Al-Ghazālī's Theory of Islamic Government," esp. pp. 232–36. The work concerned was *Moderation in Religious Belief (al-Iqtisad fi al-i'tiqad)*, on which see chapter 5, p. 99.

113 *Only a handful had ever*: See Bernard Lewis, *Muslim Discovery*, pp. 67, 312.

114 *"The just infidel"*: Paraphrasing Howorth, *History*, 3:132; Ibn al-Tiqtaqa, *al-Fakhri*, p. 14.

114 *From his perspective*: See Wilferd Madelung, "Authority in Twelver Shiism in the Absence of the Imam," in George Makdisi, *La notion d'autorité au Moyen Age*, pp. 172n9 and 165.

115 *even managed to overlook*: Hitti, *History of the Arabs*, p. 298. Gift exchanges occurred between 797 and 806.

115 *"The warm humour"*: Bernard Lewis, *Muslim Discovery*, p. 139, translating al-Mas'udi's *(Kitab) al-Tanbih wa'l-ishraf*.

115 *He portrayed them*: Ibn Munqidh, *Arab-Syrian Gentleman*, pp. 161–67.

115 *The earliest written laws*: The information on the Nablus canons in this paragraph is drawn from Kedar, "On the Origins."

116 *if a man swore*: Qur'an 24:6; Ibn Rushd, *Distinguished Jurist's Primer*, 2:140–49.

116 *"They installed a huge cask"*: Ibn Munqidh, *Arab-Syrian Gentleman*, pp. 168–69.

116 *"Those who had little money"*: Fulcher of Chartres, *History of the Expedition*, p. 272.

117 *an Arab traveler even dared*: Ibn Jubayr, *Travels*, pp. 349–50.

117 *despite efforts by panicky Muslim officials*: Lévi-Provençal, *Séville musulmane*, p. 128.

117 *and long-distance poisoning*: See Charles Burnett, "The Translating Activity in Mediaeval Spain," in Jayyusi, *Legacy of Muslim Spain*, pp. 1036–58, esp. pp. 1048–50; Irwin, *For Lust of Knowing*, pp. 30–31.

118 *Their introduction came*: See generally Charles Burnett, "Arabic into Latin: The Reception of Arabic Philosophy into Western Europe," in Adamson and Taylor, *Cambridge Companion to Arabic Philosophy*, pp. 370–404. Cf. Bernard G. Dod, "Aristotle Latinus," in Kretzmann et al., *Cambridge History of Later Medieval*

Philosophy, pp. 52, 58–61 (the author debunks the "tenacious legend that the West learnt its Aristotle via translations from the Arabic" but observes that "the legend has more basis when one considers Aristotelian doctrine in a vaguer sense").

118 *"a rational foe"*: Al-Ghazali, *Incoherence*, p. 6; cf. the discussion in his autobiographical *Deliverance from Error* (*al-Munqidh min al-dalal*) of the value of sciences such as logic and mathematics and the counterproductive consequences of opposing them in religion's name: Watt, *Faith and Practice*, pp. 32–43.

118 *One example usefully illustrates*: For al-Ghazali's argument, see *Incoherence*, pp. 166–77. For Ibn Rushd's response, see Khalidi, *Medieval Islamic Philosophical Writings*, p. 162.

119 *The Dominican friar*: Vansteenkiste, "San Tommaso d'Aquino ed Averroè," pp. 589–604.

120 *Ibn Rushd's own fortunes*: On his disgrace, see Urvoy, *Ibn Rushd (Averroes)*, pp. 34–36.

120 *Although jurists had identified*: Al-Mawardi, *Ordinances*, pp. 17–20; Binder, "Al-Ghazālī's Theory of Islamic Government," pp. 236–37.

120 *The one who came closest*: Al-Mawardi, *Ordinances*, p. 20.

120 *When Caliph al-Mutawakkil had been killed*: For the validation of al-Mutawakkil's murder, see Goldziher, *Muslim Studies*, 2:75–76; cf. Hugh Kennedy, *Court of the Caliphs*, pp. 267–68. On the abdication of Caliph al-Muʿtazz, see Ibn al-Tiqtaqa, *al-Fakhri*, p. 241; Kennedy, *Court of the Caliphs*, pp. 287–88. On the blinding of Caliph al-Qahir, see Amedroz and Margoliouth, *Eclipse*, 4:328–31.

121 *Court for the Review*: See chapter 3, p. 57.

121 *Al-Mawardi had laid down limits*: Al-Mawardi, *Ordinances*, pp. 268–74; but cf. Reza, "Islam's Fourth Amendment," esp. pp. 731–32, 744–50, where the author observes that the rules prescribed by al-Mawardi offered few practical guarantees; see also Buckley, "Muhtasib," esp. pp. 107–11.

121 *"No agent of the state"*: Lévi-Provençal, *Séville musulman*, pp. 39–42. Ibn Abdun (d. 1134) was a Malikite *muhtasib*.

121 *certain scholars have argued*: For Islamic influences on English law, see John A. Makdisi, "Islamic Origins of the Common Law," esp. pp. 1717–30; Henry Cattan, "The Law of Waqf," in Khadduri and Liebesny, *Law in the Middle East*, esp. pp. 213–18; Gaudiosi, "Influence of the Islamic Law of Waqf."

121 *Sicily's King Roger II*: Amari, *Storia dei Musulmani*, 3:451–52.

122 *Baybars expressed his undying allegiance*: On the somewhat stillborn renaissance of the caliphate, see Howorth, *History*, 3:176–79; Jackson, "Primacy," pp. 58–59; Holt, "Some Observations."

122 *issued a series of edicts*: Jackson, *Islamic Law and the State*, pp. 51–52.

122 *An authoritative thirteenth-century overview*: Ibn Rushd, *Distinguished Jurist's Primer*, 2:571–72 (sneezing), 2:41 (breast-feeding), 2:155 (manure sales).

123 *"The people of Damascus"*: Rapoport, "Legal Diversity," p. 218 (the text translated there has slightly different wording). On Baybars's reform, see also Jackson, "Primacy," and Escovitz, "Establishment."

124 *Insolvent debtors*: Ibn Rushd, *Distinguished Jurist's Primer*, 2:341–42; cf. Rapoport, "Legal Diversity," pp. 219–20.

124 *allowed a judge sometimes to rely*: Baber Johansen, "Signs," pp. 175–76, 177–78; for a general discussion about this type of proof, see Ibn Rushd, *Distinguished Jurist's Primer*, 2:565–66.

124 *Malikites were known for an expansive*: Rapoport, "Legal Diversity," p. 221. See also chapter 11, p. 242.

7. The Reinvention of Tradition: Salafism

125 *Local legend*: See Michel, *Muslim Theologian's Response*, p. 78; cf. al-Bukhari, 4.55.657; David Cook, *Studies in Muslim Apocalyptic Literature*, pp. 173–75. Other details in this paragraph are drawn from volume 3 of Howorth, *History*.

126 *which was just beginning*: Rosenthal, *Herb*, esp. pp. 44–45, 49–54, 93, 148.

126 *cemeteries were magical gateways*: On the mystical fondness for graveyards, see Karamustafa, *God's Unruly Friends*, pp. 21, 33, 44. On the enraptured of God specifically, see Meri, *Cult of Saints*, pp. 91–100; on the Qalandariyya and Haydariyya, see Karamustafa, *God's Unruly Friends*, pp. 16, 19–21, 46, 152–56.

126 *superfluous to worldly order*: Amitai-Preiss, "Sufis and Shamans," pp. 29–30 ("surplus of the earth"); Karamustafa, *God's Unruly Friends*, p. 53 ("excess of this world").

127 *eighteen cartloads*: Cooperson, *Classical Arabic Biography*, p. 169, citing a report about an erstwhile teacher of Ibn Hanbal's named Bishr al-Hafi (the Barefoot) who lived 767–840.

127 *respectable Sufi fraternities*: On the gradual institutionalization of Sufism, see Karamustafa, *God's Unruly Friends*, pp. 86–90; Ruthven, *Islam in the World*, pp. 244–60.

127 *he met the philosopher*: Urvoy, *Ibn Rushd (Averroes)*, pp. 118–20.

127 *the most ambitious written attempt*: See William Chittick, "Ibn 'Arabī," in Nasr and Leaman, *History of Islamic Philosophy*, 1:497–509, esp. pp. 504–507; A. E. Affifi, "Ibn 'Arabi," in Sharif, *History of Muslim Philosophy*, 1:398–420.

127 *still bestsellers in the United States*: Ptolemy Tompkins, "Rumi Rules!" *Time*, October 29, 2002.

128 *Exhibiting a bibliophobia*: Karamustafa, *God's Unruly Friends*, p. 42.

128 *Other mystics imagined themselves*: On the antinomianism prevalent among Sufis of this era, see ibid., pp. 17–23, 31–38, 90–96; for an account that shows how the traditions have passed down to the present, see Frembgen, *Journey to God*, pp. 66–127. On countervailing efforts by mainstream mystics to appropriate ascetic energies from the ninth century onward, see Karamustafa, *God's Unruly Friends*, pp. 28–31.

128 *"closer to [man]"*: Qur'an 50:16.

128 *"Oh, Abu al-Hasan!"*: Nicholson, *Mystics of Islam*, p. 136.

128 *"Between the spiritual Muslims"*: Nwyia, "Une cible d'Ibn Taimiya," p. 128.

129 *mentioned twice*: The 9/11 Commission Report, pp. 50 and 362, www.9-11com mission.gov.

129 *"influence in shaping"*: Aslan, *No God but God*, p. 85.

129 *several cuts above*: See the opinions of his contemporaries surveyed in Little, "Screw Loose."

129 *his instinct was never*: Ibn Taymiyya's views about the need for Muslims to differentiate themselves from infidels are expressed at length in a polemic translated in Memon, *Ibn Taimīya's Struggle*, esp. pp. 98–161.

129 *he led a protest*: Michel, *Muslim Theologian's Response*, pp. 69–71.

130 *an example illustrates*: Ibid., pp. 78–79.

131 *Ibn Taymiyya once contradicted*: See Yossef Rapoport, "Ibn Taymiyya on Divorce Oaths," in Winter and Levanoni, *Mamluks*, esp. pp. 201–203. For another example of his willingness to challenge existing doctrines on the basis of ancient practice, see his support for the imposition of fines in *Public Duties*, pp. 62–64.

131 *Considering the lawfulness of hashish*: Rosenthal, *Herb*, pp. 64, 126–27; cf. Laoust, *Essai*, pp. 111–14.

131 *he associated with a reputable*: George Makdisi, "Ibn Taimīya"; cf. Memon, *Ibn Taimīya's Struggle*, pp. ix–xii, 25–26; Michel, *Muslim Theologian's Response*, p. 33.

132 *humiliating a hashish-addled*: Nadwi, *Life*, pp. 36–37; Rosenthal, *Herb*, p. 84n7.

132 *A confrontation ensued*: Memon, *Ibn Taimīya's Struggle*, pp. 62–64; cf. Nadwi, *Life*, p. 39.

132 *letter of complaint*: See Memon, *Ibn Taimīya's Struggle*, p. 43; Michel, *Muslim Theologian's Response*, p. 13.

133 *repeatedly condemned and punished*: Ibn Taymiyya would be incarcerated six times and spend more than six years in prison between 1294 and 1328: Little, "Historical and Historiographical Significance," pp. 312–13; for a summary of the political factors underpinning his conflict with the authorities, see ibid., pp. 320–25. For a more sympathetic account and analysis of his tribulations, see Memon, *Ibn Taimīya's Struggle*, pp. 46–72, 82–87.

133 *such traditions were simply unholy*: Ibn Taymiyya's views on tomb veneration, as expressed in a lengthy polemic from the early 1320s, are set out in Memon, *Ibn Taimīya's Struggle*, pp. 251–97; cf. pp. 49–50, 82. See also Nadwi, *Life*, pp. 79–88; Michel, *Muslim Theologian's Response*, p. 36.

133 *A Cairo shrine famous*: Nadwi, *Life*, p. 88.

134 *A court was convoked*: Laoust, *Essai*, pp. 145–47; Memon, *Ibn Taimīya's Struggle*, pp. vii, 47–50, 82–85.

134 *Tens of thousands*: See Laoust, *Essai*, pp. 149–50.

135 *The deity he worshipped*: For Ibn Taymiyya's thoughts about divine omnipotence and human free will, an issue subsumed in Arabic by the word *qadar* (roughly, "power"), see Michel, *Muslim Theologian's Response*, pp. 44–55.

135 *A younger son of Hülegü's*: For the conversion of Hülegü's son Teguder Ahmad (r. 1282–84) and the role played by Sufis in proselytizing among the Mongol

elites of Persia, see Amitai-Preiss, "Sufis and Shamans"; for a good account of
their activities at a popular level there and in Anatolia, see Karamustafa, *God's
Unruly Friends*, pp. 1–23.

136 *Persians adopted Shiʿism*: Savory, *Iran Under the Safavids*, pp. 13–16, 29–30.

136 *Although Selim staked*: Legend would later claim that the caliphate was formally
transferred to Sultan Selim I in 1517, but this was a fiction first expressed by the
Turkish-born Armenian historian Ignatius Mouradgea d'Ohsson in 1787:
Arnold, *Caliphate*, pp. 142–48. On the Mughal allegiances and claims, see ibid.,
pp. 159–62; Sicker, *Islamic World in Ascendancy*, p. 189.

137 *A proposal to draft*: See chapter 3, p. 55.

137 *Shariʿa-influenced codes*: On the delineation of Ottoman law during the fifteenth
and sixteenth centuries, see Peters, *Crime and Punishment*, pp. 69–75.

138 *The statutes were often called*: See İnalcık, "Suleiman the Lawgiver," esp. pp. 107–10.

138 *The onslaught reduced*: See the vivid account of the city's destruction in Ibn
Taghri Birdi, *History of Egypt*, 2:44–51.

138 *attributed the government's heavy-handedness*: Silvestre de Sacy, *Chrestomathie*,
2:161, 164–65 (a translation of al-Maqrizi's *al-Khitat*). The full passage is on
pp. 157–67, and the Arabic text is on pp. 55–66.

138 *His selective description*: See Ayalon, "Great Yāsa (C2)," esp. pp. 121–23, 126–
27. On the actual impact of Genghis Khan's *yasa* among the Mamluks, see
Ayalon, "Great Yāsa (C1)," and Amitai-Preiss, "Ghazan, Islam, and Mongol
Tradition." Al-Maqrizi's misleading account is still cited by some Muslims as
proof of the dangers of departing from the shariʿa: see, for example, Nadwi,
Life, pp. 13–14.

139 *"even if the Prophet"*: Fauzi M. Najjar, "Islamic Political Philosophy," in Marmura,
Islamic Theology and Philosophy, p. 95, quoting words attributed by al-Qanuji
(d. 1307); for views about the *siyasa*, see also Bernard Lewis, *Political Words and
Ideas*, pp. 31–46.

139 *"[from] the caliph [to]"*: Ibn Taymiyya, *Droit public*, p. 12; see also Baber Johansen, "Perfect Law," in Bearman et al., *Law Applied*, esp. pp. 267–70.

139 *Ibn Taymiyya's account of the* siyasa: Ibn Taymiyya, *Droit public*, pp. 39, 88, 92;
Public Duties, pp. 25, 60; on trials of suspicion, see also Baber Johansen, "Signs,"
p. 190; Baber Johansen, "Perfect Law," p. 268.

140 *even more far-reaching conclusions*: For the examples given in this paragraph, see
Baber Johansen, "Signs," pp. 188–90, citing Ibn Qayyim, *al-Turuq al-hikmiya*,
pp. 48–49, 92–93, 101, 228–30.

140 *The majority of Islamic jurists*: Baber Johansen, "Signs," pp. 170–71, 178.

140 *Testimony could be beaten out*: Ibid., pp. 191–92, citing Ibn Qayyim's *al-Turuq
al-hikmiya*, pp. 7, 13, 108; Reza, "Torture and Islamic Law," pp. 24–25.

140 *It was first justified*: See Baber Johansen, "Signs," pp. 170–71, 192. The Shafiʿite
theorist al-Mawardi then took the view that executive officials could use force as
an investigative technique, even in cases involving religious law: see *Ordinances*,
pp. 94–103, 239.

141 *one historian has suggested*: Baber Johansen, "Signs," p. 193.

141 *Forceful interrogations were impermissible*: Peters, *Crime and Punishment*, pp. 82–83; Heyd, *Studies*, pp. 116–19, 252–54.

142 *Ottoman officials allegedly indulged*: DeLong-Bas, *Wahhabi Islam*, p. 247.

142 *he judged a woman*: On the stoning and its aftermath, see Philby, *Arabia*, pp. 9–12; for an account that is tendentiously sympathetic to al-Wahhab, see DeLong-Bas, *Wahhabi Islam*, pp. 24–29.

142 *One of the lesser-known facts*: Mouradgea d'Ohsson, *Tableau général*, 3:259; Heyd, *Studies*, p. 263.

142 *Saudi forces were soon desecrating*: Philby, *Arabia*, pp. 87–88.

143 *Al-Wahhab's debt*: DeLong-Bas, *Wahhabi Islam*, p. 256. On al-Wahhab's own citations of Ibn Taymiyya, see also ibid., pp. 340n74 and 341n109. For a thorough and extremely sympathetic biography of al-Wahhab, see ibid., esp. pp. 13–91; for a more hostile corrective, see Abou El Fadl, *Great Theft*, pp. 75–80.

8. Jihad: A Law-Torn World

144 *Over the course of 1295*: Rashid al-Din, *Compendium*, 3:619–30; Howorth, *History*, 3:376–87, 395–98; on Ghazan's conversion, see also Melville, *History and Literature*, pp. 159–77; Amitai-Preiss, "Sufis and Shamanism," pp. 32–35.

144 *"those charged with authority"*: See chapter 6, p. 113.

145 *"Be assured that all countries"*: See Joseph Somogyi, "Adh-Dhahabi's Record of the Destruction of Damascus by the Mongols in 1299–1301," in Löwinger and Somogyi, *Ignace Goldziher Memorial Volume*, pp. 354–55.

145 *were disallowed*: Qur'an 4:26.

145 *Apostasy was averted*: See Amitai-Preiss, "Ghazan, Islam, and Mongol Tradition," pp. 2–3.

145 *"Even if we forbid [intoxication]"*: Rashid al-Din, *Compendium*, 3:743. On Ghazan's administrative and legal reforms more generally, see ibid., 3:663–762; on his loyalty to the *yasa*, see Amitai-Preiss, "Ghazan, Islam, and Mongol Tradition," pp. 3–5.

145 *It was Mamluk soldiers who now*: Al-Maqrizi, *Histoire des sultans mamlouks*, 2:517n31, 542–45 (marginal numbers). On this first campaign (winter 1299–spring 1300), see also Howorth, *History*, 3:429–50; Somogyi, "Adh-Dhahabi's Record," pp. 360–81; Reuven Amitai, "The Mongol Occupation of Damascus in 1300: A Study of Mamluk Loyalties," in Winter and Levanoni, *Mamluks*, pp. 21–41.

146 *sixteen hundred Mongol captives*: Al-Maqrizi, *Histoire des sultans mamlouks*, 2:579 (marginal number).

146 *he led a delegation*: Ibid., pp. 544–45; see also ibid., p. 546 (marginal number); on Ibn Taymiyya's activities during the Mongol campaign, see also Somogyi, "Adh-Dhahabi's Record," esp. pp. 365, 370, 377, 380, 385; Nadwi, *Life*, pp. 28–31, 35.

146 *three legal opinions*: Extracts from the second and most substantial have been translated into French by Yahya Michot as "Textes spirituels" XI, XII, and XIII, available via www.muslimphilosophy.com/it. There is also a hard-to-obtain

English translation: Thomas Raff, *Remarks on an Anti-Mongol Fatwa of Ibn Taimiya* (Leiden: privately printed, 1973). Although it is impossible to know when it was written, it seems to date from some time after late 1308: see Aigle, "Mongol Invasions," pp. 117–18; Michot, "Textes spirituels XII," n36.

147 *"They believe that [Genghis Khan]"*: See Michot, "Textes spirituels XII," p. 1; cf. Michel, *Muslim Theologian's Response*, p. 72.

147 *Jesus was born of a virgin*: Qur'an 3:47.

147 *he contended in this context*: Aigle, "Mongol Invasions," pp. 99, 101–103; Michot, "Textes spirituels XI," "Textes spirituels XIII."

149 *"Fight and slay the [impenitent]"*: Qur'an 9:5.

149 *one even urged Muslims*: Ibid., 9:29. For other justifications of combat, see, for example, 2:216, 9:41, 49:15.

150 *One ninth-century theologian*: Abu Sulayman, *Towards an Islamic Theory*, p. 44.

150 *what place warfare should possess*: For an overview of the classical doctrines about warfare that emerged in the Abbasid caliphate, see Khadduri, *War and Peace*; for a translation of the seminal work by Muhammad ibn al-Hasan al-Shaybani (750–805), see Khadduri, *Islamic Law of Nations*.

150 *speaking of truth to an unjust ruler*: Michael Cook, *Commanding Right and Forbidding Wrong*, p. 6n18.

150 *suppression of egotism*: See chapter 5, p. 103.

150 *The jurists made clear*: Abu Sulayman, *Towards an Islamic Theory*, pp. 19–24.

151 *Non-Muslims were eligible*: See chapter 2, p. 43.

151 *al-Wahhab turned his grievance*: DeLong-Bas, *Wahhabi Islam*, pp. 246–56. For a (rather uncritical) synopsis of al-Wahhab's own ideas about jihad, see pp. 201–25.

152 *they had always theorized*: Al-Baladhuri, *Origins*, 2:221; Nizami, *Religion and Politics*, pp. 329–31.

153 *"for a terror and example"*: Harington, *Elementary Analysis*, 1:346–48; see also N. Majumdar, *Justice and Police*, pp. 100, 116, 309.

153 *root-and-branch legal reform*: See Kugle, "Framed, Blamed, and Renamed," esp. pp. 264–74, 281–86; see also Anderson, *Law Reform*, pp. 19–25.

153 *It was already widely believed*: Dalrymple, *Last Mughal*, p. 33.

153 *Ever since the fall*: See Abou El Fadl, "Islamic Law and Muslim Minorities," esp. pp. 150–51.

153 *Ibn Taymiyya had similarly advised*: Michot, *Muslims Under Non-Muslim Rule*, pp. 11–27, 63–100 (the town concerned was Mardin).

153 *"wields no authority"*: See Mujeeb, *Indian Muslims*, pp. 390–91.

154 *"There were many who advised"*: Ibid., p. 395.

154 *Sayyid Ahmed's convoluted principles*: Metcalf, *Islamic Revival*, p. 62.

154 *a statute that allowed*: On the Doctrine of Lapse that was given legal effect in 1834, see R. C. Majumdar, *History and Culture*, 1:58–95.

154 *A rumor was circulating*: On the spread of the "greased cartridges" story, see David, *Indian Mutiny*, pp. 52–66.

154 *the most militant early rebels*: Dalrymple, *Last Mughal*, pp. 439–40.

155 *"The known restless spirit"*: Ibid., p. 440.

155 *It was scholars who*: Compare ibid., pp. 228–29 and pp. 23, 159, 264–68, 285, 294, 336.

155 *Delhi's congregational mosque*: Ibid., p. 475; Spear, *Twilight of the Mughals*, pp. 218–22.

155 *a penal code came into force*: Kugle, "Framed, Blamed, and Renamed," pp. 300–301.

155 *Islamic legal scholars*: Metcalf, *Islamic Revival*, pp. 82, 142–43, 352; Syed Ahmed Khan, *Review on Dr. Hunter's Indian Musalmans*; Donohue and Esposito, *Islam in Transition*, pp. 32–34; Ali, *Leader Reassessed*, pp. 266–71.

156 *"[Its] schisms and divisions"*: Donohue and Esposito, *Islam in Transition*, p. 19; see also al-Afghani, *Réfutation*, pp. 174–85. On Jamal al-Din's life, see Abrahamian, *Iran Between Two Revolutions*, pp. 62–65; see also Nikki R. Keddie's account in Rahnema, *Pioneers*, pp. 11–29; Donohue and Esposito, *Islam in Transition*, pp. 13–19.

157 *One of Selim's successors*: On the Pan-Islamist exploitation of the caliphate by Abdulhamid II from the 1870s onward, see Arnold, *Caliphate*, pp. 173–77 (and pp. 164–66); Finkel, *Osman's Dream*, pp. 492–99.

157 *certify it a jihad*: Peters, *Jihad*, pp. 55–57.

158 *Ali Abd al-Raziq cautiously proposed*: Donohue and Esposito, *Islam in Transition*, pp. 24–31.

158 *"Muslims . . . are compelled"*: Al-Banna, *Five Tracts*, pp. 150, 155; see also Lia, *Society*, pp. 83–84, 165.

159 *Zionist-crusader alliance*: On the links drawn between Zionism and the Crusades, see Morris, *1948*, pp. 105, 187, 194, 313.

159 *"worldwide jihad in defense"*: Ibid., p. 65. Other details in this paragraph come from ibid., pp. 85, 182–83, 395–96; and Peters, *Jihad*, pp. 104–105.

160 *well over half*: See Morris, *1948*, p. 407 ("some seven hundred thousand Arab refugees").

161 *"No political system"*: Qutb, *Milestones*, p. 57. On Qutb, see Charles Tripp's biography in Rahnema, *Pioneers*, pp. 154–83; Wright, *Looming Tower*, pp. 7–31. For a thoughtful account of the Egyptian's influence, which avoids both idolization and demonization, see Abu-Rabi, *Intellectual Origins*.

161 *during the couple of years*: Kepel, *Muslim Extremism*, p. 42.

161 *"mask for the crusading spirit"*: Qutb, *Milestones*, p. 160.

162 *"My words will be stronger"*: Wright, *Looming Tower*, p. 31.

162 *first gained traction after 1948*: See Bernard Lewis, *Semites and Anti-Semites*, esp. pp. 194–97 (he notes that "the penetration of anti-Semitism in its European Christian form was at first slow and limited, and it did not become a major factor in the Arab world until the late 1950s and 1960s"). See also David Cook, *Contemporary Muslim Apocalyptic Literature*, esp. pp. 18–35, 59–71, 184–200, 223–25; Pipes, *Hidden Hand*, esp. pp. 103–20, 289–324.

163 *Takfir wa al-Hijra then imploded*: Kepel, *Muslim Extremism*, pp. 70–102; on the important refutation of judgmental extremism by members of al-Azhar and the

Muslim Brotherhood (a work titled *Du'at la qudat*, or *Preachers, Not Judges*), see Zollner, *Muslim Brotherhood*, esp. pp. 64–145.

163 *They duly provided it*: See Peters, *Jihad*, pp. 156–59.

163 *in his tract*: Jansen, *Neglected Duty*, esp. pp. 166–75, 187–88, 191–92, 199–200. Taymiyya's fatwa on the status of the town of Mardin is translated and discussed extensively in Michot, *Muslims Under Non-Muslim Rule*.

164 *"I have killed"*: See Kepel, *Muslim Extremism*, pp. 191–92.

164 *Some 280 men*: Wright, *Looming Tower*, pp. 54–55; Charles Richards, "Trial Starts of 280 Egyptian 'Plotters,'" *Financial Times*, December 6, 1982, p. 3.

166 *fixated on the religious challenge*: On the gathering Saudi-Iranian rivalry, which would culminate in a bloody confrontation between Iranian pilgrims and Saudi security forces during the 1987 hajj, see Martin Kramer, "Tragedy in Mecca," in Pipes, *Sandstorm*, pp. 241–67; Jacob Goldberg, "Saudi Arabia and the Iranian Revolution: The Religious Dimension," in Menashri, *Iranian Revolution*, pp. 155–70.

166 *"prejudicial to the Afghan people"*: Kepel, *Jihad*, p. 139; see also Robert Fisk, "UN Pressed to Drop Scheme for Mediation in Afghanistan," *Times* (London), January 28, 1981, p. 8.

166 Defense of the Muslim Lands: Azzam's text is available at www.religioscope.com /info/doc/jihad/azzam_defence_3_chap1.htm. On Azzam generally, see Kepel, *Jihad*, pp. 144–47.

166 *fatwas going back to the Crusades*: Berkey, *Formation of Islam*, p. 200.

167 *accounts of Soviet helicopters*: Wright, *Looming Tower*, pp. 96, 106; Benjamin and Steven, *Age of Sacred Terror*, p. 99.

167 *one more miracle in 1987*: This is the year given in a stipulation in *U.S. v. Usama bin Laden et al.*, referred to in the transcript of February 14, 2001, www.en.wiki source.org/wiki/United_States_of_America_v._Usama_bin_Laden.

168 *"I believe that among the many"*: *Time*, February 11, 1985 (ellipses omitted and punctuation changed in text).

168 *The tactic's only other practitioners*: Although several writers have sought to establish that the Tamil Tigers developed their suicidal skills while training alongside Shi'a paramilitaries in Lebanon during the 1980s, none has advanced evidence to prove the claim. All that can be said for sure is that there were contacts between other Tamil paramilitaries and secular Palestinian guerrilla organizations: see Fair, *Urban Battle Fields*, p. 36.

168 *the Qur'an made clear*: On suicide, see Qur'an 4:29, 2:195, 16:61; al-Bukhari, 8.73.74, 4.56.669; Goldziher, *Muslim Studies*, 2:352; Rosenthal, "On Suicide," esp. pp. 240–46. On the prohibition of fiery punishments, see al-Bukhari, 4.52.260, 9.84.57; Ibn Rushd, *Distinguished Jurist's Primer*, 1:460.

168 *Ayatollah Khomeini personally authorized*: Martin Kramer, "Redeeming Jerusalem: The Pan-Islamic Promise of Hizballah," in Menashri, *Iranian Revolution*, p. 116.

168 *Sheikh Naim Qassem*: Jaber, *Hezbollah*, pp. 87–88; Munir, "Suicide Attacks and Islamic Law," esp. pp. 73–74.

169 *He had recently helped establish*: Wright, *Looming Tower*, p. 130; Chehab, *Inside Hamas*, p. 193; Kepel, *Jihad*, pp. 153–58.

170 *his primary concern was to combat*: Ayman al-Zawahiri's autobiography purports to explain his estrangement from the Muslim Brotherhood: Mansfield, *His Own Words*, pp. 68–69, 160–69, 276.

170 *The senior muftis*: Yvonne Y. Haddad, "Operation Desert Storm and the War of Fatwas," in Masud et al., *Islamic Legal Interpretation*, pp. 301–302.

171 *joint military training*: Wright, *Looming Tower*, pp. 173–74; Bergen, *Holy War*, pp. 92–93.

171 *"[Salim] said that our time now"*: Testimony (corrected for consistency) of Jamal al-Fadl on February 6, 2001, in *U.S. v. Usama bin Laden*, www.en.wikisource.org /wiki/United_States_of_America_v._Usama_bin_Laden; cf. Benjamin and Steven, *Age of Sacred Terror*, pp. 42, 120. Mamdouh Salim's nom de guerre was Abu Hajer al-Iraqi.

172 *he had ever countenanced*: Ibn Taymiyya allowed in limited circumstances for the killing of Muslims who were being used in battle as human shields: see David Cook, "Implications," pp. 136–37.

172 *noncombatants should be spared*: See Peters, *Jihad*, p. 49; Ibn Taymiyya, *Droit public*, p. 128. Cf. the discussion of lawful and unlawful acts of war in Ibn Rushd, *Distinguished Jurist's Primer*, 1:456–61.

172 *Palestinian violence moved up*: Pedahzur, *Suicide Terrorism*, p. 54.

172 *two motorcycle-borne members*: Wright, *Looming Tower*, pp. 185–86.

172 *one of the first-ever Sunni justifications*: See Azzam, "Al-Qaeda," p. 4.

173 *"constitution, international law and norms"*: Wright, *Looming Tower*, p. 209.

173 *his inaugural fatwa*: "Declaration of War Against the Americans Occupying the Land of the Two Holy Places," July 1996. Translations are available online, for example, via www.wikisource.org.

173 *"The [requirement] to kill"*: Donohue and Esposito, *Islam in Transition*, pp. 430–32.

174 *At 10:30 a.m. on Friday*: Wright, *Looming Tower*, pp. 270–72.

174 *"these events have divided"*: Speech broadcast on October 7, 2001, www.september 11news.com/OsamaSpeeches.htm.

175 *Certain foreign scholars*: Douglas Jehl, "For Saudi Cleric, Battle Shapes Up as Infidel vs. Islam," *New York Times*, December 5, 2001; Nafi, "Fatwā and War."

175 *While the senior mufti*: Compare the condemnation of sectarian killings issued in September 2005 by Saudi Arabia's senior mufti, Sheikh Abdul Aziz al-Asheikh (reported on, for example, *Arab News*, November 19, 2005), and the anti-Shi'a fatwa of Sheikh Abd al-Rahman al-Barrak, reported by Reuters on December 29, 2006.

175 *After a twenty-seven-year-old*: Chehab, *Inside Hamas*, p. 89; for a more general fatwa on suicide bombing by Qaradawi, see Donohue and Esposito, *Islam in Transition*, pp. 469–71.

177 *The French colonial authorities*: See Yahya Michot, *Pour une tombe à Damas*, www.saphirnews.com/Pour-une-tombe-a-Damas_a4483.html.

178 *"They stop Muslims"*: Brisard, *Zarqawi*, p. 239.

178 *"Whoever kills a human being"*: Qur'an 5:32.

9. Innovation and Its Discontents: Islamic Law
and the Challenge of Change

182 *satanic verses*: There are detailed accounts of the incident recorded in al-Tabari, *History*, 6:xxxiv–xxxv, 107–12, and Ibn Ishaq, *Life of Muhammad*, pp. 165–67. Although no canonical hadith collection explicitly mentions the story, al-Bukhari attributes to Ibn Abbas a description of the Prophet at one point leading pagans in prayer: "The Prophet prostrated while reciting An-Najm and with him prostrated the Muslims, the pagans, the jinns, and all human beings" (2.19.177).

182 *A religious seminar*: Shahab Ahmed, "Ibn Taymiyyah and the Satanic Verses," p. 73.

183 *"Do you not think"*: Quoted in ibid., p. 77.

183 *After unhappily leafing through*: The work I showed him was Abd al-Qadir al-Jilani's analysis of the story in chapter 10 of his *Ghunyatul talibeen*, and he referred me to Sayeeadi, *Tibyan al-Qur'an*, 7:776–85.

184 *Muslims have always believed*: Shahab Ahmed, "Ibn Taymiyyah and the Satanic Verses," pp. 86–90.

184 *Sailors brought the Black Death*: The information in this and the following paragraph is drawn primarily from Dols, *Black Death*, and Dols, "Plague in Early Islamic History." Ibn Battuta also made brief observations about a visit to Damascus in July 1348, where he witnessed penitential fasts and processions that supposedly produced some relief: "God Most High lightened their affliction; the number of deaths in a single day reached a maximum of two thousand, whereas the number rose in Cairo and Old Cairo to twenty-four thousand in a day." Ibn Battuta, *Travels*, 1:143–44.

185 *"The existence of contagion"*: Arnold and Guillaume, *Legacy of Islam*, p. 340; cf. Ober and Alloush, "Plague at Granada," p. 422.

185 *A few years down the line*: Gibb et al., *Encyclopaedia of Islam* ("Ibn al-Khatīb"); see also Dols, *Black Death*, p. 94.

186 *had each contemplated*: On Ibn Sina, see Marmura, "Avicenna's 'Flying Man' in Context"; for a translation of Ibn Tufayl's *Hayy bin Yaqzan*, see Khalidi, *Medieval Islamic Philosophical Writings*, pp. 99–153.

186 *Even Ibn Qayyim*: Ibn Qayyim, *Medicine of the Prophet*, pp. 110–16.

186 *"the greatest work of its kind"*: Toynbee, *Study of History*, 3:322.

186 *The North African expressed no doubt*: Ibn Khaldun, *Muqaddimah*, 1:184–245.

186 *"rolling up the carpet"*: Ibn Khaldun, *Autobiographie*, p. 34.

186 *"The medicine mentioned"*: Ibn Khaldun, *Muqaddimah*, 3:150.

187 *"every innovation is heresy"*: Goldziher, *Muslim Studies*, 2:34–35.

187 *Scholars long ago acknowledged*: On "good" innovations, see Fierro, "Treatises Against Innovations," esp. pp. 205–206.

187 *Eighth-century jurists transformed*: See chapter 3, p. 60.

187 *railed against mathematics*: Ibn Taymiyya's *al-Radd* portrayed mathematics as a bogus form of knowledge that "does not bring perfection to the human soul, nor save man from castigation of God, nor lead him to a happy life." Its religious illegitimacy was such that it could not even be used to determine the beginning of religiously significant lunar months: see Nurcholish Madjid, "Ibn Taymiyya on *Kalam* and *Falsafa*: A Problem of Reason and Revelation in Islam" (Ph.D. diss., University of Chicago, 1984), pp. 235–36.

187 *most Muslim revivalists*: A comprehensive and representative collection of speeches, tracts, and articles by Islamic modernists of the late nineteenth and early twentieth centuries can be found in Kurzman, *Modernist Islam*.

188 *Malaysia's National Fatwa Council*: Mazwin Nik Anis, "Fatwa Council Says Yoga with Worshipping, Chanting Is Prohibited," *Star Online*, November 22, 2008; Mazwin Nik Anis, "Guidebook for Muslims in Space," *Star Online*, October 6, 2007.

188 *But its capacity to accommodate*: A knowledge of customary law (*urf*) was one of the qualifications required of a *mujtahid*, according to an influential work by Abu'l Husayn al-Basri (d. 1083), and he thought it "essential to determine God's law in the light of the exigencies of human life." See Hallaq, "Was the Gate of Ijtihad Closed?" p. 5.

188 *"each age is distinguished"*: Berkey, "Tradition, Innovation," p. 48.

188 *"Strange as it may seem"*: Al-Ghazali, *Book of Knowledge*, p. 206.

188 *the modern world's 1.6 billion Muslims*: On Islamic demography, see Pew Research Center, *Mapping the Global Muslim Population*; for relevant legal provisions about the constitutional status of Islamic norms, see Afghanistan Constitution, Art. 3; Egypt Constitution, Art. 2; Iran Constitution, Arts. 2–4; Iraq Constitution, Art. 2; Maldives Constitution, Art. 10(b); Pakistan Constitution, Art. 227 (and cf. Art. 2A); Qatar Constitution, Art. 1; Saudi Arabia Basic Law of 1992 (Royal Decree No. A/90), Art. 1; Sudan Interim Constitution, Art. 5; Syria Constitution, Art. 3(2); Yemen Constitution, Art. 3. As and when Libya succeeds in drafting a constitution, it will certainly make some reference to the supremacy of Islamic law; the same is true of Somalia, though a settled legal order is not likely to materialize in that country anytime soon.

189 *they established a madrasa*: See Metcalf, *Islamic Revival*, esp. pp. 87–137, 140–57.

190 *Deobandi warnings*: Fatwa 7563 (September 14, 2008) and Fatwa 9432 (December 22, 2008), www.darulifta-deoband.org.

192 *to avoid Hindu haircuts*: Metcalf, *Islamic Revival*, p. 153.

193 *"the gate of interpretation"*: See chapter 5, p. 104.

193 *"principally a means"*: Sikand, "Deoband's War on Television," www.openaccess .leidenuniv.nl/handle/1887/4946.

194 *by intuition alone*: Metcalf, *Islamic Revival*, p. 104.

197 *accepted the Mu'tazilite argument*: See chapter 5, p. 94.

198 *in a series of lectures*: Martin, *Creating an Islamic State*, pp. 115–24; Abrahamian, *Iran Between Two Revolutions*, pp. 476–79.

200 *engineer a putsch*: An account of how the covert operation was planned and put into

effect in 1953, written by a CIA operative near the top of the chain of command, is available via the *New York Times* website, www.nytimes.com/library/world /mideast/041600iran-cia-index.html.

201 sayyids *(descendants of Hussein)*: Ali and Fatima had two sons, and more-or-less untranslatable honorifics attach to the lineages of both. The direct descendants of Hussein are called *sayyids*, while those of his elder brother, Hassan, are known as *sharifs*.

201 *the Iranian state threatened*: Art. 638 of Iran's 1991 Penal Code.

202 *I spoke to many admirers*: On Shabestari (b. 1936), see Taji-Farouki, *Modern Muslim Intellectuals*, pp. 193–224.

202 *"an ocean poured into a jar"*: Soroush, *Expansion*, p. 273. The same December 2007 interview ("The Word of Mohammad") is available via his website: www .drsoroush.com. The quoted phrase, though used by Soroush, is drawn from the poetry of Rumi.

203 *an official recount*: See Michael Slackman, "Amid Crackdown, Iran Admits Voting Errors," *New York Times*, June 23, 2009.

203 *"divine assessment"*: See Fareed Zakaria, "Theocracy and Its Discontents," *Newsweek*, June 20, 2009.

203 *Jürgen Habermas himself*: The identification of the German as a coconspirator came during the prosecutor's opening on August 2, 2009. An account of the proceedings is archived at the excellent online magazine *Tehran Bureau*: www .pbs.org/wgbh/pages/frontline/tehranbureau.

204 *"Mr. Khamenei"*: See "Iran: The Revenge," dated December 2009 and posted (in English) on www.drsoroush.com.

204 *the ideas of the popular religious reformist*: On Ali Shariati, see Rahnema, *Pioneers*, pp. 208–50.

204 *protesting a secret massacre*: On Montazeri's opposition to the regime's slaughter of several thousand political prisoners in 1988, see Robertson, *Massacre*, esp. pp. 6–7, 32, 43–44, 62–63, at www.iranrights.org/english/attachments/doc_1115.pdf.

205 *"A political system based"*: The July 2009 fatwa is available via the *Tehran Bureau* at www.pbs.org/wgbh/pages/frontline/tehranbureau/2009/07/grand-ayatollah -montazeris-fatwa.html.

206 *sacred struggle to understand*: On the exercise of *ijtihad* in general, see Hallaq, *History of Islamic Legal Theories*, pp. 117–24; Aghnides, *Mohammedan Theories*, pp. 112–26.

207 *hadiths promised believers*: Al-Shafiʻi, *Risāla*, p. 299.

207 *The phenomenon is illustrated*: On *ijtihad* and the use of modern communications technology, see Bunt, *Virtually Islamic*; Bunt, *Digital Age*; Cesari, *When Islam and Democracy Meet*, pp. 111–22; Brinkley Messick, "Media Muftis: Radio Fatwas in Yemen," in Masud et al., *Islamic Legal Interpretation*, pp. 310–20.

208 *about ten a day*: Kashif ul-Huda, "Fatwas: The Big Picture," June 4, 2010, www .twocircles.net/2010jun04/fatwas_big_picture.html.

208 *Some advise correspondents*: See, for example, sources in Bunt, *Digital Age*, pp. 139–40.

208 *"It is not permissible"*: Fatwa dated March 15, 2010, at www.islam-qa.com/en/ref /131101.

208 *"the solution to this disastrous situation"*: See www.islam-qa.com/en/ref/591 /masturbation.

209 *"that doomed land"*: See www.islam-qa.com/en/ref/126523.

209 *"conjure up images"*: Fatwa issued on September 13, 2003, available via www .islamonline.net.

209 *"it is permissible for a husband"*: Fatwa issued May 19, 2004, available via www .islamonline.net.

209 *repeatedly forbidden both*: See www.fatwa-online.com/marriage/sexualrelations /sre003/index.htm; for the various opinions at www.askimam.org, search under "oral sex."

10. Punishment and Pity: The Modern Revival of Islamic Criminal Law

212 *Dozens of health centers*: See Maqbool Ahmed, "'Holy' Writ," *Herald* (Karachi), November 2008, p. 69; Zahid Hussein, "Taleban Threaten to Blow Up Girls' Schools if They Refuse to Close," *Times* (London), December 26, 2008.

212 *A proposed administration of justice*: Raja Asghar, "Sharia for Malakand as Zardari Signs Law," *Dawn*, April 14, 2009, p. 1.

212 *evidence then emerged*: See Declan Walsh, "Outcry in Pakistan After Video of a 17-Year-Old Girl's Flogging by the Taliban Is Shown on TV," *Guardian*, April 4, 2009.

214 *whereas offenses against the person*: On the distinction between a right proper to God (*huq Allah*) and one enjoyed by humanity (*huq al-abd*), which corresponds roughly to the notion of public and private rights in Western jurisprudence, see Kamali, *Principles*, p. 448; cf. Peters, *Crime and Punishment*, p. 54. The terminology goes some way to explain the hostility toward human rights discourse that is common among conservative Muslims: they argue that "human" rights necessarily violate the rights of God.

215 *This one was a pregnant woman*: Her fate is described in Muslim, 3.916, 17.4205 and 4206.

215 *Ahmad ibn Hanbal reported*: Melchert, *Ahmad ibn Hanbal*, p. 21, citing the traditionist's (*Kitab*) *al-Zuhd*, 76.97.

216 *Judges are advised to avoid*: Kamali, *Principles*, p. 293; Peters, *Crime and Punishment*, pp. 20–22.

216 *Repentance prior to arrest*: See chapter 1, p. 27; Peters, *Crime and Punishment*, pp. 27–28, 34, 57, 58, 65. On the peculiarities of remorse in apostasy cases, see chapter 11, pp. 240–42.

217 *Stonings are recorded just once*: See chapter 7, p. 142. Amputations were more

common but still rare: compare Mouradgea d'Ohsson, *Tableau général*, 3:266; Heyd, *Studies*, pp. 264–66; Çiğdem, "Corporal Punishment," esp. p. 40.

217 *the only known case*: Semerdjian, *Off the Straight Path*, p. 158.

217 *Muslim chroniclers and Christian travelers*: See, for example, Mouradgea d'Ohsson, *Tableau général*, pp. 236–81 (on the eighteenth-century Ottoman Empire); Foster, *Embassy*, pp. 87, 104, 190–91, 201 (on seventeenth-century Mughal India).

217 *"seems to be possessed of"*: Robert Fisk, "Four People Stoned to Death After Iran Trial," July 4, 1980, p. 1; see also "Four in Iran Executed by Stoning, 7 by Firing Squad," *New York Times*, July 4, 1980, p. 1.

217 *The penalty was notionally in force*: More specifically, in Saudi Arabia, Yemen, and Qatar. See Peters, *Crime and Punishment*, pp. 142–43.

218 *A fresh-faced army officer*: On Libya's reintroduction of Islamic criminal penalties, see Ann Elizabeth Mayer, "Reinstating Islamic Criminal Law in Libya," in Dwyer, *Law and Islam in the Middle East*, p. 103.

218 *Beyond the Arabian Peninsula*: The British governor-general of India, Warren Hastings, confirmed a stoning to death (along with numerous mutilations) in 1773: see N. Majumdar, *Justice and Police*, pp. 112, 314–17. Islamic criminal penalties other than stoning and flogging lingered in Nigeria until the 1960s and continued to hold sway in ungovernable parts of Afghanistan and Pakistan: Anderson, *Law Reform*, pp. 27, 87.

218 *"He can thus judge"*: Khomeini, *Sayings*, p. 31.

218 *"not so big that"*: Art. 119 of the 1982 Penal Code, later replaced by Art. 104 of the 1991 Penal Code.

218 *the tradition that Caliph Ali*: See chapter 2, p. 51.

218 *keep their palms and thumbs*: Art. 218 of the 1982 Penal Code, later replaced by Art. 201(d) of the 1991 Penal Code.

218 *a mini-guillotine*: Peters, *Crime and Punishment*, p. 163.

218 *martial law powers*: The penalties that were formally introduced in the name of martial law (a jurisdiction that owed its structure to Pakistan's colonial heritage) included not just flogging but also amputation. See Noman, "Pakistan and General Zia," p. 33; "Amputation of Hand Introduced by Pakistan's Military Rulers as Penalty for Theft and Banditry," *Times* (London), July 11, 1977, p. 4.

219 *It served historically*: See chapter 1, p. 27, and accompanying note.

219 *Most classical jurists*: Peters, *Crime and Punishment*, pp. 57–59.

219 *Saudi scholars issued a fatwa*: Vogel, *Islamic Law and Legal System*, pp. 254–55; Peters, *Crime and Punishment*, p. 151.

219 *Both Libya and Pakistan had decided*: Mayer, "Reinstating Islamic Criminal Law in Libya," p. 105; Peters, *Crime and Punishment*, p. 156. Note, however, that crucifixion is formally an option in Somalia, under Art. 168 of the country's Penal Code.

220 *"prove dangerous to"*: Mayer, "Reinstating Islamic Criminal Law in Libya," p. 105.

220 *"Such of the witnesses"*: Offence of Zina (Enforcement of Hudood) Ordinance, 1979, §§5(2), 17.

220 *The very existence of written*: See chapter 3, p. 55.

220 *the codes kept coming*: For an overview, see Peters, *Crime and Punishment*, pp. 142–73. Islamic courts also enjoy a limited criminal jurisdiction in Malaysia's Kelantan province, and to the embarrassment of many of the country's legislators Indonesia's Aceh province introduced a strict version of the shari'a in October 2009, including mandatory prayer and stoning: see "Stricter Brand of Islam Spreads Across Indonesian Penal Code," *New York Times*, October 28, 2009, p. A6.

220 *Even the Iraqi president*: Cockburn and Cockburn, *Saddam Hussein*, pp. 127–28.

220 *Saudi Arabia facilitates the removal*: See, for example, Amnesty International, "Saudi Arabia: Remains a Fertile Ground for Torture with Impunity," MDE 23/004/2002, May 1, 2002, www.unhcr.org/refworld/docid/3ccfbc114.html; Amnesty International, *Amnesty International Report 2003—Saudi Arabia*, May 28, 2003, www.unhcr.org/refworld/docid/3edb47df4.html.

221 *Its judges gave sixteen-year-old*: See BBC report of May 2, 2006, www.news.bbc .co.uk/1/hi/world/africa/4967108.stm. The principle that *qadis* may permit a murder victim's next of kin to retaliate in person is a feature of Malikite and Shafi'ite jurisprudence: Peters, *Crime and Punishment*, p. 31. A Nigerian court has pronounced a similar sentence at least once: Peters, *Crime and Punishment*, p. 172. Art. 265 of Iran's 1991 Penal Code also allows for such a procedure: Ibid., p. 162.

221 *a judge can therefore take account*: Peters, *Crime and Punishment*, pp. 65–67.

221 *Modern Iran authorizes courts*: Art. 638 (taboo violation) and Art. 637 (public immorality) of Iran's 1991 Penal Code.

221 *Saudi judges are even less*: Vogel, *Islamic Law and Legal System*, esp. pp. 83–165; cf. Peters, *Crime and Punishment*, pp. 148–53.

221 *the Qur'an's call for feminine modesty*: Qur'an 24:31, 33:59. Cf. the instruction to men to "subdue their eyes . . . and maintain their chastity" in 24:30. Article 638 of Iran's 1991 Penal Code authorizes fines and jail terms for women who appear in public without a "proper *hijab*" (it also allows courts to punish other "religious taboos" with up to seventy-four lashes, but *hijab* violations were removed from this general prohibition in 1997). On Sudan, see Tristan McConnell, "Sudanese Woman Lubna Hussein Freed After Union Pays 'Trouser' Fine," *Times* (London), September 9, 2009.

222 *"How near is what God"*: Al-Jahiz, *Epistle*, p. 26.

222 *On the strength of an ambiguous*: Iran addresses the subject of lesbianism in some detail in its 1991 Penal Code, Arts. 128, 129, 134. The most egregious form of the offense, defined as "genital," can earn a culprit one hundred lashes. The chances of convicting someone who pleads not guilty are diminished by the testimonial requirements—four male eyewitnesses—but lesser evidence allows for up to ninety-nine *ta'zir* lashes if a judge concludes that two unrelated women shared a bed. The only possible reference to lesbianism in the Qur'an comes in an injunction (at 4:15) that "if any of your women are guilty of lewdness, take the evidence of four witnesses from amongst you; and if they testify confine them to houses until death claims them or God ordains for them some other way."

On the position taken among classical jurists, see Farah, *Marriage and Sexuality*, pp. 37–38.

222 *At least six allow for*: Iran, Saudi Arabia, Mauritania, Sudan, northern Nigeria, and Yemen maintain the death penalty for (homosexual) sodomy. Several other Muslim states authorize prison terms for sexual deviations of a very broadly defined kind: see, e.g., §§407 and 408 of Libya's Penal Code ("consensual sexual relations outside marriage"; §377 of Malaysia's Penal Code ("carnal intercourse against the order of nature" and "gross indecency"); and §377 of Pakistan's Penal Code ("unnatural intercourse"). The Qur'an itself contains only one specific reference to punishment, and it is relatively mild: "If two men among you commit indecency punish them both. If they repent and mend their ways, let them be. God is forgiving and merciful" (4:16). For the more hostile stance taken up by some classical jurists, see Farah, *Marriage and Sexuality*, pp. 37–39; Peters, *Crime and Punishment*, pp. 61–62.

222 *a hadith that warns*: Tirmidhi, 3118.

222 *An outcry finally caused*: Abdullah Shihri, "Saudi King Pardons Woman Who Was Gang Raped," *Guardian*, December 18, 2007; Ebtihal Mubarak, "Qatif Girl's Lawyer Gets His License Back," *Arab News*, January 20, 2008. The defense lawyer's website, which includes a link to his Facebook page, is at www.allahem.net.

224 *The peaceful introduction*: See the discussions in Ostien, *Sharia Implementation*, 3:3–75; Harnischfeger, *Democratization*, pp. 170–78.

224 *Pakistan's first open-air whippings*: "100,000 Pakistanis See Flogging," *New York Times*, October 21, 1977; "100,000 Watch as Child Rapist Gets 15 Lashes," *Daily Telegraph*, March 2, 1978. For accounts of the other spectacles described in this paragraph, see Anwar Iqbal, "Fifteen Lashes," *Granta* 63 (Autumn 1998); "Lahore Crowd Sees Three Men Being Hanged," *Times* (London), March 23, 1978, p. 10; Marcia Gauger, "Whips of God," *Time*, November 5, 1979.

225 *Parties that directly credit God*: Tanwir, "Religious Parties," p. 252 ("In the 2002 elections . . . the religious parties increased their percentage of the vote from less than 2 percent to over 11 percent").

226 *the court sidestepped*: Jehan Mina v. State, PLD 1983 FSC 183; Jahangir and Jilani, *Hudood Ordinances*, pp. 55, 186.

226 *Sudan's courts have been known*: Sidahmed, "Problems in Contemporary Applications," p. 198; cf. Art. 76 of Iran's 1991 Penal Code ("The testimony by women alone or along with the testimony of a just man does not prove adultery but the witnesses will be subject to the punishment for false accusation [*qazf*] as specified by the law").

226 *The Qur'an and hadiths frequently enjoin*: Numerous traditions attest to the Prophet's opposition to the beating of women, and many early Muslim scholars challenged customary restrictions on a woman's freedom to marry: see, for example, his valedictory sermon as recorded in Ibn Ishaq, *Life of Muhammad*, p. 651; Ibn Sa'd, *Women of Madina*, pp. 143–44; Levy, *Social Structure*, p. 63; Melchert, *Ahmad ibn Hanbal*, p. 2.

226 *A series of debates*: Lau, "Twenty-Five Years of Hudood Ordinances," pp. 1304–306.

227 *an era of "free sex"*: See the BBC report of November 16, 2006, www.news.bbc.co .uk/1/hi/6153994.stm.

227 *"enlightened moderation"*: Al-Zawahiri made the remark in a video addressed to the Pakistani people that was released in April 2006.

227 *"no one has the right"*: Taqi Usmani's remarks were made in an article that circulates online under the title "The Reality of 'Women Protection Bill,'" para. 4.2.

227 *The Qur'an teaches that God values*: Qur'an 5:46, 21:107.

228 *the vexed subject of televisions*: See www.albalagh.net/qa/video_chips.shtml. Taqi Usmani's dominance has made his views as controversial as they are lucrative. Although his financial expertise is much valued in the corporate sector, rival Deobandis issued a fatwa in August 2008 declaring every supposedly Islamic bank in Pakistan to be in contravention of the shari'a. In case their target was not obvious, they also observed that no Muslim should ever appear on religious television shows. See "Islamic Banking, TV Channels Against Shariah, Declare Religious Scholars," *News* (Karachi), August 30, 2008.

228 *"the gate of* ijtihad": See chapter 5, p. 104.

229 *"a double-edged sword"*: Usmani, *Islam and Modernism*, pp. 114–16; see also pp. 73–89, 113–22.

229 *judges had ruled in an adultery appeal*: Hazoor Baksh v. Federation of Pakistan, PLD 1981 FSC 145, reversed as *Federation of Pakistan v. Hazoor Baksh*, PLD 1983 FSC 255.

229 *Every court in Pakistan*: See Enforcement of Shari'ah Act 1991, §4.

230 *the Federal Shariat Court had ruled*: Suo Moto No. 1/K of 2006.

230 *his successor's court struck down*: See the declaration at www.pakistani.org/paki stan/judgments/2010/fsc_wpb.pdf.

230 *It had found that the trial judge*: Criminal Appeal No. 93/L of 2006.

231 *Classical jurists long ago developed*: Ibn Rushd, *Distinguished Jurist's Primer*, 2:433; Ibn Sa'd, *Men of Madina*, 2:358.

231 *The Hanbalites acknowledged*: Baroody, *Crime and Punishment*, p. 68.

231 *In March 2002, an appellate court*: Ostien, *Sharia Implementation*, 5:45, 105.

232 *Even Saudi Arabia managed*: Vogel, *Islamic Law and Legal System*, p. 246. The figure of four stoning executions and forty-five theft amputations refers to the period from May 1981 to April 1992.

232 *Colonel Qaddafi's Libya*: Amnesty International, *Amnesty International Report 2003—Libya*, May 28, 2003, www.unhcr.org/refworld/docid/3edb47da4.html.

232 *Northern Nigeria has claimed*: This is an estimate based on news reports. On the dearth of official records, see Harnischfeger, *Democratization and Islamic Law*, p. 35.

232 *stonings to death were in "suspension"*: "Iran to Abolish Death by Stoning," *Financial Times*, December 20, 2002, p. 6; see also the Amnesty International press release of August 2008 titled "Iran: Suspension of Stoning a Welcome Step if Carried Out."

233 *erasing them in heaven*: See Peters, *Crime and Punishment*, pp. 30–31; cf. p. 172. One dubiously sourced hadith holds that "the hand of the repentant thief precedes him to heaven": see Vogel, *Islamic Law and Legal System*, p. 241.

233 *"a reward in the hereafter"*: Interview with Asghar Hussein Shaheedi, April 22, 2009.

234 *two Iranian dissenters were hanged*: AFP report of January 28, 2010. Their names were Mohammad Reza Ali Zamani and Arash Rahmani Pour.

234 *on top of a pole*: See Amnesty International report index number MDE 23/035/2009, December 7, 2009.

234 *"A good punishment"*: "Paedophile to Be Beheaded and Crucified in Saudi Arabia for String of Sex Attacks Where He Left Toddler to Die in Desert," *Daily Mail*, November 4, 2009 (online comment section), available via www.dailymail.co.uk.

235 *global death penalty league tables*: See Amnesty International's annual death penalty reports available at www.amnesty.org/en/death-penalty.

235 *"Unless and until we get"*: Interview with Syed Munawar Hassan, April 13, 2009.

236 *"If men had been forbidden"*: Al-Ghazali, *Book of Knowledge*, p. 142.

11. "No Compulsion in Religion"? Apostasy, Blasphemy, and Tolerance

237 *an incriminating document*: Accounts of the precise opinions that Massignon was said to have espoused are contested and contradictory: see discussion in Massignon, *Passion*, 1:539–51. Except when otherwise noted, the account of al-Hallaj's life and trial is drawn from this work.

238 *Other Sufis turned to God*: On the classical Sufi doctrines of *fana* (the passing away of the self) and uniting with the divine (a state known as *hulul*), see Fakhry, *History of Islamic Philosophy*, pp. 242–44.

238 *"Even if he says to you"*: Massignon, *Passion*, 1:558. On the execution, see ibid., 1:560–625; Amedroz and Margoliouth, *Eclipse*, 4:90–91.

238 *"if You had revealed"*: Massignon, *Passion*, 1:600.

239 *His acolytes would soon be*: Ibid., pp. 571, 589–93; Amedroz and Margoliouth, *Eclipse*, 4:91; Margoliouth, *Table-Talk*, 2:90.

239 *it drew pilgrims for a millennium*: Levy, *Baghdad Chronicle*, p. 146; cf. Massignon, *Passion*, 1:231. On his posthumous intellectual influence, see Massignon, *Passion*, 1:36–51.

239 *A couple of hadiths prescribed*: Al-Bukhari, 4.52.260, 9.83.17; cf. 9.84.57, 9.84.58, 9.89.271.

239 *"Who will absolve you"*: See Ibn Ishaq, *Life of Muhammad*, p. 667; al-Bukhari, 5.59.568; Muslim, 1.176.

239 *an earlier brush with the law*: see Massignon, *Passion*, 1:475.

239 *He was sought out*: Ibid., pp. 502, 504; Amedroz and Margoliouth, *Eclipse*, 4:88.

240 *several made clear*: Massignon, *Passion*, 1:496–501; Amedroz and Margoliouth, *Eclipse*, 4:84–85. The condemnation was possible nevertheless because most of the witnesses were Malikites: Massignon, *Passion*, 1:500.

241 *it would be gradually narrowed*: See chapter 10, p. 219.

241 *But during these early years*: On the fluidity of late-eighth-century rules about apostasy, see Goldziher, *Muslim Studies*, 2:199. On the origins of *zandaqa* and its linkage to Islamic heresies, see Massignon, *Passion*, 1:378–85.

241 *unsure of the dividing line*: The lawfulness of magic would continue to be contested among Hanafites for centuries: Peters and de Vries, "Apostasy in Islam," p. 4.

241 *"[Zindiqs] are killed"*: Malik ibn Anas, *al-Muwatta*, p. 304; cf. Goldziher, *Muslim Studies*, 2:200.

242 *Caliph al-Mahdi appointed an inquisitor*: Browne, *Literary History of Persia*, 1:159–64; 307; al-Tabari, *History*, 29:214, 237, 241; 30:69–70.

242 *at the fore*: The prominent role of Malikites should not be understood to mean that other jurists took apostasy lightly. Fourteenth-century Hanbalites adopted the Malikite approach toward repentance (see Rapoport, "Legal Diversity," p. 223), and each school of jurisprudence developed its own expansive definitions of the crime. A sixteenth-century Hanafite text stated that apostasy might occur if a believer showed respect to a non-Muslim or uttered God's name while rolling backgammon dice, for example, and it identified several ways in which ridiculing a religious scholar might justify execution: Peters and de Vries, "Apostasy in Islam," p. 4; see also Peters, *Crime and Punishment*, pp. 64–65.

242 *the order for execution stood*: Dols, *Majnūn*, p. 451.

242 *They were the first*: See chapter 7, p. 140.

243 *At least twenty-six more people*: See Rapoport, "Legal Diversity," pp. 223–26; table of cases at p. 224.

243 *The Talmud envisioned a hell*: Schäfer, *Jesus in the Talmud*, esp. pp. 13, 82–94, and sources cited therein.

243 *Gospels repeatedly blamed Jews*: Matthew 27:24–25; cf. 1 Thessalonians 2:14–16; Acts 2:22–23, 2:36, 3:12–15, 8:30.

243 *"until [the Muslim] religion"*: Quoted in Norman Daniel, *Arabs and Mediaeval Europe*, p. 252.

243 *has begun in the past three decades*: See Peters and de Vries, "Apostasy in Islam," p. 13, where the authors state (in 1975) that "there is no evidence that apostates are still being put to death in Islamic countries" and that "in the Ottoman Empire and Egypt, the last cases of capital punishment for apostasy date from the first half of the last century."

244 *amputating thieves' limbs*: There were at least sixty-five instances during 1984: Peters, *Crime and Punishment*, p. 167; see also Peters, "Islamization of Criminal Law," pp. 263–66.

244 *Taha was arrested for sedition*: See an-Na'im, "Islamic Law of Apostasy," pp. 207–10; Peters, *Crime and Punishment*, p. 165.

244 *Thirteen days after his arrest*: "Nimeiry Lets Man of 76 Hang," *Times* (London), January 17, 1985, p. 4.

244 *six Muslim countries now acknowledge*: The countries that formally regard

apostasy as a capital offense are Afghanistan, Mauritania, Qatar, Saudi Arabia, Sudan, and Yemen.

244 *avoided the embarrassment*: In June 2000, Yemen put on trial a man named Mohammed Omer Haji, a.k.a. George, who had converted to Christianity two years previously, but he "escaped" three months later only to reemerge in New Zealand. An Afghan named Abdul Rahman, charged with apostasy in March 2006 for converting to Christianity, was permitted to slip into exile by way of the fiction that he was mentally deranged.

244 *decapitated an Egyptian pharmacist*: The execution of Mustafa Ibrahim was reported by Reuters on November 2, 2007. There seems to have been a more general crackdown on foreign witches and wizards in progress. It was reported a month earlier that an entire department of moral enforcers in the city of Ta'if was at work detecting sorcery and that they had found twenty-five evil magicians in a year. Twenty-four of them were foreigners. See "Virtue Commission's Special Wing Fights Charlatans," *Arab News*, October 27, 2007.

245 *a charge of capital sorcery*: "Lebanese TV Psychic Condemned to Death in Saudi to Be Reprieved," *Guardian*, April 21, 2010.

245 *"Anyone who claims this"*: See Reuters report of March 15, 2008.

245 *unfortunate consequences*: See Qur'an 16:106–109; cf. 2:218, 3:86–90, 4:137.

245 *"let him who will"*: Ibid., 18:29.

245 *"Let there be no compulsion"*: Ibid., 2:256.

245 *hanged upside down or wrapped*: Kadri, *Trial*, pp. 63–64, 152.

246 *If they were killed*: Ibn Rushd, *Distinguished Jurist's Primer*, 2:500.

247 *"nations and tribes"*: Qur'an 49:13.

247 *"the investigation of individuals' beliefs"*: Iran Constitution, Art. 23. On the right to equality, see also Arts. 19 and 20.

247 *it has not officially executed*: The last person killed as an apostate after an ordinary trial was Hossein Soudmand, a father of four, who was hanged on December 3, 1989, after converting to Christianity in 1960 at the age of thirteen. Apostasy was also one pretext used by the Iranian state to justify the execution of many thousands of political prisoners during the autumn of 1988: see Robertson, *Massacre*, pp. 65–67, available at www.iranrights.org/english/attachments /doc_1115.pdf.

248 *"Zoroastrian, Jewish, and Christian Iranians"*: Iran Constitution, Art. 13.

248 *The community claims to have*: See www.question.bahai.org/002.php.

248 *at least two converts to Christianity*: Marzieh Amirizadeh and Maryam Rustampoor were in jail in May 2009. Ramtin Soudmand had spent two months in jail a year earlier; his father was the last Iranian executed for apostasy (in 1989), as observed three notes above. On unsolved murders during the 1990s, see, for example, the obituary of Mehdi Dibaj in *The Independent*, July 7, 1994.

249 *The sense that wrongdoers compound*: Discretion in the wake of wrongdoing is explicitly sanctioned in several hadiths: see, for example, al-Bukhari, 8.73.95, which has the Prophet declaring that every sinner is forgivable "except those who com-

mit a sin openly or disclose their sins to the people"; 8.81.775, which claims that an undiscovered *hadd* crime is necessarily being concealed by God and "it is up to God whether to excuse or punish [the perpetrator]." See also chapter 1, pp. 29–30. For a discussion of the public/private distinction in Islamic law, see Rosen, *Justice of Islam*, pp. 187–99.

251 *a fatwa that was adventurous*: Robert Tait, "A Fatwa for Freedom," *Guardian*, July 27, 2005; see also the segment of a documentary that aired on al-Arabiya on July 2, 2005, available at www.youtube.com/watch?v=8rj8HM5G_ow.

252 *Believers are urged*: See Qur'an 4:140, 7:199, 25:63, 28:55, 50:39, 73:10.

252 *Certain hadiths report*: On the Muslim conquest of Mecca in 632, see chapter 1, p. 32, and corresponding endnotes.

252 *a crime so heinous*: Peters, *Crime and Punishment*, pp. 27, 65, 180.

252 *one of the few known cases*: See chapter 7, p. 129.

252 *within the Muslim world itself*: Pakistan has become the epicenter of modern Islamic blasphemy laws, as discussed in this chapter, but several other states penalize the sin. Saudi Arabia allows for death sentences in general, and Art. 513 of Iran's 1991 Penal Code prescribes execution for abuse of the Prophet in particular. The last Iranian convicted was Hashem Aghajari, a disabled war veteran and history professor, who spent the better part of two years in a condemned cell for a 2002 speech that had included a single fleeting mention of the Prophet. His primary concern had been to argue that people should forge a personal relationship with God and acknowledge that clerics were not infallible. For a translation of his remarks, see www.memri.org/report/en/0/0/0/0/0/0/770.htm.

253 *"belong to any religion or caste"*: Burke, *Jinnah*, p. 28.

253 *"Pakistan is not going to be"*: Ibid., p. 125.

253 *"as contradictory a term"*: Aziz, *Making of Pakistan*, p. 106. On the opposition to Pakistan among religious conservatives, see also discussion in Nasr, *Vanguard*, pp. 103–15; Munir et al., *Report*, pp. 19–20, 243, 253–56, 259. The latter report was produced by a court of inquiry set up to investigate the anti-Ahmadi agitation in Punjab between 1949 and 1953 and can be found at www.thepersecution.org/dl/report_1953.pdf.

253 *the nation's Infidel-in-Chief*: See Munir et al., *Report*, p. 11; cf. pp. 14–15, 254–56.

253 *"This country was created"*: Akbar, *India*, p. 53. The 1985 reform was enacted as the Revival of the Constitution of 1973 Order, 1985. On the incorporation and its aftermath, see Lau, *Role of Islam*, pp. 47–73; for a contemporary critique, see Pervez Hoodbhoy and Abdul Hameed Nayyar, "Rewriting the History of Pakistan," in Mohammad Asghar Khan, *Islam, Politics, and the State*, pp. 164–77.

254 *"the sacred name"*: Pakistan Penal Code, §295-C. On the other amendments to the 1927 blasphemy law (which is now §295-A), see Siddique and Hayat, "Unholy Speech."

254 *Forty-four prosecutions*: Siddique and Hayat, "Unholy Speech," pp. 380–81; cf. pp. 324, 326.

254 *to be lynched*: See, for example, ibid., pp. 327–35, containing an account of the

trial of the Christians Salamat and Rehmat Masih, during which a codefendant was killed and murder attempts were made on the defense lawyer Asma Jahangir and her sister Hina Jilani. The judge was fatally shot after the conclusion of the case. See generally Jahangir, *From Protection to Exploitation*.

254 *mentally ill defendants*: Siddique and Hayat, "Unholy Speech," pp. 342–50; see also Jahangir, *From Protection to Exploitation*, pp. 55–56, 58, 59, 74, 109, 136; for a more recent case, involving incarceration in a mental asylum without trial, see "LHC Frees Blasphemy Accused Zaibunnisa After 14 Years," *Dawn*, July 22, 2010.

255 *A Muslim preacher named*: On Mirza Ghulam Ahmad's views, see Friedmann, *Prophecy Continuous*, esp. pp. 172–76; Munir et al., *Report*, esp. pp. 9–10, 195–96. His followers sometimes blur the full extent of his claims to spiritual authority, but he ended his life explicitly claiming to be a successor to Jesus and Muhammad and a divinely inspired messenger: see discussion in Friedmann, *Prophecy Continuous*, pp. 119–34; Munir et al., *Report*, pp. 187–89.

255 *"absolute and unqualified finality"*: Constitution (Second Amendment) Act, 1974; cf. Constitution of Pakistan, Art. 260(3).

256 *they would be charged*: Peters, *Crime and Punishment*, p. 158 ("more than a hundred" awaiting trial under §295-C at the end of 2003). For a more recent breakdown of reported convictions, see Siddique and Hayat, "Unholy Speech," pp. 323–26; see also the Ahmadis' own website at www.thepersecution.org.

256 *a 1984 amendment to the blasphemy law*: Pakistan Penal Code, §§298-B and 298-C.

257 *The other one was then obliged*: "'No Option' but to Abide by PM's Decision on Blasphemy: Sherry," *Dawn*, February 3, 2011.

257 *well represented by a couple of cases*: Both defendants coincidentally have the same name, Younus Sheikh, and the vagaries of transliteration make it easy to confuse them. On the author, see "Writer of Sacrilegious Book Gets Jail Term," *Dawn*, August 12, 2005; "Blasphemy Convict to Serve Sentences Concurrently," *News* (Karachi), February 10, 2011. For an account of the doctor's trial, see Siddique and Hayat, "Unholy Speech," pp. 342–44.

257 *Supreme Court upheld an argument*: *Muhammad Ismail Qureshi v. Pakistan*, PLD 1991 FSC 10, upheld by Supreme Court on April 21, 2009: *Dawn*, April 22, 2009. The following day's edition of *Dawn* carried a critical editorial.

258 *A well-known hadith warns*: One formulation can be found in Abu Dawud, 3.4580; see also Aghnides, *Mohammedan Theories*, p. 128, and accompanying discussion.

258 *While Mongols menaced*: Michel, *Muslim Theologian's Response*, p. 82; Memon, *Struggle*, p. 211.

258 *copper Muslim pots*: Metcalf, *Islamic Revival*, p. 153.

258 *And the first Ahmadi to fall*: Munir et al., *Report*, p. 14.

260 *Anne Frank in bed*: See www.arabeuropean.org.

260 *best cartoons about the Holocaust*: www.irancartoon.com/120/holocaust/index .htm.

261 *"When I was coming up"*: Weisberg, *Bushisms*, p. 48 (speech to Iowa Western Community College, January 21, 2000).

12. Heaven on Earth

263 *legend records that Caliph Umar*: Taylor, *Vicinity of the Righteous*, pp. 56–57. This is the best source on the history and religious significance of Cairo's cemeteries; for an anthropological account, see Nedoroscik, *City of the Dead*.

263 *It became a major pilgrimage destination*: Caroline Williams, "Cult of 'Alid Saints."

263 *a sociologist had leafed through*: See Ruthven, *Islam in the World*, pp. 122–24. Cf. Amina Abdul Salam, "Asking the Saints for Help," *Egyptian Gazette*, October 18, 2006, p. 2.

263 *used to be publicly burned*: Julian Johansen, *Sufism and Islamic Reform*, pp. 150–52; cf. Fayza Hassan, "You've Got Mail," *Egypt Today*, March 2005.

263 *Fourteenth-century polemicists warned*: See, for example, the criticisms by the Malikite jurist Ibn al-Hajj detailed in Berkey, "Tradition, Innovation," esp. pp. 57–58, and Ibn Taymiyya's opinions discussed at chapter 7, p. 133.

264 *Several Shafi'ites themselves*: Omer, *Origins and Significance*, p. 134.

264 *The man who gave al-Shafi'i*: On the monument's architectural history, see Caroline Williams, *Islamic Monuments*, pp. 134–35.

264 *City cemeteries more generally*: Omer, *Origins and Significance*, p. 218; Guest, "Cairene Topography," p. 57.

264 *Two of the most cosmopolitan*: Ibn Jubayr, *Travels*, pp. 36–42; Ibn Battuta, *Travels*, 1:45–48.

265 *the graveyard was a forest*: Ibn Jubayr, *Travels*, p. 203.

265 *That changed for the first time*: On the partial destruction in 1803–1806, see Burckhardt, *Travels*, 2:222–26; for a vivid description of the site soon after the systematic violence of the mid-1920s, see Rutter, *Holy Cities*, 2:256–58. On August 13, 2002, Saudi authorities dynamited the mosque and tomb of Ja'far al-Sadiq (d. 765): Beranek and Tupek, "From Visiting Graves to Their Destruction," p. 4, www.brandeis.edu/crown/publications/cp/CP2.pdf. For relatively recent accounts of the cemetery's state, see Nordin and Nordin, *Life That Matters*, pp. 39–40; Hammoudi, *Season in Mecca*, pp. 94–95.

265 *Only about twenty structures*: Daniel Howden, "The Destruction of Mecca: Saudi Hardliners Are Wiping Out Their Own Heritage," *Independent*, August 6, 2005.

265 *Debates meanwhile rage*: Beranek and Tupek, "From Visiting Graves to Their Destruction," pp. 4–5.

266 *The revulsion for headstones*: On the pagan cult of stone markers for the dead (*ansab*, sing. *nusub*), see Qur'an 5:3, 5:90; Goldziher, *Muslim Studies*, 1:211–17. On the domed tents (*qubba*), see ibid., 1:231–33.

267 *hearings devoted specifically*: Raymond Hernandez, "Muslim 'Radicalization' Is Focus of Planned Inquiry," *New York Times*, December 16, 2010.

268 *a recent New York Times op-ed*: "President Apostate?" *New York Times*, May 12, 2008. The critical observations by the newspaper's public editor were published on June 1, 2008.

268 *swiftly overturned on appeal*: S.D. v. M.J.R., 415 N.J.Super. 417, 2 A.3d 412 (2010).

268 *a "pre-emptive strike"*: Mark Schlachtenhaufen, "Sharia Law, Courts Likely on 2010 Ballot," *Edmond (Okla.) Sun*, June 4, 2010.

269 *more than three hundred*: See Center on Law and Security, *Terrorist Trial Report Card*, pp. 4–7.

269 *A survey of opinions*: Pew Research Center, *Muslim Americans*, p. 53.

269 *a more recent poll shows*: Abu Dhabi Gallup Center, *Muslim Americans*, p. 30.

269 *two and a half million Muslims*: Pew Research Center, *Mapping the Global Muslim Population*, pp. 24–25. Considerably higher estimates circulate in the media, but this figure seems to be a well-informed estimate: see discussion in Pew Research Center, *Muslim Americans*, pp. 9–14.

269 *a third of them are native-born and*: Pew Research Center, *Muslim Americans*, p. 15.

270 *American Muslims have disproportionately lost faith*: On suspicions among American Muslims of U.S. law-enforcement and military agencies, see Abu Dhabi Gallup Center, *Muslim Americans*, pp. 23–24.

270 *Most of the serious conspiracies*: See Center on Law and Security, *Terrorist Trial Report Card*, p. 20; see also Chesney, "Beyond Conspiracy?"

271 *"step by step, to the gallows"*: Bawer, *While Europe Slept*, p. 236. Other material in this paragraph can be found on pp. 33, 77–86, 152, and 187.

271 *The citations were an understandably unwelcome*: Bruce Bawer, "Inside the Mind of the Oslo Murderer," *Wall Street Journal*, July 25, 2011.

272 *Oklahoma legislators justified*: Schlachtenhaufen, "Sharia Law, Courts Likely on 2010 Ballot."

272 *opinion polls that suggest*: See, for example, Patrick Hennessy, "Survey's Finding of Growing Anger in the Islamic Community . . . ," *Daily Telegraph*, February 19, 2006; Policy Exchange, *Living Apart Together*, pp. 5, 46; Centre for Social Cohesion, *Islam on Campus*, p. 40. Although the sources cited would doubtless characterize their findings as politically neutral, it should perhaps be noted that all are generally considered right of center.

272 *more than twice as favorable*: See Policy Exchange, *Living Apart Together*, pp. 5, 46.

272 *Fifty percent of respondents*: Centre for Social Cohesion, *Islam on Campus*, pp. 39–40.

272 *the evolving structure of British Islam*: See generally Philip Lewis, *Islamic Britain*; Philip Lewis, *Young, British, and Muslim*.

274 *Turn-of-the-century Russian immigrants*: Dench, Gavron, and Young, *New East End*, p. 16.

274 *Social reformers used to lament*: See, for example, Russell and Lewis, *Jew in London*, esp. pp. 8–9, 144–48 (the authors were optimistic that the forces of assimilation would eventually win out); cf. Dench, Gavron, and Young, *New East End*, p. 17.

274 *a campaign that reached its nadir*: *Daily Mail*, August 20, 1938. "'The way stateless Jews from Germany are pouring in from every port of this country is becoming an outrage . . .' In these words, Mr. Herbert Metcalfe, the Old Street magistrate, yesterday referred to the number of aliens entering the country

through the 'back door'—a problem to which the Daily Mail has repeatedly pointed."

275 *According to the draft constitution*: See www.hizb.org.uk/wp-content/uploads /2011/02/Draft-Constitution.pdf. For its provision on apostasy, see Art. 7(c); on discrimination see Arts. 19, 31, 42, 67, 69, 87, 108–18; on slavery see Art. 19. On the group's founder, see Commins, "Taqi al-Din al-Nabhani"; on Hizb ut-Tahrir generally, see Baran, "Fighting the War of Ideas."

275 *a legal manual*: The constitution draws its provisions from the work of the eleventh-century Baghdad jurist al-Mawardi, on whom see chapter 6, p. 120.

277 *while surveys suggest*: Maxwell, "Trust in Government," pp. 96–98.

279 *Muslim Arbitration Tribunal*: See www.matribunal.com.

279 *A U.K.-trained lawyer*: For the requirement that panels include a solicitor or barrister, see Rule 10 of the MAT rules; on judicial review, see Rule 23 of the MAT rules and §66 of the Arbitration Act 1996.

279 *There has been a federal arbitration law*: Federal Arbitration Act, 9 USC §§1–16 (2000); see generally Shippee, "Blessed Are the Peacemakers"; see also Grossman, "Is This Arbitration?" esp. pp. 177–87; Rafeeq, "Rethinking," pp. 128–35. On the rules followed by rabbinical tribunals, see the document posted on the Beth Din website at www.bethdin.org/docs/PDF1–Layman%27s_Guide.pdf. See also Wolfe, "Faith-Based Arbitration," pp. 448–50, for a discussion of the far more hostile approach to Islamic arbitration tribunals in Ontario, Canada.

279 *it formally forbids*: See (Rabbi) Yaacov Feit, "The Prohibition Against Litigating in Secular Court," at www.bethdin.org/docs/Arkaos%20Article.pdf.

280 *Oklahoma's amendment stalled*: Mark Schlachtenhaufen, "Judge Extends SQ 755 Decision Time," *Edmond (Okla.) Sun*, November 22, 2010; *Awad v. Ziriax et al.*, Dist. Court, WD Oklahoma 2010, Case No. CIV-10-1186-M. The preliminary injunction granted the plaintiff is being appealed at the time of writing.

281 *he ruled musicians and board gamers*: See MacDonald, "Emotional Religion in Islam," p. 201.

281 *His followers later became*: Omer, *Origins and Significance*, p. 134; Berkey, "Tradition and Innovation," pp. 57–58.

282 *Qur'anic ring tones*: Mohammed Khalil, "A Look at the Quran Ringtones Fatwa," *Al-Sharq al-Awsat*, February 23, 2010, at www.asharq-e.com.

282 *The American female scholar*: Barbara Ferguson, "Woman Imam Raises Mixed Emotions," *Arab News*, March 20, 2005. See also chapter 4, p. 86.

282 *a theory of secular citizenship*: See Ramadan, *Western Muslims*, esp. pp. 62–77.

283 *Academics elsewhere are retrieving*: See, for example, Reza, "Islam's Fourth Amendment," pp. 803–806, where the author argues that Islam's traditional concern to protect privacy and personal integrity can today form the basis for a general limit on state power; Baderin, "Identifying Possible Mechanisms," which seeks to identify a range of Islamic legal institutions that could be used to protect and promote human rights principles.

283 *the kingdom went so far*: Reza, "Torture and Islamic Law," p. 29n26; for details

of the criminal procedure code's regulation of torture prior to 2001, see Vogel, *Islamic Law and Legal System*, pp. 238–39.

283 *No matter how overwhelming*: Kamali, *Principles*, p. 204.

283 *"If there's a war between us"*: The words were attributed to Mesbah-Yazdi by Abdolkarim Soroush in a 2006 interview. See www.drsoroush.com/English /Interviews/E-INT-HomaTV.html.

283 *It is fairly easy to piece together*: See Ibn Rushd, *Distinguished Jurist's Primer*, 2:443–74; an-Na'im, *Toward an Islamic Reformation*, pp. 172–75.

283 *it has been publicly renounced*: See Clarence-Smith, *Islam and Abolition*, p. 11. The author makes clear that the institution survives in parts of the Muslim world, notwithstanding its universal abolition in theory.

285 *"No one ever says"*: Interview with Asghar Shaheedi, April 22, 2009.

Bibliography

This book draws on three translations of the Qur'an: an annotated text by Abdullah Yusuf Ali, which dates from 1934; the Penguin rendition by N. J. Dawood, first published in 1956; and a recent work—which is easily the most fluid and comprehensible to modern ears—by M.A.S. Abdel Haleem, first published by Oxford University Press in 2004. There are no English compilations of the six authoritative Sunni hadith collections, but the works of al-Bukhari and Muslim, along with parts of Abu Dawud's compilation and the text of Malik ibn Anas's *al-Muwatta*, have been put online by the Muslim Students Association at the University of Southern California: see www.usc .edu/dept/MSA. The same site contains several translations of the Qur'an, including the one by Yusuf Ali mentioned above.

Books

Abbot, Nadia. *Aishah: The Beloved of Mohammed*. Chicago, 1942.

Abdul-Jabbar, Ghassan. *Bukhari*. New Delhi, 2007.

Abou El Fadl, Khaled. *The Great Theft*. New York, 2005.

Abrahamian, Ervand. *Iran Between Two Revolutions*. Princeton, N.J., 1983.

Abu al-Faraj [Bar Hebraeus]. *Historia compendiosa dynastiarum*. Translated by Edward Pocock. London, 1663.

Abu-Rabi, Ibrahim M. *Intellectual Origins of Islamic Resurgence in the Modern Arab World*. Albany, N.Y., 1996.

Abu Sulayman, Abdul Hamid. *Towards an Islamic Theory of International Relations*. 2nd ed. Herndon, Va., 1993.

Adamson, Peter, and Richard C. Taylor, eds. *The Cambridge Companion to Arabic Philosophy.* Cambridge, U.K., 1985.

Adler, Marcus N., ed. *The Itinerary of Benjamin of Tudela.* London, 1907.

Afghani, Jamal ad-Din al-. *Réfutation des matérialistes.* Translated by A.-M. Goichon. Paris, 1942.

Aghnides, Nicolas P. *Mohammedan Theories of Finance.* Lahore, 1961.

Ahmed Ali, Mir. *A Commentary on the Holy Qur'an.* 2nd ed. Qom, 2000.

Ahsan, Muhammad M. *Social Life Under the 'Abbāsids, 170–289 A.H., 786–902 A.D.* London, 1979.

Akbar, M. J. *India: The Siege Within.* 2nd ed. New Delhi, 1996.

Ali, S. B. Sheik. *A Leader Reassessed: Life and Work of Sir Syed Ahmed Khan.* Mysore, 1999.

Allard, Michel. *Le problème des attributs divins.* Beirut, 1965.

Amari, Michele. *Storia dei Musulmani di Sicilia.* 2nd ed. Edited by Carlo Alfonso Nallino. 3 vols. Catania, 1933–39.

Amedroz, H. F., and D. S. Margoliouth. *The Eclipse of the 'Abbasid Caliphate.* 7 vols. Oxford, 1920–21.

Anderson, Norman. *Law Reform in the Muslim World.* London, 1976.

Arnold, Thomas W. *The Caliphate.* Oxford, 1924.

Arnold, Thomas W., and A. Guillaume, eds. *The Legacy of Islam.* Oxford, 1931.

Arnold, Thomas W., and Reynold A. Nicholson, eds. *A Volume of Oriental Studies Presented to Edward G. Browne.* Cambridge, U.K., 1922.

Aslan, Reza. *No God but God.* London, 2005.

Awdah, Abd al-Qadir. *Al-Tashri al-jina'i al-Islami muqaranan bi al-qanun.* 2 vols. Beirut, 1986.

Ayoub, Mahmoud M. *The Crisis of Muslim History: Religion and Politics in Early Islam.* Oxford, 2003.

Aziz, K. K. *The Making of Pakistan: A Study in Nationalism.* Lahore, 2002.

Baladhuri, Abu-l Abbas Ahmad al-. *The Origins of the Islamic State.* Translated by Philip Hitti and F. C. Murgotten. 2 vols. New York, 1916–24. (A translation of his *[Kitāb] Futūh al-buldān.*)

Banna, Hasan al-. *Five Tracts of Hasan al-Bannā' (1906–49): A Selection from the "Majmū'at Rasā'il al-Imām al-Shahīd Hasan al-Bannā."* Translated by Charles Wendell. Berkeley, Calif., 1978.

Baroody, George M. *Crime and Punishment Under Hanbali Law.* Cairo, 1961.

Barral, J. M., ed. *Orientalia Hispanica: Sive studia F. M. Pareja octogenario dicata.* Leiden, 1974.

Barthold, W. [Vasilii]. *Turkestan Down to the Mongol Invasions.* 2nd ed. Translated by H. A. R. Gibb. London, 1928.

Bawer, Bruce. *While Europe Slept: How Radical Islam Is Destroying the West from Within.* New York, 2006.

Bearman, Peri, et al., eds. *The Law Applied: Contextualizing the Islamic Shari'a.* London, 2008.

Benjamin, Daniel, and Simon Steven. *The Age of Sacred Terror: Radical Islam's War Against America.* New York, 2002.

Bergen, Peter L. *Holy War, Inc.* London, 2002.

Berkey, Jonathan P. *The Formation of Islam: Religion and Society in the Near East.* Cambridge, U.K., 2003.

Bosworth, C. E., et al., eds. *The Islamic World: From Classical to Modern Times.* Princeton, N.J., 1989.

Brisard, Jean-Charles. *Zarqawi: The New Face of al-Qaeda.* Cambridge, U.K., 2005.

Browne, Edward G. *A Literary History of Persia.* 4 vols. Cambridge, U.K, 1928.

Bunt, Gary R. *Islam in the Digital Age: E-jihad, Online Fatwas, and Cyber Islamic Environments.* London, 2003.

———. *Virtually Islamic: Computer-Mediated Communication and Cyber Islamic Environments.* Cardiff, 2000.

Burckhardt, John L. *Travels in Arabia.* 2 vols. London, 1829.

Burke, S. M., ed. *Jinnah: Speeches and Statements, 1947–48.* Karachi, 2000.

Burton, John. *The Collection of the Qur'ān.* Cambridge, U.K., 1977.

———. *The Sources of Islamic Law: Islamic Theories of Abrogation.* Edinburgh, 1990.

Butler, Alfred J. *The Arab Conquest of Egypt and the Last Thirty Years of the Roman Dominion.* 2nd ed. Oxford, 1978.

Cesari, Jocelyne. *When Islam and Democracy Meet: Muslims in Europe and in the United States.* New York, 2004.

Chehab, Zaki. *Inside Hamas.* London, 2007.

Clancy-Smith, Julia Ann, ed. *North Africa, Islam, and the Mediterranean World.* London, 2001.

Clarence-Smith, William Gervase. *Islam and the Abolition of Slavery.* London, 2006.

Clot, André. *Harun al-Rashid and the World of "The Thousand and One Nights."* Translated by John Howe. London, 1986.

Cockburn, Andrew, and Patrick Cockburn. *Saddam Hussein: An American Obsession.* London, 2002.

Colville, Jim, ed. *Sobriety and Mirth: A Selection of the Shorter Writings of al-Jāhiz.* London, 2002.

Cook, David. *Contemporary Muslim Apocalyptic Literature.* Syracuse, N.Y., 2005.

———. *Studies in Muslim Apocalyptic Literature.* Syracuse, N.Y., 2002.

———. *Understanding Jihad.* Berkeley, Calif., 2005.

Cook, Michael. *Commanding Right and Forbidding Wrong in Islamic Thought.* Cambridge, U.K., 2000.

Cooperson, Michael. *Classical Arabic Biography: The Heirs of the Prophets in the Age of al-Ma'mūn.* Cambridge, U.K., 2000.

———. *Al-Ma'mun.* Oxford, 2005.

Dalrymple, William. *The Last Mughal: The Fall of a Dynasty, Delhi, 1857.* London, 2006.

Daniel, Elton L. *The Political and Social History of Khurasan Under Abbasid Rule, 747–820.* Minneapolis, 1979.

Daniel, Norman. *The Arabs and Mediaeval Europe.* London, 1975.

David, Saul. *The Indian Mutiny: 1857*. London, 2002.

DeLong-Bas, Natana J. *Wahhabi Islam: From Revival and Reform to Global Jihad*. New York, 2004.

Dench, Geoff, Kate Gavron, and Michael Young. *The New East End: Kinship, Race, and Conflict*. London, 2006.

Dennett, Daniel C. *Conversion and the Poll Tax in Early Islam*. Cambridge, Mass., 1950.

Dodge, Bayard, ed. *The Fihrist of al-Nadīm: A Tenth-Century Survey of Muslim Culture*. 2 vols. New York, 1970.

Dols, Michael W. *The Black Death in the Middle East*. Princeton, N.J., 1977.

——. *Majnūn: The Madman in Medieval Islamic Society*. Oxford, 1992.

Donner, Fred M. *Narratives of Islamic Origins: The Beginnings of Islamic Historical Writing*. Princeton, N.J., 1998.

Donohue, John J., and John L. Esposito. *Islam in Transition: Muslim Perspectives*. 2nd ed. Oxford, 2007.

Dwyer, Daisy H., ed. *Law and Islam in the Middle East*. New York, 1990.

Elliot, Henry M. *The History of India, as Told by Its Own Historians: The Muhammadan Period*. 8 vols. London, 1867–77.

Fair, C. Christine. *Urban Battle Fields of South Asia: Lessons Learned from Sri Lanka, India, and Pakistan*. Santa Monica, Calif., 2004.

Fakhri, Majid. *A History of Islamic Philosophy*. 2nd ed. New York, 1983.

Farabi, Abu Nasr al-. *Al-Farabi on the Perfect State* (Mabādi' ārā' ahl al-madīnat al-fāḍila). Translated by Richard Walzer. Oxford, 1985.

Farah, Madelain. *Marriage and Sexuality in Islam*. Salt Lake City, 1984.

Fierro, Maribel. *'Abd al-Rahman III: The First Cordoban Caliph*. Oxford, 2005.

Finkel, Caroline. *Osman's Dream: The Story of the Ottoman Empire, 1300–1923*. New York, 2006.

Foster, William. *The Embassy of Sir Thomas Roe to India, 1615–19, as Narrated in His Journal and Correspondence*. London, 1926.

Frembgen, Jürgen Wasim. *Journey to God: Sufis and Dervishes in Islam*. Translated by Jane Ripkin. Karachi, 2008.

Friedmann, Yohanan. *Prophecy Continuous: Aspects of Ahmadī Religious Thought and Its Medieval Background*. New Delhi, 2003.

Fulcher of Chartres. *A History of the Expedition to Jerusalem, 1095–1127*. Translated by Frances R. Ryan. Knoxville, Tenn., 1969.

Ghazali, al-. *The Book of Knowledge*. Edited by Nabih A. Faris. New Delhi, 2002.

——. *Imam Gazzali's "Ihya Ulum id-Din."* Translated by Fazul ul-Karim. 4 vols. Lahore, 1978–.

——. *The Incoherence of the Philosophers*. Translated by Michael E. Marmura. 2nd ed. Provo, Utah, 2000.

——. *The Marvels of the Heart*. Translated by Walter J. Skellie. Louisville, Ky., 2010.

Gibb, Hamilton A. L. R., et al., eds. *Encyclopaedia of Islam*. 12 vols. 2nd ed. Leiden, 1960–2009.

Gibbon, Edward. *The History of the Decline and Fall of the Roman Empire.* 6 vols. London, 1776–88.

Gleave, Robert, and Eugenia Kermeli, eds. *Islamic Law: Theory and Practice.* New York, 2001.

Goldziher, Ignaz. *Muslim Studies.* Translated by C. R. Barber and S. M. Stern. 2 vols. London, 1967–71.

Grunebaum, Gustave E. von. *Medieval Islam.* Chicago, 1946.

Gutas, Dimitri. *Greek Thought, Arabic Culture: The Graeco-Arabic Translation Movement in Baghdad and Early 'Abbāsid Society (2nd–4th/8th–10th Centuries).* London, 1998.

Hallaq, Wael B. *A History of Islamic Legal Theories.* Cambridge, U.K., 1997.

Hamid, Abdul Ali. *Moral Teachings of Islam: Prophetic Traditions from "Al-Adab al-Mufrad" by Imam al-Bukhari.* Lanham, Md., 2003.

Hammoudi, Abdellah. *A Season in Mecca: Narrative of a Pilgrimage.* Cambridge, U.K., 2006.

Harington, John H. *An Elementary Analysis of the Laws and Regulations in Council at Fort.* 3 vols. Calcutta, 1805–17.

Harnischfeger, Johannes. *Democratization and Islamic Law: The Sharia Conflict in Nigeria.* Chicago, 2008.

Heyd, Uriel. *Studies in Old Ottoman Criminal Law.* Edited by V. L. Ménage. Oxford, 1973.

Hitti, Philip K. *History of the Arabs.* 10th ed. New York, 1970.

Howorth, Henry H. *History of the Mongols.* London, 1876–88.

Hurvitz, Nimrod. *The Formation of Hanbalism: Piety into Power.* London, 2002.

Hussain, Aftab. *Status of Women in Islam.* Lahore, 1987.

Hutchins, William M., ed. *Nine Essays of al-Jahiz.* New York, 1989.

Ibn al-Athir. *Annals of the Saljuq Turks.* Translated by D. S. Richards. London, 2002.

——. *The Chronicle of Ibn al-Athīr for the Crusading Period from "al-Kāmil fī'l-ta'rīkh."* Translated by D. S. Richards. 3 vols. Aldershot, 2006–2008.

Ibn al-Tiqtaqa. *Al-Fakhri.* Translated by C.E.J. Whitting. London, 1947.

Ibn al-Zubair. *Book of Gifts and Rarities.* Translated by Ghada Hijjawi al-Qaddumi. Cambridge, Mass., 1996.

Ibn Aqil. *The Notebooks of Ibn 'Aqil: Kitāb al-Funūn.* Edited by George Makdisi. 2 vols. Beirut, 1970–71.

Ibn Battuta. *The Travels of Ibn Battuta, A.D. 1325–1354.* Translated by H.A.R. Gibb. 5 vols. Cambridge, U.K., 1958–2000.

Ibn Ishaq. *The Life of Muhammad: A Translation of Ibn Ishāq's "Sīrat rasūl Allāh."* Translated by A. Guillaume. Karachi, 2006.

Ibn Jubayr. *The Travels of Ibn Jubayr.* Translated by R. J. C. Broadhurst. London, 1952.

Ibn Khaldun. *Autobiographie.* Translated by Abdessalam Cheddadi. Algiers, 2008.

——. *The Muqaddimah.* Translated by Franz Rosenthal. 3 vols. 2nd ed. Princeton, N.J., 1967.

Ibn Khallikan. *Ibn Khallikan's Biographical Dictionary.* Edited by Mac Guckin de Slane. 4 vols. Paris, 1842–71.

Ibn Munqidh. *An Arab-Syrian Gentleman and Warrior in the Period of the Crusades: Memoirs of Usamah ibn-Munqidh.* Translated by Philip K. Hitti. 1929. Reprint, New York, 2000.

Ibn Qayyim al-Jawziyya. *Medicine of the Prophet.* Translated by Penelope Johnson. Cambridge, U.K., 1998.

Ibn Qutayba. *Le traité des divergences du hadīt d'Ibn Qutayba: Traduction annotée du "Kitāb ta'wīl muhtalif al-hadīt."* Translated by Gérard Lecomte. Damascus, 1962.

Ibn Rushd. *The Distinguished Jurist's Primer: A Translation of "Bidayat al-mujtahid."* Translated by Imran Ahsan Khan Nyazee. 2 vols. Reading, 1994–96.

Ibn Saʿd, Muhammad. *Kitab al-Tabaqat al-kabir.* Translated by S. Moinul Haq. 2 vols. Karachi, 1967–72.

———. *The Men of Madina.* Translated by Aisha Bewley. 2 vols. London, 2000. [A translation of vols. 5 and 7 of his (*Kitab*) *al-Tabaqat al-kabir.*]

———. *The Women of Madina.* Translated by Aisha Bewley. London, 1995. [A translation of vol. 8 of his (*Kitab*) *al-Tabaqat al-kabir.*]

Ibn Taghri Birdi. *History of Egypt, 1382–1469 A.D.* Translated by William Popper. 8 vols. Berkeley, Calif., 1954–63.

Ibn Taymiya [*sic*]. *Public Duties in Islam: The Institution of the Hisba.* Translated by Muhtar Holland. Leicester, 1982.

Ibn Taymiyya. *Le traité de droit public d'Ibn Taimiya.* Translated by Henri Laoust. Beirut, 1948.

Irwin, Robert. *The Arabian Nights: A Companion.* London, 1995.

———. *For Lust of Knowing: The Orientalists and Their Enemies.* London, 2006.

Jaber, Hala. *Hezbollah: Born with a Vengeance.* London, 1997.

Jackson, Sherman A. *Islamic Law and the State: The Constitutional Jurisprudence of Shihāb al-Dīn al-Qarāfī.* Leiden, 1996.

Jahangir, Asma. *From Protection to Exploitation: The Laws Against Blasphemy in Pakistan.* Lahore, n.d.

Jahangir, Asma, and Hina Jilani. *The Hudood Ordinances: A Divine Sanction?* Lahore, 2003.

Jahiz, al-. *The Book of Misers [Kitāb al-Bukhalā].* Translated by R. B. Serjeant. Reading, 1997.

———. *The Epistle on Singing Girls of Jāhiz.* Translated by A. F. L. Beeston. Warminster, 1980.

Jansen, Johannes J. G. *The Neglected Duty: The Creed of Sadat's Assassins and Islamic Resurgence in the Middle East.* New York, 1986.

Jayyusi, Salma K., ed. *The Legacy of Muslim Spain.* Leiden, 1992.

Johansen, Julian. *Sufism and Islamic Reform in Egypt: The Battle for Islamic Tradition.* Oxford, 1996.

Juvaini, Ala-ad-Din Ata-Malik. *The History of the World Conqueror.* Translated by John A. Boyle. 2 vols. Manchester, 1958.

Kadri, Sadakat. *The Trial: A History, from Socrates to O. J. Simpson.* New York, 2005.

Kamali, Mohammad Hashim. *Principles of Islamic Jurisprudence.* 3rd ed. Cambridge, U.K., 2003.

Karamustafa, Ahmet T. *God's Unruly Friends: Dervish Groups in the Islamic Later Middle Period, 1200–1550.* Salt Lake City, 1994.

Kennedy, Hugh. *The Court of the Caliphs.* London, 2004.

———. *The Early Abbasid Caliphate: A Political History.* London, 1981.

———. *Muslim Spain and Portugal: A Political History of al-Andalus.* Harlow, 1996.

Kepel, Giles. *Muslim Extremism in Egypt: The Prophet and Pharaoh.* Translated by Jon Rothschild. 2nd ed. Berkeley, Calif., 1993.

Khadduri, Majid. *War and Peace in the Law of Islam.* Baltimore, 1955.

———, trans. *The Islamic Law of Nations: Shaybānī's "Siyar."* Baltimore, 1966.

Khadduri, Majid, and Herbert J. Liebesny, eds. *Law in the Middle East: Origin and Development of Islamic Law.* Washington, D.C., 1955.

Khalidi, Muhammad A., ed. *Medieval Islamic Philosophical Writings.* Cambridge, U.K., 2005.

Khan, Mohammad Asghar, ed. *Islam, Politics, and the State: The Pakistan Experience.* London, 1985.

Khan, Syed Ahmed. *Review on Dr. Hunter's Indian Musalmans: Are They Bound in Conscience to Rebel Against the Queen?* Benares, 1872.

Khomeini, Ruhallah. *Sayings of the Ayatollah Khomeini.* Translated by Harold J. Salemson. New York, 1980.

Kraemer, Joel L. *Humanism in the Renaissance of Islam: The Cultural Revival During the Buyid Age.* Leiden, 1986.

Kremer, Alfred von. *The Orient Under the Caliphs.* Translated by S. Khuda Buksh. Calcutta, 1920.

Kretzmann, Norman, et al., eds. *The Cambridge History of Later Medieval Philosophy.* Cambridge, U.K., 1982.

Krey, August C., ed. *The First Crusade: The Accounts of Eye-Witnesses and Participants.* Princeton, N.J., 1921.

Kurzman, Charles, ed. *Modernist Islam, 1840–1940: A Sourcebook.* New York, 2002.

Lamberton, Robert. *Homer the Theologian.* London, 1986.

Lane-Poole, Stanley. *Mediaeval India Under Mohammedan Rule (A.D. 712–1764).* Lahore, 2007.

Laoust, Henri. *Essai sur les doctrines sociales et politiques de Takī-d-Dīn Ahmad b. Taimīya.* Cairo, 1939.

Lassner, Jacob. *The Topography of Baghdad in the Early Middle Ages: Text and Studies.* Detroit, 1970.

Lau, Martin. *The Role of Islam in the Legal System of Pakistan.* Leiden, 2005.

Lerner, Gerda. *The Creation of Patriarchy.* Oxford, 1986.

Le Strange, Guy. *Baghdad During the Abbasid Caliphate*. Oxford, 1900.

Lévi-Provençal, É., ed. *Séville musulmane au début du XIIe siècle: Le traité d'Ibn 'Abdun sur la vie urbaine et les corps de métiers*. Paris, 1947.

Levy, Reuben. *A Baghdad Chronicle*. Cambridge, U.K., 1929.

———. *The Social Structure of Islam*. Cambridge, U.K., 1962.

Lewis, Bernard. *The Assassins: A Radical Sect in Islam*. London, 2003.

———. *The Muslim Discovery of Europe*. London, 1982.

———. *Political Words and Ideas in Islam*. Princeton, N.J., 2008.

———. *Semites and Anti-Semites: An Inquiry into Conflict and Prejudice*. London, 1997.

Lewis, Philip. *Islamic Britain: Religion, Politics, and Identity Among British Muslims*. 2nd ed. London, 2002.

———. *Young, British, and Muslim*. London, 2007.

Lia, Brynjar. *The Society of the Muslim Brothers in Egypt: The Rise of an Islamic Mass Movement, 1928–1942*. Reading, 1998.

Lindgren, Uta, ed. *Europäische Technik im Mittelalter, 800 bis 1400: Tradition und Innovation*. Berlin, 1996.

Lippman, Thomas W. *Inside the Mirage: America's Fragile Partnership with Saudi Arabia*. Boulder, Colo., 2004.

Löwinger, Samuel, and Joseph Somogyi. *Ignace Goldziher Memorial Volume*. Budapest, 1948.

Lucas, Scott C. *Constructive Critics, Hadīth Literature, and the Articulation of Sunnī Islam: The Legacy of the Generation of Ibn Sa'd, Ibn Ma'īn, and Ibn Hanbal*. Leiden, 2004.

Lyons, Jonathan. *The House of Wisdom: How the Arabs Transformed Western Civilization*. London, 2009.

Madelung, Wilferd. *The Succession to Muhammad*. Cambridge, U.K., 1997.

Majumdar, N. *Justice and Police in Bengal, 1765–1793: A Study of the Nizamat in Decline*. Calcutta, 1960.

Majumdar, R. C., ed. *The History and Culture of the Indian People: British Paramountcy and Indian Renaissance*. 2 vols. Bombay, 1963–65.

Makdisi, George. *History and Politics in Eleventh-Century Baghdad*. Aldershot, 1990.

———. *La notion d'autorité au Moyen Age: Islam, Byzance, Occident*. Paris, 1982.

Makkari, Ahmed ibn Mohammed al-. *The History of the Mohammedan Dynasties in Spain*. Translated by Pascual de Gayangos. 2 vols. London, 2002.

Malik ibn Anas. *Al-Muwatta of Imam Malik ibn Anas: The First Formulation of Islamic Law*. Translated by Aisha Bewley. London, 1989.

Mango, Andrew. *Atatürk*. London, 1999.

Mansfield, Laura. *His Own Words: Translation and Analysis of the Writings of Dr. Ayman Al Zawahiri*. TLG Publications, 2006.

Maqrizi, Ahmad ibn Ali. *Histoire des sultans mamlouks, de l'Égypte*. Translated by É. Quatremère. 2 vols. Paris, 1845.

Margoliouth, D. S., trans. *The Table-Talk of a Mesopotamian Judge*. 2 vols. London, 1921–22.

Marmura, Michael E. *Islamic Theology and Philosophy: Studies in Honor of George F. Hourani.* Albany, N.Y., 1984.

Martin, Vanessa. *Creating an Islamic State: Khomeini and the Making of a New Iran.* London, 2000.

Massignon, Louis. *The Passion of al-Hallaj, Mystic and Martyr of Islam.* Translated by Herbert Mason. 4 vols. Princeton, N.J., 1982.

Masud, Muhammad K., et al., eds. *Islamic Legal Interpretation: Muftis and Their Fatwas.* Cambridge, Mass., 1996.

Mas'udi, al- [Maçoudi]. *The Meadows of Gold.* Translated by Paul Lunde and Caroline Stone. London, 1989.

———. *Les prairies d'or.* Translated by C. Barbier de Meynard and P. de Courteille. 9 vols. Paris, 1861–73.

Mawardi, al-. *The Ordinances of Government.* Translated by W. H. Wahba. Reading, 1996.

Melchert, Christopher. *Ahmad ibn Hanbal.* Oxford, 2006.

———. *The Formation of the Sunni Schools of Law.* Leiden, 1997.

Melville, Charles, ed. *History and Literature in Iran: Persian and Islamic Studies in Honour of P. W. Avery.* 2nd ed. London, 1998.

Memon, Muhammad Umar. *Ibn Taimīya's Struggle Against Popular Religion.* With an annotated translation of his *Kitāb iqtidā' as-sirāt al-mustaqīm mukhālafat ashāb al-jahīm.* The Hague, 1976.

Menashri, David. *The Iranian Revolution and the Muslim World.* Boulder, Colo., 1990.

Meri, Josef W. *The Cult of Saints Among Muslims and Jews in Medieval Syria.* Oxford, 2002.

Metcalf, Barbara Daly. *Islamic Revival in British India: Deoband, 1860–1900.* Princeton, N.J., 1982.

Mez, Adam. *The Renaissance of Islam.* Translated by S. K. Buksh and D. S. Margoliouth. 3rd ed. New Delhi, 1995.

Michel, Thomas F., ed. *A Muslim Theologian's Response to Christianity: Ibn Taymiyya's "Al-Jawab al-Sahih."* New York, 1984.

Michot, Yahya. *Muslims Under Non-Muslim Rule.* Oxford, 2006.

Migne, Jacques-Paul. *Patrologiae cursus completus . . . Series Græca etc.* 162 vols. Paris, 1857–1912.

Milani, Abbas. *Lost Wisdom: Rethinking Modernity in Iran.* Washington, D.C., 2004.

Milliot, Louis. *Introduction à l'étude du droit musulman.* 2nd ed. Paris, 1987.

Minhaj al-Siraj Juzjani. *Tabakāt-i-Nāsirī: A General History of the Muhammadan Dynasties of Asia, Including Hindustan.* Translated by H. G. Raverty. 2 vols. London, 1881–97.

Mitha, Farouk. *Al-Ghazālī and the Ismailis: A Debate on Reason and Authority in Medieval Islam.* London, 2001.

Mitri, Tarek, ed. *Religion, Law, and Society: A Christian-Muslim Discussion.* Geneva, 1995.

Modarressi, Hossein. *Crisis and Consolidation in the Formative Period of Shi'ite Islam*. Princeton, N.J., 1993.

Morris, Benny. *1948*. London, 2008.

Mouradgea d'Ohsson, Ignatius. *Tableau général de l'Empire othoman*. 3 vols. Paris, 1787–1820.

Mujeeb, Muhammad. *The Indian Muslims*. London, 1967.

Munir, Muhammad, et al. *Report of the Court of Inquiry Constituted Under Punjab Act II of 1954 to Enquire into the Punjab Disturbances of 1953*. Lahore, 1954.

Muqaddasi, al-. *The Best Divisions for Knowledge of the Regions*. Translated by Basil A. Collins. Reading, 1994.

Nadwi, Sayyed Abul Hasan Ali. *Shaikh-ul-Islam Ibn Taimiyah: Life and Achievements*. Leicester, 2005.

Na'im, Abdullahi Ahmed an-. *Toward an Islamic Reformation: Civil Liberties, Human Rights, and International Law*. Syracuse, N.Y., 1990.

Nasawi [Nesawi], Muhammad al-. *Histoire du sultan Djelal ed-din Mankobirti*. Translated by O. Houdas. 2 vols. Paris, 1891–95.

Nasr, Seyyed Hossein, and Oliver Leaman. *History of Islamic Philosophy*. 2 vols. Tehran, 1996.

Nasr, Seyyed Vali Reza. *The Vanguard of the Islamic Revolution: The Jama'at-i Islami of Pakistan*. London, 1994.

Nedoroscik, Jeffrey A. *The City of the Dead: A History of Cairo's Cemetery Communities*. Westport, Conn., 1997.

Nicholson, Reynold A. *A Literary History of the Arabs*. New Delhi, 2006.

———. *The Mystics of Islam*. London, 1914.

Nizami, Khaliq A. *Religion and Politics in India During the Thirteenth Century*. Oxford, 2002.

Nöldeke, Theodor. *Sketches from Eastern History*. Translated by John S. Black. London, 1892.

Nordin, Norani, and Nordin Yusof. *A Life That Matters: A Spiritual Experience*. Selangor, 2008.

O'Leary, De Lacy. *A Short History of the Fatimid Khalifate*. London, 1923.

Ostien, Philip, ed. *Sharia Implementation in Northern Nigeria, 1999–2006: A Sourcebook*. 5 vols. Ibadan, 2007.

Oudah, Abdul Qadir. *Criminal Law of Islam*. Translated by S. Zakir Aijaz. 4 vols. New Delhi, 1999.

Patton, Walter M. *Ahmed ibn Hanbal and the Mihna*. Leiden, 1897.

Pedahzur, Ami. *Suicide Terrorism*. Cambridge, U.K., 2005.

Pedersen, Johannes. *The Arabic Book*. Translated by Geoffrey French. Princeton, N.J., 1984.

Pellat, Charles. *The Life and Works of Jāhiz*. Translated by D. M. Hawke. London, 1969.

Peters, Rudolph. *Crime and Punishment in Islamic Law*. Cambridge, U.K., 2005.

———. *Jihad in Classical and Modern Islam*. Princeton, N.J., 1996.

Philby, Harry St. J. B. *Arabia*. London, 1930.

Pipes, Daniel. *The Hidden Hand: Middle East Fears of Conspiracy*. Basingstoke, 1996.

———, ed. *Sandstorm: Middle East Conflicts and America*. Lanham, Md., 1993.

Polo, Marco. *The Book of Ser Marco Polo, the Venetian*. Translated by Henry Yule. Cambridge, U.K., 2010.

Quasem, M. Abul. *Al-Ghazali on Islamic Guidance*. Bangi, Selangor, 1979.

Qutb, Sayyid. *Milestones*. New Delhi, 2001.

Rahnema, Ali, ed. *Pioneers of Islamic Revival*. 2nd ed. London, 2005.

Ramadan, Tariq. *Western Muslims and the Future of Islam*. Oxford, 2004.

Rashid al-Din. *Rashiduddin Fazlullah's "Jami't-tawarikh" Compendium of Chronicles: A History of the Mongols*. Translated by W. M. Thackston. 3 vols. Cambridge, Mass., 1998–99.

Reynolds, Gabriel Said, ed. *The Qur'ān in Its Historical Context*. Abingdon, 2008.

Robson, James, ed. *Tracts on Listening to Music*. London, 1938.

Rosen, Lawrence. *The Justice of Islam*. Oxford, 2000.

Rosenthal, Franz. *The Classical Heritage in Islam*. London, 1975.

———. *The Herb: Hashish Versus Medieval Muslim Society*. Leiden, 1971.

Roth, Cecil. *A Short History of the Jewish People*. 2nd ed. London, 1953.

Russell, Charles, and H. S. Lewis. *The Jew in London: A Study of Racial Character and Present Day Conditions*. London, 1901.

Ruthven, Malise. *Islam in the World*. 3rd ed. London, 2006.

Rutter, Eldon. *The Holy Cities of Arabia*. 2 vols. London, 1928.

Savory, Roger. *Iran Under the Safavids*. Cambridge, U.K., 1980.

Sayeedi, Ghulam Rasul. *Tibyan al-Qur'an*. 12 vols. Lahore, 2009.

Sayılı, Aydın. *The Observatory in Islam and Its Place in the General History of the Observatory*. Ankara, 1960.

Schacht, Joseph. *An Introduction to Islamic Law*. Oxford, 1964.

Schäfer, Peter. *Jesus in the Talmud*. Princeton, N.J., 2007.

Scott, S. P., ed. *The Visigothic Code*. Boston, 1910.

Semerdjian, Elyse. *"Off the Straight Path": Illicit Sex, Law, and Community in Ottoman Aleppo*. Syracuse, N.Y., 2008.

Shaban, M. A. *The 'Abbāsid Revolution*. Cambridge, U.K., 1970.

———. *Islamic History: A New Interpretation*. 2 vols. Cambridge, U.K., 1971–76.

Shāfiʿī. *Islamic Jurisprudence: Shāfiʿī's "Risāla."* Translated by Majid Khadduri. Baltimore, 1961.

Sharf, Andrew. *Byzantine Jewry*. London, 1971.

Sharif, M. M., ed. *A History of Muslim Philosophy*. 2 vols. Karachi, 1963–66.

Shayzari, Abd'al Rahman b. Nasr al-. *The Book of the Islamic Market Inspector: Nihāyat al-Rutba fī Talab al-Hisba (The Utmost Authority in the Pursuit of Hisba)*. Edited by R. P. Buckley. Oxford, 1999.

Sicker, Martin. *The Islamic World in Ascendancy: From the Arab Conquests to the Siege in Vienna*. Westport, Conn., 2000.

Silvestre de Sacy, ed. *Chrestomathie Arabe*. 3 vols. 2nd ed. Paris, 1826–27.

Sklare, David E. *Samuel ben Hofni Gaon and His Cultural World: Texts and Studies.* Leiden, 1996.

Soroush, Abdulkarim. *The Expansion of Prophetic Experience.* Leiden, 2009.

Spahic, Omer. *The Origins and Significance of Funerary Architecture in Islamic Civilization.* Kuala Lumpur, 2006.

Spear, Percival. *Twilight of the Mughals.* Karachi, 1973.

Spellberg, Denise A. *Politics, Gender, and the Islamic Past: The Legacy of 'Aisha bint Abi Bakr.* New York, 1994.

Tabari, al-. *The History of al-Tabari.* 40 vols. New York, 1989–2007.

Taji-Farouki, Suha. *Modern Muslim Intellectuals and the Qur'an.* Oxford, 2004.

Taylor, Christopher Schurman. *In the Vicinity of the Righteous.* Leiden, 1999.

Tha'alibi, al-. *The Book of Curious and Entertaining Information.* Translated by C. E. Bosworth. Edinburgh, 1968.

Toynbee, Arnold J. *A Study of History.* 12 vols. London, 1934–61.

Tritton, A. S. *The Caliphs and Their Non-Muslim Subjects: A Critical Study of the Covenant of 'Umar.* Mysore, 1930.

Tyan, Emile. *Histoire de l'organisation judiciaire en pays d'Islam.* 2nd ed. Leiden, 1960.

Urvoy, Dominique. *Ibn Rushd (Averroes).* Translated by Olivia Stewart. London, 1991.

Usmani, Muhammad Taqi. *Islam and Modernism.* Translated by Muhammad S. Siddiqui. Karachi, 1999.

Vasiliev, A. A. *History of the Byzantine Empire.* Translated by S. Ragozin. 2 vols. Madison, Wis., 1928.

Vogel, Frank E. *Islamic Law and Legal System: Studies of Saudi Arabia.* Leiden, 2000.

Vyse, Howard. *Operations Carried on at the Pyramids of Gizeh in 1837: With an Account of a Voyage into Upper Egypt.* 3 vols. London, 1840–42.

Walton, J. Michael. *Found in Translation: Greek Drama in English.* Cambridge, U.K., 2006.

Wasserstein, David. *The Caliphate in the West: An Islamic Political Institution in the Iberian Peninsula.* Oxford, 1993.

Watt, William Montgomery. *The Faith and Practice of al-Ghazali.* London, 1953.

———. *The Formative Period of Islamic Thought.* Oxford, 1998.

Weisberg, Jacob. *George W. Bushisms: The "Slate" Book of the Accidental Wit and Wisdom of Our Forty-Third President.* New York, 2001.

Wiet, Gaston. *Baghdad: Metropolis of the Abbasid Caliphate.* Norman, Okla., 1971.

Williams, Caroline. *Islamic Monuments in Cairo: The Practical Guide.* 6th ed. Cairo, 2008.

Winter, Michael, and Amalia Levanoni, eds. *The Mamluks in Egyptian and Syrian Politics and Society.* Leiden, 2004.

Wright, Lawrence. *The Looming Tower: Al-Qaeda's Road to 9/11.* London, 2006.

Zein, Amira el-. *Islam, Arabs, and the Intelligent World of the Jinn.* Syracuse, N.Y., 2009.

Zollner, Barbara H. E. *The Muslim Brotherhood: Hasan al-Hudaybi and Ideology.* New York, 2009.

Articles

Abou El Fadl, Khaled. "Islamic Law and Muslim Minorities: The Juristic Discourse on Muslim Minorities from the Second/Eighth to the Eleventh/Seventeenth Centuries." *Islamic Law and Society* 1, no. 2 (1994), pp. 141–87.

Ahmed, Leila. "Women and the Advent of Islam." *Signs* 11, no. 4 (1986), pp. 665–91.

Ahmed, Shahab. "Ibn Taymiyyah and the Satanic Verses." *Studia Islamica* 87 (1998), pp. 67–124.

Aigle, Denise. "The Mongol Invasions of Bilād al-Shām by Ghāzān Khān and Ibn Taymiyya's Three 'Anti-Mongol' Fatwas." *Mamluk Studies Review* 11, no. 2 (2007), pp. 89–120.

Ali-Karamali, Shaista P., and Fiona Dunne. "The Ijtihad Controversy." *Arab Law Quarterly* 9, no. 3 (1994), pp. 238–57.

Amedroz, H. F. "The Hisba Jurisdiction in the Ahkam Sultaniyya of Mawardi." *Journal of the Royal Asiatic Society* (1916), pp. 77–101, 287–314.

———. "The Office of Kadi in the Ahkam Sultaniyya of Mawardi." *Journal of the Royal Asiatic Society* (1910), pp. 761–96.

Amitai-Preiss, Reuven. "Ghazan, Islam, and Mongol Tradition: A View from the Mamlūk Sultanate." *Bulletin of the School of Oriental and African Studies* 59, no. 1 (1996), pp. 1–10.

———. "Sufis and Shamans: Some Remarks on the Islamization of the Mongols in the Ilkhanate." *Journal of the Economic and Social History of the Orient* 42, no. 1 (1999), pp. 27–46.

Arjomand, Said Amir. "The Consolation of Theology: Absence of the Imam and Transition from Chiliasm to Law in Shi'ism." *Journal of Religion* 76, no. 4 (1996), pp. 548–71.

Ayalon, David. "The Great Yāsa of Chingiz Khān: A Reexamination (Part B)." *Studia Islamica* 34 (1971), pp. 151–80.

———. "The Great Yāsa of Chingiz Khān: A Reexamination (Part C1)." *Studia Islamica* 36 (1972), pp. 113–58.

———. "The Great Yāsa of Chingiz Khān: A Reexamination (Part C2): Al-Maqrīzī's Passage on the Yāsa Under the Mamluks." *Studia Islamica* 38 (1973), pp. 107–56.

Azzam, Maha. "Al-Qaeda: The Misunderstood Wahhabi Connection and the Ideology of Violence." *Royal Institute of International Affairs Briefing Paper No. 1* (2003).

Baderin, Mashood A. "Identifying Possible Mechanisms Within Islamic Law for the Promotion and Protection of Human Rights in Muslim States." *Netherlands Quarterly of Human Rights* 22, no. 3 (2004), pp. 329–46.

Bagnall, Roger S. "Alexandria: Library of Dreams." *Proceedings of the American Philosophical Society* 146, no. 4 (2002), pp. 348–62.

Baran, Zeyno. "Fighting the War of Ideas." *Foreign Affairs* 84, no. 6 (2005), pp. 68–78.

Beranek, Ondrej, and Karel Tupek. "From Visiting Graves to Their Destruction: The Question of *Ziyara* Through the Eyes of Salafis." *Crown Papers* (Brandeis), July 2009.

Berkey, Jonathan P. "Tradition, Innovation, and the Social Construction of Knowledge in the Medieval Islamic Near East." *Past and Present* 146 (1995), pp. 38–65.

Binder, Leonard. "Al-Ghazālī's Theory of Islamic Government." *Muslim World* 45 (1955), pp. 229–41.

Blair, Ann. "Reading Strategies for Coping with Information Overload, ca. 1550–1700." *Journal of the History of Ideas* 64, no. 1 (2003), pp. 11–28.

Boyle, John A. "The Death of the Last 'Abbasid Caliph: A Contemporary Muslim Account." *Journal of Semitic Studies* 6, no. 2 (1961), pp. 145–61.

Buckley, R. P. "The Muhtasib." *Arabica* 39, no. 1 (1992), pp. 59–117.

Calder, Norman. "Doubt and Prerogative: The Emergence of an Imāmī Shī'ī Theory of Ijtihād." *Studia Islamica* 70 (1989), pp. 57–78.

Carney, Frederick S. "Some Aspects of Islamic Ethics." *Journal of Religion* 63, no. 2 (1983), pp. 159–74.

Chesney, Robert M. "Beyond Conspiracy? Anticipatory Prosecution and the Challenge of Unaffiliated Terrorism." *Southern California Law Review* 80 (2007), pp. 425–502.

Çiğdem, R. "Corporal Punishment (Amputation of a Hand): The Concept of *Sariqa* (Theft) in Theory and in Practice." *Ankara Law Review* 4, no. 1 (2007), pp. 25–41.

Commins, David. "Taqi al-Din al-Nabhani and the Islamic Liberation Party." *Muslim World* 81, nos. 3–4 (1991), pp. 194–211.

Cook, David. "The Implications of 'Martyrdom Operations' for Contemporary Islam." *Journal of Religious Ethics* 32, no. 1 (2004), pp. 129–51.

Cook, Michael. "Ibn Qutayba and the Monkeys." *Studia Islamica* 89 (1999), pp. 43–74.

———. "The Opponents of the Writing of Tradition in Early Islam." *Arabica* 44, no. 4 (1997), pp. 437–530.

Coulson, Noel J. "Doctrine and Practice in Islamic Law." *Bulletin of the School of Oriental and African Studies* 18, part 2 (1956), pp. 211–26.

Dols, Michael W. "Plague in Early Islamic History." *Journal of the American Oriental Society* 94, no. 3 (1974), pp. 371–83.

Escovitz, Joseph H. "The Establishment of Four Chief Judgeships in the Mamlūk Empire." *Journal of the American Oriental Society* 102, no. 3 (1982), pp. 529–31.

Fierro, Maribel. "The Treatises Against Innovations (*Kutub al-Bida'*)." *Der Islam* 69, no. 2 (1992), pp. 204–36.

Fischel, Walter. "The Origin of Banking in Mediaeval Islam." *Journal of the Royal Asiatic Society* (1933), pp. 339–52, 569–603.

Gaudiosi, Monica M. "The Influence of the Islamic Law of Waqf on the Development of the Trust in England: The Case of Merton College." *University of Pennsylvania Law Review* 136 (1988), pp. 1231–61.

Gleave, Robert. "Between *Hadīth* and *Fiqh*: The 'Canonical' *Imāmī* Collections of *Akhbār*." *Islamic Law and Society* 8, no. 3 (2001), pp. 350–82.

Grossman, Michael C. "Is This Arbitration? Religious Tribunals, Judicial Review, and Due Process." *Columbia Law Review* 107 (2007), pp. 169–209.

Guest, R. "Cairene: Topography: El Qarafa According to Ibn Ez Zaiyat." *Journal of the Royal Asiatic Society* 1 (1926), pp. 57–61.

Hallaq, Wael B. "On the Origins of the Controversy About the Existence of Mujtahids and the Gate of Ijtihad." *Studia Islamica* 63 (1986), pp. 129–41.

——. "Was the Gate of Ijtihad Closed?" *International Journal of Middle East Studies* 16, no. 1 (1984), pp. 3–41.

Hinds, Martin. "The Murder of the Caliph 'Uthman." *International Journal of Middle East Studies* 3, no. 4 (1972), pp. 450–69.

Holt, P. M. "Some Observations on the 'Abbāsid Caliphate of Cairo." *Bulletin of the School of Oriental and African Studies* 47, no. 3 (1984), pp. 501–507.

Horii, Satoe. "Reconsideration of Legal Devices (*Hiyal*) in Islamic Jurisprudence: The Hanafīs and Their 'Exits' (*Makhārij*)." *Islamic Law and Society* 9, no. 3 (2002), pp. 312–57.

Hourani, George F. "A Revised Chronology of Ghazālī's Writings." *Journal of the American Oriental Society* 104, no. 2 (1984), pp. 289–302.

Hurvitz, Nimrod. "Mihna as Self-Defense." *Studia Islamica* 92 (2001), pp. 93–111.

İnalcık, Halil. "Suleiman the Lawgiver and Ottoman Law." *Archivum Ottomanicum* 1 (1969), pp. 105–38.

Jackson, Sherman A. "The Primacy of Domestic Politics: Ibn Bint al-A'azz and the Establishment of Four Chief Judgeships in Mamlūk Egypt." *Journal of the American Oriental Society* 115, no. 1 (1995), pp. 52–65.

Johansen, Baber. "Signs as Evidence: The Doctrine of Ibn Taymiyya (1263–1328) and Ibn Qayyim al-Jawziyya (d. 1351) on Proof." *Islamic Law and Society* 9, no. 2 (2002), pp. 168–93.

Kedar, Benjamin Z. "On the Origins of the Earliest Laws of Frankish Jerusalem: The Canons of the Council of Nablus, 1120." *Speculum* 74, no. 2 (1999), pp. 310–35.

Kennedy, Charles H. "Islamization in Pakistan: Implementation of the Hudood Ordinances." *Asian Survey* 28, no. 3 (1988), pp. 307–16.

Khan, Siadat Ali. "The Mohammedan Laws Against Usury and How They Are Evaded." *Journal of Comparative Legislation and International Law* 11 (1929), pp. 233–44.

Kohlberg, Etan. "The Development of the Imami Shi'i Doctrine of *Jihad*." *Zeitschrift der Deutschen Morgenländischen Gesellschaft* 126 (1976), pp. 64–86.

——. "From Imāmiyya to Ithnā-'ashariyya." *Bulletin of the School of Oriental and African Studies* 39, no. 3 (1976), pp. 521–34.

Kugle, Scott A. "Framed, Blamed, and Renamed: The Recasting of Islamic Jurisprudence in Colonial South Asia." *Modern Asian Studies* 35, no. 2 (2001), pp. 257–313.

Landau-Tasseron, Ella. "The 'Cyclical Reform': A Study of the *Mujaddid* Tradition." *Studia Islamica* 70 (1989), pp. 79–117.

Lapidus, Ira M. "The Separation of State and Religion in the Development of Early Islamic Society." *International Journal of Middle East Studies* 6, no. 4 (1975), pp. 363–85.

Lassner, Jacob W. "Some Speculative Thoughts on the Search for an 'Abbāsid Capital." *Muslim World* 55 (1965), pp. 135–41, 203–10.

Lau, Martin. "Twenty-Five Years of Hudood Ordinances—A Review." *Washington and Lee Law Review* 64, no. 4 (2007), pp. 1291–314.

Leonard, Karen. "American Muslims and Authority: Competing Discourses in a Non-Muslim State." *Journal of American Ethnic History* 25 (2005), pp. 5–30.

Le Strange, Guy. "A Greek Embassy to Baghdad in 917 A.D." *Journal of the Royal Asiatic Society* (1897), pp. 35–45.

Lewis, Bernard. "Translation from Arabic." *Proceedings of the American Philosophical Society* 124, no. 1 (1980), pp. 41–47.

Little, Donald P. "Did Ibn Taymiyya Have a Screw Loose?" *Studia Islamica* 41 (1975), pp. 93–111.

———. "The Historical and Historiographical Significance of the Detention of Ibn Taymiyya." *International Journal of Middle East Studies* 4, no. 3 (1973), pp. 311–27.

MacDonald, Duncan B. "Emotional Religion in Islam as Affected by Music and Singing." *Journal of the Royal Asiatic Society* (1901), pp. 195–252.

Makdisi, George. "Ibn Taimīya: A Sūfī of the Qādiriya Order." *American Journal of Arabic Studies* 1 (1973), pp. 118–29.

Makdisi, John A. "The Islamic Origins of the Common Law." *North Carolina Law Review* 77 (1999), pp. 1635–739.

Marmura, Michael E. "Avicenna's 'Flying Man' in Context." *Monist* 69 (1986), pp. 383–95.

Maxwell, Rahsaan. "Trust in Government Among British Muslims: The Importance of Migration Status." *Political Behavior* 32 (2010), pp. 89–109.

Munir, Muhammad. "Suicide Attacks and Islamic Law." *International Review of the Red Cross* 90, no. 869 (2008), pp. 71–89.

Nafi, Basheer M. "Fatwā and War: On the Allegiance of the American Muslim Soldiers in the Aftermath of September 11." *Islamic Law and Society* 11, no. 1 (2004), pp. 78–116.

Naʿim, Abdullahi Ahmed an-. "The Islamic Law of Apostasy and Its Modern Applicability: A Case from the Sudan." *Religion* 16 (1986), pp. 197–224.

Nawas, John A. "A Reexamination of Three Current Explanations for al-Mamun's Introduction of the Mihna." *International Journal of Middle East Studies* 26, no. 4 (1994), pp. 615–29.

Noman, Omar. "Pakistan and General Zia: Era and Legacy." *Third World Quarterly* 11, no. 1 (1989), pp. 28–54.

Nwyia, P. "Une cible d'Ibn Taimiya: Le moniste al-Tilimsānī (m. 690/1291)" *Bulletin d'Études Orientales* 30 (1978), pp. 127–45.

Ober, William B., and Nabil Alloush. "The Plague at Granada, 1348–1349: Ibn al-Khatīb and Ideas of Contagion." *Bulletin of the New York Academy of Medicine* 58, no. 4 (1982), pp. 418–24.

Peters, Rudolph. "The Islamization of Criminal Law: A Comparative Analysis." *Die Welt des Islams* 34, no. 2 (1994), pp. 246–74.

Peters, Rudolph, and Gert J. J. de Vries. "Apostasy in Islam." *Die Welt des Islams* 17, no. 1/4 (1975), pp. 1–25.

Rafeeq, Mona, "Rethinking Islamic Law Arbitration Tribunals: Are They Compatible with Traditional American Notions of Justice?" *Wisconsin International Law Journal* 28 (2010), pp. 109–39.

Rapoport, Yossef. "Legal Diversity in the Age of *Taqlīd*: The Four Chief *Qāḍīs* Under the Mamluks." *Islamic Law and Society* 10, no. 2 (2003), pp. 210–28.

Renard, John. "*Al-Jihad al-Akbar*: Notes on a Theme in Islamic Spirituality." *Muslim World* 78 (1988), pp. 225–42.

Reza, Sadiq. "Islam's Fourth Amendment: Search and Seizure in Islamic Doctrine and Muslim Practice." *Georgetown Journal of International Law* 40 (2009), pp. 703–806.

———. "Torture and Islamic Law." *Chicago Journal of International Law* 8 (2007), pp. 21–41.

Rosenthal, Franz. "On Suicide in Islam." *Journal of the American Oriental Society* 66, no. 3 (1946), pp. 239–59.

Rowson, Everett K. "The Effeminates of Early Medina." *Journal of the American Oriental Society* 111, no. 4 (1991), pp. 671–93.

Serjeant, R. B. "The Caliph ʿUmar's Letters to Abū Mūsā al-Ashʿarī and Muʿāwiya." *Journal of Semitic Studies* 29, no. 1 (1984), pp. 65–79.

Shippee, R. Seth, "'Blessed Are the Peacemakers': Faith-Based Approaches to Dispute Resolution." *ILSA Journal of International and Comparative Law* 9 (2002), pp. 237–55.

Sidahmed, Abdel Salam. "Problems in Contemporary Applications of Islamic Criminal Sanctions: The Penalty for Adultery in Relation to Women." *British Journal of Middle Eastern Studies* 28, no. 2 (2001), pp. 187–204.

Siddique, Osama, and Zahra Hayat. "Unholy Speech and Holy Laws: Blasphemy Laws in Pakistan—Controversial Origins, Design Defects, and Free Speech Implications." *Minnesota Journal of International Law* 17, no. 2 (2008), pp. 302–85.

Sourdel, Charles. "La biographie d'Ibn al-Muqaffaʿ d'après les sources anciennes." *Arabica* 1, no. 3 (1954), pp. 307–23.

Sourdel, Dominique. "La politique religieuse du calife ʿabbaside al-Maʾmun.'" *Revue des Études Islamiques* 30 (1962), pp. 27–48.

Sprenger, Aloys. "On the Origin and Progress of Writing Down Historical Facts Among the Musalmans." *Journal of the Asiatic Society of Bengal* 25 (1856), pp. 303–29, 375–81.

Tanwir, Farooq. "Religious Parties and Politics in Pakistan." *International Journal of Comparative Sociology* 43 (2002), pp. 250–68.

Tritton, A. S. "Islam and the Protected Religions." *Journal of the Royal Asiatic Society* 2 (1931), pp. 311–38.

Vansteenkiste, Clemens. "San Tommaso d'Aquino ed Averroè." *Rivista degli Studi Orientali* 32 (1957), pp. 585–623.

Wendell, Charles. "Baghdād: *Imago Mundi*, and Other Foundation-Lore." *International Journal of Middle East Studies* 2 (1971), pp. 99–128.

Williams, Caroline. "The Cult of 'Alid Saints in the Fatimid Monuments of Cairo Part II: The Mausolea." *Muqarnas* 3 (1985), pp. 39–60.

Williams, Wesley. "Aspects of the Creed of Imam Ahmad Ibn Hanbal: A Study of Anthropomorphism in Early Islamic Discourse." *International Journal of Middle East Studies* 34, no. 3 (2002), pp. 441–63.

Wolfe, Caryn L. "Faith-Based Arbitration: Friend or Foe? An Evaluation of Religious Arbitration Systems and Their Interaction with Secular Courts." *Fordham Law Review* 75 (2006), pp. 427–69.

Yalaoui, Mohammed. "Controverse entre le Fatimide al-Mu'izz et l'Omeyyade al-Nasir, d'après le 'Kitab al-majalis w-al musayarat' du Cadi Nu'man." *Les Cahiers de Tunisie* 26 (1978), pp. 7–33.

Zaman, Muhammad Q. "The Caliphs, the 'Ulamā', and the Law: Defining the Role and Function of the Caliph in the Early 'Abbāsid Period." *Islamic Law and Society* 4, no. 1 (1997), pp. 1–36.

Online Publications

Abu Dhabi Gallup Center. *Muslim Americans: Faith, Freedom, and the Future.* Abu Dhabi, August 2011. www.abudhabigallupcenter.com/148772/REPORT-Muslim-Americans-Faith-Freedom-Future.aspx.

Center on Law and Security, NYU School of Law. *Terrorist Trial Report Card, September 11, 2001–September 11, 2010* (2010). www.lawandsecurity.org/Portals/0/documents/01_TTRC20101.pdf.

Centre for Social Cohesion. *Islam on Campus: A Survey of UK Student Opinions.* London, 2008. www.socialcohesion.co.uk/files/1231525079_1.pdf.

Pew Research Center. *Mapping the Global Muslim Population.* Washington, D.C., October 2009. www.pewforum.org/newassets/images/reports/Muslimpopulation/muslimpopulation.pdf.

Pew Research Center. *Muslim Americans: Middle Class and Mostly Mainstream.* Washington, D.C., May 2007. http://pewresearch.org/pubs/483/muslim-americans.

Policy Exchange. *Living Apart Together: British Muslims and the Paradox of Multiculturalism.* London, 2007. www.policyexchange.org.uk/assets/Living_Apart_Together_text.pdf.

Robertson, Geoffrey. *The Massacre of Political Prisoners in Iran, 1988.* Washington, D.C., 2010. www.iranrights.org/english/attachments/doc_3434.pdf.

Acknowledgments

Exploring the extent of divine justice was always going to take work, and the task would have been a lot tougher without the solid support of my family. The foremost debt is owed my dad, who consistently firmed up my thoughts and kept at bay the temptation to pussyfoot around. My uncle Junaid, my aunt Rakshan, and the welcoming households of her brothers Feroz and Taj made it almost relaxing to travel through northern India; my uncle Iqbal and his brother Aslam generously put me up in Dubai; and the people of Badaun received me with great congeniality, twice. At the cost of failing to mention several very friendly relatives who live in the town, I am especially grateful for the practical help given me by Hazrat Salim Miah, Affan Haque, Arslan Qadri, the charming Tanveer Saab, and his sons, Hummi and Abad.

I had disagreements with some of the scholars and students I met, but it was a privilege to talk to them all. A few figure in the text of this book, and among those who do not, I benefited in particular from the assistance of Mufti Muhammad Naeem from Karachi's Jamia Binoria, Zafar Abbas Shah at the Sehwan shrine, and Javed Ahmad Ghamidi and Khalid Zaheer of Lahore's prestigious al-Mawrid Institute. Aysha Kidwai and her late father, Khalid Kidwai, provided very useful introductions before my visit to Lucknow, and I was much helped within the city by Farid Faridi, Colonel Shamsie, Maulana Syed Hamidul Hassan at the Jamia Nazmia, and Maulana Khalid Rashid of the Islamic Centre of India.

Habib Jan regularly took my life in his hands in Karachi; Farooq Moin facilitated meetings with tact and humor; and Iqbal Haider, Khurram Jafri, Shimaila Matri-Dawood, and Ayaz Dawood were as knowledgeable as they were fun to be with. Nadeem Anthony helped me see how Pakistan looks to its religious minorities in Lahore, and the owner of that city's convivial Regale Internet Inn, Malik Saab, was an excellent host. Amer Siddiqui merits one of the biggest nods of them all. In return for not much more than my thoughts on *Britain's Got Talent*, his family kept me entertained, accommodated, and fed for weeks on end in Karachi—thanks again, Amer, Soni, Raafay, Sundas, and Sehr.

In Istanbul, Iason Athanasiadis very kindly loaned me an apartment and several friends; and I was hothoused through modern Turkish history by Nursuna Memecan and İbrahim Yildirim of the Justice and Development Party; and Professor Haluk Kabaalioğlu, Professor Feroz Ahmad, and Dr. Sultan Üzeltürk of Yeditepe University. For their legal insights, thanks to Georges Assaf and Chawkat Houalla in Lebanon; Mohamed Madkour in Cairo; and Muhammed Khalid Sayed, now in Cape Town. It would not be sensible to identify the Iranians and Syrians who helped me along the way, but I am extremely grateful to all of them. Two people merit particular, if elliptical, thanks: Hossein, for putting me in touch with some excellent people and helping me comprehend the real meaning of religious expediency in Iran; and Mazin, who understood better than anyone else how important it was to find Ibn Taymiyya's tomb.

Courtney Hodell was an excellent editor, whose enthusiastic support and perceptive revisions saw me through many a wobbly moment. Her efforts, along with the unfailing assistance of Mark Krotov and the work of my British editor, Jörg Hensgen at Bodley Head, improved my own by several orders of magnitude. Much respect to Paul Moss and Aileen McColgan for their gently constructive comments on an early draft, and a resounding shout out, as they almost say, to everyone else who contributed to my equilibrium, knowledge, or itinerary as I researched and wrote. Thanks especially and alphabetically to Amir

Amirani, Rachel Aspden, Kate Beattie, Kerry Glencorse, Justine Hardie, Mary Harper, Frances Harrison, Paul Lewis, Liz Mermin, Kamin Mohammadi, Pru Rowlandson, Roxanna Shapour, and Kitty Sterling. Derek Johns meanwhile agented me with his customary aplomb; colleagues at Doughty Street Chambers were as supportive as ever; and without the British Library, the Institute of Advanced Legal Studies, and the School of Oriental and African Studies, this book would not have got far off the ground.

Finally, I ought to mention my niece, Natasha Haider, and my nephew, Kiyan Haider. They contributed nothing to the text and seemed almost indifferent at times to its subject matter. They want to see their names in print, however. It is not worth my while to disregard their wishes.

Index

Page numbers beginning with 289 refer to notes.

A Note About the Author

Sadakat Kadri is a practicing English barrister and qualified New York attorney, with law degrees from Cambridge University and Harvard Law School. He is the author of *The Trial: A History, from Socrates to O. J. Simpson*; he has contributed to *The Guardian, The Times* (London), and the *London Review of Books*; and he is the winner of the 1998 Shiva Naipaul Memorial Prize for travel writing. He lives in London.